Managing Across Diverse Cultures in East Asia

G000093518

Why 'Managing across diverse cultures in East Asia'? In this book we re-examine the link between culture and management across the region vis-à-vis the new economic, political and social landscape that has appeared over the last decade. We accordingly present a set of chapters on East Asian cultures, economies, societies and their management across the board, focusing on countries such as China, Japan and South Korea, as well as the Overseas Chinese enclaves of Hong Kong SAR, Macau and Taiwan. The contributors to this edited book are all specialists in their respective fields; they hail from a variety of universities and business schools across the world, located in a wide range of countries in the East and in the West. The chapters, we believe, reflect a balance between the past and present, theory and practice, as well as the general and the particular.

Malcolm Warner is Professor and Fellow Emeritus, Wolfson College and Judge Business School, University of Cambridge, UK. He has published extensively in the field of Asian management.

Managing Across Diverse Cultures in East Asia

Issues and challenges in a changing globalized world

Edited by Malcolm Warner

LONDON AND NEW YORK

First published 2013
by Routledge
2 Park Square, Milton Park, Abingdon, Oxon OX14 4RN

Simultaneously published in the USA and Canada
by Routledge
711 Third Avenue, New York, NY 10017

Routledge is an imprint of the Taylor & Francis Group, an informa business

© 2013 selection and editorial material, Malcolm Warner; individual
chapters, the contributors.

The right of the editor to be identified as the author of the editorial
material, and of the authors for their individual chapters, has been asserted
in accordance with sections 77 and 78 of the Copyright, Designs and
Patents Act 1988.

All rights reserved. No part of this book may be reprinted or reproduced or
utilised in any form or by any electronic, mechanical, or other means, now
known or hereafter invented, including photocopying and recording, or in
any information storage or retrieval system, without permission in writing
from the publishers.

Trademark notice: Product or corporate names may be trademarks or
registered trademarks, and are used only for identification and explanation
without intent to infringe.

British Library Cataloguing in Publication Data
A catalogue record for this book is available from the British Library

Library of Congress Cataloging in Publication Data
Managing across diverse cultures in East Asia : issues and challenges in a
changing globalized world / edited by Malcolm Warner.
    p. cm.
    Includes bibliographical references and index.
    1. Management—East Asia.   2. Management—Cross-cultural studies.
    3. East Asia—Economic conditions.   I. Warner, Malcolm.
    HD70.E22M36 2013
    658.3008'095—dc23

                                                    2012010258

ISBN: 978-0-415-68089-9 (hbk)
ISBN: 978-0-415-68090-5 (pbk)
ISBN: 978-0-203-10695-2 (ebk)

Typeset in Times New Roman
by RefineCatch Limited, Bungay, Suffolk

MIX
Paper from
responsible sources
FSC
www.fsc.org FSC® C004839

Printed and bound in Great Britain by the MPG Books Group

Contents

17 Managing across diverse cultures in East Asia: conclusions 277
MALCOLM WARNER (UK)

Figures and graphs

Figures

Graphs

Tables

About the editor

Malcolm Warner is Professor and Fellow Emeritus, Wolfson College, Cambridge and the Judge Business School, University of Cambridge. He has been a Research Fellow at Stanford University, as well as Columbia University, in the USA and has held appointments at the London Business School and the Brunel University-Henley Management College in the UK, before joining Cambridge. He was also a past Halevy Visiting Professor at 'Sciences Po' (L'Institut d'Etudes Politiques (IEP)) in Paris, as well as being a Visiting Associate at the Wissenschaftszentrum in Berlin. He has, in addition, been a frequent Visiting Academic at many Chinese campuses and business schools, including the China-Europe International Business School (CEIBS) in Shanghai, and at Nanjing, Tsinghua and Zhejiang Universities, as well as at the University of Hong Kong and the City University of Hong Kong. Professor Warner has also been Editor-in-Chief of the *International Encyclopedia of Business and Management* (London: Thomson, 2002, 8 volumes). He has published many books and articles over the years in the field of Asian management and HRM. His most recent publication is an edited book on *Society and HRM in China* (London and New York: Routledge, 2012). He is currently co-editor of the *Asia Pacific Business Review*, a SSCI-rated journal.

List of contributors

Benson, John. Professor and Dean, School of Management, University of South Australia, Adelaide, Australia.

Chung, Sun-wook. Doctoral Candidate, Department of International & Comparative Labor, Cornell University, Ithaca NY, USA.

Cooke, Fang Lee. Professor, Faculty of Business and Economics, Monash University, Melbourne, Australia.

Cunningham, Li Xue. Lecturer, Centre for Research in Asian Management, Cass Business School, City University, London, UK.

Das, Dilip, K. Professor, Sol-Bridge International School of Business, Woosong University, Daejeon, Republic of Korea.

Debroux, Philippe. Professor, Doshisha Business School, Soka University, Kyoto, Japan.

Du, Juan. Lecturer, Shanghai International Studies University, Shanghai, PRC.

Ip, Olivia. Associate Professor, Management Department, City University of Hong Kong, Hong Kong SAR.

Jackson, Keith. Tutor, School of African and Asian Studies, SOAS, University of London, UK.

Khilji, Shaista, E. Associate Professor, George Washington University, Washington, DC, USA.

Kuruvilla, Sarosh. Professor, Department of International & Comparative Labor, Cornell University, Ithaca, NY, USA.

Minkov, Misho. Associate Professor, International University College, Sofia, Bulgaria.

Ng, Sek-Hong. Reader, HKU Business School, University of Hong Kong, Hong Kong SAR.

Nolan, Jane. Lecturer, Centre for Labour Studies, University of Leicester University of Leicester, Leicester, UK.

Rowley, Chris. Professor, Centre for Research in Asian Management, Cass Business School, City University, London, UK and Research Director, 'HEAD' Foundation, Singapore.

Tung, Rosalie L. Professor, Beedie School of Business, Simon Fraser University, Barnaby, BC, Canada.

Warner, Malcolm. Professor and Fellow Emeritus, Wolfson College and Judge Business School, University of Cambridge, Cambridge, UK.

Witt, Michael, A. Professor, INSEAD Business School, France and Singapore.

Zhao, Shuming. Professor and Dean, NJU Business School, Nanjing University, Nanjing, PRC.

Preface

How managers cope with cultural diversity has been an interest of mine for many years now. I have produced a number of works comparing management in different cultures in the last few decades or so, notwithstanding the multi-volume edited *Regional Encyclopedia of Business and Management – IEBM Handbook Series* (London and New York, NY: Thomson, 1999) and an edited book, *Culture and Management in Asia* (London and New York, NY: Routledge, 2003).

This new volume attempts to both update and deepen knowledge of that region, specifically focusing on East Asia, the new 'powerhouse' of the globalised world economy. In this edited tome, we will accordingly present a set of chapters on East Asian cultures, economies, societies and their management across the board, but with a particular focus on the key players in the region, China, Japan and South Korea. The work may be used as a text, or a reference resource, for those at both undergraduate and postgraduate levels in business studies, economics, management, sociology and so on, particularly for MBA students and DBAs, as well as for academics and practitioners alike interested in the region.

I would like here to offer my thanks to all of the contributors to the volume who have been so committed to this endeavour and have given of their talent and time. Some hail originally from East Asia itself; a number of these now live and work abroad; yet others are Western-born and based. They are all specialists in their respective fields; they come from a variety of universities and business schools across the world, located in a wide range of countries in the East and in the West, such as Australia, Bulgaria, Canada, France, Hong Kong, Japan, PRC, Singapore, South Korea, the UK and the USA, amongst others.

Acknowledgements must be given to the past and present Presidents and Fellows of Wolfson College, Cambridge, as well as the previous and current Directors and Faculty of the Judge Business School, University of Cambridge for their invaluable support over the years.

My special thanks to my Editor of many years' standing at Routledge, Peter Sowden, whose support has been unflinching and all those others at this publishing-house who have helped to make this book possible.

Malcolm Warner,
Cambridge,
January, 2012

Abbreviations

AACSB International, The Association to Advance Collegiate Schools of Business.
ACFTU, All-China Federation of Trade Unions.
ACWF, All-China Women's Federation.
ADB, Asian Development Bank.
AOM, Academy of Management.
APEC, Asia Pacific Economic Community.
ASEAN, Association of South East Asian States.
BRIC, Brazil, Russia, India and China.
CASS, Chinese Academy of Social Sciences.
CCAC, Comissariado Contra a Corrupção (Commission Against Corruption).
CCP, Chinese Communist Party.
CD, Confucian Dynamism.
CEMA, Chinese Enterprise Management Association.
CEMI, China Europe Management Institute.
CEO, Chief Executive Officer.
CLB, China Labour Bulletin.
CLSY, China Labour Statistical Yearbook.
COE, Collectively-Owned Enterprise.
DOE, Domestically-Owned Enterprise.
DPE, Domestic Private Enterprise.
DPRK, Democratic People's Republic of Korea.
EFMD, European Foundation for Management Development.
EMBA, Executive Masters of Business Administration.
EME, Emerging Market Economies.
EPZ, Export processing Zone.
ER, Employment Relations.
EU, European Union.
FDI, Foreign Direct Investment.
FIE, Foreign-Invested Enterprise.
FYP, Five-Year Plan.
GDP, Gross Domestic Product.
HKFTU, Hong Kong Federation of Trade Unions.
HKSAR, Hong Kong Special Administrative Region.

HKSB, Hong Kong and Shanghai Bank.
HKU, University of Hong Kong.
HKUST, Hong Kong University of Science and Technology.
HPMS, High Performance Management System.
HPWS, High Performance Work Systems.
HR, Human Resources.
HRM, Human Resource Management.
ICAC, Independent Commission Against Corruption.
ILC, International Labour Conventions.
ILO, International Labour Organization.
ILR, Industrial and Labour Relations.
IMF, International Monetary Fund.
IR, Industrial Relations.
JDP, Japanese Democratic Party.
JETRO, Japanese External Trade Organization
JIT, Just in Time.
JMA, Japanese Management Association.
JR, Japan Railways.
JV, Joint Venture.
KAIST, Korea Advanced Institute of Science and Technology.
KCTU, Korean Confederation of Trade Unions.
KMA, Korean Management Association.
KMT, Kuomintang.
LDP, Liberal Democratic Party of Japan.
M&A, Mergers and Acquisitions.
MBA, Masters of Business Administration.
MNC, Multinational Corporation.
MOHR, Ministry of Human Resources.
MOLSS, Ministry of Labour and Social Security.
NIE, Newly Industrialised Economy.
NPC, National People's Congress.
NUDM, Nueva Unión para el Desarrollo del Macao (New Union for Macao's Development).
OEM, Original Equipment Manufacturer.
PA, Personnel Administration.
PM, Personnel Management.
PRC, People's Republic of China.
QC, Quality Circle.
R&D, Research and Development.
RENGO, Japanese Trade Union Federation.
RMB, Renminbi.
ROK, Republic of Korea.
SAR, Special Administrative Region.
SEZ, Special Economic Zone.
SFC, Securities and Future Commission.

SME, Small and Medium-sized Enterprise.
SNU, Seoul National University.
SOE, State-Owned Enterprise.
SSB, State Statistical Bureau.
SWC, Staff and Workers' Congress.
TQC, Total Quality Circle.
TNC, Transnational Corporation.
TQM, Total Quality Management.
TVE, Town and Village Enterprise.
USSR, Union of Soviet Socialist Republics.
WOFE, Wholly-Owned Foreign Enterprise.
WRC, Workers' Representative Congress.
WTO, World Trade Organization.
ZD, Zero-Defects policy.

Part I

Introduction

Is it not pleasant to learn with a constant perseverance and application?

(Confucius: Analects, I, i)

1 Managing across diverse cultures in East Asia

Introduction

Malcolm Warner

Introduction

Why 'Managing across diverse cultures in East Asia'? We hope in this chapter to re-examine the link between culture and management across the region. A new economic, political and social landscape has been emerging in Asia over the last decade (see earlier work, including my own, Warner, 2003) given the increasing influence of the People's Republic of China (Zhonghua renmin gongheguo) (hereafter China or PRC) vis-à-vis its neighbours – Japan and South Korea, as well as Hong Kong SAR, Macau and Taiwan (see chapters 5, 6, 7 and 8 in this book). The recent global financial crises have, in their turn, led to speculation about a 'reordering' of the world economic system, both internationally and regionally. An alternative economic order may indeed be in the making, with the 'Beijing Consensus' becoming a rival to the Washington version. The inter-relationships between the players in East Asia itself have additionally become more complex – given the increasing economic integration between the PRC and its neighbours in East Asia in the context of the wider growth in the region.

As Lee and Hong (2010:1) put it:

> Developing Asian economies have grown impressively over a period of nearly 30 years. The region's real GDP in purchasing power parity (PPP) terms climbed from about $3.3 trillion in 1980 to an estimated $24.5 trillion in 2009. That is an increase of 7.5 times, compared with just three times for the world economy during the same period. Real per capita GDP expanded in excess of four times during the period, while average global income registered less than a two-fold increase. Such robust, prolonged growth has clearly raised incomes, lifted millions out of poverty, and expanded developing Asia's global economic influence.

The 'Twenty-first Century' is thus likely to be the century of Asia. In this volume, we will accordingly present a set of chapters on Asian cultures, economies, societies and their management across the board, but with a particular focus on East Asia as this is increasingly, it would be true to say, the emerging fulcrum of economic power. We have decided to concentrate on this part of the wider

Asia-Pacific, as it is home to many of the fastest growing economies in our increasingly globalised world. Leading the pack is China, now seen as the 'powerhouse' of the world economy, with a fifth of the world's population (see chapter 5). Its economy has been growing at unprecedented pace for the last three decades, since Deng Xiaoping introduced his economic reforms at the end of the 1970s.

Many of these Asian countries were formerly called the 'Little Tigers' or 'Dragons' (see Vogel, 1991) tracking what was then the 'bigger' one, which was Japan, now a significant economic power but increasingly overshadowed by what had become known as the 'Middle Kingdom' (Chongghuo) over the centuries, in terms of aggregate levels of population, resources and wealth. The so-called 'Asian miracle', which led to their growth, it is said, mainly came about through the 'work ethic', through perhaps what one economist has seen as 'perspiration' rather than 'inspiration' (see Krugman, 1994). The contributions presented in this volume are all intended to explore this perceptive observation in greater detail and to update our knowledge of the region's achievements, deepen our understanding of its ways and enhance what we can learn from it.

As economic power is now seen as moving from 'West' to 'East' (see chapter 2) with nations like China even being seen as potential global bankers of last resort, there is an increasing degree of interest in how these Eastern economies have come to the forefront of international attention and how their management and managers contribute to their success. China is now recovering the economic hegemony it formerly enjoyed for centuries until the Industrial Revolution took root in Western Europe (see Maddison, 2007). It was once the 'Workshop of the World' and is now once again taking over this niche. In the tenth century AD, it had been the world's leading economy in terms of per capita income. The West once imported most of its manufactured products from the East, many at bargain-basement prices. But a new 'Silk Road', whether material or digital, will probably be passing on goods and services to the West, higher and higher up the 'value-chain', in future years.

We are well aware that there is no single entity called 'Asia' or even 'East Asia'. The constituent parts have had a long and difficult history, going back millennia (see Fairbank *et al.*, 1973). There is a complex tapestry of cultures, many of them originating from the deep and distant past (see Goody, 1996). We will be looking at where there are overlays, given that for example China had already conquered and/or influenced many of its neighbours over the centuries. Its cultural influence has been extensive in countries like Japan, Korea and Vietnam, to cite but a few (see Holcombe, 2011). The Confucian inheritance has in its turn been noteworthy (see chapter 3). In later centuries, imperial expansion by powers in the region, whether from the East or the West, had profound impacts.

Is there a 'winning', 'killer-app' Asian management model to copy? At one stage, the Japanese were held up as an example and their management was said to be de rigueur. But there are no easy answers. Management has often had both an *exogenous,* as well as an *indigenous,* origin. We find that there was sometimes even a two-way flow between different national ways of managing. Western, Taylorist management was mainly imported into Japan after the First World War (as indeed it was into China) and then again after the Second World War (as a US government-led Scientific Management training programme for Japanese managers, for instance) and was then reimported back to North America and Western Europe in the form, amongst others, of total quality management practices (TQM), such as 'Zero-Defects' (ZD) policies, amongst others (see Warner, 1994). What was once just 'Western', now became 'Eastern'.

For a long time, management theory and practice had already diffused from the West to the East (see Westney, 1987). In the early phases of modernisation, exogenous influences were dominant. These entered the new environments through foreign invested firms, joint ventures, management consultants and the like. In the later phases of modernisation, these may well be integrated into local practices and then modified and re-exported back to their source. This phenomenon has been seen in the Japanese case but has not yet occurred in the Chinese one. As Japan has been in a state of economic stasis in recent years (see chapter 7), there has been less emphasis on promoting its management models as ones to emulate. Although China is now in the ascendant, its management has not as yet been promoted externally as an exemplar. Of course, this may change with time, as the latter country is building a number of top global MNCs, such as Haier, Huawei and Lenovo (see Nankervis *et al.*, 2013, in press).

The heterogeneity of Asia represents an issue but then the diversity of local environments may also be a problem in most parts of the world. But we will look for common characteristics which will help to explain why they look different from their Western counterparts. Even within East Asia, there are, additionally, specific management practices according to the location studied. It is perfectly permissible to talk about 'Chinese', 'Japanese' or 'South Korean' management, for example and many do (see chapters 4, 5, 6, 7 and 8). Hong Kong, Macau and Taiwan may in turn present difficulties, because they have generic Chinese characteristics (see chapter 6), as well as their own local ones. Some even bundle them together as 'Overseas (*Nanyang*) Chinese' management, which is also a phenomenon found outside East Asia, as in the case of Singapore and indeed elsewhere wherever Chinese do business.

Although the Asian societies used to have considerable differences in national wealth and income between each other, with Japan having the lead over the others, the gap is narrowing (see Table 1.1). All the countries of East Asia have, however, seen a relative increase in their standard of living in recent years, with the possible exception of North Korea. China, for example, has now a much improved level of GDP per capita in purchasing power parity (PPP) terms compared with the past, although this is less the case in money terms. It is, however, likely that there will be a weaker differential in future years. The Chinese economy grew over the last three decades at around 10 per cent per annum but the growth rates of Hong Kong, Singapore, South Korea and Taiwan, all with relatively higher levels of initial income per capita, somewhat declined relatively over the period. It is said that as countries get richer they do so less rapidly over time and their growth rates slow down (Lee and Hong, 2010:2). Table 1.1 shows their key economic indicators for 2010.

Table 1.1 Key economic indicators, China, Japan and South Korea, 2010.

	China	Japan	S. Korea
Population total	1,338,300,000	127,450,459	48,875,000
GDP, aggr.	$5,878,629m	$5,497,812m	$1,014,483m
GDP growth, p.a.	10.3%	5.1%	6.2%
GDP per capita/US$	$4,393 [7,600, PPP]	$43,137	$20,757

Source: World Bank (2011) Available at http://web.worldbank.org/WBSITE/EXTERNAL/EXTABO UTUS/0,pagePK:50004410~piPK:36602~theSitePK:29708,00.html (accessed 11.11.11).

There is another, wider debate which deals with what has been called 'convergence', on the one hand and 'divergence' on the other (see Warner 2002, 2011). As far as the former is concerned, the argument centres on industrial societies and their economies, as a result of the modernisation process, becoming more like each other and consequently their enterprises appearing to be increasingly similar as the modernisation process proceeds (see chapter 11). Managerial ideas are transmitted across frontiers very quickly these days and are adopted by indigenous firms and then spread as new forms of enterprise structure are cloned through a process of institutional and organisational isomorphism. By a process of copycat 'convergence' behaviour, new organisational templates become established.

The counter-argument, relating to 'divergence', would present the case for societies and their enterprises retaining their distinctly national characteristics, plus or minus (see chapter 3). The 'societal effect' (see Maurice *et al.*, 1980) would ensure national differences remain in place. Unlike where societies and constituent enterprises were becoming more and more like each other, they and their firms might even become more and more distinct. The *reductio ad absurdum* would be where all countries and institutions were totally different from each other, which is an unlikely scenario. There are, of course, refinements of these states of play, such that there can be either 'hard' (absolute) or 'soft' (relative) versions of each. There might be, for example, 'soft convergence' where enterprises may look increasingly like those found elsewhere in the world but retaining many local characteristics (see Rowley *et al.*, 2005). The truth probably lies somewhere in the middle of the 'convergence–divergence' spectrum. In spite of the degree of possible 'convergence', however, when you are in Tokyo for example, the way of doing business over there still remains very much Japanese, as it does in Beijing in terms of its 'Chinese characteristics'.

Some writers, nonetheless, point to a common cultural legacy across Asia (see chapters 3, 10 and 16) but this is an argument different from the convergence one. In recent years, there has been a debate about the importance of 'Asian values' (see chapter 16) the motivation for which may have been political in part. Even so, there is little doubt that Confucianism has played a major role in influencing how many Asian societies work, over the *longue durée* and in recent times.

The philosopher, Confucius, (551–479 BC) (Kong Fuzi) may well be regarded as the uncrowned emperor of China (Ronan, 1978:79). There are other major streams of thought in Chinese thinking, such as the Legalists and the Daoists but the Confucians may still retain their niche (see Bell, 2008). The current Chinese leadership has even recently promoted what is in effect a synthesis of Confucianism, Capitalism and Marxism as a path to what they call the 'Harmonious Society', an ideological variation that was first officially proclaimed by [the former President] Hu Jintou in 2006 and is now widely used in China (see Warner, 2011). The Chinese government had even set up Confucius Institutes around the world to teach Chinese culture and language (see chapter 15). Another co-opted figure has been Sun Tzu (see *The Economist*, 2011) as the CCP has attempted to project 'soft power'.

However, some caution must be used here, as it was not that long ago that Confucianism was seen as a backward philosophy and a negative factor as far as modernisation and economic growth were concerned. Confucius is problematic in another way: 'Mao and his colleagues regarded Confucius's philosophy as the ideological glue of the feudal system they destroyed; and so attempts to promote him are vulnerable to the growing split in the Communist Party' (*The Economist*, 2011).There are also many kinds of belief-systems, let alone varieties of Confucian thought in Asia, so there may be no simple 'cause-and-effect' relationships between values and economic variables. Again, Confucianism is only one amongst several other competing belief-systems in the region, (such as Buddhism, Christianity, Islam and Shintoism, for instance). It has, however, more recently been recognised as having a positive influence compared with earlier opinion. This advantage may be due to an emphasis on the 'interdependent self' in the East, rather the 'independent' one dominant in Western thought (see Luo, 2000:8). Earlier, individualism was seen as linked to the Protestant work ethic and this was regarded as a potential motor of modernisation. Today, we are less sure about this; collectivism is now seen as having its virtues and interdependence is more highly regarded. More than a few chapters will reflect this debate, which is still ongoing.

A number of fundamental questions may now be posed at this juncture:

- What are the underpinning influences at the macro (-economy) level, as well as at the micro (-firm) level, which are related to the economy, culture and management in these economies?
- How does each societal case provide a unique story and experience regarding the global challenges and the pressures vis-à-vis reforming its management systems?
- How far are dysfunctions in each rooted in systemic problems (for example, widespread executive corruption in Japan, corporate bad behaviour in South Korea, or crony favouritism in China)?
- To what degree are such issues linked to changing values, business ethics and related issues such as 'face culture' in their respective societies?
- How may we evaluate positive and negative aspects of traditional value-systems, as well as their impact on management thinking and behaviour in East Asia?

Whilst we would not wish to over-generalise from the evidence presented in this volume, specific Chinese, Japanese, South Korean and other managerial examples in East Asia may enable readers to acquire insights into what was going on in the past, still continues to exist and may persist in the future. We would, however, recommend critical caution at all times in coming to terms with and interpreting possible general trends in management in the region, as well as more widely.

Structure of the book

The work is divided into three sections, establishing the structure of the book, each with a number of relevant chapters covering different aspects of international business in the region under their respective headings. We have tried to be as comprehensive as possible in covering the many dimensions of Asian management which we see as of potential interest to both teachers and students of this subject, as well as interested practitioners.

The first part of the book will deal with general themes common to specific terrains in East Asia, such as economy, culture and management (see chapters 2 to 4); the second, with specific locally-focused studies, looks at China, Hong Kong, Japan, South Korea and others (chapters 5 to 8); the third examines a range of issues such as business networks, employment relations, gender barriers, human resource management, SMEs and so on (chapters 9 to 15). At the end of the volume, we attempt to summarise the findings of these contributions and present some conclusions regarding the possible models of Asian management which are appropriate, what they have in common and where they are different (chapters 16 and 17).

The chapters in the volume are largely qualitative in nature, although some quantitative data is included. The general themes dealt with are mainly cross-national and cross-cultural in nature. Those relating to specific localities are mainly centred on this or that geographical area. The chapters dealing with wider issues are, in turn, where appropriate, comparative. Many of these will present their case in the context of Asia as a whole; some will only cover East Asia; whilst others may also refer in passing to specific regions further afield such as in South East Asia or even in South Asia.

In conceiving this volume, we approached a set of authors with the necessary expertise to cover the issues and topics we thought relevant to the study of Asian management. We decided to choose a number of the latter which we thought inter-esting and relevant. The list is not absolutely comprehensive in terms of covering all possible fields but we believe we have chosen wisely. All of the authors are specialists in their respective fields; they hail from a variety of universities and business schools across the world, located in a wide range of countries in the East and in the West, such as Australia, Bulgaria, Canada, China, France, Hong Kong, Japan, Singapore, South Korea, the UK and the USA, amongst others. Given their backgrounds, and expertise on Asia, they offer a good cross-national and interdisciplinary mix of scholars.

The authors were asked to write their contributions on the basis of a pre-scribed, if relatively flexible, brief; in this sense, the book was devised to follow a previously worked-out plan designed to examine the present realities of the economic, political and social achievements of the specific geographical locations in East Asia included, as well as their historical and cultural backgrounds, but at the same time to allow the contributors a degree of freedom in approaching their subject. They have all, we believe, acquitted themselves well in this respect. The chapters, we believe, reflect a fair balance between the past and the present, theory and practice, as well as the general and the particular.

Contributions to this volume

We will now present a short summary of each of the chapters in this volume.

Chapter 2 by Das suggests that the Asian economies were struck late by the crisis and recession (2007–9) and that they spearheaded the recovery from the crisis. Since the second quarter of 2009 Asian economies began to lead the global recovery. In the advanced industrial economies recovery was not only tepid but they also continued to suffer from serious economic and financial setbacks. Asia's post-recession rapid growth took place at the expense of the EU-15 and the US economies. An important development is China's unremitting rise and overwhelming dominance of the regional economy in the post-crisis period. It emerged as a more important trade partner of several regional econ-omies and stimulated intra-regional trade substantially. Also, trade resulting from the vertical fragmentation of production in Asia expanded much faster than in the other regions of the global economy. China also played a decisive role in the operations and spread of production networks in the region. In the post-crisis period, both intra-regional and extra-regional FDI flows spurted in Asia. FDI flows to China began to structurally transform. They shifted to high-technology and services sectors. Asian economies, particularly China, became outward investors of reasonable proportion. It became amply clear that in the post-crisis period the impact of the advanced industrial economies over the fast globalising Asian EMEs has declined. With rapid global integration, some Asian EMEs have become important global players in their own right. In the materialisation of this new trend, once again the Chinese economy played a unique role. In the pre-Asian crisis period, it became conventional to think of the Asian EMEs as decoupled from the advanced industrial economies. This scenario altered during both the crisis and post-crisis periods. Business cyclical co-movements between Asia and the G-3 became somewhat more synchronised.

In chapter 3 by Minkov, he notes that the study of culture has enjoyed unprec-edented interest recently, as the intensifying globalisation process has revealed important cultural differences across the globe, including the management field. The chapter dwells on some of the most salient cultural characteristics that distinguish the East Asian societies from those of the rest of the world and examines some of their internal differences as well. It presents the results of large-scale cross-cultural studies that situate the East Asian countries on measures of values, beliefs, personality traits (the 'Big Five'), cognitive patterns, communication patterns, social behaviour indicators (such as road death-tolls, corruption, murder rates, educational achievement and sexual behaviour) and work-related cultural characteristics. The East Asian countries are often found to have extreme positions on many of these indicators, the other extreme being typically occupied by African, Arab, or Latin American societies.

Chapter 4 by Jackson profiles, in turn, East Asian management in terms of its distinct systems and styles. Brief illustrations from management practice are developed in order to trace the patterns of similarity and difference that emerge when scholars attempt to discern, attribute and compare the management systems and styles of China, Hong Kong, Japan, South Korea, Taiwan and so on. The terms 'management systems' and 'management styles' are defined before exploring the extent to which systematic reference to these terms – along with the cultures and subcultures that give context to them – can tell us something meaningful about how managers operating within and across these diverse East Asian economies appear to be responding to the pressures driving change globally and/or regionally. Here, change is discussed in terms of how East Asian managers in particular appear to respond to the shifts they perceive as relevant in the political, economic, technological and sociocultural macro-environments within which they and their organisations compete and do international business: specific examples are highlighted. The discussion draws on a range of established and current literature relevant to the field, balancing both Asian and non-Asian perspectives. Overall, this chapter is designed to give direction and encouragement to current and future students of East Asian management. Simultaneously, it offers a broad-brush foundation to the more in-depth discussions presented elsewhere in this book.

In chapter 5, Zhao and Du set out to describe the relationship between culture and management in the People's Republic of China. This country is now playing an increasingly important global role as one of the biggest markets in the world, since the economic reforms and opening-up to the outside world that started in 1978. As China transforms its economy, understanding *culture* is seen as one of the main variables propelling this advancement and accounting more specifically for the distinct management developments that have evolved in China over the last few decades. In a rapidly changing and varied context, such as contemporary China, it is very difficult to assess the degree to which traditional culture continues to exert an influence on management values and behaviour. We need to bear a number of issues and questions in mind when addressing this subject. First, we must recognise China's great diversity and start by asking 'to which China are we referring? Which sector, which region, which generation?' Second, what is taking place in China – keen to learn from the outside world yet also conscious of its history – may force us to abandon the notion that people necessarily conform to a simple notion of 'culture'. In these circumstances, they may not necessarily fit neatly with the cultural dimensions chosen, but instead may display apparent paradoxes. The social identity of modern Chinese managers may indeed be more complex than appreciated.

In chapter 6 by Ip and Ng, Hong Kong, Macau and Taiwan, the three Overseas Chinese (*Nanyang*) societies on the fringe of the Mainland, which have each experienced spectacular economic growth over the last few decades, are examined as newly industrialised economies (NIEs) of East Asia. In spite of their common Confucian heritage and signs of mutual institutional convergence, the authors argue that there are visible diversities which make each distinctive in their cultural, socio-political, economic and management systems – which are in the final analysis, according to the authors, historical. Both Hong Kong and Macau were formerly under colonial rule, until the PRC introduced the novel political formula of 'one country, two systems' in the 1980s prior to their reunification in 1997 and 1999. Important differences do however remain. The legacies left behind by the British on Hong Kong are evidently different from the Portuguese influences in Macau. On the other hand, the successive regimes of the Dutch, Japanese and Americans in Taiwan have made it a hybrid society.

In chapter 7 by Benson and Debroux, Japanese management practices are seen as undergoing change as they respond to a variety of pressures occurring over the past two decades. The seemingly increasing pace of these changes raises a number of important questions such as what are the key underpinning factors influencing Japanese management now; how has management responded to the current challenges presented over the past two decades; what are the constraints operating in Japan to systematic change; and what conclusions can we draw in terms of the structure and form of present-day Japanese management? This chapter will address such issues, although it must be stressed that change in the management practices of Japanese companies is not uniform or clearly transparent. The focus throughout will be on the management of human resources, as this is where significant change is taking place and where the environmental contexts are dynamic and fluid. The chapter commences with a brief outline of the historical and cultural context of Japan which is then followed by a discussion of the development of Japanese business and management and recent economic development. This discussion provides the backdrop for the following section which discusses why change has been necessary and the difficulties of transitioning to a 'new' management system. The slow and varied rate of transition in Japan demonstrates how corporate and societal culture modifies and reinforces managerial values and behaviour. The chapter concludes with a discussion on how far the dysfunctional aspects of the current Japanese management system are rooted in systemic problems.

In chapter 8, Rowley examines the changing nature of management and culture in South Korea. Post-1960s South Korea (hereafter Korea) developed rapidly from a poor agricultural society into a rich, industrialised 'Asian Tiger' economy after the end of the Korean War in the early 1950s but began to have problems after the Asian Financial Crisis in the early 1990s. Here, the development and influence of management and culture in Korea is important for a number of reasons. First, management plays a key role in business, economic development and society but it does not exist in a vacuum. Key works in the field indicate management variations may arise as stemming from culture. Second, even for some non-culturalists, the concept of culture is recognised (see chapter 3). Cultural underpinnings have major consequences for institutional environments. So, institutional perspectives need to be based in cultural contexts. Third, in contrast to the implications of universalism and convergence-related concepts, culture remains not only important and diverse, but may be portrayed as ingrained, deep and slow moving.

Chapter 9 by Cooke compares the patterns of women's participation in employment and management in China, Japan, South Korea and Taiwan. It examines the political environment and institutional context within which women in these countries/regions have been facilitated as well as hindered in pursuing their managerial careers. The chapter shows that while significant progress has been made in the last three decades in women's education in all four societies, which in some cases surpasses that of men of the same age groups, this achievement has not been matched by the same level of earnings and organisational/corporate positions. Although affirmative action programmes in various forms have been introduced by the State in each location, which are aimed to enhance gender equality, the implementation of these policy interventions is hampered by a number of societal, organisational and individual factors. The comparison reveals a common historical trend of women's disadvantages, although progress has been made in each location to varying degrees. Institutional structures, persistent patriarchal gender norms and stereotypes and ineffective representation limit women's bargaining power in the labour market and hold down their financial rewards as well as career progression. However, the various institutional and cultural factors are not played out to the same strength and each employment system contains unique features.

In chapter 10 by Nolan, the author reviews the academic literature on the use of *guanxi* networks in China and on business networks in East Asia more generally. The review has three core aims. The first is to develop a critical understanding of the influence that a Confucian cultural heritage has had on East Asian business networks in China, Japan and South Korea. Here, the chapter demonstrates that while 'maintaining harmonious relations' is a key uniting theme across all nations, there are varying degrees of emphasis which guide social networking behaviour in different ways in different countries. For example, *guanxi* in Chinese communities emphasises the development of long-term personal relationships based on kinship and regional connections, whereas in Japan business networking places more emphasis on corporate connections rather than those based on individual associations. In South Korea the emphasis is on maintaining harmony, or *inhwa,* through kin-based hierarchies and authority relationships, a pattern which is reflected in the 'clan-like' nature of the nation's largest organisations. The second aim of the chapter is to consider the interaction between national culture and institutional structures with a particular focus on the case of Chinese *guanxi*. Here the key question is whether or not the region is experiencing a decline in the importance of *guanxi* networks in the light of far-reaching reforms and a shift towards a more rational-bureaucratic market economy. The third section will offer some evaluation of this debate by arguing that, in global business at least, the continuing need of MNCs to establish links with government officials is a form of *guanxi* networking that needs to be maintained, but that is also one that can prove particularly hazardous for the foreign manager. In conclusion, the chapter evaluates continuity and change in *guanxi* in the post-reform period in China examining both what it is now used for and who it is used by.

Chapter 11 by Witt draws on business systems analysis to offer a comparative overview of business and its cultural and institutional underpinnings in East Asia and particularly in China, Japan and South Korea. The overall picture that emerges is one of considerable variety in such economies. China presents itself as a mixed economy combining several distinct business systems, including a strong private sector and a possibly resurgent state-controlled sector, both operating by different sets of rules. Despite minor institutional changes in recent years, the Japanese business system remains highly coordinated and employee-centric. South Korea retains a business-group-led form of capitalism. The future may see China evolve some resemblance with the present-day South Korean system. Little change is likely in Japan and South Korea may possibly develop structural similarities with continental European business systems.

In Cunningham's chapter 12, the author argues that with a sustained high-single to double-digit economic growth and development in recent decades, East Asian economies are increasingly playing the role of a global growth-pole, and are fast emerging as a manufacturing and information technology hub of the world economy. One of the key characteristics of the East Asia region is the presence and importance of a large small and medium-sized enterprises (SME) sector comprising the majority of enterprises in all of the region's economies. Although it is important to recognise that the challenges SMEs face, and the corresponding policies aimed at strengthening their competitive performance, may vary due to a great diversity of economies and development experiences among the countries in the region, the broad contexts faced by East Asian SMEs are similar. Thus, the paper examines the issues and challenges to East Asian SMEs in a renewed global market environment, with special focus on four economies in the region – China, Hong Kong, South Korea and Taiwan. The importance of SMEs in their nation's economy is demonstrated. The difficulties, challenges and opportunities for SMEs in the new economic environment after the 2008 global financial crisis are discussed. In order to enhance SMEs' competitiveness in the changing business environment, it argues that not only the industrial structure but also the labour market and management systems in which SMEs operate need to be reshaped and transformed. In so doing, a transitionary and evolutionary change in SMEs across East Asian economies should occur, and simultaneously, distinctive management systems, institutional structures and business models may emerge.

Chapter 13 by Kuruvilla and Chung argues that firm-level human resource strategies in East Asia which emphasise workplace flexibility in response to increased global competition, coupled with institutional and legal changes that encourage and facilitate such strategies, have resulted in a dramatic increase in the use of informal employment strategies (the use of casual, temporary and contract workers) in China, Japan and South Korea. In all three countries, such informal employment accounts for over 35 per cent of the workforce. This externalisation of the employment relationship represents the dominance of the 'logic of competition' that underlies employment relations systems in East Asia. Given the inability of traditional labour unions to provide increased protection (most unions do not represent temporary, casual and contract workers) and given the absence of 'high road' employment relations strategies of firms that promote stable employment, governments have taken the lead to alleviate, if not improve, the working conditions of this large 'informal' workforce through new regulations that seek to control the growth of informal labour that older regulations facilitated. Although this attempt at 're-regulation' denotes a growing 'logic of labor protection' in these countries, we are sceptical about its success in controlling the growth of flexibility strategies that rely on 'informal' labour.

Chapter 14 by Khilji focuses upon contemporary management behaviour and culture in South Asia and compares it with several countries in East Asia and Southeast Asia. It presents a detailed overview of the socio-economic and cultural environment in many South Asian economies and shows that following a period of deregulation, the region has witnessed impressive economic growth. It is reflected in increased multinational activity, a growing private sector and a spree of international acquisitions initiated by South Asian (in particular, Indian) companies. The recent fascination of the West with the 'India Way', a management philosophy that caters to social mission, investment in human capital and developing innovative new products in the face of competition and lack of resources, is described, whereby Indian companies are being labelled as offering a compelling new business model that faltering companies in the West should emulate. However, it is also argued in this chapter that despite much economic progress and business development in South Asia, not all companies pursue exemplary management practices. The majority struggle with balancing tradition and modernity. Their challenges in terms of rapidly changing individual values, population explosion, talent shortages, inadequate infrastructure, slow and bureaucratic political governance and extremism in society are highlighted. A comparison with East Asia and Southeast Asia indicates that management and culture throughout Asia is being constantly reshaped by globalisation that is reflected in new practices and changing employee expectations, attitudes and behaviours. It is concluded that managers need to learn from each other and embrace an ambicultural model that incorporates the best of Eastern and Western values. The chapter concludes that such a model is likely to help Asian organisations succeed and position them as role models for the future generations of global managers.

In chapter 15, Warner looks at management education and training in Asia, focusing in particular on three countries, namely China, Japan and South Korea. All are core economies in East Asia and all are major players in the expanding trade and growing well-being of that part of the world. He also refers to a number of Overseas Chinese domains in the region, such as Hong Kong, Macau and Taiwan, if only in passing. Business schools and similar institutions in Asia are now to be found almost everywhere. The fastest expansion of management education and training in the world is now to be found in that region. There are indeed precedents for contemporary developments in management education and training, in terms of the notion of highly selective elite schools stemming from the Confucian tradition but with varying degrees of continuity linking past and present. There may of course be 'family resemblances' from one country to another. But 'convergence' theory does fully not resolve the issue in this context. Modernisation and industrialisation do not have the same impact on these countries' systems of management education and training. Neither does the cultural and historical legacy of Confucianism point to overly common outcomes. The cultural resilience of the Japanese system seems to protect it more from exogenous influences compared with the Chinese or South Korean systems. One irony is that American-style business schools have diffused more widely in communist China than in anti-communist Japan. If 'soft' convergence does occur, the author argues, it might be likely to do so within cultural parameters but possibly in unanticipated ways.

In chapter 16 by Tung, we see a view of the future of management in East Asia. Since the Industrial Revolution, Western industrial/business practices have been emulated worldwide. This situation began to change after the Second World War. The 2008–9 global financial crises and the sovereign debt debacle in the European Union have accelerated the transition from 'West leads East' to 'West meets East'. This chapter first examines the factors that have contributed to this changed calculus of global competition. These include:

- the widening disparity in economic growth rates;
- the rising competitiveness of non-Western multinationals;
- the growing share of research and publications from emerging markets, particularly China.

The chapter then speculates on the future of East Asian management. While Western management theories and practices will most likely not be totally eclipsed and replaced by East Asian management paradigms and styles, the latter (particularly Chinese management) will most likely exhibit the following characteristics:

- more intense scrutiny of Western management practices, particularly their pitfalls, and as they apply to the context of the institutional environment specific to a given society;
- more bidirectional flow of knowledge from East to West and vice-versa as distinguished from the more unilateral flow from West to East prevalent in the past;
- diversity of styles and practices characterised by eclecticism.

Chapter 17 by the Editor attempts to sum up what has been said in the book, why it was important and where it is leading to. The 'devil' it concludes is always 'in the details'.

Conclusions

In this edited volume, we have tried to present the many dimensions of Asian management relevant to the region's growing economic power, particularly focusing on East Asia. We have also seen how the region is rapidly changing with respect to its economies, cultures and management and how these affect the way it does business. To better come to terms with these developments, we have throughout emphasised an eclectic interdisciplinary approach, bringing together approaches derived from economics, management studies, politics, sociology and so on, to shed light on managerial behaviour across the region. The debate on 'Asian values' has also been noted, as well as the long-standing influence of Confucianism. The contributors aim to shed light on the diverse aspects of Asian management in which they specialise. The result we hope will enable the reader to have a richer understanding of the 'whole' as well as the 'parts'!

References

Bell, D. (2008) *China's New Confucianism: Politics and Everyday Life in a Changing Society*. Princeton, NJ: Princeton University Press.

Economist, The (2011) 'Sun Tzu and the art of soft power', *The Economist*, 17 December, pp. 97–9.

Fairbank, J. K. Reischauer, E. O. and Craig, A. M. (1973) *East Asia: Tradition and Transformation*. Boston: Houghton Mifflin.

Goody, J. (1996) *The East in the West*. Cambridge: Cambridge University Press.

Holcombe, C. (2011) *A History of East Asia: From the Origins of Civilization to the Twenty-First Century*. Cambridge: Cambridge University Press.

Krugman, P. (1994) 'The Myth of Asia's Miracle', *Foreign Affairs*, 73: 62.

Lee, J. W. and Hong, K. (2010) 'Economic Growth in Asia: Determinants and Prospects'. *ADB Economics Working Paper Series 220*. Manila: Asian Development Bank.

Luo, Y. (2000) *Guanxi and Business*. Singapore: World Scientific.

Maddison, A. (2007) *Chinese Economic Performance in the Long Run, 960–2030 AD*, Development Centre Studies. Paris: OECD.

Maurice, M., Sorge, A. and Warner, M. (1980) 'Societal differences in organizing manufacturing units: A comparison of France, West Germany, and Great Britain', *Organization Studies*, 1: 59–86.

Nankervis, A., Cooke, F. L., Chatterjee, S. R. and Warner, M. (2013) *New Human Resource Management Models from China and India*. London: Routledge (in press).

Ronan, C. (1978) *The Shorter Science and Civilization in China* (with J. Needham). Vol. 1. Cambridge: Cambridge University Press.

Rowley, C., Benson, J. and Warner, M. (2005) 'Towards an Asian model of human resource management? A comparative analysis of China, Japan and South Korea', in Warner, M. (ed.) *Human Resource Management in China Revisited*. London: Routledge, pp. 301–18.

Vogel, E. F. (1991) *The Four Little Dragons: The Spread of Industrialization in East Asia*. Cambridge, MA: Harvard University Press.

Warner, M. (1994) 'Japanese culture, Western management: Taylorism and human resources in Japan', *Organization Studies*, 15: 509–33.

Warner, M. (2002) 'Globalization, labour markets and human resources in Asia Pacific economies: An overview', *International Journal of Human Resource Management*, 13: 384–98.

— (ed.) (2003) *Culture and Management in Asia*. London: RoutledgeCurzon.

— (ed.) (2011) *Confucianism HRM in Greater China; Theory and Practice*, London and New York: Routledge.

Westney, D. E. (1987) *Imitation and Innovation: The Transfer of Western Organizational Patterns to Meiji Japan*. Cambridge, MA: Harvard University Press.

World Bank (2011) Miscellaneous. Available at http://web.worldbank.org/WBSITE/EXTERNAL/EXTABOUTUS/0,pagePK:50004410~piPK:36602~theSitePK:29708,00.html (accessed 11.11.11).

Part II

Themes

To rule a country of a thousand chariots, there must be reverent attention to business, and sincerity, economy in expenditure, and love for men; and the employment of people at the proper seasons.

(Confucius: Analects, I, v)

2 East Asian economy

An overview

Dilip K. Das

Introduction

A momentous economic event of historic significance is that the Asian economies, particularly those of East and Southeast Asia, grew at a vertiginous rate over the last four decades. The West took 300 years to industrialise and innovate and Japan 100, but the newly-industrialised economies (NIEs) of Asia[1] took only 40 years, while China took merely 30 (Lin, 2011). The Asian economies went through an unprecedented process of economic development, industrialisation and urbanisation. They were *inter alia* driven by the forces of regionalisation and globalisation. One indicator of their rapid growth is the trend in per capita income in Asia, which surpassed the world average per capita income in the early 1980s and has maintained a higher growth rate since (Bai, *et al.*, 2009). By the dawn of the twenty-first century, they had been transformed manifestly, which in turn had a decisive impact over the global economy. That Asia has begun to play a pivotal role in global sustainability is demonstrated by its role during the global financial crisis of 2007–9, the Great Recession and the recovery.

The objective of this chapter is to focus on the economic landscape in Asia that has altered over the recent past, particularly during the global financial crisis and the newly emerged Asian economic scenario of the post-global-financial-crisis period. The Asian economic landscape of the post-global-financial-crisis period has markedly different characteristics from that of the previous period.

Global financial crisis and Asian economy

The global financial crisis of 2007–9 was the first veritable and full-sized financial and economic crisis of this century. It was ignited in the financial sector and spilt into the real economy. It was perhaps the most virulent crisis of the last seven decades. Paul A. Samuelson (2010; p. xvi) termed it a state of 'terrible meltdown'. Ben Bernanke called it, 'the worst financial crisis in global history, including the Great Depression' (Chan, 2011).[2] A crisis of this magnitude naturally has a massive all-round impact.

In a globalised economy the crisis propagated rapidly, albeit Asia was well positioned to weather the financial and economic storm. Asian financial institutions were not exposed to the so-called 'toxic assets' and macroeconomic reforms and financial restructuring initiated after the Asian crisis (1997–8) had structurally fortified Asian economies and financial markets. Additionally, due to attractive economic fundamentals a large inflow of portfolio capital had taken place in the Asian economies – before the onset of the global financial crisis. These financial inflows also reflected the demand conditions in the prominent international financial centres. For the most part, the regional economy was resilient to the global financial crisis. During the initial phase, though, the crisis did not affect Asia and some even believed that it would pass Asia by without being excessively detrimental to the region.

Somewhat belatedly, the crisis and recession affected the real economy and financial markets in Asia. The regional economies were hit extremely hard in the last quarter of 2008, after the collapse of Lehman Brothers. The crisis had a massive impact over contours of the Asian economies. Governments and central banks in Asia responded promptly and persuasively. Although the Asian economy contracted during the first quarter of 2009, towards the end of the first quarter and beginning of the second signs of the so-called green-shoots of recovery became visible in several Asian economies. This event applied a fortiori to the emerging-market economies (EMEs) of the region. They began giving faint albeit distinct indications of a recovery. The two indicators that began to abstemiously look up were exports and industrial production.

The slow recovery picked up gradual momentum. It became more distinct and explicit in the more open economies of Asia that were large exporters of electronics and other high-technology manufactured products. Those that had a large domestic demand base were also relatively swift in recovering. China, Indonesia and the Republic of Korea (hereinafter Korea) recorded the briskest recovery in industrial production. When these and other Asian economies began their rebound, the global economy was still mired in recession. An early indication of rebound in Asia seemed to validate the so-called decoupling hypothesis for the region. That is, Asia was *not in synch* but leading the global economic cycle.

Asia spearheads the resurgence of the global economy

From the second quarter of 2009, Asian EMEs began to lead the global recovery. At this point the European Union (EU), the United States (US) and the rest of the global economy were not out of recession. In 2009, Asia was the only region that posted positive real GDP growth of 3.6 per cent (Table 2.1). It outperformed the other regions of the global economy (Das, 2011). For an outward-oriented regional economy, whose growth was largely export-based, this was indeed unusual.

Since the first quarter of 2010, trade in Asia was recovering at a strong pace, albeit multilateral trade recovery was not so strong. At this point, monthly trade statistics for Asia had returned to their pre-crisis level. Merchandise trade in the region recorded a 30 per cent leap in 2010, higher than the average global merchandise trade increase of 21 per cent (ESCAP, 2011). Thus, Asia worked as a

Table 2.1 Real GDP growth rates: Asia spearheading the global growth

	2008[1]	2009	2010	2011	2012 (Projections)
Asia	5.2	3.6	8.3	6.8	6.9
Newly-industrialised Asian Economies (NIEs)[2]	1.8	−0.8	8.4	4.9	4.5
ASEAN-5[3]	4.7	1.7	6.9	5.4	5.7
Euro Area	0.6	−4.1	1.7	1.6	1.8
United States	0.4	−2.6	2.8	2.8	2.9
World	3.0	−0.5	5.0	4.4	4.5

1   For 2008, real effective exchange rates are assumed to be constant at the levels prevailing during 23 February–23 March 2010. From 2009–2012 (projections), the real effective exchange rates applied are at the levels prevailing during 8 February–8 March 2011.
2   Hong Kong SAR, the Republic of Korea, Singapore and Taiwan.
3   Indonesia, Malaysia, the Philippines, Thailand and Vietnam.

stabilising force in the global economy. It provided a 'pull-force' to the global recovery. Export growth rates in the region began tapering off in early 2011.

The global economy was no longer in recession in 2010 (Table 2.1). However, the recovery was highly uneven or, as it began to be called, multi-speed. Different regions of the global economy were recovering at different paces. Asia continued to lead the global economy forward. In 2010, it grew at the rate of 8.3 per cent. Comparable growth rate in the EU was 1.7 per cent and in the US 2.8 per cent.

According to the estimates made by the Conference Board (CB), Asia accounted for 47 per cent of global GDP growth in 2010 (Conference Board, 2011). The performance of the Chinese economy was particularly noteworthy in this regard. Its contribution to the recovery endeavours was maximal (see chapter 5). It not only did not suffer a recession in 2009 but also grew by 9.3 per cent. In 2010, it turned in a stellar double-digit (10.3 per cent) growth performance (IMF, 2011a). The global financial crisis, recession and recovery set in motion forces that are reshaping the structure of the Asian and global economies and policy-making framework. For instance, wise men acknowledged that unregulated capitalism cannot run modern economies efficiently. Errors on the Left and Right both mandated what Samuelson (2010) called 'centrism'. The global financial crisis rendered the Group-of-Seven (G-7) unrepresentative of the global economy and irrelevant. It was supplanted by the G-20. This shift was a highly consequential change in the global strategic landscape.

New Asian economic landscape

Over the preceding half century, per capita incomes increased in all the developing regions, but only Asia could achieve the unique distinction of achieving income convergence towards the high-income industrial countries (see chapters 5, 6, 7 and 8). This applies particularly to the Asian NIEs and the EMEs. As seen in Table 2.2, the heft of the Asian economy in the global economy is rising. Over the

Table 2.2 GDP as a proportion of world GDP (%)

	1990	2000	2009
Asia	18.67	23.27	22.28
EU-15	32.13	25.09	26.03
US	26.27	30.73	24.23

Sources: (The World Bank, 2011)
Data for Taiwan comes from (*Economy Watch*, 2011)

1990–2009 period, Asia's GDP as a proportion of the global GDP increased, with Asia now accounting for close to a quarter of the global GDP. It needs to be reiterated here that Asia is defined to include only the dynamic economies of East and Southeast Asia. Conversely, the GDP of the EU-15 and the US as a proportion of global GDP declined over the same period. The increasing importance of the developing economies in the global economy is almost totally driven by the robust growth performance of Asia, notably that of China.

Considerable reorienting of global and regional systems occurred during the last decade, also during the post-global financial crisis period. The inter-relationship between the principal economic players in Asia became more complex. As China continued on its brisk growth-path, economic and financial integration between the Asian economies intensified. Regional cooperation among the three large players, namely, China, Japan and Korea, is on the rise (see chapters 5, 7 and 8).

China's increasing role

One of the most conspicuous developments was China's inexorable rise and overwhelming dominance of the regional economy.[3] A comparison of GDP growth rates, trade and other indicators of the important regional economies testifies to this fact (Table 2.3). Judged in an absolute sense, China's economic performance

Table 2.3 China is growing faster than Japan and the NICs (in billions of $)

	GDP		Exports		Imports	
	1990	2010	1990	2009	1990	2009
China	356.94	5,745.13	57.37	1,333.30	46.71	1,113.20
Japan	3,058.04	5,390.90	316.75	636.14	287.93	620.79
Korea	263.78	1,371.33	73.74	415.43	76.57	382.81
Taiwan	164.75	430.10	67.42	203.67	54.79	174.37
Hong Kong SAR	76.89	316.03	100.43	408.13	93.79	393.07
Singapore	36.84	217.38	38.43	426.36	42.38	391.67
			(1988)	(2008)	(1988)	(2008)

Sources: (The World Bank, 2011); (National Statistics, Republic of China (Taiwan), 2011); (IMF, 2011a); (Mongobay, 2011)

was nothing short of phenomenal. When China began its transition to a market-oriented economy in 1978 its per capita income was a paltry US$182 and trade dependence (trade-to-GDP ratio) was 11.2 per cent. It has recorded 9.9 per cent annual GDP growth over the last three decades and 16.3 per cent growth rate in international trade. According to the *World Development Indicator 2011* (The World Bank, 2011), China's 2009 GDP at current prices and exchange rate was $4.98 trillion and in terms of purchasing power parity (PPP) $9.22 trillion. Its per capita GDP at current prices and exchange rates was $3,744 in 2009 and in terms of PPP $6,828. Its trade dependence ratio crossed 65 per cent, the highest among the world's large systemically significant economies. It succeeded in lifting 600 million people out of poverty.

China's regional importance started growing long before it edged past Japan to become the second largest economy in the world at market prices and exchange rates in mid-2010. This feat was, and continues to be, an event of enormous economic and geopolitical significance. China's ebullient growth performance is continuously influencing and transforming the regional economy. In the near future it will create exceptional growth opportunities for the other Asian economies to upgrade their pattern of growth and move up the value chain. China may well have a similar impact on the global economy.

Openness and rapid trade growth

Asian economies, particularly the EMEs and the NIEs, are well known for being successful traders as well as for being open economies. Over the last quarter century, the share of Asia, excluding Japan, in total world trade increased much faster than that of North America and the EU-15. Openness is defined as trade (exports + imports) as a percentage of GDP. According to *International Trade Statistics 2010*, Asia was not a particularly strong trading region until the early 1970s. However, in 2009 it was the second largest trading region after the EU, accounting for 29.4 per cent of total multilateral exports and 27.4 per cent of total imports. The largest trading regional economy, China alone accounted for 9.9 per cent of multilateral exports and 8.1 per cent of imports in 2009 (WTO, 2010). An interesting fact in this regard is that the increasing importance of Asia as a trading region is partially due to the rising trade in parts, components and intermediate goods (Aminian *et al.*, 2007).

Due to rapid trade growth relative to GDP growth, the openness of the Asian economies went on increasing. It was 74.65 per cent of GDP in 1985, 138.16 per cent in 2005 and 129.48 per cent in 2009 (The World Bank, 2011). The retreat in 2009 can be explained by the fact that it was the global financial crisis year, and multilateral trade recorded a wrenching contraction. The fast expansion of China's trade, both intra-regional and multilateral, favourably influenced the openness of the Asian economies. The increasing trend in regional trade has intensified the regional and global integration of the Asian economy.

Escalating regionalisation of trade

According to *International Trade Statistics 2010,* Asia is its own largest trading partner; 51.6 per cent of its exports are intra-regional. In 2000 intra-regional exports were 49 per cent. As trading partners, the significance of the EU (17.9 per cent) and North America (17.5 per cent) for Asia was much less in 2009 than its intra-trade (WTO, 2010).

Over the 2000–9 period, the growth of intra-regional trade in Asia was faster than Asia's trade with the rest of the world. While Asian exports almost doubled over this period, intra-regional exports increased three times (IMF, 2011b).[4] China's role in intra-regional trade expansion was vital. It was the principal player in intra-regional trade during this period, accounting for more than half of total trade within the region. The increase in intra-regional trade was the result of an increase in trade with the developing Asian economies. Over 2000–9, the share of exports to developing Asian economies increased to one quarter of total regional exports. China accounted for 12 per cent of regional exports in 2009 and 50 per cent of exports to regional developing economies. Conversely, the role of Japan and the NIEs as a major export destination for the Asian exporters declined (ESCAP, 2011).

Vertically integrated production networks

Production fragmentation-based trade in Asia expanded much faster than in the other regions of the global economy, namely the EU and the North American Free Trade Area (NAFTA). Over the preceding two decades, Asia has come to dominate network production and the trade emanating from it. This trend is contrary to earlier expectations when Asia's relative position was to erode vis-à-vis Mexico and the countries at the periphery of Europe. Global and regional production networks became strong in Asia and were responsible for the emergence of 'Factory Asia'.

China has played a decisive role in the operation and spread of production networks. Although China was to participate in them late, production networks spread over southern and eastern China, and the surrounding Asian economies have reorganised the industrial production structure of Asia. They have turned China into a manufacturing and exporting powerhouse. (IMF, 2011b; Gaulier *et al.*, 2007). Essentially due to the operations of these networks, Asian trade increasingly grew China-centred. China relies on inputs from the Asian economies, particularly Japan and the NIEs. The reverse relationship holds equally well. That is, the surrounding Asian economies rely increasingly on inputs from China. It acts as a base or hub for firms located in technologically more advanced Asian economies like Japan and the NIEs. As the finished products are exported to the advanced industrial economies from China, the value and volume of exports from China has skyrocketed. The trade surplus of the region vis-à-vis the rest of the world has grown large. The same applies to the trade surplus of China vis-à-vis the advanced industrial economies, in particular the US.

The principal reasons behind the rapid evolution in the fragmentation of value chains were, first, Asia has diverse labour supply conditions in the region (see chapter 13). They range from high-wage Japan and the NIEs to the low-wage Southeast Asian economies. Manufacturing wages in China and many other Asian economies are lower than those in Mexico and the countries at the periphery of Europe. Second, having a favourable trade and investment policy regime, better ports and a better communications infrastructure gave an edge to the Asian economies. They provided Asian economies with a decisive cost advantage. Therefore transnational corporations (TNCs) preferred Asia as a site for their production bases over the other regions of the global economy. Third, several Asian economies got started early in the network production operation. Japan and the NIEs were the pioneers in this regard. Therefore, they can now offer agglomeration advantages to the large foreign companies and TNCs. Fourth, although China was a latecomer to vertically integrated production, it has now evolved as the centre of low-cost assembly operations. Its large labour endowment *inter alia* gives it an advantage of steady factor prices (Athrukorala, 2011). Also, China's strategy of devising and successfully running the special economic zones (SEZs) saw rich pay-offs in this area.

The increase and spread of fragmentation of value chains has materially influenced trade flows. Parts, components and intermediate goods have evolved as a large trading sector. In 2009, this was the most dynamic sector in multilateral trade. It represented more than half of the non-fuel merchandise trade (WTO, 2011). Growing trade in parts, components and intermediate goods intensified specialisation in international trade and added value along the production chain. It also stimulated intra-regional foreign direct investment (FDI).

Surge in foreign direct investment

Both regionally and globally FDI suffered a sharp decline during the global financial crisis. FDI inflows made a spurt in 2010 in Asia. They increased by 24 per cent, to $300 billion, in 2010. These FDI flows were both intra-regional and extra-regional. In terms of FDI receipts, the major Asian economies performed in a dissimilar manner. FDI flows to the Association of Southeast Asian Nations (ASEAN)[5] economies more than doubled in 2010. Also, China and Hong Kong SAR enjoyed large double-digit growth, but Korea and Taiwan recorded a marked decline. Several ASEAN economies made proactive endeavours to liberalise several industrial sectors to attract more FDI. Indonesia, Malaysia and Singapore were particularly successful in this regard. Therefore, the ASEAN economies received $79.4 billion in 2010, which was higher than the previous record receipt of $76 billion in 2007. The Philippines also liberalised more industries and strengthened supportive policy measures.

FDI flows to ASEAN increased because production costs and wages in China have been rising and Indonesia and Vietnam have been gaining ground as low-cost production centres, particularly in low-end manufactures. Low-income countries in ASEAN, like Lao PDR, received a lot of investment from China and Thailand.

Offshoring of low-cost manufacturing activities to China has been decelerating. Even disinvestment took place in the coastal provinces. FDI flows to China have been structurally transforming. They have been shifting to high-technology and services sectors. Singapore received $39 billion in 2010, almost half of the total receipt by the ASEAN group. The reasons such large FDI flows went to Singapore are, first, in the post-global financial crisis period financial flows to the EMEs in general rose and second Singapore has the reputation of being an important global financial centre, as well as the regional headquarters of numerous TNCs. China received $105.7 billion in 2010 and Hong Kong SAR $69 billion. In both cases, the statistics were at a historic high.

Asian economies have now become outward investors of reasonable proportion. Outward foreign direct investment (OFDI) from Asia increased from $193.2 billion in 2009 to $231.6 billion in 2010, a 19.9 per cent increase. The principal outward investment-making Asian economies are China, Hong Kong SAR, Malaysia, Korea, Singapore and Taiwan. China invested $68 billion as OFDI in 2010 and Hong Kong $76 billion. Asian business firms have been acquiring overseas assets in numerous industries in geographically widespread countries. China was the largest outward investor. For the first time, China's OFDI in 2010 exceeded that of Japan. Cross-border M&A purchases by Asian business firms surged to nearly $94 billion in 2010, the highest level reached by Asian firms. Accounting for over 30 per cent of the total, China made the largest amount of M&A purchases.[6]

Decoupling and re-coupling Asia

Panel regression framework analysis reveals that the impact of the advanced industrial economies over the fast globalising EMEs has declined during the present phase of globalisation, which is believed to have begun in the first half of the 1980s. Driven by their brisk GDP growth rates, the EMEs have developed their own momentum and vitality. Some of them have become important players in the global economy in their own right. Therefore, the old relationship of one group of economies depending upon the other has changed into multifaceted interdependence between these two groups (Akin and Kose, 2008). In the materialisation of this new trend, China has played a unique role and has developed a special niche in the global economy. In part, this trend has developed because China has expanded its exports into the advanced industrial economies and has received a large investment from them. Other Asian EMEs may follow China in this endeavour (Fidrmuc and Korhonen, 2010).

In the pre-Asian crisis period, it became conventional to think that economic activity in the Asian economy, particularly the Asian EMEs, was not dependent on the advanced industrial economies. That is, they had decoupled from the three advanced industrial economies, namely the EU, Japan and the US, or the so-called G-3. Asian economies, particularly the EMEs, seemed to be advancing under their own momentum, without needing a locomotive for their growth. They appeared to be a self-contained economic entity. According to this hypothesis, rapid growth in the region could work as a growth impetus for the Asian EMEs. This became known as the decoupling hypothesis.

This scenario altered in the post-Asian crisis period when cyclical co-movements between Asia and the G-3 initially became somewhat more synchronised and then this trend strengthened. Calculations of decadal correlations between GDP growth in Asia and that in the G-3 by the Asian Development Bank (2007) confirmed this trend. After remaining negative in the 1990s, the correlation became positive (0.64) for the 2000–7 period. The correlation was higher at 1.0 for 2008. The global financial crisis of 2007–9 further discredited the so-called decoupling hypothesis. After becoming independent of the G-3 economies in the 1900s, synchronisation of the business cycle in Asia with those of the G-3 economies increased. Computations of Granger causality also confirmed that movements in the G-3 business cycle affected Asian business cycles after a lag of two to three years (Brooks and Hua, 2009).

Post-global crisis Asia

As elaborated earlier, Asian recovery from the global financial crisis and the Great Recession was swift. By the last quarter of 2010, the GDP growth rate had picked up in the ASEAN-5[7] economies and the NIEs of Asia. The Chinese economy grew at a double-digit rate in 2010 (Table 2.1). Economic performance in the region was supported by both strong domestic demand and flourishing exports. However, this pick-up was delayed in Japan; it did not occur until early 2011. The earthquake and tsunami of March 2011 caused enormous loss of life and property in Japan. They substantially disrupted the economic activity in the region as well; in particular, the supply-chain operations were seriously interrupted. That said, the disturbance in the regional economy was not unmanageable. Commodity exporters of Asia benefited from high prices in the global commodity markets. The Asian economy began 2011 in a healthy state, but by 2012, less so.

Unevenness in the global recovery continued. The advanced industrial economies, particularly the EU and the US, not only recovered slowly but also continued having additional economic difficulties of ominous proportions. The former was plagued by sovereign debt crises in several economies. Notwithstanding the listlessness of the recovery and sovereign debt-related disturbances, investment in machinery and equipment in the advanced industrial economies recovered. It began to rise due to the onset of the global investment cycle. The Asian economies were able to take full advantage of this recovery in investment because, first, they have become large exporters of machinery and transport equipment. Approximately 60 per cent of their total exports fall into these two categories. Second, import elasticity of investments in the advanced industrial economy is high. Third, for several Asian economies, electronics goods are an important export sector. This category of export benefited from the long-term trend of large and increasing consumption by consumers in the advanced industrial economies, particularly the US. Fourth, Asian export performance was also strengthened by a strong demand for final goods from the Asian EMEs.

Several extra-regional EMEs also contributed to this demand. Fifth, the Chinese economy has become progressively well-integrated with the rest of the Asian economy. Its increasing demand for both final and intermediate goods has begun playing a material role in stimulating the export performance of the Asian economies. As Asian exports picked up momentum, their industrial production began rising as well.

Due to moderately accommodative financial conditions and favourable fiscal policies, private demand in the Asian economies was high. China and the ASEAN-5 economies recorded particularly strong retail sales. They were encouraged by strengthening consumer confidence and growth in real wages. Due to sharp increases in capacity utilisation, investment in capital spending by Asian business firms was on the rise. Also, the trend in infrastructure spending continued. This trait applied mostly to China and Hong Kong SAR.

In comparison to the pre-global financial crisis period, the cost of capital remained lower in 2011 in Asia. Banks' credit expanded at a rapid rate in the region. Equity and debt issuance in the ASEAN-5 countries increased in 2010 and 2011. The same trend was observed in China and Korea. This shift also occurred in both local and foreign markets. Foreign investors felt comfortable in investing in Asia. Currencies in the region were under pressure to appreciate in the final quarter of 2010. The *yen* appreciated after the Japanese earthquake in March 2011 to an exceedingly high level, but the synchronised Group-of-Seven (G-7) intervention depreciated it somewhat. The real effective exchange rates in China and ASEAN-5 economies weakened in the final quarter of 2010. However, due to the high inflation rate in many of these economies the real currency depreciation was not much. In contrast, nominal effective exchange rates strengthened in the NIEs. Due to a strong current account surplus, Hong Kong SAR was an exception in this regard (see chapter 6).

Although the unemployment situation had improved since the recovery from the Great Recession, vulnerable groups still suffered high unemployment rates in many subregions. Indonesia and Thailand were two prime examples. High unemployment rates among youth did not show much improvement. It remained close to twice the average unemployment rate in the economies. Other worries of the policy-makers were income inequality and social exclusion, which remained obstinately high. Asian economies have benefited a great deal from economic globalisation, which in turn has promoted the well-being of workers in general. However, globalisation failed to benefit all workers. It passed certain categories of workers in Asia and has not benefited them at all (see chapter 13).

The medium-term growth projection of the EMEs of Asia by the International Monetary Fund (IMF) is 8 per cent (IMF, 2011a). They are projected to grow at this rate in both 2011 and 2012. This projection is close to the potential output growth for the Asian EMEs but a trifle below the 8.5 per cent growth rate achieved during 2002–7, the quinquennium before the global financial crisis. Although China's growth is expected to be moderate due to the tightening of investment, it is expected to be the lead economy in Asia during the medium term. Conversely in Indonesia growth rate is projected to accelerate.[8]

Conclusions

To sum up, the emergence of the Asian economy as a dynamic economic growth-pole over the preceding four decades is an event of historic significance. The global financial crisis of 2007–9 was exceedingly severe and it transformed the scenario further. The Asian economies were struck late by the crisis and recession and they spearheaded the recovery from the crisis. Since the second quarter of 2009, the Asian economies began to lead the global recovery. In the advanced industrial economies recovery was not only tepid but they also continued to suffer from serious economic and financial setbacks. China, Indonesia and Korea recorded the briskest recovery in industrial production. The Asian economies began to play a role in global economic sustainability. This fact favourably influenced their heft in the global economy. The economic landscape of Asia has significantly and comprehensively altered over the recent past. In the post-crisis period, Asia contributed a great deal to global economic growth. The global financial crisis, recession and recovery set in motion forces that are reshaping the structure of the Asian and global economies and policy-making frameworks, but China's growth-rate may be now slowing down.

Several Asian economies began to converge towards the high-income industrial countries. Asia now accounts for almost a quarter of global GDP. Its global economic expansion is taking place at the expense of the EU-15 and the US. An important development is China's unremitting rise, leading to overwhelming dominance of the regional economy. China's regional importance started growing long before it edged past Japan to become the second largest economy in the world at market prices and exchange rates in mid-2010. The Chinese economy became more prominent both regionally and globally than Japan and the NIEs. The Asian economies, particularly the EMEs and the NIEs, are well known for being successful traders, as well as for being open economies.

Over the last quarter of a century, the share of Asia excluding Japan in total world trade has increased much faster than that of North America and the EU-15. China emerged as a successful trading economy. The fast expansion of China's trade, both intra-regional and multilateral, has favourably influenced the openness of the Asian economies.

Intra-regional trade in Asia has expanded briskly, particularly since 2000. Asia is its own most important trading partner. China has emerged as an important trade partner of several regional economies and has stimulated intra-regional trade substantially. Production fragmentation-based trade in Asia has expanded much faster than in the other regions of the global economy. Over the preceding two decades, Asia has thus come to dominate network production and the trade emanating from it. Global and regional production networks became strong in Asia and were responsible for the emergence of 'Factory Asia'.

China played a decisive role in the operations and spread of production networks (see chapters 5, 11 and 12). Production networks spread over southern and eastern China and the surrounding Asian economies. They have reorganised the industrial production structure of Asia as well as turning China into a manufacturing and exporting powerhouse. Considerable reorienting of global and regional systems occurred during the post-global financial crisis period. Inter-relationship between the principal economic players in Asia became more complex (see chapter 16).

After the global financial crisis, the FDI flows spurted in Asia. They were both intra-regional and extra-regional FDI flows. No doubt there was a wide diversity in FDI receipt in the Asian economies. Growth of FDI to China has been decelerating. Even disinvestment took place in the coastal provinces. FDI flows to China have been structurally transforming. They have been shifting to high-technology and services sectors. Asian economies have become outward investors of reasonable proportion. China is the largest outward investor. In 2010, China's OFDI exceeded that from Japan. This was a 'first' for the Middle Kingdom.

The impact of the advanced industrial economies over the fast globalising EMEs has declined during the present phase of globalisation and some EMEs have become important global players in their own right. In the materialisation of this new trend, China played a unique role. In the pre-Asian crisis period, it became conventional to think of the Asian EMEs as decoupled from the advanced industrial economies. This scenario altered in the post-Asian crisis period and cyclical co-movements between Asia and the G-3 initially became somewhat synchronised and then this trend strengthened.

Notes

1   The NIEs comprise Hong Kong SAR, the Republic of Korea, Singapore and Taiwan.
2   As quoted by Chan (2011) in *The New York Times*, January 27.
3   Several scholarly accounts of it are available. For instance, see Das (2008), Lardy (2002 and 2003), Lau *et al.* (2000), Naughton (2007) and Song *et al.* (2011).
4   See chapter 3, IMF (2011b).
5   The Association of Southeast Asian Nations (ASEAN) was founded by five Southeast Asian economies, namely, Indonesia, Malaysia, the Philippines, Singapore and Thailand in August 1967. Since then its membership has expanded to include Brunei, Myanmar, Cambodia, Laos and Vietnam.
6   The source of statistical data relating to FDI and OFDI is the *World Investment Report* 2011, chapter 2 (UNCTAD, 2011).
7   The ASEAN-5 economies comprise Indonesia, Malaysia, the Philippines, Thailand and Vietnam.
8   This section draws on IMF (2011b), chapter 1.

References

Akin, C. and Kose, M. A. (2008) 'Changing Nature of North-South Linkages: Stylized Facts and Explanation', *Journal of Asian Economics*, 19: 1–28.
Aminian, N., Fung, K. C. and Iizaka, H. (2007) 'Foreign Direct Investment, Intra-Regional Trade and Production Sharing in East Asia'. Research Institute of Economy, Trade and Industry/ *RIETI Discussion Paper,* No. 07-E-064. Tokyo: RIE.
Asian Development Bank (ADB) (2007) *Asian Development Outlook.* Manila: ADB.
Athrukorala, P. C. (2011) 'Production Networks and Trade Patterns in East Asia', *Asian Economic Papers*, 10: 65–95.

Bai, X., Wieczorek, A. J. and Kaneko, S. (2009) 'Enabling Sustainability Transition in Asia: Importance of Vertical and Horizontal Linkages', *Technological Forecasting and Social Change*, 76: 255–66.

Brooks, D. H. and Hua, C. (2009) 'Asian Trade and Global Linkages', *Asian Development Review*, 26: 103–28.

Chan, S. (2011) 'Crisis Panel's Report Parsed Far and Wide', *The New York Times*, January 27, p.1.

Conference Board (2011) *Global Economic Outlook 2011*. New York: CB, April.

Das, Dilip K. (2008) *The Chinese Economic Renaissance: Apocalypse or Cornucopia?* Basingstoke: Palgrave Macmillan.

— (2011) *Asian Economy: Spearheading the Recovery from the Global Financial Crisis.* London and New York: Routledge.

Economy Watch (2011) Taiwan Economic Statistics and Indicators. Available at http://www.economywatch.com/economic-statistics/country/Taiwan

ESCAP (Economic and Social Commission for Asia and the Pacific) (2011) 'Asia-Pacific Trade and Investment Report 2011'. New York: ESCAP, July.

Fidrmuc, J. and Korhonen, I. (2010) 'The Impact of the Global Financial Crisis on Business Cycles in Asian Emerging Economies', *Journal of Asian Economics*, 21: 293–303.

Gaulier, G., Lemoine, F. and Unal-Kesenci, D. (2007) 'China's Emergence and Reorganization of Trade Flows in Asia', *China Economic Review*, 18: 209–43.

IMF (International Monetary Fund) (2011a) *World Economic Outlook.* Washington, DC: IMF, April.

— (2011b) *Regional Economic Outlook: Asia and Pacific.* Washington, DC: IMF, April.

Lardy, N. R. (2002) *Integration of China in the Global Economy.* Washington, DC: The Brookings Institution.

— (2003) 'Trade Liberalization and its Role in Chinese Economic Growth'. Paper presented at the International Monetary Fund conference on *A Tale of Two Giants: India and China*, New Delhi, November 14–16.

Lau, L., Qian, Y. and Roland, G. (2000) 'Reform without Losers: An Interpretation of China's Dual-Track Approach', *Journal of Political Economy*, 108: 120–43.

Lin, J. Y. (2011) 'From Flying Geese to Leading Dragons'. Washington, DC: World Bank, Policy Research Working Paper No. 5702, June.

Mongobay (2011) *Singapore – The Economy.* Available at http://www.mongabay.com/reference/country_studies/singapore/ECONOMY.html (retrieved 26 July 2011).

National Statistics, Republic of China (Taiwan) (2011) *Statistical Indicator Online Database.* Available at http://eng.stat.gov.tw/mp.asp?mp=5

Naughton, B. (2007) *The Chinese Economy: Transition and Growth.* Cambridge, MA: MIT Press.

Samuelson, P. A. (2010) 'A Centrist Proclamation' in *Economics*, New York: McGraw-Hill, pp. xvi–xvii.

Song, Z., Storesletten, K. and Zilibotti, F. (2011) 'Growing Like China', *American Economic Review*, 101: 202–41.

UNCTAD (United Nations Conference on Trade and Development) (2011) *World Investment Report,* 2011. New York, NY: UNCTAD.

The World Bank (2011) *World Development Indicators 2011 (WDI).* Washington, DC: World Bank.

WTO (World Trade Organization) (2010) *International Trade Statistics 2010.* Geneva: WTO.

— (2011) *Trade Patterns and Global Value Chains in East Asia.* Geneva: WTO.

3 East Asian culture

An overview

Misho Minkov

Introduction

The expansion of globalisation has led to increased contacts between members of different societies, particularly in the world of business and politics. As a result, the study of culture has enjoyed unprecedented interest and development in the past few decades and much has been learned about the cultures of the East Asian societies through research by local and foreign scholars. While some findings about the cultural differences between East Asia and the rest of the world seem intuitively logical, as they partly confirm popularly held impressions and stereotypes (examples of these are available in Boster and Maltseva, 2006), others have come as striking revelations to Westerners and Asians alike. This chapter dwells on some of the most salient cultural characteristics that distinguish East Asian societies from those of the rest of the world and examines some of their internal differences as well.

Historical background

For thousands of years, East Asian societies have shared a combination of features that is not found as a whole in any other cultural region: an economy based on wet-rice cultivation, centralised imperial government, official endorsement of Confucianism as an ethical code, the prominent role of Buddhism, cohabitation of diverse philosophies and religions rather than a single official dogma and the use of the Chinese script (see Warner, 2011). Other commonalities can also be added to this list, such as shared architectural styles and diets, the most conspicuous of these probably being the absence of dairy products and bread. It is therefore natural to expect that these shared East Asian experiences have resulted in similar cultural values, beliefs and norms.

Indeed, a number of large-scale cross-cultural studies, such as the Chinese Culture Connection (1987), Project GLOBE (House *et al.*, 2004) and the World Values Survey (Inglehart and Baker, 2000) have identified a Confucian or East Asian cultural cluster. The countries in that group are often found near the extremes of a number of important cultural and societal indicators. The best known of these are the region's spectacular economic growth and the unrivalled educational achievement of its schoolchildren, especially in mathematics. These indicators are associated with various cultural measures on which East Asia also gravitates toward extreme positions. Although these characteristics of Chinese, Korean and Japanese culture (see chapters 5, 7 and 8) are less widely known, they are crucially important for understanding the East Asian phenomenon.

Cultural values

The World Values Survey (WVS) is the largest study of human values, beliefs and norms, carried out longitudinally since 1980 in nearly 100 countries. It is also the most reliable cross-cultural project since its samples are nationally representative.[1] The questionnaire contains a list of ten basic values; the respondents are asked to select those of them that they consider important for children. Graph 3.1 shows how nine of these values relate to each other in the latest WVS round, carried out from 2005 to 2008 in 57 countries. Items that are close together are highly and positively correlated: when people in a particular country select one of those values, they also tend to choose the adjacent ones. Items that are situated across from each other are opposites: if one is deemed important in a particular society, the opposite is not.[2]

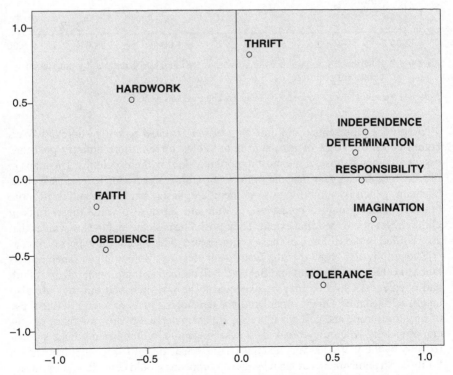

Graph 3.1 Positions of nine basic values for children from the World Values Survey in a two-dimensional space

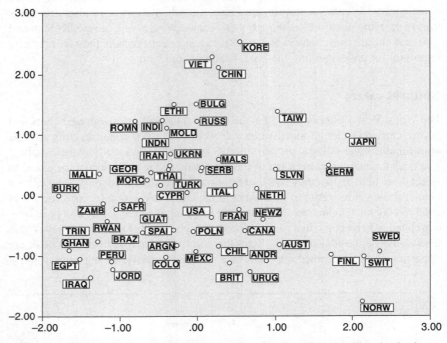

Graph 3.2 Positions of 56 countries in a two-dimensional space defined by nine basic values for children

Note: See Appendix, pp. 47–8, for a list of country abbreviations used.

Graph 3.2 represents a cultural map of the 56 most recently surveyed WVS countries on the basis of the same nine values for children: country positions essentially match those of the most important values in their societies. The maps in the two graphs suggest that the cultures of China and South Korea, as well as Vietnam, which is culturally close to them, emphasise hard work and thrift more than any other group of countries. Taiwan and Japan also value these traits in children, yet not to the same extent. Their positions indicate that the key values that are instilled in the children of those countries are independence and perseverance.

The graphs also show that the East Asian countries do not attach much importance to values that Inglehart and Baker (2000) defined as traditional: religious faith and obedience. Children may be expected to be well-behaved but they are also taught self-reliance. On the other hand, the developing parts of Asia, just like those of Eastern Europe and perhaps more so, are characterised by low tolerance of others, especially when they break the laws. Singapore, which has not been studied recently by the WVS, has retained this characteristic despite its wealth: it is known for its harsh punishments of what Western Europeans would consider minor infractions. Japan appears to have shifted somewhat closer to Northern Europe on this indicator: it values tolerance to a considerably greater extent but is still far from the positions of the Scandinavian countries.

The graphs demonstrate that Vietnam is culturally very close to mainland China and South Korea, at least in terms of its value system and value structure. Hard work and thrift are key Vietnamese values, tolerance is not. Although Vietnam is not traditionally classified as an East Asian country, it probably should be. It has experienced diverse cultural influences from the Middle Kingdom and today shares many cultural characteristics with its giant neighbour.

Hong Kong's raw scores on the WVS values for children make that country an outlier with an improbable position by any standards; therefore it is absent from Graph 3.2. Yet, a completely different picture emerges when the scores are ipsatized (standardised by case). The resulting scores reveal not only inter-cultural comparisons but also intra-cultural value structures, reflecting the way in which values are prioritised within a particular society. That statistical transformation would place Hong Kong next to Taiwan on the map in Graph 3.2. That means that although Hong Kong respondents indicate that they attach an improbably low importance to all nine values for children, they prioritise them much like the other East Asian countries, placing responsibility, independence, and hard work at the top and religious faith at the bottom of their priority list (cf., chapters 10, 12 and 14).

These findings from the WVS are confirmed by various other sources. The Chinese Culture Connection (1987) studied the values of over 2,000 university students from 23 nations. It found that mainland China, Hong Kong, Taiwan, Japan and South Korea had the highest scores of all countries on a cultural dimension defined by a high importance of thrift and perseverance and a low importance of traditional values such as personal stability (a tendency to adhere to immutable values and beliefs as advocated by the Middle Eastern religions) and, notably, tradition. 'Reciprocation of favours' was also a negative value on this dimension; consequently, it is considered far less important in East Asia than in the countries that appeared at the opposite end of this cultural continuum: Pakistan, Nigeria, and the Philippines. This dimension was called 'Confucian work dynamism', subsequently renamed 'long-term orientation' by Hofstede (2001). It is strongly correlated with the dimension defined by the North versus South (or Northwest versus Southeast) diagonal in Graphs 3.1 and 3.2.

Green *et al.* (2005) studied the values and beliefs of 2,546 undergraduate students in 20 countries. They obtained a psychological dimension called 'self-reliance' and provided average national scores for it. High-scoring countries were those whose respondents endorsed items such as 'Only those who depend on themselves get ahead in life'. The dimension index created a contrast between China, Lebanon, Russia and Singapore, where self-reliance was most strongly embraced, and Latin America, where it received the weakest support. 'Self-reliance' is strongly correlated with the North versus South dimension in Graphs 3.1 and 3.2.

The earlier versions of the WVS administered a crucially important item, asking the respondents to assess the importance that they attached to 'service to others' as a personal value (discontinued in 2005–8). The significance of this item cannot be overstated. At the national level, it yields a high negative correlation with thrift as a value and would be found right across from it if it were placed on the map in

Graph 3.1. This demonstrates that 'thrift' is associated with a concern for self-reliance rather than depending on the services of others, and explains why 'thrift' is negatively correlated with 'unselfishness' (thus, positively with selfishness) across the WVS respondents of some sub-Saharan countries. These associations confirm that East Asian culture emphasises individual self-reliance in economic matters rather than dependence on help from others. In Latin America, but also in the Middle East and throughout Africa, the reverse situation is observed: it is important to help others and – consequently – to receive assistance.

We must note that this operationalisation of self-reliance has nothing to do with individualism in the sense of Hofstede's (2001) cultural dimension, subsequently replicated by Project GLOBE (Gelfand *et al.*, 2004). The latter dimension stands, among other things, for individual liberation from the bonds of social conformism; it is not about giving a high priority to individual achievement of economic goals through hard work, thrift and perseverance, which is what self-reliance is about. On the maps in Graphs 3.1 and 3.2, the individualism dimension would correspond to the East versus West diagonal; thus the most individualist and least conformist societies would be those of the richest countries of the world. The African nations, found at the opposite end of the map, are evidently the most collectivist and socially conservative. Emerging Asia is in between, whereas Japan is obviously no longer characterised by the conformism and collectivism that it used to be associated with some generations ago. Nowadays, Japan leans strongly towards the individualist values in the eastern part of the map on Graph 3.1, such as personal responsibility. This is one of the predictable effects of the strong economic development that took place in Japan after the Second World War.

These cultural characteristics that distinguish East Asia from the rest of the world have tremendous societal implications. After the findings of the Chinese Culture Connection, Hofstede and Bond (1988) saw a link between the values that defined Confucian work dynamism and fast economic growth (see chapter 11). Not everybody was convinced by the statistical correlation though: if there is something special in East Asian culture that can fuel miraculous economic growth, and if culture is a very stable phenomenon, why did this miracle fail to occur earlier?

Development economists have pointed out that what is an advantage for economic growth in a given historical period may become irrelevant in another period (Gallup and Sachs, 1998). There is strong evidence that economic growth is positively correlated with savings rates across developing countries but not across rich countries (Dornbusch *et al.*, 2004). Thus, a culture of thrift may be an advantage for China, South Korea, Vietnam, Eastern Europe and India but not for Japan where this factor has exhausted its potential (see chapter 7). Also, fast economic growth requires non-cultural factors as well, such as free markets, which were missing in China, Vietnam and Eastern Europe for a long time, as well as the adoption of new technology. The East Asian countries are excellent adopters but not great radical innovators. As we see from the maps in Graph 3.1 and Graph 3.2, imagination is not a typical East Asian value; it is mostly cherished in the rich Western world. The East Asian countries had to wait for the West to produce the technologies that they needed to catalyse their culture of hard work, saving and perseverance.

The Chinese Culture Connection (1987) provided cultural indices for a very limited number of countries. Subsequently, Hofstede *et al.* (2010), Hofstede and Minkov (2010), Minkov (2011), and Minkov and Hofstede (2012) analysed WVS data and provided indices for cultural dimensions that essentially replicated Confucian work dynamism or long-term orientation and were good predictors of economic growth across over 40 countries.

Hofstede (2001) noted that the long-term orientation dimension predicted not only economic growth but also educational achievement, especially in mathematics. Although it is clear that East Asian schoolchildren always top the rankings of the Trends in International Mathematics and Science (TIMSS) project, especially in mathematics (latest data from Mullis *et al.*, 2007), this hypothesis was hard to substantiate for the previously mentioned reason: the limited number of countries for which long-term orientation scores were available. A solution to this problem was provided by Minkov (2008) who showed that educational achievement, as measured by TIMSS, is strongly and negatively correlated with WVS items that measure religiousness, national pride and parental pride and form a single dimension of national culture called 'monumentalism'.[3] It appears that societies that emphasise pride and stable values and beliefs, as advocated by the Middle Eastern religions, are characterised by a self-complacency that does not encourage self-improvement through modern education; in fact such education may even be viewed as a threat to the existing social system of values and beliefs (Minkov, 2011). Vice-versa, the East Asian societies emphasise modesty, humility, adaptability and a willingness to learn from others. This gives them a strong advantage in education.

If the monumentalism dimension were plotted on the maps in Graphs 3.1 and 3.2, it would run exactly from the Southwest (the Middle East), where pride and adherence to immutable values and beliefs is strongly emphasised, to the Northeast (East Asia) where – apart from the focus on thrift and perseverance – humility looms large and individual polymorphism and adaptability to shifting circumstances are viewed as desirable. Rather than see Western influence as a threat to their identity, East Asians avidly absorb it and incorporate it into their cultures. It is a firmly established fashion among the overseas Chinese to adopt English personal names. This Westernisation trend has reached mainland China as well where many people have two names: a Chinese one for domestic use and an English one for interaction with Westerners. Consumption of Western art and fashion is also growing strongly in East Asia as opposed to the Middle East and North Africa where it is seen by many as incompatible with the local customs.

The monumentalism dimension provides a sophisticated, albeit partial, explanation of national differences in educational achievement. Its sophistication stems from its complex theoretical basis: a series of treatises by Canadian psychologist Steven Heine who sees a link between self-enhancement (a feeling of personal superiority, such as pride), self-stability (a focus on an invariant self) and a lack of interest in self-improvement through education. Grasping these concepts and their associations may not be easy; yet there is direct evidence of cultural differences in the way that different societies view the importance of education. Noorderhaven and Tidjani (2001) asked African scholars and students to draw up a list of values and administered it to 1,100 respondents: students in Cameroon, Ghana, Senegal, Tanzania and Zimbabwe, South Africa (white), Belgium, Germany, the United Kingdom, Guyana, Hong Kong, Malaysia, the Netherlands and the United States. The study revealed a cultural dimension that opposed the African countries to Hong Kong and Malaysia. Africans were most likely to emphasise hospitality (which is similar to service to others and reciprocation of favours) and traditional wisdom; they attached a low importance to acquisition of wisdom through modern education. In Hong Kong and Malaysia, the situation was precisely the opposite.

East Asian values were also studied by Schwartz (1994) as part of his large cross-cultural project, using data from 38 nations. Unlike the previously discussed analyses, Schwartz's findings did not highlight any conspicuous East Asian characteristics that give the region a distinct cultural identity.

It did provide some additional glimpses into the East Asian cultures though. As a whole, they, and especially mainland China, were found to be strongly hierarchical and low on egalitarianism. This seems to reflect acceptance of differences in social status rather than support for socio-economic inequality – relatively low in East Asia despite its recent growth in China. Schwartz also found low intellectual autonomy in East Asia; a dimension that is mostly about creativity and broad-mindedness. This confirms the low emphasis on individual imagination known from the WVS. East Asia also scored low on harmony which stands for protection of the environment.

Schwartz also highlighted some differences between the East Asian countries. Japan did not share the low interest in intellectual autonomy that was reported for Hong Kong, China, Taiwan and Singapore. China and Japan had high scores on mastery but Singapore scored low.

Personality traits

Mean Big-Five personality traits for nations and ethnic groups have been reported in three large cross-cultural studies: McCrae (2002), McCrae and Terracciano (2005), and Schmitt et al. (2007). Some of the results are strongly discordant, which raises the question of which study should be believed and what the reported group-level measures actually mean.[4] Nevertheless, the first and third studies concur on some of their findings about East Asians: Japanese, South Koreans, mainland Chinese (missing in the third study), Hong Kong Chinese and Taiwanese. Respondents from these societies describe themselves as strongly neurotic and introverted. Thus, East Asians are prone to experience anxiety, stress and worry. Relative to other ethnic groups, they are less likely to be characterised by warmth, gregariousness, excitement-seeking tendencies and positive emotions. Additionally, East Asians describe themselves as very low on Big-Five conscientiousness. This finding may come as a surprise. Yet, it is perfectly logical.

At the national and ethnic level, the conscientiousness dimension correlates with religiosity and reflects a respect for the past and its traditions; it does not measure anything like reliability or personal responsibility. The evidence concerning the other Big-Five traits in East Asia is less clear.[5]

Emotional and cognitive patterns

A number of authors have discussed an important cultural contrast in emotion and cognition (see chapter 16): dialecticism versus analyticism or absolutism (Choi and Choi, 2002; Heine, 2001; Hofstede, 2001; Minkov, 2011; Nisbett *et al.*, 2001; Peng and Nisbett, 1999; Peng and Nisbett, 2000; Peng *et al.*, 2006). East Asians have been described as possessing dialectical feelings and thoughts: an inclination to experience emotions of opposite valence ('I am sad and happy') at the same time or within short periods, to present ambivalent self-descriptions ('I am strict and lenient'), and to reconcile apparent contradictions ('This is both good and bad'). The North Americans to whom they have been compared are typically less likely to exhibit such forms of dialecticism. While most studies of this type compare only a few cultural groups, Schimmack *et al.* (2002) studied the frequency of pleasant and unpleasant emotions in 5,866 university students from 38 nations and found that East Asians (Hong Kong Chinese, Japanese, mainland Chinese and South Koreans) as well as Thais and Nepalese, were least likely to dissociate the two types of emotions, whereas Arabs, Latin Americans and Anglos were most likely to experience either of the two but not both within a short period. The study provided strong evidence for a cultural contrast in emotional patterns across many ethnic groups, ranging from East Asian dialecticism (at least in relative terms) to Arab, Anglo and Latin absolutism.

Minkov (2009) surmised that East Asian dialecticism would have societal implications. It would be associated with a tendency to avoid extreme statements concerning socially important issues, such as 'The government of this country is very good' or 'Our government is very bad'. If one starts from such an extreme position, dialectical reconciliation of opposites becomes more difficult than if the initial position is 'The government is somewhat good', which is easy to reconcile with an opponent's stance: 'The government is somewhat bad'. Minkov (2009) analysed nationally representative cross-cultural data from the Pew Research Center and found strong support for this hypothesis. South Korea, China, Japan and Indonesia had the lowest social polarisation index, expressed as low percentages of respondents who adopt extreme positions in judgements on socially sensitive issues. The Middle Eastern countries, Tanzania and Pakistan had the highest social polarisation, expressed as a high percentage of respondents adopting extreme positive positions and high percentages adopting extreme negative positions on the same items. The United States exhibited the same trend. The social polarisation index was highly and negatively correlated with the emotional dialecticism index of Schimmack *et al.* (2002), cross-validating both measures and showing that dialecticism is a multifaceted phenomenon. Minkov (2009) concluded that the East Asian societies have a tendency to seek dialectical reconciliation of conflicting opinions so as to avoid social tension, whereas the Middle East, sub-Saharan Africa, Pakistan and other nations are characterised by an absolutism that can easily breed internal conflict, especially if it is coupled with social factors such as poverty (see chapter 14).

These findings may help explain some differences in communication and expression style between Anglo and other Western countries on the one hand and East Asia on the other. In the West, East Asians are often perceived as having a frustrating tendency to avoid answering questions with a categorical 'yes' or 'no'. In East Asia, such categorical statements, and especially a flat 'no', may be viewed as impolite and an invitation to a confrontation.

Social behaviour indicators

Using data from the UN Office on Drugs and Crime (2010), including official police records and estimates by public health organisations, Minkov (2011) compiled a national murder index for 173 countries and studied the structure of the relationships between that variable and its main correlates. He obtained two factors. The first was called 'exclusionism versus universalism'. The exclusionism pole was defined mainly by high corruption, high road death tolls and high percentages of adults living with parents.[6] As this dimension was strongly and negatively correlated with national wealth, it highlighted important differences between the East Asian societies, reflecting their unequal wealth: relatively high road death tolls and corruption in China versus careful driving and relative transparency in Singapore and Japan.

The second factor that emerged in this analysis was called 'hypometropia versus prudence'. The hypometropia pole was defined by high murder rates and high HIV rates. Adolescent fertility and low IQ (thus, low general education and especially low mathematical skills) were also strongly associated with this factor,[7] but also with the first. Minkov associated this dimension with mating competition theory which discusses a link between free and intense competition for women with intra-societal violence and risk acceptance. The highest scores on this dimension were obtained for the sub-Saharan and Central American countries, the lowest were those of China, Korea, Japan and Singapore. This analysis explained a well-known combination of East Asian societal characteristics: high performance on IQ tests, low intra-societal violence, low adolescent fertility, infrequent sexual networking and low HIV rates. A large cross-cultural study by Schmitt *et al.* (2004) confirmed that sexual competition and networking are atypical of East Asia. That region had the lowest scores on mate-poaching: attempting to attract somebody who is already involved in a romantic relationship with someone else.

Work-related cultural characteristics

Countless studies have investigated various work-related values, beliefs and ideologies in East Asia but relatively few of these are large cross-cultural comparisons that can be used to place the East Asian societies on a world cultural map. Still, a few studies provide precisely that information. Unlike the previously discussed research on values, abilities and behavioural indicators, comparisons of work-related traits have not revealed any strong peculiarities or extremes that set East Asia apart from the rest of the world. Nevertheless, the findings may be of interest to international managers and consultants.

Smith *et al.* (1996) analysed questionnaire answers from 8,841 manual, clerical, managerial and professional workers from 43 countries. One of the dimensions that they extracted was called 'egalitarian commitment versus conservatism'. It highlighted various contrasts which essentially distinguished the West European and Anglo countries, where egalitarian commitment was found to be the strongest, from the developing countries, where conservatism loomed large. Interestingly, all of the East Asian countries in the sample gravitated toward the conservatism pole; this was mostly true of China and South Korea, but to some extent also true of wealthy Singapore, Hong Kong and Japan.

In the developing countries (high on conservatism), as well as in the rich East Asian nations, respondents expressed a stronger agreement that the company should be involved in the employees' private lives and take into account the size of their families when determining their salaries. In the rich Western countries (high on egalitarian commitment), the prevalent opinion was that jobs and private lives should be strictly separated.

Respondents in developing countries, as well as in wealthy East Asia, were more likely to agree to work overtime hours without financial compensation, expressing the view that the boss's appreciation would be a sufficient reward. The ideal manager was described as a benevolent father figure. He was expected to know the answers to most problems and was allowed to adopt an authoritarian style. Respondents in the Western countries did not share these views. They expected a participative management style.

The second dimension discussed by Smith *et al.* was called 'utilitarian involvement versus loyal involvement'. It created a clear geographic contrast. The former Soviet bloc and mainland China were found at the utilitarian involvement extreme. All Asian countries (except China), some African countries and the Middle East were at the loyal involvement pole. The respondents from countries at the utilitarian involvement extreme perceived organisations as loose amalgamations of individuals coming together to pursue individual interests rather than commit to group goals. The respondents from countries at the loyal involvement extreme viewed organisations as organic entities where people share the consequences of collective fortune and setbacks.

Project GLOBE (Dorfman *et al.*, 2004) studied the views of 17,370 middle managers in 951 organisations, operating in 59 countries. Among other things, the respondents were asked to describe the ideal leader by answering a questionnaire. Relative to their peers in other countries, and especially in Northwestern Europe and the Anglo world, respondents in East Asia (China, Hong Kong, Japan, Singapore, South Korea and Taiwan), Southeast Asia and the Middle East were found to attach a low importance to a participative leadership style and to be more tolerant of an evasive, self-protective style. Also, there was no strong appreciation of charismatic leadership in East Asia, although the Middle East scored even lower in that respect.

Smith *et al.* (2002) studied middle managers in 53 countries, the average sample size being about 100 per country. The respondents were asked how different types of managerial decisions were made in different circumstances in their organisations. East and Southeast Asia (as well as Iran, Bulgaria and Romania) had the highest scores in the world on reliance on widely accepted beliefs as to what is right. Also, South Korea, Hong Kong, Macau and Singapore were among the countries with the strongest reliance on unwritten rules. In Japan and China this trend was considerably weaker, whereas Taiwan had the lowest score on that measure of all in the sample (see chapters 5, 6, 7 and 8). Relative to the rest of the world, reliance on superiors was also found to be high throughout the East Asian region, except in Singapore. Also in a relative perspective, the East Asian countries showed a low reliance on guidance from subordinates, specialists, co-workers and the managers' own experience. Thus, compared to the prevalent management style in other regions, East Asian management can be summarised as authoritarian rather than consultative.

Conclusions

To sum up, this chapter provides an overview of culture and management in East Asia. It provides a definitive introduction to the literature on the subject which is now voluminous relating to the comparative research in the field. Amongst other subjects, it looks at 'Confucian Dynamism' which has been invoked to explain economic success in the region and its impact on business. It also covers the tension between 'traditional' and 'modern' cultural values and their impact on management. While some findings about the cultural differences between East Asia and the rest of the world seem intuitively logical, as they partly confirm popularly held impressions and stereotypes, others have come as striking revelations to Westerners and Asians alike. The chapter examines some of the most salient cultural characteristics that distinguish East Asian societies from those of the rest of the world, as well as at the same time also examining some of their internal differences.

Notes

1   The data are freely available in the official WVS website: http://www.world valuessurvey.org
2   Graph 3.1 represents a two-dimensional plot of nine values for children from the WVS. 'Unselfishness' was not included in the analysis as it does not correlate significantly with any of the other nine values and represents an odd variable. The plot was produced after z-score standardisation by variable. The plot can be obtained in nearly identical forms through multidimensional scaling or factor analysis.
    Graph 3.2 plots the 56 WVS countries on the two dimensional space defined by the nine values. Because Hong Kong is a strong outlier with unusually low scores on all variables, it was dropped from this analysis.

3   The term 'monumentalism' reflects the fact that the human self in societies with strong religion and pride is like a proud and stable monolithic monument.
4   The first and second of these studies are similar in that they used self-reports, whereas the second relied on peer-reports; this may explain some of the discrepancies.
5   It is also interesting to note that a Chinese personality inventory revealed a somewhat different structure from the Big Five, as well as an indigenous Chinese dimension without an equivalent in the American model (Cheung and Leung, 1998; Cheung *et al.*, 1996; Cheung *et al.*, 2001).
6   Minkov interpreted exclusionism versus universalism as a contrast between concern for one's in-group coupled with exclusion and neglect of out-groups versus in-group disintegration and universal rule of law.
7   Minkov explained hypometropia (meaning 'near-sightedness') as a short-term vision in reproductive matters: a focus on risky and potentially violent mating competition for the purpose of early and abundant procreation, ensuring the survival of society, often at the expense of an individual's life. Prudence was defined as a long-term strategy that bets on risk avoidance and individual longevity.

References

Boster, J. S. and Maltseva, K. (2006) 'A crystal seen from each of its vertices: European views of European national characters', *Cross-Cultural Research*, 40: 47–64.

Cheung, F. M. and Leung, K. (1998) 'Indigenous personality measures: Chinese examples', *Journal of Cross-Cultural Psychology*, 29: 233–48.

Cheung, F. M., Leung, K., Fan, R. M., Song, W. Z., Zhang, J. X. and Zhang, J. P. (1996) 'Development of the Chinese Personality Assessment Inventory', *Journal of Cross-Cultural Psychology*, 27: 181–99.

Cheung, F. M., Leung, K., Zhang, J. X., Sun, H. F., Gan, Y. Q., Song, W. Z. and Xie, D. (2001) 'Indigenous Chinese personality constructs: Is the Five-Factor Model complete?', *Journal of Cross-Cultural Psychology*, 32: 407–33.

Chinese Culture Connection (1987) 'Chinese values and the search for culture-free dimensions of culture', *Journal of Cross-Cultural Psychology*, 18: 143–64.

Choi, I. and Choi, Y. (2002) 'Culture and self-concept flexibility', *Personality and Social Psychology Bulletin*, 28: 1508–17.

Dorfman, P. W., Hanges, P. J. and Brodbeck, F. C. (2004) 'Leadership and cultural variation: The identification of culturally endorsed leadership profiles' in House, R. J., Hanges, P. J., Javidan, M., Dorfman, P. W. and Gupta, V. (eds) *Culture, leadership, and organizations. The GLOBE study of 62 societies*. Thousand Oaks, CA: Sage, pp. 669–719.

Dornbusch, R., Fischer, S. and Startz, R. (2004) *Macroeconomics*. New York: McGraw-Hill/Irwin.

Gallup, J. L. and Sachs, J. (1998) 'Geography and economic growth'. Paper prepared for the annual World Bank conference on development economics. Washington DC: World Bank, April 20–1, 1998. Online publication. Retrieved 18 September 2005 from www.worldbank.org/html/rad/abcde/sachs.pdf

Gelfand, M., Bhawuk, D., Nishii, L. H. and Bechtold, D. (2004) 'Individualism and collectivism' in House, R. J., Hanges, P. J., Javidan, M., Dorfman, P. W. and Gupta, V. (eds) *Culture, leadership, and organizations. The GLOBE study of 62 societies*. Thousand Oaks, CA: Sage, pp. 437–512.

Green, E. G. T., Deschamps, J. C. and Paez, D. (2005) 'Variation of individualism and collectivism within and between 20 countries: A typological analysis', *Journal of Cross-Cultural Psychology*, 36: 321–39.

Heine, S. J. (2001) 'Self as cultural product: An examination of East Asian and North American selves', *Journal of Personality*, 69: 881–906.

Hofstede, G. (2001) *Culture's consequences: Comparing values, behaviours, institutions and organizations across nations*. Thousand Oaks, CA: Sage (first published 1980).

Hofstede, G. and Bond, M. H. (1988) 'The Confucian connection: From cultural roots to economic growth', *Organizational Dynamics*, 16: 5–21.

Hofstede, G. and Minkov, M. (2010) 'Long- versus short-term orientation: New perspectives'. *Asia Pacific Business Review*, 16: 493–504.

Hofstede, G., Hofstede, G. J. and Minkov, M. (2010) *Cultures and organizations: Software of the mind*. 3rd edition. New York: McGraw-Hill.

House, R. J., Hanges, P. J., Javidan, M., Dorfman, P. W. and Gupta, V. (eds) (2004) *Culture, leadership, and organizations. The GLOBE study of 62 societies*. Thousand Oaks, CA: Sage.

Inglehart, R. and Baker, W. E. (2000) 'Modernization, cultural change, and the persistence of traditional values', *American Sociological Review*, 65: 19–51.

McCrae, R. R. (2002) 'NEO-PI-R data from 36 cultures: Further intercultural comparisons' in McCrae, R. R. and Allik, J. (eds) *The five-factor model of personality across cultures*. New York: Kluwer Academic/Plenum, pp. 105–26.

McCrae, R. R., and Terracciano, A. (2005) 'Personality profiles of cultures: Aggregate personality traits', *Journal of Personality and Social Psychology*, 89: 407–25.

Minkov, M. (2008) 'Self-enhancement and self-stability predict school achievement at the national level', *Cross-Cultural Research*, 42: 172–96.

— (2009) 'Nations with more dialectical selves exhibit lower polarization in life quality judgments and social opinions', *Cross-Cultural Research*, 43: 230–50.

— (2011) *Cultural differences in a globalizing world*. London: Emerald.

Minkov, M. and Hofstede, G. (2012) 'Hofstede's fifth dimension: New evidence from the World Values Survey', *Journal of Cross-Cultural Psychology*, 43: 3–14.

Mullis, I. V. S., Martin, M. O. and Foy, P. (2007) *TIMSS 2007 international mathematics report: Findings from IEA's Trends in International Mathematics and Science Study at the fourth and eighth grades*. Chestnut Hill, MA: TIMSS and PIRLS International Study Center.

Nisbett, R. E., Peng, K., Choi, I. and Norenzayan, A. (2001) 'Culture and systems of thought: Holistic vs. analytic cognition', *Psychological Review*, 108: 291–310.

Noorderhaven, N. G. and Tidjani, B. (2001) 'Culture, governance, and economic performance: An explorative study with a special focus on Africa', *International Journal of Cross-Cultural Management*, 1: 31–52.

Peng, K. and Nisbett, R. E. (1999) 'Culture, dialectics, and reasoning about contradiction', *American Psychologist*, 54: 741–54.

— (2000) 'Dialectical responses to questions about dialectical thinking', *American Psychologist*, 55: 1067–8.

Peng, K., Spencer-Rodgers, J. and Nian, Z. (2006) 'Naive dialecticism and the Tao of Chinese thought' in Kim, U., Yang, K. S. and Huang, K. K. (eds) *Indigenous and cultural psychology: Understanding people in context*. New York: Springer, chapter 11, pp. 247–62.

Schimmack, U., Oishi, S. and Diener, E. (2002) 'Cultural influences on the relation between pleasant emotions and unpleasant emotions: Asian dialectic philosophies or individualism-collectivism?', *Cognition and Emotion*, 16: 705–19.

Schmitt, D. P. *et al.* (2004) 'Patterns and universals of mate poaching across 53 nations: The effect of sex, culture, and personality on romantically attracting another person's partner', *Journal of Personality and Social Psychology*, 86: 560–84.

Schmitt, D. P., Allik, J., McCrae, R. R. and Benet-Martinez, V. (2007) 'The geographic distribution of Big Five personality traits: Patterns and profiles of human self-description across 56 nations', *Journal of Cross-Cultural Psychology*, 38: 173–212.

Schwartz, S. H. (1994) 'Beyond individualism/collectivism: New cultural dimensions of values' in Kim, U., Kagitcibasi, C., Triandis, H. C., Choi, S. C. and Yoon, G. (eds) *Individualism and collectivism: Theory, method, and application*. Thousand Oaks, CA: Sage, pp. 85–119.

Smith, P. B., Dugan, S. and Trompenaars, F. (1996) 'National culture and the values of organizational employees: A dimensional analysis across 43 nations', *Journal of Cross-Cultural Psychology*, 27: 231–64.

Smith, P. B., Peterson, M. and Schwartz, S. H. (2002) 'Cultural values, sources of guidance, and their relevance to managerial behaviour: A 47-nation study', *Journal of Cross-Cultural Psychology*, 33: 188–208.

Warner, M. (2011) (ed.) *Confucian HRM in Greater China: Theory and Practice*. London and New York, NY: Routledge.

Appendix

Expansions of the country name abbreviations in Graph 3.2.

ANDR	Andorra
ARGN	Argentina
AUST	Australia
BRAZ	Brazil
BULG	Bulgaria
BURK	Burkina Faso
CANA	Canada
CHIL	Chile
CHIN	China
COLO	Colombia
CYPR	Cyprus
EGPT	Egypt
ETHI	Ethiopia
FINL	Finland
FRAN	France
GEOR	Georgia
GERM	Germany
GHAN	Ghana
GUAT	Guatemala
INDI	India
INDN	Indonesia
IRAN	Iran
IRAQ	Iraq
ITAL	Italy
JAPN	Japan
JORD	Jordan
KORE	Korea

MALS	Malaysia
MALI	Mali
MEXC	Mexico
MOLD	Moldova
MORC	Morocco
NETH	Netherlands
NEWZ	New Zealand
NORW	Norway
PERU	Peru
POLN	Poland
ROMN	Romania
RUSS	Russia
RWAN	Rwanda
SAFR	South Africa
SERB	Serbia
SLVN	Slovenia
SPAI	Spain
SWED	Sweden
SWIT	Switzerland
TAIW	Taiwan
TRIN	Trinidad and Tobago
THAI	Thailand
TURK	Turkey
BRIT	United Kingdom
UKRN	Ukraine
URUG	Uruguay
USA	US
VIET	Vietnam
ZAMB	Zambia

4   East Asian management

An overview

Keith Jackson

Introduction

The discussion in this chapter profiles East Asian management both as an entity and in terms of its distinct systems and styles. It is structured in pursuit of the following three main sets of questions:

- To what extent do East Asian management systems and styles continue to differ among themselves?
- To what extent do East Asian management systems and styles appear to influence each other?
- What specific challenges are likely to shape the development of East Asian management systems and styles?

Addressing these questions offers readers a broad-brush foundation to the more in-depth discussions presented elsewhere in this book.

Management systems

Reference to distinct national or regional management *systems* relevant to East Asia is established in the relevant literature (cf. Whitely, 1990; Koike, 1995; Warner and Joynt, 2002; Child and Warner, 2003; Chen, 2004). In etymological terms, the English word 'system' denotes something that is 'brought together' with the result that many diverse parts or 'subsystems' are perceived to form a coherent whole. We refer to systems when we attempt to describe, explain, compare and (albeit speculatively) predict patterns of change; or, from a management perspective, perceived or discerned *needs* to change. The underlying theory is that each system develops towards a dynamic state of equilibrium as it responds to pressures that emerge both from within and from outside the system (cf. Von Bertalanffy, 1968). The management system of any one industry or economy is under constant pressure to respond and adapt to changes emerging from its macro-business environment. In strategic terms, this environment might be described using a *PESTEL* analysis of the Political, Economic, Socio-cultural, Technological, Ecological and Legal factors that – singly and in combination – appear to act and interact as forces prompting change within and across national management systems.

The dynamic of how management systems evolve might be visualised as a basic 'I > P > O' pattern, whereby *Inputs* influence discernible *Processes* of change which, when managed, generate *Outputs* that become inputs to future change processes. To illustrate, Japan's 'national innovation system' (NIS) is currently challenged to develop new forms of political, economic, technological and legal partnering arrangements between government, university research centres, venture capital providers and new technology-based start-ups in order to remain competitive with its East Asian neighbours across a range of what were previously regarded in Japan as highly successful business sectors: e.g. the manufacture of semiconductors and consumer electronics (cf. Jackson and Debroux, 2009; Taplin, 2007).

Comparing management systems

One basic conceptual approach towards comparing systems is to identify those that appear relatively closed to inputs driving change and those that appear relatively open or permeable (Córdoba-Pachón, 2010). Each national or industrial system – and, by extension, each organisation as a subsystem supporting that superordinate system (Morgan, 1989) – might be interpreted as a distinct social, economic and technological entity compelled to respond to 'globalisation' (however defined) and to the rapid expansion and extension of cross-border business interests and activities. To illustrate, East Asian societies are characterised by a demographic trend whereby a dwindling number of employees is taxed (literally) to subsidise the welfare of rapidly ageing populations. Another significant trend in the People's Republic of China (PRC) or hitherto 'China', is the migration of anything up to 200 million workers from the provinces towards new urban and industrial developments (cf. Liu, 2010). Given that East Asian societies are perceived to remain – in cultural and ethnic terms – relatively traditional or impermeable compared to Western societies, these demographic shifts act as 'inputs' towards the evolution of established systems and styles of management.

In his comprehensive comparison of 'Asian management systems' Chen (2004) draws on Parsons (1956) to emphasise the 'P' element of the aforementioned I > P > O dynamic. Chen defines a management system structurally as a process of interaction across 'three distinctive layers' (2004: 18). These include managing technical core activities such as planning and supervising, influenced by variables such as fluctuating market conditions, size and history of organisation along with current management policy or philosophy. The second 'layer' is shaped by attempts to manage the social-cultural systems within an organisation – an endeavour influenced by national, regional and industry-specific cultures (cf. Hofstede, 1980, 2001; Hofstede *et al.*, 2010). The third layer comprises the types of external relationships that all organisations need in order to survive, including relationships to stakeholders such as customers, competitors, suppliers, distributors, local and national governments along with regulatory bodies such as the World Trade Organization (WTO).

In his introduction, Chen (2004) presents a number of models designed to describe and compare national and regional systems of management before settling on one that links management philosophy and environmental factors as input factors to the development and expression of distinct processes of competitive strategy development supported by operational management practices – processes emphasised in this current discussion as distinct management styles. The performance outcomes of these interdependent processes become evident in measures standard to business practice: Chen (2004: 18) defines performance dually in terms of operational management effectiveness and more strategic enterprise effectiveness – a distinction adopted in this current discussion. In summary Chen distinguishes between national and regional systems of management by the manner in which each system appears to respond – uniquely – over time to the challenges generated across the global business environment: e.g. the PESTEL factors highlighted above.

Management styles and cultures

The notion of 'culture' relevant to East Asian management is discussed in chapter 3. Here, it is salient to recognise how reference to management 'philosophies' (Chen, 2004) or the beliefs and values that inform 'management practices' (Warner, 2003a; Warner, 2011) specific to one or other Asian culture might inform our discussion of distinct management *styles*. We might reflect on how the English word 'style' originates from Latin for a writing instrument (*stilus*) and came to signify a pattern or 'style' of handwriting that could be observed to distinguish the behaviour and (speculatively) attitudes of one individual or social-cultural group from another (Ayto, 1990). A management 'style' can thus be understood as a 'subsystem' to a management system in that it expresses a patterned 'coming together' of behavioural choices that (when observed) distinguish one group of managers from another. These diverse styles become evident as groups of East Asian managers seek to respond to the forces for change generated from across their strategic *and* their operational working environments (Warner, 2003b).

Comparing management styles

Embedded in cultures, management systems evolve over time (see chapter 11) and notably in response to economic policy changes initiated by governments and/or as a system-wide response to changing market opportunities. To illustrate, Cooke (2012: 180) traces the evolution of 'Chinese leadership and management styles' relevant to State-Owned Enterprises (SOEs) from the 'state-planned economy period (1947–78)' to the ensuing 'marketisation period' initiated in the PRC by Deng Xiaoping. Observing how both Chinese and non-Chinese managers respond to the opportunities that these political and economic changes created should give some indication of their relative or preferred styles. Specific to post-marketisation China, Si *et al.* (2009) offer a striking illustration of how management styles might be identified and compared. Building on previous research by Turnley and

Feldman (1999) focusing on the 'psychological contracts' negotiated by US American managers with their employers, Si and his colleagues in Shanghai elicited the behaviours and values expressed by Chinese managers who, like their US American counterparts, perceived their individual career development to be dependent on the attentiveness and competence of senior line-managers. In the US American case, the mid-career respondents admitted to reducing their commitment to current tasks after deciding to seek another job. In contrast, the Chinese managers in the Si *et al.* survey claimed to commit more overtly to current tasks in the expectation that this would merit a more positive character reference as they too looked to exit their current employer. In both cases, the managers involved expected more recognition, reward and (not least) 'voice' (cf. Marchington *et al.*, 2001). Echoing Child and Warner (2003), it is relevant here to explore the extent to which the senior managers involved might respond to this emergent challenge of professional expectation: e.g. whether the embedded culture-specific values and social structures associated with Confucian tradition might hinder these senior managers towards allowing more voice to subordinates (cf. Warner, 2003b).

How East Asian management systems and styles differ

In the 1980s, the co-founder of Honda Motor Corporation (T. Fujisawa) observed how US American and Japanese management systems were 'ninety-five per cent the same', and yet 'different in all important respects' (Adler, 1986; op. cit. Chen, 2004: 265). This type of elliptical comment prompted Western management researchers to work out how Japanese multinational corporations (MNCs) had begun competing so effectively and globally in business sectors as diverse as consumer electronics, white goods and automobile manufacturing: these large Japanese organisations (*kaisha*) had begun penetrating markets formerly dominated by US American and other Western MNCs (cf. Abeglen and Stalk, 1985; Whitehill, 1991).

How was this possible? One answer to this question is to invoke the systems and styles of management considered by scholars to be distinctive and, indeed, 'unique' to Japan (cf. Haghirian, 2010; Bebenroth and Kanai, 2011). This claim to uniqueness might be illustrated in reference to Japan's Toyota Motor Corporation. Founded in 1937, it directly employs over 260,000 people worldwide. Members of the founding Toyoda family continue to hold positions on the executive board. In terms of system outputs Toyota is an organisation with a reputation for driving innovation (cf. Nonaka and Takeuchi, 1995; Liker, 2004; Takeuchi and Nonaka, 2004). As a legacy to manufacturing and innovation management systems worldwide, Toyota has given us new standard concepts such as *kanban*-style 'just-in-time' (JIT) inventory and supply chain management, and 'quality circles' whereby mid-level managers and supervisors are allowed space to identify and communicate upwards opportunities for process and product improvement, and *kaizen* which (even without translation) has become widely interpreted as a management philosophy relentlessly seeking process and product improvement, not least in the reduction of product defect rates and the processes of resource waste management (Rose, 2002). These distinctive elements became recognised as the formidable Toyota Production System (TPS) and subsequently underpinned what became heralded in Western management circles as *TQM* (cf. Burman, 1995; Trott, 2004).

More recently, a similar analysis of management systems and styles in Japan (see chapter 7) might indicate over time how system strengths can become weaknesses, especially if they remain too closed. One result was the so-called 'lost decade' of the 1990s, extending now into a period of slow-burning economic recession (cf. Porter *et al.*, 2000; Jackson and Debroux, 2009). However, a number of new entrants to global market prominence include Nintendo, Uniqlo and Sanrio – creators of the now ubiquitous 'Hello Kitty' brand. Their emergence might be attributed to the 'cool Japan' effect (cf. Storz, 2009) evident also in the global spread (note: with little direct promotional support) of *sushi, bento, manga* and other 'Asian fusion' lifestyle choices readily associated with a cross-nationally mobile and cross-culturally aware cadre of young professionals (cf. Ohmae, 2001; Jackson, 2010). However, another interpretation emphasises a set of management practices that might begin to explain the distinctive 'five per cent' alluded to by Fujisawa and subsequently highlighted by Chen (2004). These involve emphasising trusting as opposed to controlling (i.e. over-supervising) employees in core operational roles (cf. Ouchi, 1981; Jackson and Tomioka, 2004).

To illustrate, within TPS a team of assembly workers could (in theory) stop an entire production line if they believed the components input did not match the required quality standards. This social-cultural emphasis on trusting in the competence and commitment of operational level employees to generate and assess process outcomes relevant to measures of enterprise effectiveness is developed by Takeuchi and Nonaka (2004) into the intriguing concept of *ba* which they describe as a physical and or virtual 'place' designed by managers or innovation leaders for creating and sharing knowledge. It provides a forum for 'enhancing mutual trust among participants' (2004: 56). They cite the development of the Toyota Prius as a product of *ba*. It was introduced to market in 1997 and at a time when the innovation systems supporting manufacturing giants such as Ford and GM were visibly crumbling. Unusually for a traditional Japanese *kaisha,* the project team behind the Prius were instructed by project leaders to 'evaluate the new technology', regardless of professional background or 'speciality' and to 'think what is best for the product, instead of representing one's department's interests' and, in doing this, 'not care about one's age or rank' (Takeuchi and Nonaka, 2004: 109). Here, as elsewhere, the organisation's key resources are human, and both management and enterprise effectiveness might be measured by the extent to which teams of Toyota employees are able to create and share the knowledge that feeds processes of product and production innovation – a space made available also to SMEs entrusted as the organisation's key strategic suppliers (cf. Sako, 1992) As a strength this style of innovation management appears effective. However, its relative impermeability (i.e. its essential Japanese-ness) might over time prove to be a weakness as patterns and practices become embedded and unresponsive to key environmental changes (cf. Jackson and Debroux, 2009).

Consequently, the pattern of innovation management in Japan continues to emphasise intra-preneurial (i.e. closed subsystem) styles rather than the more open entrepreneurial styles currently attributed to Chinese management systems (cf. Storz and Schäfer, 2011).

With *trust* comes *space* 'to make mistakes' (Handy, 1993), and in East Asian contexts particularly the potential to 'lose face' (cf. Trompenaars and Hampden-Turner, 1998; Ambler *et al.*, 2009). We can imagine an intense pressure to perform to preordained expectations – a pressure that both competent and less competent senior managers might exploit. To illustrate, as Toyota Motor Corporation sought to become the world's leading automobile manufacturer (by volume) it was (like its competitors) working to absorb rising commodity prices for oil and aluminium. The pressure on some mid-level managers became evident in an unprecedented level of media reporting in Japan about *karoshi* or the process whereby aspiring and committed managers work themselves to an untimely death (Takeda, 2002). This type of gritty, life-threatening commitment to work might reflect an indigenous Japanese management philosophy such as the 'community or fate' (*unmei kyodotai*) notion commonly attributed by scholars to a people inhabiting an island continually formed and re-formed by a hostile natural environment (cf. Koike, 1995; Debroux, 2003). Others might invoke *samurai* traditions and values of *bushido* or 'the way of warriors'. Against the background of current political and economic developments in Japan, both invocations appear simplistic.

How East Asian management systems and styles compete

Against this background, we can also consider the type of management systems and styles that support the long-term management of strategic business risk. Similar to the *keiretsu*-type organisations in Japan such as Toyota and Mitsubishi, South Korean Hyundai is a *chaebol*-type organisation that over time has engaged in chemicals, steel and aluminium manufacture, shipbuilding, marketing, construction and financial services (Lansbury *et al.*, 2007). The Japanese term *keiretsu* translates roughly as a 'linked together' system of organisation (cf. Chen, 2004) while *chaebol* has been interpreted as a system of business organisation 'held together by cross-shareholdings, subsidies and loan guarantees in an opaque fashion' (Rowley and Bae, 2003: 189) – 'opaque', that is, to non-Koreans and organisational outsiders, including non-Korean competitors. The integrated structure of both systems serves to support long-term planning while simultaneously offering a basis for responding to risks generated in the strategic business environment – that is, for as long as these risks appear relatively predictable. In the late 1990s, South Korea became swept up in the then 'Asian economic crisis' and the fragility of the 'opaque' financial and commercial credit systems became exposed by global financial markets, as chapter 8 spells out. For a short period, the South Korean economy effectively came under the administration of the International Monetary Fund (IMF) – a humiliating experience for a people who had achieved an unprecedented rate of national economic and technological progress since the ceasefire that interrupted (but did not formally end) the Korean War in 1953. However, in order to emerge from the crisis and rebalance the national currency the financial system was both rethought and reformed, and the capital supporting the continuing export drives of *chaebol* such as Hyundai, LG and Samsung became more 'real' and sustainable in global economic terms (cf. Coe and Kim, 2002).

Like Toyota, the Hyundai *chaebol* is a major employer and thus a pillar of a national social economy. Senior management systems tend to overlap with national political systems, thus supporting comparatively assured access to commercial credits and (potentially) to sources of high-level corruption. The senior managers of *keiretsu* and *chaebol* are likely to be male: however, and, quite unlike their Japanese counterparts, senior Korean managers are likely to have experienced command responsibilities in the national army – an experience that informs their in-group style of management communication (cf. Merkin, 2005). Consequently, when comparing Japanese and Korean management systems and styles some understanding of the historical context is relevant. First, there is the legacy of Japanese colonialism and cultural oppression on the Korean peninsula between 1910 and 1945. Second, there was the aforementioned Korean War and the observation that Japanese *kaisha* – supported by the United States of America – benefited in business and technological terms from both the war and the subsequent peace dividends generated by that conflict (cf. Allinson, 1997). Since 1953 industrial development in the South Korean *chaebol* retraced a pattern of export-orientation set by rival Japanese *keiretsu*, albeit delayed by events for around fifteen years (Chen, 2004). Correspondingly, Western observers of South Korean management styles identify a nationalistic 'catch up' mentality and a 'can do' entrepreneurial spirit almost fatalistically prepared for adversity (cf. Rowley and Bae, 2003; Rowley and Paik, 2009; Rowley and Jackson, 2011). The humiliation of the 'IMF period' prompted a freshly capitalised burst of creative export energy (cf. Coe and Kim, 2002). South Korean *chaebol* such as Samsung Electronics and *LG* excel in the marketing and export of, for example, memory chips, mobile phone technology and consumer electronics such as flat-screen televisions. In global terms both producers currently outperform their nearest Japanese rivals. As a vivid illustration of this trend, the rolling neon advertisement for Sanyo, a Japanese consumer electronics manufacturer, had (since 1984) been an iconic feature over Piccadilly Circus in London – similar to New York's Times Square as a prime location for global advertising. In September 2011, the iconic Sanyo banner was replaced by an advertisement for Hyundai.

How East Asian management systems and styles influence each other

One primary source of influence shaping the expression and development of management styles across East Asia can be found in a shared legacy of Confucian philosophy (see chapters 1, 5, 6 and others). Echoing Warner (2003b), this enduring legacy accounts for the 'family resemblances' evident across East Asian management. The extent to which this legacy might influence the development of diverse management systems might be traced by following recent flows and patterns of 'foreign direct investment' (FDI) across the region. Along with FDI, comes the transfer of new knowledge and technologies: i.e. assuming the systems targeted for FDI are open to such inputs. Here it is relevant to highlight the contribution made in East Asia (as elsewhere in the world) by the managers of small and medium-sized enterprises (SMEs). Of particular relevance to the aforementioned Confucian legacy is the 'Chinese Family Business' (CFB) type (Chen, 2004) of SME (see chapter 12). The CFB is accepted as one of the most successful models for business organisation in the history of global commerce (Redding, 1990). Consequently, the CFB continues to form the bedrock of successful economies such as Singapore, Taiwan and Hong Kong SAR (see chapters 6 and 12) (cf. Ambler and Witzel, 2000, Selmer and de Leon, 2003; Chou, 2003; Ambler *et al.*, 2009; Mead and Andrews, 2009).

As a system for doing business, the CFB emulates the social economic unit that is the family and, beyond this, the extended network of relationships commonly referred to in Chinese as *guanxi* or a system of social and business relationships that extend across Chinese societies (as chapter 10 clearly shows) and as perhaps unspoken obligations across generations of family members (cf. Pye, 1992; Dunfee and Warren, 2001). This concept is discussed in more detail in chapter 10. For now, we can refer to *guanxi* in order to highlight some of the systemic consequences of the 'family resemblances' that characterise Asian as opposed to non-Asian contexts for the development of management philosophies and practices. Here, we can cite Tian who defines *guanxi* as a 'favour seeking pragmatic social practice' (2007: 51). While admitting that the practice is not unique to Chinese societal cultures – in Western cultures we might refer to 'connections' – Tian recognises its salience to business across Chinese cultures, and in Mainland China particularly since the economic reforms of the late 1970s. A management style to complement the effective working of the *guanxi* system is *mianzi* or the type of social and business behaviour designed to avoid causing or experiencing loss of 'face' (cf. Child and Warner, 2003). Combining self-perceptions and social attributions as complex as integrity, dignity, respect and social reputation, the *mianzi* concept is fundamental to Confucian notions of social harmony and is a core strategic asset in the development and maintenance of business relationships both within and beyond the economic, social-cultural, technological and legal spaces defined by the CFB (cf. Chen, 2004; Tian, 2007).

During the late 1970s, CFBs along with MNCs headquartered in 'Chinese Circle' economies such as Taiwan, Hong Kong and Macau began investing heavily in the southern and coastal regions of Mainland China (Naughton, 2007). With the PRC now 'open for business', many CFBs sought to reinvest in the Mainland areas from which their families had originated (Peterson, 2012). The strategic focus initially was on exploiting government subsidies to manufacture low-value goods such as shoes and textiles for export (Hsing, 1998). The government in Beijing had long sought to protect the established State-Owned Enterprises (SOEs) from direct foreign competition as SOEs were (and remain) major employers across China and, in the absence of an adequate welfare system, remain major pillars in the enduring 'iron rice bowl' (*tie fan wan*) contract between the state and its people to provide them with work and a basic income for life. As a result of their enmeshment in socially and historically anchored *guanxi* systems, FDI from neighbouring Chinese/Confucian economies could be regarded in sociocultural terms as 'non-foreign' – a process almost of 'repatriating' family fortunes (cf. Graham and Wada, 2001; Naughton, 2007).

The precise form and impact of SMEs such as the CFB are discussed in more detail in chapter 12. Here, we can observe how the flow of FDI from within the China Circle economies soon served (in Western terms) to 'professionalise' the preferred styles and expectations of managers across the Chinese Mainland. To illustrate, 'expatriate' managers from Taiwan-based CFBs could pass on a competitively honed perspective on international marketing and logistics for manufactured goods (cf. Chou, 2003). Similarly, their counterparts from Hong Kong could offer internationally benchmarked services in commercial financing and law (cf. Selmer and de Leon, 2003), a process of cross-border collaboration that supports the rapid and spectacular infrastructure development around the Pearl River Delta region and assures Hong Kong a role at the mouth of one of the world's busiest conduits for manufacturing and international trade. As the institutional context for trade and business across China has become more differentiated, managers based in the Chinese Mainland have become more adept at positioning their goods in key global markets, notably in the USA and Europe. The likes of Lenovo, Haier, Huawei and Tsingtao have become global brands in both developed and emerging markets, while global players such as Geely Automobile have become active in the acquisition of established brands such as Volvo. Swedish managers are now challenged to adapt to Chinese styles of management and of doing business (cf. Isaksson, 2009), allowing us to look forward to the emergence of further hybrid styles and systems of management.

By achieving and successfully maintaining these positions, Mainland Chinese managers have developed distinct styles of cross-cultural business negotiations (cf. Pye, 1992; Child and Warner, 2003; Chen, 2004; Tian, 2007). Their recent achievements might be attributed to the outcomes of investment at national, regional, organisational and individual levels of management training and development in China (cf. Warner and Goodall, 2009; Warner, in this current collection). To illustrate, 'Shanghai-China' tops the OECD (2010a) rankings for secondary school educational outputs, with 'Korea' second and 'Hong Kong-China' fourth. Finland, a hardy perennial in such rankings, holds on to third place. This represents an accumulation of evidence describing a 'knowledge premium' that the criss-cross flows of FDI within and between East Asian social economies serve to generate (cf. Naughton, 2007). However, as a systemic output of Chinese FDI these developments in education and professionalisation might be understood – during the formative stages, at least – as a result of the 'expatriate' Chinese managers involved being more culturally attuned to observing practices emphasising *mianzi*, unlike initially (and perhaps inevitably) their non-Chinese rivals. On the basis of family resemblance – and, indeed, rivalry – both parties might be willing to learn effectively from each other. Through *mianzi* and related indigenous value systems, parties to business negotiations might influence each others' management styles sufficiently to support choices in practice where establishing long-term business relationships become prioritised over measures of short-term gain (cf. Tian, 2007). This 'family resemblance' became acknowledged subsequently in managers of South Korean and Japanese MNCs, notably around the north-eastern city of Dalian (Chen, 2004; Naughton, 2007).

The economic crises currently challenging the management systems and styles distinct to so-called 'developed' (e.g. Western) economies serve to spotlight how global flows and sources of FDI have shifted dramatically as China invests increasingly heavily in other developing economies in Southeast Asia, Africa and Latin America, thereby securing competitive access to valuable and rare commodities and to lower cost labour markets than those available at home. On the wave of such trends Chinese management systems and styles, whether in their culturally embedded or emerging hybrid forms, look set to command our attention for many years to come.

Conclusions

Applying a PESTEL analysis allows us briefly to highlight issues likely to challenge the current state of management systems and styles in East Asia. For example, political decisions made by PRC leaders increasingly shape what politicians worldwide term 'the global economy'. Meanwhile, Japanese managers witness prime ministers who come and go and in their wake leave a regional diplomatic framework that appears incoherent and lacking clear identity or direction. Strategic planners in South Korea await the implications of the North Korean leadership succession. The political climate generally is one of heightened and prolonged uncertainty.

In contrast, the economic outlook is (if anything) more certain. The engine for global economic growth remains in Asia (OECD, 2010b). The Japanese yen remains strong as global investors seek a reserve currency alternative to the US dollar: the euro meanwhile falters. Japanese exporters struggle to manage costs, while South Korea remains exposed to the turbulence of external financial markets, not least in the USA and Europe (cf. Cho, 2009). Organisations such as Hyundai increasingly rely on markets in China (including Hong Kong) for exports: a share now risen to 30 per cent from 10 in 1997 (OECD, 2010c: 46). As Mainland Chinese FDI becomes targeted ever more globally, similar challenges of performance dependency arise: e.g. in relation to managing commodities sourced in Africa (cf. Raine, 2009). In Mainland China itself, social inequality is set to grow, even though average wages are moving up. Leveraging the advantage of a government controlled exchange rate for the yuan, the central government will likely continue their policy of imposing price controls while passing on the cost of higher imports (e.g. fuel) to consumers, possibly leading to social unrest. Where political and economic factors interact, the long-term consequences are uncertain, and both business and ethical questions arise about the sustainability of current economic growth rates.

Ecological systems across the region are in a precarious state. For example, while projects in China such as the controversial Three Rivers Dam attract global headlines, less reported attention is given to the dramatic fall in groundwater table levels across China (Naughton, 2007), the critical challenges of managing industrial waste safely (Suttmeier, 2012) and the impact locally and globally of the casino-based economy of Macau SAR, the business turnover of which now exceeds Las Vegas (UKHK, 2008). After the 2011 Tohoku tsunami and nuclear plant disaster in Japan, the Japanese *kaisha* faces challenges to source energy; simultaneously, major conurbations across Korea are experiencing forms of energy rationing.

Nonetheless, national innovation systems across East Asia are likely to remain vibrant: creativity in adversity. Given the common Western view that East Asian economies (above all Chinese) are routinely assumed to be 'sinners' in relation to Intellectual Property Rights (IPR), it may come as a surprise to some that the number of globally enforceable technology patents registered by Chinese-owned enterprises is soon to outstrip patents registered by US American competitors (Zhou and Stembridge, 2008): the sinners may soon become the sinned against. Meanwhile, the predominant language of the Internet is soon to become Mandarin Chinese (OECD, 2010d).

This latter observation reminds us that the focus for discussion in this book is people. In terms of numbers the global business focus inevitably is on China and the challenges and opportunities generated by mass migration and unprecedented urbanisation (cf. Devan *et al.*, 2008). Established family ties are being stretched; a new expression of 'cultural identity' among managers is emerging across East Asia, at once global and professional (cf. Jackson and Tomioka, 2004; Debroux, 2011) and local and personal (cf. Chen, 2006). CFBs along with SOEs, *keiretsu* and *chaebol* now compete in an increasingly global and socially mobile market for managers designated as 'talent' (cf. Sun *et al.*, 2007; Ngo *et al.*, 2008; Cooke, 2012; Jackson – forthcoming). And in doing this there is an opportunity to find and include the missing piece from the talent jigsaw relevant to future developments in East Asian management systems and styles: women. Women continue to be under-represented in East Asian management systems and styles (see chapter 9) and notably those defined by reference to Confucian values (cf. Warner, 2011). For now we can conclude that, whether from male or female perspectives, there are many fine stories about East Asian management still to be told – stories developed in the chapters that follow.

References

Abeglen, J. C. and Stalk, G. (1985) *Kaisha: The Japanese Corporation.* New York: Basic Books.

Adler, N. J. (1986) 'From the Atlantic to the Pacific Century: Cross-cultural management reviewed', *The Journal of Management* 12: 295–316.

Allinson, G. D. (1997) *Japan's Postwar History.* Ithaca, NY: Cornell University Press.

Ambler, T. and Witzel, M. (2000) *Doing Business in China.* London: Routledge.

Ambler, T., Witzel, M. and Xi, C. (2009) *Doing Business in China.* London: Routledge.

Ayto, J. (1990) *Bloomsbury Dictionary of Word Origins.* London: Bloomsbury.

Bebenroth, R. and Kanai, T. (eds) (2011) *Challenges of Human Resource Management in Japan.* London and New York: Routledge.

Burman, R. (1995) *Manufacturing Management: Principles and Systems.* London: McGraw-Hill.

Chen, L. L. (2006) *Writing Chinese: Reshaping Chinese Cultural Identity.* New York: Palgrave Macmillan.

Chen, M. (2004) *Asian Management Systems.* Stamford (CT): Cengage.

Child, J. and Warner, M. (2003) 'Culture and management in China' in Warner, M. (ed.) 2003, *Culture and Management in Asia.* London and New York: Routledge, pp. 24–47.

Cho, D. (2009) The Republic of Korea's economy in the swirl of global crisis. *Asian Development Bank Institute Working Paper Series.* No. 147. Tokyo: ADBI.

Chou, W-C. G. (2003) 'Culture and management in Taiwan' in Warner, M. (ed.) 2003, *Culture and Management in Asia.* London and New York: Routledge, pp. 210–27.

Coe, D. T. and Kim, S-J. (eds) (2002) *Korean Crisis and Recovery.* Seoul: International Monetary Fund/Korea Institute for International Economic Policy.

Cooke, F. L. (2012) *Human Resource Management in China: New Trends and Practices.* London: Routledge.

Córdoba-Pachón, J-R. (2010) *System Practice in the Information Society.* London: Routledge.

Debroux, P. (2003) 'Culture and management in Japan' in Warner, M. (ed.) 2003, *Culture and Management in Asia.* London and New York: Routledge, pp. 99–114.

— (2011) 'Human resource management and employment systems in Asia: directions of change and new challenges' in Bebenroth, R. and Kanai, T. (eds) (2011) *Challenges of Human Resource Management in Japan.* London: Routledge, pp. 79–96.

Devan, J., Negri, S. and Woetzel, J. (2008) 'Meeting the challenges of China's growing cities', *McKinsey Quarterly* (July). Available at https://solutions.mckinsey.com/insightschina, accessed 25 September 2011.

Dunfee, T. W. and Warren, D. E. (2001) 'Is guanxi ethical? A normative analysis of doing business in China', *Journal of Business Ethics,* 32: 191–204.

Graham, E. M. and Wada, E. (2001) 'Foreign Direct Investment in China: Effects on Growth and Economic Performance', *Working Paper, Washington DC Institute for International Economics 01–3.* Available at http://www.iie.com/publications/wp/2001/01–03.pdf, accesssed 2 December 2011.

Haghirian, P. (ed.) (2010) *Innovation and Change in Japanese Management*, Basingstoke: Palgrave Macmillan.

Handy, C. (1976) *Understanding Organizations.* London: Penguin, p. 322.

Hofstede, G. (1980) *Culture's Consequences: International Differences in Work-related Values.* Beverly Hills (CA): Sage.

— (2001) *Culture's Consequences.* London: Sage.

Hofstede, G., Hofstede, G. J. and Minkov, M. (2010) *Cultures and Organizations; Software of the Mind.* 3rd edition. New York: McGraw-Hill.

Hsing, Y-T. (1998) *Making Capitalism in China: the Taiwan Connection.* Oxford: Oxford University Press.

Isaksson, P. (2009) 'Chinese views on Swedish management – consensus, conflict-handling and the role of the team'. Stockholm: Vinnova/Swedish Institute.

Jackson, K. (2010) 'Talent management' in Rowley, C. and Jackson, K. (eds) (2011) *Human Resources Management: The Key Concepts.* London: Routledge, pp. 206–13.

— (forthcoming) 'Challenges and prospects for managing human resources sustainably across countries, cultures and business sectors: Suggestions towards a practitioner-driven research agenda' in Ehnert, I., Harry, W. Zink, K. (eds) (forthcoming) *Managing Human Resources Sustainably.* Heidelberg: Springer (in press).

Jackson, K. and Tomioka, M. (2004) *The Changing Face of Japanese Management.* London and New York: Routledge.

Jackson, K. and Debroux, P. (2009) *Innovation in Japan: Emerging Patterns, Enduring Myths.* London: Routledge.

Koike, K. (1995) *Nihon no koyo system* (The Japanese Employment System). Tokyo: Toyo Keizai Shimposha.

Lansbury, R. D. Suh, C-S and Kwon, S-H (2007) *The Global Korean Motor Industry: The Hyundai Motor Company's Global Strategy.* London: Routledge.

Liker, J. (2004) *The Toyota Way: Fourteen Management Principles from the World's Greatest Manufacturer.* New York: McGraw-Hill.

Liu, W. (2010) *Social capital and urbanization: the case of 'villages within city' in Shenzhen, China.* Available at www.universitas21.com/GRC/GRC2009/Weibin.pdf, acccessed 1 December 2012.

Marchington, M., Wilkinson, A. and Ackers, P. (2001) *Management choice and employee voice.* London: CIPD.

Mead, R. and Andrews, T. A. (2009) *International Management: Culture and Beyond.* Chichester: John Wiley.

Merkin, R. (2005) 'The influence of masculinity-femininity on cross-cultural facework', *Journal of Intercultural Communication Research*, 34: 267–89.

Morgan, G. (1989) *Creative Organization Theory: A Resource Book.* London: Sage.

Naughton, B. (2007) *The Chinese Economy: Transitions and Growth.* Cambridge (MA): MIT Press.

Ngo, H-Y., Lau, C.M. and Foley, S. (2008) 'Strategic human resource management, firm performance, and employee relations climate in China', *Human Resource Management* 47: 73–90.

Nonaka, I. and Takeuchi, H. (1995) *The Knowledge-Creating Company.* Oxford: Oxford University Press.

OECD (2010a) *Programme for international student assessment (PISA).* Paris: OECD Publications. Available at http://www.oecd.org/dataoecd/54/12/46643496.pdf, accessed 23 September 2011.

— (2010b) *OECD Economic Outlook.* Paris: OECD Publishing.

— (2010c) *OECD Economic Surveys: Korea.* Paris: OECD Publishing.

— (2010d) *OECD Information Technology Outlook.* Paris: OECD Publishing

Ohmae, K. (2001) *The Invisible Continent: Four Strategic Imperatives for the New Economy.* London: Nicholas Brealy.

Ouchi, W. G. (1981) *Theory Z: How American Management can Meet the Japanese Challenge.* Reading (MA): Addison Wesley.

Parsons, T. (1956) 'Suggestions for a sociological approach to the theory of organizations', *Administrative Science Quarterly*, 1: 62–85.

Peterson, G. (2012) *Overseas Chinese in the People's Republic of China.* London: Routledge.

Porter, M. E., Takeuchi, H. and Sakakibara, M. (2000) *Can Japan Compete?* Cambridge (MA): Perseus.

Pye, L. (1992) *Chinese Negotiating Style: Commercial Approaches and Cultural Principles.* New York: Quoron.

Raine, S. (2009) *China's African Challenges*. Abingdon: Routledge/IISS.

Redding, S. G. (1990) *The Spirit of Chinese Capitalism*. Berlin: Walter de Gruyter.

Rose, E. L. (2002) 'Toyota production system' in Bird, A. (ed.) (2002) *Encyclopedia of Japanese Business and Management*. London and New York: Routledge, pp. 450–3.

Rowley, C. and Bae, J. (2003) 'Culture and management in South Korea' in Warner, M. (ed.) *Culture and Management in Asia*. London and New York: Routledge, pp. 187–209.

Rowley, C. and Paik, Y. (2009) *The Changing Face of Korean Management*. London and New York: Routledge.

Rowley, C. and Jackson, K. (eds) (2011) *Human Resources Management: The Key Concepts*. London: Routledge.

Sako, M. (1992) *Prices, Quality and Trust. Interfirm Relations in Britain and Japan*. Cambridge: Cambridge University Press.

Selmer, J. and de Leon, C. (2003) 'Culture and management in Hong Kong SAR' in Warner, M. (ed.) (2003), *Culture and Management in Asia*. London and New York: Routledge, pp. 48–65.

Si, S. X., Feng, W. and Li, W. (2009) 'The effect of organizational psychological contract violation on managers' exit, voice, loyalty and neglect in the Chinese context' in Warner, M. (ed.) op. cit., pp.162–74.

Storz, C. (2009) 'Innovation, institutions and entrepreneurs: The case of "cool Japan" ' in Jackson, K. and Debroux, P. (eds) *Innovation in Japan: Emerging Patterns, Enduring Myths*. London: Routledge, pp. 401–24.

Storz, C. and Schäfer, S. (2011) *Institutional Diversity and Innovation: Continuing and Emerging Patterns in Japan and China*. London and New York: Routledge.

Sun, L-Y., Aryee, S. and Law, K. S. (2007) 'High-performance human resource practices, citizenship behavior, and organizational performance: A relational perspective', *Academy of Management Journal*, 50: 558–77.

Suttmeier, R. P. (2012) 'China's management of environmental crises: risks, recreancy, and response' in Chung, J. H. (ed.) *China's Crisis Management*. Abingdon: Routledge, pp. 108–29.

Takeda, M. (2002) *'Karoshi'* in Bird, A. (ed.) (2002) *Encyclopedia of Japanese Business and Management*. New York: Routledge, pp.265.

Takeuchi, H. and Nonaka, I. (2004) *Hitotsubashi on Knowledge Management*. New York: John Wiley.

Taplin, R. (ed.) (2007) *Innovation and Business Partnering in Japan, Europe and the United States*. Abingdon: Routledge.

Tian, X. (2007) *Managing International Business in China*. Cambridge: Cambridge University Press.

Trompenaars, F. and Hampden-Turner, C. (1998) *Riding the Waves of Culture: Understanding Diversity in Global Business*. New York: McGraw-Hill.

Trott, P. (2004) *Innovation Management and New Product Development*. London: Financial Times/Prentice-Hall.

Turnley, W. H. and Feldman, D. C. (1999) 'The impact of psychological contract violations on exit, voice, loyalty, and neglect', *Human Relations*, 52: 895–922.

UKHK (2008) 'Business and trade in Macao', *British Consulate-General Hong Kong*. Available at http://ukinhongkong.fco.gov.uk/en/about-us/uk-in-macao/about-macao/business-profile, accessed 12 November 2012.

Von Bertalanffy, L. (1968) *General System Theory: Foundations, Development, Applications*. New York: Brazilier.

Warner, M. (ed.) (2003a) *Culture and Management in Asia*. London: Routledge.
— (2003b) 'Introduction: Culture and Management in Asia' in Warner, M. (ed.) (2003), *Culture and Management in Asia*. London: Routledge pp.1–23.
— (ed.) (2011) *Confucian HRM in Greater China: Theory and Practice*. London: Routledge.
Warner, M. and Joynt, P. (eds) (2002) *Managing Across Cultures: Issues and Perspectives*. London: Thomson Learning.
Warner, M. and Goodall, K. (eds) (2009) *Management Training and Development in China: Educating Managers in a Globalized Economy*. Abingdon: Routledge.
Whitehill, A. (1991) *Japanese Management: Tradition and Transition*. London: Routledge.
Whitely, D. (1990) 'Eastern Asian enterprise structures and comparative analysis of forms of business organizations', *Organization Studies*, 11: 47 – 74.
Zhou, E-Y. and Stembridge, B. (2008) 'Patented in China: the current and future state of innovation in China'. London: Thomson Reuters. Available at http://ip.thomsonreuters.com/media/pdfs/WIPTChina08.pdf, accessed 1 December 2012.

Part III

Societal case studies

To govern means to rectify. If you lead on the people with correctness, who will dare not to be correct?

(Confucius: Analects, XII, xvii)

5 The changing nature of management and culture in China[1]

Shuming Zhao and Juan Du

Introduction

This chapter sets out to describe the relationship between culture and management in the People's Republic of China (see Child and Warner, 2003). With a history of more than 5,000 years and a current population of more than 1.3 billion people, China is today considered a 'transitional economy' (see Warner *et al.*, 2005), moving from a highly centrally planned economic system towards a market-oriented economy with unique Chinese characteristics. China is now playing an increasingly important global role as one of the biggest markets in the world, since the economic reforms and opening-up to the outside world that started in 1978. As China transforms its economy, understanding its *culture* is key as it is one of the main variables propelling this advancement and accounting more specifically for the distinct management developments that have evolved in China over the last few decades (Warner, 2005, 2008, 2009, 2011).

Since China became a member of the World Trade Organization (WTO) in December 2001, Chinese firms have been facing more competition and challenges from foreign countries, as more overseas companies are investing and doing business in China. Many Chinese companies have taken measures to meet the new challenges, such as attracting talent internationally and implementing foreign advanced management techniques and technologies. For any organisation, culture and management are interdependent elements which influence the organisation's success. 'Culture' plays a significant part in creating a supportive environment for accomplishing the goals of the enterprises. If culture and management can be aligned, it will be helpful for setting strategic goals and achieving success (see chapter 3)

Although much attention is given in the management literature to societal as well as organisational culture and management (see Warner, 2011), it is recognised that cultural implications are sometimes overlooked by organisations. Management works within an organisational culture, even in a diverse global environment. As many scholars have indicated, the impact of societal and organisational culture on organisations around the globe has become a more important consideration for cross-cultural and multinational business management (Hofstede, 1980, Hofstede *et al.*, 2010; Warner, 2011).

'Culture' is a more general term that refers to the set of shared values within an organisation. Management refers to the organisational activities and infrastructure, and the various methods and practices within it, that help an organisational culture run with the efficiency and consistency that should be the hallmark of any healthy entity, whether it is a corporation, a government, a university or any other organisation.

Attention to culture also has important meaning for practising international managers, for whom it serves as a convenient and effective tool for understanding the many obstacles they may experience when working with people from different countries. Management practices have derived from different institutional foundations in different societies and cultures. And culture will play different roles in all kinds of institutions which constitute the distinctive social organisation of a country and its economy. The norms and habits that these institutions form will in turn affect organisational performance and they may also impact significantly on corporate and managerial behaviour.

For a country, history is embedded in its social structure and values. This implies that nations have their own logic of social and economic organisation (see Hofstede, 1980, Hofstede *et al.*, 2010; Chinese Culture Connection, 1987; Hofstede and Bond, 1988). In China, for example, the foundation of the Chinese respect for hierarchy and the family social collective is based on the relational norms expounded by philosophers such as Confucius, as well as legal codes such as those developed during the Tang Dynasty. Meanwhile, culture and institutions tend to influence different aspects of management and organisation. Culture also impacts primarily on individual attitudes and behaviour, including interpersonal behaviour.

Institutions, by contrast, impact directly on features that are shaped or constrained by formal norms and rules. These include systems of corporate ownership, accountability and governance, conditions of employment and collective bargaining and the reliance on formal contracts for intra- and inter-organisational transactions.

In addition to managerial behaviour, history, societal culture and institutions also influence organisational cultures. They make the structure an integral part of organisational culture. Organisational structure deals primarily with the set-up of the culture. How management works, which specific responsibilities supervisors have, how a complaint is passed through the ranks – these are all issues within the organisational culture that are directly tied to how an organisational structure works. Another common way to describe how culture works in an organisation is to say that organisational culture is the way in which the interrelated groups within an organisation are set up to allow them to function smoothly.

The relationship between organisational culture and management is always important for these two functions and behaviours. This chapter introduces China's historical background, economic background, social culture background, corporate culture, managerial behaviour, managerial values, labour–management conflict resolution; and their implications for managers. Through these descriptions, we hope readers will better understand Chinese culture and management style.

Historical background

China is home to the oldest and most continuous civilisation of the world. One of the earliest and the most complicated State structures has evolved, as well as social and personal management philosophies (see Goody, 1996). Before the Opium War in 1840, despite incursions and invasions, the core cultural values of Chinese society had been very stable and intact for over 2,000 years. However, after 1840 Western ideas started to influence the Chinese, and meanwhile the Chinese began a re-evaluation of their own tradition and were eager to learn from the outside world. In today's China, people's lifestyles have become quite Westernised in many ways. Even so, traditional ideas are still deeply embedded in managerial, social and work values (see Lamond and Leung, 2010).

Confucianism

Developed from the teachings of Confucius, Confucianism has strongly influenced the culture and history of China, as well as many other East Asian countries (see chapters 6, 7, 8), and it remains influential even today (see Lin and Ho, 2009). Whereas some Westerners may consider Confucianism as a religion similar to Christianity and Buddhism, the Chinese view Confucianism as an ethical and philosophical system. People do not worship Confucius; instead they follow his teachings and thoughts in their personal behaviour and social activity (see Bell, 2008).

State management

The first accountable kingdom in China was the Xia dynasty founded around 2,000 BC, near the Huang River (the Yellow River) region. During the period from 770 BC to 256 BC (the Spring and Autumn period and the War Kingdoms period) Chinese culture entered its first golden age. It was in that time that many of the most important philosophies, including Confucianism, emerged. Scholars started to study the art of Statecraft and management; different schools began to develop and spread. The three most important schools from the time period were Legalism, Taoism and Confucianism.

Legalism claims that only strict laws and a centralised government could lead to a State becoming a powerful country. The Qin kingdom, which adapted Legalism, conquered the rest of the kingdoms and founded the first united empire in China's history. Although Legalism was abandoned and never adopted again after Qin collapsed, the idea of a strong central government and unification has been deeply embedded in Chinese culture until the present day.

Taoism claims that government should interfere as little as possible, according to the notion of *wu-wei*, to let nature's laws happen. After reuniting China again, the second empire (the Han) adapted this smaller-scale government notion and non-interference approach, to recover from the war.

Confucianism claims that moral education will lead the people to honour and the country to harmony. In 140 BC the emperor of Han announced that Confucianism would become the official State ideology and that the government would only employ scholars who studied Confucianism. Since then Confucianism has become the dominant ideology in China. Moral norms replaced laws, becoming the primary means of governing. This helps to explain why the Chinese heavily rely on *guanxi* (relationship) and *mingsheng* (reputation) rather than contracts and laws (see chapter 10).

Social and personal management

The ideas and philosophy of social and personal management are mainly influenced by Confucianism (Rarick, 2009). The early widely accepted social norms came from the ideas of Three Bonds of Loyalty (loyalty to the ruler, filial obedience and the fidelity of a wife to her husband) and Three Basic Guides (the ruler guides the subject, the father guides the son and the husband guides the wife) from Confucianism. This démarche led to a hierarchical structure in Chinese society. By moral standards, the subordinate has to follow the instruction of the superior, instead of challenging it; however, this is neither absolute nor enforced by laws. The entire society lives according to moral norms. This standard encouraged interpersonal relations to become stronger and more important.

Confucius believed that by teaching and education, a person could become perfect. With wisdom, the person could distinguish between honour and shame and behave properly and willingly. Thus, there need be no laws to force people to do 'the right thing'. Greatly influenced by this idea, the Chinese were to become very serious and careful about education and behaviour. Family members are closely bonded by filial piety and social groups (people who work together, study together and so on) are closely bonded by loyalty. In China, as is well-known, the family is the most important social entity. The Chinese consider filial piety towards parents to be a key responsibility, the same as parents to their children. In society, the relationship is built on trust, and this trust is based on one's social behaviour, age, credibility and possible common experience.

Business management

Historically, business persons have been discriminated against as a social class in China. Moral standards, for instance, were set strongly against the alleged greed of business people. An individual's social position was not measured by wealth, but by success in politics or knowledge. Although those in business were seen as low in social class, from the State's point of view commerce was still a very important matter.

Three common approaches were used widely. State monopoly emerged very early and was widely used. For example, salt, precious metal mining and coinage became permanent monopolies. Other fields such as winemaking and metal-smelting (iron earlier and steel later) were also frequent subjects. The concept of market interference was first addressed in the Spring and Autumn periods, and was first practised in the Han dynasty. The government set up a special structure to purchase grain in good harvest years, when the market price was low, in order to lift the price and sell grain in poor harvest years when the market price was high, in order to stabilise the level. The last common approach was the main tool of taxation. Sang Hongyang (152 BC–80 BC), an economist in the Han dynasty, first implemented a complex and dynamic taxation system. One of his most famous ideas was that a continuous heavy tax upon peasants would lead to revolt and a periodical heavy tax upon business activity would benefit and enrich the government, because there will always be new businesses to replace the bankrupt ones.

Economic background

China's current economic growth rate is approximately 9 per cent annually. Its contribution to global GDP growth since 2000 has been almost twice as large as that of the next three biggest emerging economies (Brazil, India and Russia) combined. In 2011, China still maintained a rapid economic growth rate, and the estimated GDP growth rate was about 9.8 per cent, which was slightly lower than that in 2010. China's GDP growth was 10.3 per cent in 2010. Directly or indirectly, the Chinese economy has influenced interest rates, prices for raw materials and wages in the Western established economies. Currently, China is the most R&D intense emerging market country and is seventh of all the countries in the world. With its high growth rate, the presence and impact of the Chinese economy will only increase in the world (see chapter 2). Its economic power is exemplified by the fact that it was expected to be the fifth largest source of outward foreign direct investment during 2004–7. China attracted US$105.74 billion in foreign direct investment in 2010 while it invested US$590 million abroad in the same year, not including the financial sectors.

Since adopting the 'Economic Reforms' and 'Open Door' policy of Deng Xiaoping 30 years ago, China has moved from a traditional planning economy to a market economy. In 1978, Deng made a significant decision that China should focus on socialist modernisation. He pointed out that in the new period of change the historical task of the Party was to build China into a modern, powerful socialist society. Ever since that key moment, China has stepped on to a fast-growing track and has made remarkable achievements. Thus, since 1978, China has made rapid progress in industrialisation and urbanisation. The Chinese economy has sustained rapid economic growth. From the year 1978 to the present day, China's GDP has grown relentlessly at an average rate of close to 10 per cent (*People's Daily*, 2010; World Bank, 2010). At present, China is the second largest economy in the world.

China's foreign exchange reserves have burgeoned to US$3.2 trillion. This figure exceeds the sum of the world's major seven countries (United States, Japan, Britain, Germany, France, Canada and Italy, referred to as the G7). China has gained a rapid increase in living standards. For urban residents, the benefits have been significant. For rural areas, the problem of feeding hundreds of millions of poor people has been solved in a relatively short period of time.

The socialist market economy has thus dramatically expanded and improved. China's economic reforms first started in the rural areas, and gradually advanced to the cities. The 'Open Door' policy saw the establishment of 'Special Economic Zones' along the coast. In rural reforms, Anhui Province took the lead in adopting the 'Household Contract Responsibility System'. This démarche was a great success, gained official support and then spread across the country. In enterprise reforms, the Chinese government conducted various forms of autonomy experiments with State-owned enterprises to expand pilot-sites such as those originally in Sichuan Province; at the same time, collective and private enterprises were gradually reformed. Management training was reintroduced and business schools were established (Warner and Goodall, 2009).

Commodity, financial and labour markets have since evolved, and gradually a modern market system has taken root. With the continuous deepening of the reforms, the market system has been greatly expanded. Factor-markets have gradually been introduced with the abolition of dual-pricing systems of production and with further liberalisation of the competitive price-mechanisms for goods and services. With the shrinking of the scope of government investment, businesses have filled the gap. Despite the relatively short history of the capital market, China's stock market size, GDP market value, volume and trading systems have risen sharply. Relevant financial laws and regulations continue to improve. The development of capital-market reform has played a great role in promoting State-owned enterprises and reducing financial risk.

China has become an important member of the global economic system. From 1978 to 2011, foreign trade volume increased from US$109 billion to over US$3 trillion, an almost 300 fold increase, and will reach US$5.3 trillion by the year 2020. With its accession to the World Trade Organization (WTO), China cannot only coordinate and resolve trade disputes by the rules of international trade organisations, but also better safeguard its economic interests and promote a fairer world economic order through participation in the formulation of world trade rules.

China is now ranked amongst the top emerging market economies for attracting foreign capital. Products which are now made in China (and assembled) are exported widely, which has won China the accolade 'workshop of the world'. Exports of labour-intensive products once exploited the comparative advantage of cheap labour in China, but such costs are now rising dramatically.

In the past 30 years, China has *pari passu* neglected the protection of natural resources, the environment and the labour rights of its workers. To be specific, environmental resources have been over-consumed. Economic development has been achieved at the cost of severe damage to China's environment and resources. The gap between the rich and poor has deepened and the Gini-coefficient is now as high as in Western countries.

Societal culture

We will now discuss the societal culture of China through the examination of education, social values, consumption behaviour, religious belief and subcultures.

Education

China has a long history and tradition of educating its talent. Chinese people attach great importance to education for their offspring. Although China had an early, well-established education system in Imperial times for the few, the transformation from a traditional elite education system to a modern broad-based one encountered many difficulties and was not able to make significant progress until the founding of the People's Republic of China (PRC) in 1949. Today, China is building a high-quality modern education system. The illiteracy rate has dropped to 3 per cent in 2010, from 80 per cent in 1900. Today, China has over 20 million university undergraduate and postgraduate students. It also has a growing number of business schools and MBA graduates (see chapter 15).

Social values

Social values refer to the attitudes and perceptions of people towards the world in which they live. The traditional Chinese value-system is formed with Confucianism at its core and with Buddhism and Taoism at the periphery. The central domination of Confucianism is long-lasting, stable and solid (see Warner, 2011).

The traditional Confucianism ideology addresses the idea of loyalty to the ruler, filial obedience and the fidelity of the wife to the husband as well as various types of personal behaviour, social conduct and rites. In the nineteenth century, China entered a phase of comprehensive historical change, and the traditional value-system was severely challenged. In the last century, we have seen both the disintegration of traditional values and the emergence of modern ideas.

Nowadays, the Chinese people still place great importance on loyalty in social relations, filial piety in family relations and fidelity in marriage, although these may be weakening. While Chinese people are eager to learn from the rest of the world and open their minds to accept Western notions, the very essence of being Chinese lingers.

Consumption behaviour

The Chinese are famous for being thrifty and are keen on saving. After the Opium War, the disintegration of the traditional lifestyle and the influx of foreign goods gradually changed the consumption behaviour of the Chinese. While recently becoming the world's second largest consumer market and the largest luxury market, the Chinese still paradoxically have the world's largest bank savings. The gross domestic savings rate is now around 50 per cent per annum.

Religious belief

Today's China is said to be a 'multi-religious' country. Where citizens freely choose and express their religious beliefs and religious identity. The most popular religions are Buddhism, Taoism and Islam. There are others, such as Catholicism within Christianity, but their number remains relatively small. However, many Chinese are neither atheists nor believers of any religion. The dominant ideology in China is, we would argue, Confucianism. Although many Westerners see Confucianism as a religion, the Chinese consider it as a 'philosophy of life' (see Child and Warner, 2003; Bell, 2008).

An interesting phenomenon is that many Chinese are both believers of all and believers of none, at the same time. A person who never goes to a Tao temple to pray for anything may piously prepare and perform a Tao ritual before the opening of business and the same person may pray to Buddha for prosperity another day, when passing a Buddhist temple. Many Chinese used to believe in Communism in Chairman Mao's day, before the Cultural Revolution, but have now lost much of their faith (see Bell, 2008).

Subcultures

The majority of Chinese are Han people (over 90 per cent). Because of the wide geographic distribution and the absorption of many other ethnic groups throughout history, the subcultures within this category may vary greatly, while also sharing many traditions and ideologies.

Geographically, the Chinese may be roughly divided into northern people and southern people by the Huai River. The northern people are said to be more generous and straightforward, while the southern people tend to be more dedicated and persistent. After the 'Open Door' policy in the last 30 years or so, another difference between coastal areas and inland areas has begun to emerge. The coastal people appear to attach greater importance to individualism and openness to change and are hence more likely to be entrepreneurial, whilst the inland people attach more importance to collectivism and tradition.

The subcultures of the Chinese exist in every domain. Different provinces have different subcultures, different cities within a province have different subcultures and even some different areas within a city have different subcultures. This difference of subcultures generates a very strong concept of *laoxiang* (meaning people from the same place). People from the same village, the same city, the same province stay together even when placed in different situations. Trust relationships are usually much stronger among kith and kin.

Both Western and Japanese management modes have their advantages. Many Chinese enterprises like to apply and get lessons from both management modes. But any country and nation has its specific culture, which is the accumulation of wealth during the process of long-term historical development; it is the sum of customs, values, ethics, code of conduct and the idea of the people which is refined and formed in the common social life.

In modern enterprise management, although possessing a sound business operation system is the key to success and failure, the influence of culture cannot be underestimated. Chinese traditional culture is the crystallisation of the wisdom of 5,000 years of Chinese history, and it reveals the goodness of human nature, establishes enterprise ethics, builds an effective corporate culture and creates Chinese-type management.

Corporate culture

Under the impetus of the economic reforms, Chinese business is changing rapidly. At the same time, as a result, Chinese enterprises also vary extensively, ranging from State-owned enterprises [SOEs] to collectively-owned enterprises and private firms. In late 1978, corporate culture emerged in the landmark changes that took place when the 'new' Chinese managerial model was first piloted in Sichuan Province. State-owned enterprises (SOEs) had once dominated industrial production and their work-units (*danwei*) had embodied the so-called 'iron rice-bowl' (*tie fan wan*) regime (see Child, 1994).

Since 1979, economic changes have resulted in the formation of new corporate cultures (see Hawes, 2008). In many SOEs, the residue of the 'iron rice-bowl' model continues to persist and collective enterprises may vary greatly between conservative, unsophisticated cultures to more modern entrepreneurial ones. Different corporate cultures also arise through links with foreign firms and their different national ownerships. The greatest impact on Chinese enterprise-cultures and practices is from multinational enterprises.

By inheriting a culture with strong feudalistic origins, China provides a favourable context for paternalistic corporate cultures. Enterprises at both extremes of the range, traditional SOEs and private firms, exhibit corporate cultures that reflect paternalistic cultural values. In traditional SOEs, the culture has been one of 'top-down' leadership and authority, collectivism and mutual dependence, with an emphasis on conformity and attachment to the organisation based on moral rather than material incentives (Child, 1994). A kind of '*noblesse oblige*' has prevailed in many of these firms. Loyalty to superiors and to the work unit has been complemented by employment protection and the provision of welfare benefits. This 'moral contract' is now fast breaking down as SOEs either reform or go bankrupt. There is little evidence as yet of what the corporate culture of reformed SOEs may turn out to be, although case-studies suggest that it might combine an emphasis on personal achievement with a strong collective spirit.

In the private sector, most firms are still small and their culture is much centred on the owner. Only among some larger and longer-established private firms is there evidence of decisions being made by more formal bodies such as a board of directors or a management team. In rural private firms, the direction of these firms is almost exclusively in the hands of their owner-managers.

Within private firms, be they urban (e.g. SOEs) or rural (e.g. TVEs), workers do not normally participate in decision-making, even on questions concerning benefits. In the typical urban private firm, employees can be divided into two groups. The first comprises local people and externally recruited university graduates. These employees generally hold better positions in the firms, enjoy superior wages and benefits and stay with the firm longer. They are regarded as long-term primary members of the 'corporate collectivity' and are likely to identify with its culture.

The second group consists of migrants from rural areas, who occupy a much more marginal position.

After the reform and opening-up, the entry of foreign capital has created many joint ventures and wholly foreign-owned enterprises. The culture in Chinese enterprises, at first influenced by Chinese traditional culture and specific products of historical development, has started to experience collision and fusion and has gradually become diversified. For example, in many joint ventures, an important role in the organisational structure belongs to employees possessing cross-cultural skills, who are not just interpreters or translators, but those who are capable of giving timely advice to leaders and managers on how certain things should be handled with the Chinese personnel and in China in general. Organisational structures should be differentiated depending on an enterprise's life cycle and growth. While committing to work in the People's Republic of China, it is very important to consider the factors of organisational change, due to existing adaptation to the Chinese leadership style. It is strongly desirable to have a team of people with in-depth knowledge of Chinese language and culture as a safety layer against these potential challenges (Pedyash and Shi, 2010).

Managerial behaviour

China, a country with a long historical tradition, has evolved its own 'typical' managerial behaviour which is greatly influenced by traditional Chinese culture (see Lamond and Leung, 2010). Thus, in order to explore managerial behaviour in China, we need to probe into this legacy of Chinese values. Yu *et al.* (2000) have proposed a number of key cultural factors – the patriarchal system, putting principles first, exhibiting politeness, being politics-oriented, having a 'petty' producers' mentality, having patience and patriotic sensitivity – that Chinese culture has imposed on business operation and communicating activities, which furnishes the fullest explanation of managerial behaviour under the influence of Chinese culture. Since it is hard to identify or summarise one single stereotypical management model in China, the most effective approach to investigating the subject is to target the two contrasting types of firm: State-owned Enterprises (SOEs) and private firms (Child and Warner, 2003).

Chinese culture is characterised by hierarchies (Hamilton, 1991) and a firm in China is said to be usually tightly controlled by its 'top boss' (Redding and Wong, 1986), which is particularly true in SOEs, large enterprises invested in or owned by central government or local governments. In SOEs, there are elaborate structures with many specialised departments among which necessary communication and coordination are inadequate. The irrational setting of departments further affects the realisation of business goals. Information and authority travels one way – from the top down – in SOEs, since vertical links within hierarchies are emphasised (Rarick, 2009). Being a society with high power distance, the top boss in China automatically establishes his/her authoritative position and is respected by other members. The decisions are always made by the authorities with little or no participation by other members of the corporation. And while dissensions among superiors and subordinates do occur, subordinates are inclined to be obedient to their superiors to show their respect. The largest problem in SOEs has been rooted in the patriarchal system in China. Patriarchy features prominently in the perception of Chinese staff who see the workplace as the equivalent of the family unit in Chinese culture (Child, 1994).

Thus, Chinese personnel are highly group-oriented and prefer to share responsibilities among group members, rather than accept job duties that allocate performance on an individual basis. However, these attitudes tend to be weakening among members of the urban younger generation who have received higher education and are exposed to Western culture (see Lin and Ho, 2009). Furthermore, in order to conform to social development and the market economy, SOEs have been undergoing reforms that absorb modern management methods. Privatisation and foreign acquisition impels SOEs to shoulder the responsibility for their own economic survival, which provokes their exploration of new managerial behaviour. And in the acquisition process, new problems occur in cross-culture teams. Wang (1998) discovered that when confronted with different opinions or conflict, Chinese managers are reluctant to solve the problem through direct communication with their foreign colleagues, while foreign managers feel offended if their Chinese colleagues make the conflict public through discussing the issue with superiors, raising it in a formal meeting or telling their friends.

Private firms in China have been developed mainly from self-employed enterprises, family-run enterprises and partnership enterprises, with family-run enterprises being the pervasive form. Being deeply influenced by Confucian ideas that emphasise a strict hierarchy of primary relationships between either family members or the people and their rulers, owners of private firms tend to run their businesses in a highly centralised manner (Child and Warner, 2003). This can be explained partly by a 'petty producers' mentality. Petty producers refers to peasants in China who were for a long time under the influence of the natural economy and are conservative, selfish and show distrust (Fan, 2004). Thus, enterprise owners maintain their authoritative position in the firm by making all decisions by themselves without effective supervision, feedback or control. And while conflicts arise between subordinates and members of the owning family, a high value is attached to preserving loyalty to the owner. As Chen (1995) notes, compared with their performance the owners of private firms in China are inclined to attach greater significance to the loyalty of their subordinates. The owners favour those who are loyal and pay special attention to them and develop special ties with them. Those loyal people are more likely to be assigned with vital tasks and be promoted.

SOEs and private firms in China share one similarity in their managerial behaviour; that is, they are all 'politics-oriented' and depend on *guanxi* to develop their external networks and acquire business opportunities (Tsang, 1998). These opportunities include the smooth running of routine business operations, obtaining information about government policies, achieving success in business negotiations and gaining the receipt of administrative approvals. When China first embarked on reform and opening-up in 1978, new ways of doing business were primarily initiated through the *guanxi* system, when there was no market-driven system to guide the economic flow. Business transactions in China are carried on relying more on the mutual responsibilities implicitly expressed by *guanxi* between two parties than on legal contracts, since the Chinese cultural preference is for a moral basis rather than a formal one. Besides business transactions among firms, internal employment mechanisms and performance appraisal systems are reliant on *guanxi* as well. Lacking talent selection and motivation mechanisms, enterprise owners may appoint and promote people by favouritism, in which process *guanxi* plays a major role (see chapter 10).

However, as market competition has become increasingly fierce, the value and effectiveness of the *guanxi* system has greatly deteriorated. *Guanxi* has been neutralised or marginalised in industries where there is vigorous competition. Since more SOEs are privatised or acquired by foreign ventures, contracts in business transactions are gaining increasing importance. As Luo (2002) states, while personal relationships may still be a key factor affecting business transactions between local Chinese firms, contractual principles become significant in joint ventures with foreign firms and are even welcomed by Chinese partners. Moreover, Gong *et al.*, (2007) found an immediate increase in the efficiency of labour use following the ownership change of SOEs. Thus, in such a competitive market, enterprises, no matter if they are State-owned, collective or privately owned, have to operate according to the rules of economic efficiency.

Chinese managers' behaviour has long been influenced by traditional culture and social character, and the individual reflects many typical characteristics. In addition to the previous discussion, we can also identify further social behaviours which are acquired by the individual in the process of socialisation. For example, conformity, which may be one of the expressions of lack of confidence; self-examination; and self-control, which in turn is affected by the ideal role model of *'Jun Zi'*, originating from Confucianism. Mild and gentle individual behaviour is in accordance with the harmonious moral norms of society; conservative behaviour has the same meaning as the long-term-oriented cultural dimension described by Hofstede and Bond (1988); and finally there are those behavioural changes and trends aroused by 'the face' problem and complex relationships, which unconsciously influence daily life and management practices.

Managerial values

As business has become increasingly global, the transferability of management theories and practices across national borders and different cultures has become an increasingly debated topic. Societal values, managerial practices and the congruence between the two entities have increasingly been shown to influence critical organisational outcomes. Research designed to assess the degree to which nations differ in terms of attitudes, beliefs and values has resulted in widely different findings. Attitudes toward business practices and priorities have also been found to differ by nationality.

Managerial values in China are remarkably affected by traditional Chinese cultural factors like Confucianism. However, when Chinese people are exposed to

Western culture on the way to realising economic superpower status, will traditional values be abandoned or kept? China's entry into the WTO has aroused experts' interest in studying managerial values in China, because a comprehension of Chinese managerial values as well as Chinese thinking is essential for Westerners who plan to engage in business in China (Tung, 1994).

Initially, Confucianism, whose major ideas include three basic guides (ruler guides subject, father guides son and husband guides wife), five constant virtues (benevolence, righteousness, propriety, wisdom and fidelity), and the doctrine of the mean (harmony), has been identified as the primary force that shapes Chinese values. The Chinese cultural preference is thus laid upon a *moral* basis rather than a formal footing like contracts. Thus, business transactions in China are more likely to be based upon the quality of interpersonal relationships and disputes are settled through mediation in order to achieve harmonious interpersonal relations, which can be seen to stem from the philosophy of Confucianism (see Rarick, 2009).

In the early 1990s, economic modernisation in China rekindled the pride of Chinese people in their nation and culture, which is explained by Mackerras *et al.* (2000) who see the resurgence of Confucianism as part of a new type of cultural nationalism, targeting moral and family values (Bell, 2008). In the meantime, Western business policies, values and management behaviour are now increasingly introduced into China, impacting and influencing Chinese managers. More recently, new types of managers have emerged who combine both traditional Confucian values and Western values in management practice.

Theories of convergence and divergence have been applied to explain whether one's values change in new circumstances or keep constant regardless of the changing environment (see Warner, 2009, 2011). Supporters for the convergence theory state that values are driven by the ideology of the workplace. When a nation, especially an underdeveloped one, embraces capitalism, its value-system will be changed to resemble that of Western capitalistic economies. Vertinsky *et al.* (1990) have found that traditional Chinese values prove to be more intensive in Mainland China than in Hong Kong, which is more industrialised. Chiu *et al.* (1998) discovered in another study that traditional values are more pervasive in citizens in Guangzhou than in those of Hong Kong. Closer to the present day, Lin and Ho's study (2009) sees values as being in flux. Those who support the divergence theory insist that the key factor determining individual values is the national culture rather than workplace ideology. Thus, whether a nation adopts capitalism or not, the value-system of the workforce will be stable. A more recent perspective is 'cross-vergence' theory which takes both national culture and workplace ideology into consideration in shaping value-systems.

There are also empirical studies conducted to examine the influence of Western workplace ideology on managerial values in China. Since China is a huge country with many regions, thus, on the way to industrialisation, coastal regions may witness more evident changes in managerial values than inland regions. Ralston *et al.* (1996) surveyed the managerial values of 704 managers from six cities in China. While individualistic attitudes (individualism, openness to change and self-enhancement) are found to be more prevalent among the cosmopolitan Chinese than in local Chinese, commitment to Confucianism (societal harmony, virtuous interpersonal behaviour and personal and interpersonal harmony) is found to be the same among managers from all six cities. The result supports the view that individualism tends to be greater in managers from coastal areas than those from inland areas. The outcome of a further comparison focusing on the individualism–collectivism construct of Chinese managers from the relatively cosmopolitan city of Guangzhou compared with those from the more traditional city of Chengdu was in accordance with the view that developing economies would create their own hybrid version of a market economy under the influence of traditional culture interacting with new workplace ideology (Ralston *et al.*, 1999b). That Guangzhou managers attach greater importance to individualism, while collectivism is better preserved by Chengdu managers, further supports the view that coastal and inland areas are permeated by individualism to different extents.

Ralston *et al.* (1999b) also compared the managerial values of 869 Chinese managers and professionals employed in SOEs, focusing on the individualism, collectivism and Confucianism aspects of Chinese values. Three generational groups were compared in the research: the 'new generation' of the Chinese managers, comprising subjects who were 40 years old or younger; the current generation of managers, comprising 41- to 51-year-old subjects; and the older generation, comprising subjects who were 52 years of age and older. Results show that the new generation of managers scored higher on individualism and lower on collectivism and Confucianism. These younger Chinese managers, who will be leading China into the twenty-first century, possess greater mobility and are more inclined to act independently and take risks in the pursuit of profits since their values are more individualistic, less collectivistic and less committed to Confucian philosophy than their previous generation counterparts (Ralston *et al.*, 1999b). However, Heffernan and Crawford (2001), who conducted a survey of 210 Chinese managers employing a more comprehensive assessment of Confucian values, challenged the previous conclusion. Among the new generation of Chinese managers, some elements of Confucianism are weakening while others (benevolence, temperance and persistence) are maintained (see Chen, 2008; Lin and Ho, 2009).

These studies of managerial values in China suggest that younger managers in more cosmopolitan coastal regions exposed to Western ideas are adopting new values. However, to what extent traditional Confucian values are being forsaken or discarded still remains open to question (see Warner, 2009). Apparently a unique value-system is being formed in China, integrating new Western notions and traditional Confucian culture, which reflects that on the one hand Chinese society is struggling to preserve its social tradition that has passed down from generation to generation for over 2,000 years, while on the other hand it strives to be competitive by absorbing Western elements in the new global economic competition (see Pedyash and Shi, 2010).

More and more Chinese managers are adjusting their managerial values according to the enterprise mission and vision. Managerial values existing in an organisation are the strength which can save the organisation from a hopeless situation. These kinds of values cannot be learned or duplicated by a series of behaviours, such as stories, norms, policies, rules and strategies, and they should be combined with the formation of an organisational mission and vision, which can be described as the goals that founders possess, other than for making profits. Organisational missions and visions are very important elements but easy to ignore. Managers pay most attention to organisational profits, process and growth, which modifies their behaviours in short-term orientation, while effective management, but not efficient management, actually needs more organisational behaviour modification from the perspective of strategy and long-term orientation. Therefore, all of the traditional culture, social norms and situational factors can help to form managerial values which improve organisational effectiveness (see Warner, 2011).

Labour–management conflict resolution

Western labour–management relationships (both formal and informal), with their respective rights, obligations and negotiating frameworks, have been well-established for most of the last century (see chapter 13). In advanced economies, and some less advanced ones, the relationship is more or less universally understood and supported by a complex body of associated legislation, despite recent attempts to modify or erode employee conditions and benefits in some countries in the name of enhanced efficiency, effectiveness or competitiveness. However, in many developing countries, including China, Vietnam and Indonesia in Asia, historical, sociocultural, ideological or political factors have constrained the development of such formalised labour–management (LM) systems (Collins *et al.*, 2011).

In 1949, based on the Soviet Union model, the Chinese built a 'top-down' structured labour–management conflict resolution system. All workers were enrolled in this single trade union automatically, namely the All-China Federation of Trade Unions [ACFTU]. Most of its members were to be found in SOEs until recently. The ACFTU currently has over 230 million members and is the largest in the world in terms of numbers. No other work organisations or unions are allowed outside ACFTU. Instead of using 'strikes' as the ultimate weapon, a complex arbitration and conciliation system for dealing with disputes was introduced (Brown, 2009).

The rate of unionisation varies between one SOE and another. Many of the State-owned plants formerly had official union membership as great as 100 per cent, with an average of 92 per cent found on many sites. However, membership is socially encouraged but not mandatory, and it is actually possible and legal for a worker to opt out at any time, in theory if not in practice. The rate of unionisation is much lower in firms outside the State sector, is very limited in foreign-invested enterprises [FIEs] and is almost completely absent among rural private firms. Many urban private firms will usually choose to have a union within the company. This gives them the advantage of dealing with disputes internally, rather than being handled externally by a court or a government agency.

The ACFTU was set up in 1925, organising workers on industrial lines although with occupational groupings. After 1949, this set-up prevailed and was legalised by the Trade Union Law of 1950. It was designed on Leninist lines, as a 'transmission-belt' between the Party and the 'masses', when it was set up. Trade union organisations, at least prima facie, may be said to have institutionalised the power of the workers as 'masters' (*zhuren*). The most important role among most of the unions, including those of today, is fostering labour–management relations in enterprises to boost production output. But most importantly, they provide adequate collective welfare services and organise after work activities. The ACFTU receives 2 per cent of its members' payroll for welfare and other purposes.

During the Cultural Revolution in 1966, the unions were officially dismantled. With the onset of the economic reforms at the end of the 1970s, the ACFTU was encouraged to promote economic development and maintain social stability. The trade unions were officially reinstalled in 1978 along with economic reforms through the influence of Deng Xiaoping. They gradually recovered influence over the 1980s and played a supportive role in helping the economic reforms. Labour laws were recast to regulate the emergent labour market (see Brown, 2009).

Worker representation was closely connected with the above institutional framework of the 'iron rice-bowl' welfare system, which existed mainly in Chinese SOEs and urban collectives. In this pre-reform system, wages were evenly distributed, the pace of work was steady and dismissals were extremely rare events. Extra financial incentives besides wages were very minimal or even did not exist in many plants; it was sometimes referred to as eating 'out of one big pot' (*daguofan*). However, despite the location or the degree of protection, only about one in seven Chinese workers out of the entire workforce enjoyed this protected status.

Social critics (Chan, 2001; Chan and Siu, 2010) point to shortfalls in labour standards, especially in FIEs in the coastal areas, such as those near Hong Kong and in Shenzen. It was almost impossible to conduct independent studies of living- and work-conditions for a very long period. Those in the cities, especially in public employment, appeared at least to have some degree of protection, with the virtually lifetime-employment system being in operation until recently. But life has changed in the last decade or so and the social costs of economic restructuring, as in other parts of Asia, are now being increasingly felt in China. The oversized workforce became a major issue for both the government and private firms. Downsizing and unemployment have become quite common.

Implications for managers

The implication of the shift from a centrally planned economy to so-called market socialism has been considerable for managers. Translating high-level macroeconomic policy into microeconomic detail has led to many key shifts. Before the early 1980s, managers had very limited autonomy and could neither hire nor fire workers. Like their employees, their performance was not linked to effort; motivation was low and mobility was restricted. Today, all that has changed and managers have significantly expanded powers. Over the 1980s and 1990s, China underwent a 'managerial revolution'. The enterprise and management reforms of 1984, the labour contract reforms of 1986, the personnel reforms of 1992 and the labour laws of 1994 and more recently 2008 and so on, have proved to be major landmarks on the 'Long March' to market-driven management. After the reforms of the 1980s and 1990s promoted by Deng, managers found their roles became more central and market-driven.

At the same time, managerial mindsets were radically transformed. Chinese executives became responsible for financial performance targets and could be more significantly rewarded if they did well. Some larger formerly State-owned firms have been floated on the internal and external stock exchanges.

A strong element of particularism is to be found in Chinese culture and this has practical significance for business transactions. This trait accounts for the considerable attention given to the notion of *guanxi*. It contrasts with universalism, which denotes that it is culturally appropriate to apply the same rules and standards whoever the person may be. Given the latitude that local officials generally enjoy in dealing with the foreign firms located within their purview, particularism makes China an 'uncertain' place vis-à-vis international business standards.

Now, it is difficult for China to adjust to competitive environments with effective management when fully engaged in international trade and investment. Whilst Chinese management values and behaviour have been importantly conditioned by the country's political and economic system, Chinese culture is free of the active hostility it experienced under Maoism. The big issue has become the extent to which management in China will be fashioned according to international 'best practice' as opposed to following its own principles and practices.

Given the external competitive pressures to adopt new forms of organisation such as teamwork, it will be instructive to see whether Chinese cultural attributes help or hinder this process. The collectivist orientation, importance of relationships and concern for harmony in Chinese culture might assist crucial aspects of teamwork such as common purpose, task interdependence and group orientation. On the other hand, the Confucian emphasis on rigid hierarchies and upward deference to leaders could maintain top-down control.

Conclusions

China has been shaped by its history and in turn modern Chinese management has been influenced by deep cultural roots. We have seen that the Dengist reforms of the last two decades have changed the management system from one based on a command-economy to one that is more market-driven, with increased private ownership.

In a rapidly changing and varied context, such as contemporary China, it is very difficult to assess the degree to which traditional culture continues to exert an influence on management values and behaviour (see Warner, 2011). When addressing this subject we need to reiterate a number of issues and questions. First, we must recognise China's great diversity and start by asking 'to which China are we referring? Which sector, which region, which generation?' Second, what is taking place in China, keen to learn from the outside world yet also conscious of its history, may force us to abandon the notion that people necessarily conform to a simple notion of 'culture'. In these circumstances, they may not necessarily fit neatly with the cultural dimensions chosen, but instead display apparent paradoxes (see chapter 16). The social identity of modern Chinese managers may indeed be more complex than appreciated (see Chen, 2008).

A third possibility deserving of further investigation, is that Chinese managers, are more flexible in their cultural referents than theorists such as Hofstede (1980, 2010) assume is normal for adults. Chinese people who are exposed to 'Western' values through their roles at work, or equally as consumers, may choose to segment their cultural mindsets. For instance, if conforming to certain Western norms and practices, such as higher pay in return for individual performance, then Chinese staff may decide to go along with them within the confines of their workplace roles. They may also be encouraged to accept practices imported from another culture if these are perceived to be part of a more comprehensive policy, offering other benefits such as equitable treatment, comprehensive training and good prospects for advancement. At the same time, as they switch social identity in 'converting' to their non-work roles in the family and community, they might well revert to a more traditional Chinese cultural mindset.

In summary, China offers a challenging and fascinating arena for the further exploration of the theoretical and practical issues associated with culture and management. Whether the future will lead to a degree of convergence is not the question; it is what will be the pace and ultimate limit of such change.

Note

1   This is a part of research funded by the National Natural Science Foundation of China (Project No.: 70732002).
The authors would like to thank Professors Malcolm Warner and Betty Coffey for their review comments on a previous version of the chapter.

References

Bell, D. (2008) *China's New Confucianism: Politics and Everyday Life in a Changing Society*. Princeton, NJ: Princeton University Press.
Brown, R. (2009) *Understanding Labor and Employment Law in China*. Cambridge: Cambridge University Press.
Chan, A. (2001) *China's Workers under Assault: The Exploitation of Labor in a Globalizing Economy*. Armonk, NY: M. E. Sharpe.
Chan, A. and Siu K. (2010) 'Analyzing Exploitation: The Mechanisms Underpinning Low Wages and Excessive Overtime in Chinese Export Factories', *Critical Asian Studies*, 42 (2): 167–90.
Chen, M. (1995) *Asian Management Systems*. London: Routledge.
Chen, S. J. (2008) 'The Adoption of HR Strategies in a Confucian Context' in Lawler, J. J. and Hundley, G. (eds) *The Global Diffusion of Human Resource Practices: Institutional and Cultural Limits, Advances in International Management*. Vol. 21. Amsterdam: Elsevier, pp. 145–169.
Child, J. (1994) *Management in China during the Age of Reform*. Cambridge: Cambridge University Press.

Child, J. and Warner, M. (2003) 'Culture and Management in China' in Warner, M. (ed.) *Culture and Management in Asia*. London and New York, NY: Routledge, pp. 24–47.

Chinese Culture Connection (1987) 'Chinese Values and the Search for Culture-Free Dimensions of Culture', *Journal of Cross Cultural Psychology*, 18: 143–64.

Chiu, C. H., Ting, K., Tso, G. K. F. and He, C. (1998) 'A Comparison of Occupational Values between Capitalist Hong Kong and Socialist Guangzhou', *Economic Development and Cultural Change*, 46: 749–70.

Collins, N., Nankervis, A., Sitalaksmib, S. and Warner, M. (2011) 'Labour–management relationships in transitional economies: convergence or divergence in Vietnam and Indonesia?', *Asia Pacific Business Review*, 17: 361–77.

Fan, Z. (2004) *Cross-Culture Management: The Balance of Globalization and Localization*. Shanghai: Shanghai Foreign Language Education Press.

Goody, J. (1996) *The East in the West*. Cambridge: Cambridge University Press.

Gong, Y., Gorg, H. and Maioli, S. (2007) 'Employment Effects of Privatization and Foreign Acquisition of Chinese State-owned Enterprises', *International Journal of the Economics of Business*, 14: 197–214.

Hamilton, G. C. (1991) 'The Organizational Foundations of Western and Chinese Commerce: Historical and Comparative Analysis' in *Business Networks and Economic Development in East and Southeast Asia*. Hong Kong: Centre of Asian Studies, University of Hong Kong, pp: 48–65.

Hawes, C. (2008) 'Representing Corporate Culture in China: Official and Academic Perspectives', *The China Journal*, 59, January: 31–62.

Heffernan, K. and Crawford, J. (2001) The Relationship between Managerial Values and the Adoption of Western Lifestyle Practices in the People's Republic of China. Paper presented to the Australia and New Zealand Academy of Management [ANZAM] Conference, Auckland.

Hofstede, G. (1980) *Culture's Consequence: International Differences in Work-Related Values*. Newbury Park, CA: Sage.

Hofstede, G., Hofstede, G. J. and Minkov, M. (2010) *Cultures and Organizations; Software of the Mind*. 3rd edition. New York: McGraw-Hill.

Hofstede, G. and Bond, M.H. (1988) 'The Confucius Connection: From Cultural Roots to Economic Growth', *Organizational Dynamics*, 16: 5–21.

Lamond, D. and Leung, C. (2010) 'HRM Research in China: looking back and looking forward', *Chinese Human Resource Management*, 1: 6–16.

Lin, L. H. and Ho, Y. L. (2009) 'Confucian dynamism, culture and ethical changes in Chinese societies – a comparative study of China, Taiwan, and Hong Kong', *International Journal of Human Resource Management*, 20: 2402–17.

Luo, Y. (2002) 'Partnering with Foreign Firms: How Do Chinese Managers View the Governance and Importance of Contracts?', *Asia Pacific Journal of Management*, 19: 127–51.

Mackerras, C., Taneja, P. and Young, G. (2000) *China since 1978*. Sydney: Longman.

Negandi, A. R. 1975 'Comparative Management and Organizational Theory: A Marriage Needed', *Academy of Management Journal*, 18: 334–44.

Pedyash, D. and Shi, C. (2010) 'Management Problems at Manufacturing Enterprises with 100% Russian Capital in the People's Republic of China: Challenges and Mistakes in Organization Design and Organizational Culture', *International Conference on E-business, Management and Economics*, 3: 249–53.

People's Daily (2010) 'China's economy to grow 9.5% in 2010: World Bank forecast', *People's Daily*, 17 March. Available at http://english.peopledaily.com.cn/90001/90778/90862/6922340.html (accessed 31 May).

Ralston, D. A., Gustafson, D. J., Terpsta, R. H. and Holt, D. H. (1995) 'Pre-post Tiananmen Square: Changing Values of Chinese Managers', *Asia Pacific Journal of Management*, 12: 1–20.

Ralston, D. A., Yu, K., Wang, X., Terpstra, R. H. and He, W. (1996) 'The Cosmopolitan Chinese Manager: Findings of a Study of Managerial Values Across the Six Regions of China', *Journal of International Management*, 2: 79–109.

Ralston, D. A., Van Thang, N. and Napier, N. K. (1999a) 'A Comparative Study of the Work Values of North and South Vietnamese Managers', *Journal of International Business Studies*, 30: 655–72.

Ralston, D. A., Egri, C. P., Stewart, S., Terpstra, R. H. and Yu Kaicheng (1999b) 'Doing Business in the 21st Century with the New Generation of Chinese Managers: A Study of Generational Shifts in Work Values in China', *Journal of International Business Studies*, 30: 415–28.

Rarick, C. (2009) 'The Historical Roots of Chinese Cultural Values and Managerial Practices', *Journal of International Business Research*. http://www.thefreelibrary.com/ The+historical+roots+of+Chinese+cultural+values+and+managerial. . .-a0219002339 (accessed 4 May 2010).

Redding, S. G. and Wong, Gilbert Y. Y. (1986) 'The Psychology of Chinese Organizational Behavior', in *The Psychology of the Chinese People*, Bond, Michael H. (ed.) Hong Kong: Oxford University Press, pp. 267–95.

Tsang, E. W. K. (1998) 'Can Guanxi be a Source of Sustained Competitive Advantage for Doing Business in China?', *Academy of Management Executive*, 12: 64–73.

Tung, R. L. (1994) 'Strategic Management Thought in East Asia', *Organizational Dynamics*, 22: 55–65.

Vertinsky, I., Tse, D. K., Wehrung, D. A. and Lee, K. H. (1990) 'Organization Design and Management Norms: A Comparative Study of Managers' Perceptions in the People's Republic of China, Hong Kong and Canada', *Journal of Management*, 30: 5–18.

Wang, Z. M. (1998) 'Team Management Conflict' in Selmer, J. (ed.) *International Management in China: Cross-Cultural Issues*. London: Routledge, pp. 29–44.

Warner, M. (2005) (ed.) *Human Resource Management in China Revisited*. London and New York, NY: Routledge.

— (2008) 'Reassessing Human Resource Management "with Chinese characteristics": an Overview', *International Journal of Human Resource Management*, 19: 771–801.

— (2009) ' "Making Sense" of HRM in China: Setting the Scene', *International Journal of Human Resource Management*, 20: 2169–93.

— (2011) *Confucian HRM in Greater China: Theory and Practice*. London and New York: Routledge.

Warner M., Edwards, V., Polansky, G., Pucko, D. and Zhu, Y. (2005) *Management in Transitional Economies: From the Berlin Wall to the Great Wall of China*. London and New York, NY: Routledge-Curzon.

Warner, M. and Goodall, K. (2009) (eds) *Management Training and Development in China: Educating Managers in a Globalized Economy*. London and New York, NY: Routledge.

World Bank (2010) *China Quarterly Update*, March 2010. World Bank: Washington, DC. Available at http://web.worldbank.org/WBSITE/EXTERNAL/COUNTRIES/ EASTASIAPACIFICEXT/CHINAEXTN/0,contentMDK:22502137~pagePK:1497618 ~piPK:217854~theSitePK:318950,00.html (accessed 31 May).

Yu, K. C. *et al.* (2000) *Human Resource Management*. Dalian: Dalian University of Technology Press.

6   The changing nature of management and culture in Hong Kong, Macau and Taiwan

Olivia Ip and Sek-Hong Ng

Introduction

Hong Kong, Macau and Taiwan are the three Overseas Chinese societies on the fringe of the Mainland which have each experienced spectacular economic growth as newly industrialised economies (NIEs) of East Asia. In spite of their common Confucian heritage and signs of mutual institutional convergence, we will argue in this chapter that there are visible diversities which make each distinctive in their cultural, socio-political, economic and management systems. A salient source of these differences, we go on to suggest, is in the final analysis historical. Both Hong Kong and Macau were under colonial rule, until the PRC promulgated the novel political formula of 'one country, two systems' in the 1980s to pave the way for their reunification in 1997 and 1999. The legacies left behind by the British on Hong Kong are evidently different from the Portuguese influences which envelop Macau. Conversely, the mixed imprints of successive regimes of the Dutch, Japanese and Americans in Taiwan have converted it into a hybrid society which now yearns for an identity of its own, as epitomised by the contest between the bid for independence and the sentiments of reintegration with the Mainland.

Economic affluence and post-industrialism have taken root in Hong Kong and Taiwan, while Macau has caught up recently with a swift pace when its 'core' hospitality- and leisure-industries modernised. Branded as Asia's 'Little Dragons' since the 1980s, Hong Kong and Taiwan have achieved spectacular economic growth as lead examples of the league of newly industrialised economies (NIEs) (see chapter 2).

The Hong Kong Special Administrative Region (SAR) now excels as one of the world's largest cities and financial centres. Backed by advanced technology borrowed from the United States and Japan, Taiwan in its turn has entered the realm of Original Design Manufacture (ODM) in its production activities – notably computer making and an associated electronics industry. Many Taiwanese firms became partners in transnational high-value-adding production chains and networks. Hong Kong has whistled through a staggering period of painful adjustment to almost complete recovery after the global shock of the 2008 Financial Tsunami (see chapter 2). Conversely, Taiwan appears to be still trapped in a low growth syndrome. By contrast, during the last five years Macau has stridden ahead swiftly because of the sizeable inflow of foreign capital to its bulwark 'casino' industry, alongside the commissioning of an array of infrastructural construction projects by the government.

Against the above backdrop, this chapter will set out to look at how the management of business (and public organisations) has evolved in these three places in relation to their cultural backgrounds.

Common shaping and constraining factors

Late-developing economies

The three societies of Hong Kong, Macau and Taiwan are all 'late-developers'. As such, they have the strategic advantage of borrowing advanced technology from the 'First-World' nations and emulating the latter's successful practices in managing businesses and the people whom they hire. The risks besetting such late-developing technological and institutional transplants, however, are those of non-discriminatory borrowing and excessive zeal in copying the examples of the exalted arrangements and patterns from the highly developed economies. Taiwan in the late 1980s appeared to have been trapped in such a dilemma in the domain of labour law. Anxious to revamp and modernise its inventory of labour legislation as economic development was underway, the government introduced the labour standard law extensively modelled upon the Japanese precedent. However, its promises, especially those governing redundancy payments, were considered to be too burdensome by business. Subsequent hectic haggling between the State and capital eventually led to the former's capitulation and amendments to the law, liberalising the provisions on redundancy pay (cf. chapter 13).

The hallmark of the 'strategic edge' enjoyed by the late-developers is probably the building of physical infrastructural facilities, inasmuch as they are able to choose the best mix of technology and hardware from what the providers in the First World can offer.

Hong Kong hence excels as a cosmopolitan international city with a 'lead' airport which probably ranks as the world's best, designed by a distinguished British architect, Norman Foster, alongside an efficient network of highways, a mass-transit underground rail system and an inexpensive web of telephone services. Macau has also been catching up on its infrastructural investment since its reunification with China in 1999. And now under construction is a highway-cum-bridge complex which will link up, trilaterally, Hong Kong, Macau and Zhuhai, a key outpost of the Pearl River Basin. Importing technology from Japan, Taiwan has also built a modern and extensive highway-cum-rail network which connects the northern and southern parts of the island.

However, there are always a host of constraints which pose an impediment to the pace of late development. A common source of resistance is the conservation upheld by the traditional elite and stakeholders who have a vested interest in the status quo. Besides, modern institutions and normative values, like those propagating gender and ethnic equality (see chapter 9) may conflict with preexistent beliefs, tradition and ideological systems across Asia, as well in Islamic societies (see chapter 14). As a refugee haven, Hong Kong has been a fluid society admissive to changes, especially given a British administration prior to 1997 which was permissive rather than interventionist vis-à-vis the private sector (Turner *et al.*, 1981). By comparison, Macau as a Portuguese colony before 1999 had been traditional and lukewarm about change. Taiwan, in its turn, was trapped in a Confucian 'doldrum' of status quo and had not stridden ahead on a modernisation agenda until the 'democratisation' decree issued by President Jiang Jing-guo in 1987 (Maeda and Ng, 1996).

The role of the state

Any endeavour to map the late development experiences of a society can hardly be dissociated from a concomitant discussion of the role of the State. The presence of the State has been consistently conspicuous in backing businesses in Taiwan. Tax-holidays and stock-subsidies are extended to those industries which are considered to be strategic or which engender high linkage effects in nurturing other industries. Substantial government funds are also channelled to manpower training to groom the human resources needed to sustain economic development. By contrast, the government has always expressly abstained from active inter-vention in private sector businesses in Hong Kong, reputed to be the world's bastion of 'freewheeling capitalism' – a place where Adam Smith would have felt at home. The British administration prior to the 1997 dateline of reunification with China purported to pursue a policy of 'positive non-intervention'. A typical example was the rhetorical distinction made by the authority between technical education as falling under the government's jurisdiction and industrial training as private business's responsibility. However, there were also occasions on which the pre-SAR government departed from such a principle. Of landmark significance in the contemporary history of Hong Kong were two incidents, namely:

- The inception in the 1970s of the Independent Commission Against Corruption (ICAC) which now polices against corrupt and fraudulent practices in both the civil service and the private sector.[1]
- The pegging of the Hong Kong currency to the US dollar since 1983. This was originally a 'stopgap' measure designed and implemented by the government to arrest the heavy fall in local confidence amidst the thorny Sino-British negotiations on the future of Hong Kong.

The post-1997 SAR government has essentially inherited the above approach. It pledges to pursue the policy of a 'free' economy and allow maximum latitude to private businesses. However, it has drifted steadily towards extending its 'visible hands', especially in aiding small businesses and petty capital. Such a policy shift is probably prudent, as it helps enhance Hong Kong's competitiveness in an age of 'globalisation'. But it is also explicable by the chain of crises which have beset the SAR since its inauguration.

Inflicted on its economy and society were the 'financial-cum-currency' upheaval of East Asia of 1997, the epidemic of SARS in 2003 and the worldwide financial tsunami of 2008. The government was proactive here and intervened, for example, in the labour market by funding the retraining of the unemployed and providing unemployment subsidies to the jobless. It also 'proactively' canvassed the reinstatement of an en masse intake of guest-workers to stimulate the revival of the garment production industry, although the 'motion' did not materialise because of opposition from organised labour.

In Macau, the Portuguese administration, prior to its reunification with its motherland in 1999, essentially adopted a laissez-faire policy vis-à-vis a basically one-industry economy dominated by the casino business. The post-1999 SAR government appears to have steered steadily away from such an approach. Public funds are heavily deployed, for instance, to sustain an extensive programme of infrastructural investment. A 'lead' example amidst these projects is the newly commissioned Macau airport, which helps to provide a bridge between the Mainland and Taiwan, as well as playing the role of a 'feeder' complementing Hong Kong International Airport. Backed by the government, the once monolithic 'casino industry' branched into a pluralistic hospitality sector, the enhancement of which in turn helps stimulate the tourist trade. And the officially sponsored intake of guest workers, especially those recruited from Hong Kong, helps sustain a booming building and construction industry. It may be postulated that the State has been pivotal in assisting private industry to take off and enter a realm of rapid growth since 1999 when the SAR government came into incumbency.

Culture

It is evident that the many-faceted factor of 'culture' is a pervasive force shaping management assumptions, ideologies and behaviour among enterprises in East Asia (see chapters 3, 12, 14 and 16). Simultaneously, such an imperative also gives rise to a wide latitude of diversity in business practices within this region (see Warner, 2003). As Chinese societies, Hong Kong, Macau and Taiwan share a common heritage. There already exists an ample literature exploring the thesis that the Confucian prescriptions nurture a successful ethos of 'family capitalism'. In the 1980s and early 1990s, popular management writings extolled the legendary efficacy of Asian values, which pivot around Confucian ethics in a way similar to the exalted relationship between Protestantism and Western capitalism, itself a controversial link. According to such a perspective, the modern practice and application of a Confucian approach towards the etiquette of people-governance at workplaces has yielded a 'local preference for managerial paternalism, cooperation, mutual trust, harmony and aversion from open conflict' (Ng *et al.*, 1997: 81–2). The argument goes further in suggesting that such an Asian trait favours 'labour-management collaboration and helps explain the relative quiescence of the workforce in accepting technological and productivity innovations initiated by the management at the workplaces . . .' (ibid., 82–83).

Such a culturist thesis exalting Asian values appears to have been a key imperative behind the success of Taiwan, Hong Kong and other East Asian NIEs. This was, however, thrown into question by the eruption of the 'financial-cum-currency' crisis in 1997. Doubts have also been shed upon the normative efficacy of the reputed Asian approach to enterprise and management by the sceptics. For example, Hong Kong's last British Governor, Christopher (now, Lord) Patten, lamented upon the Asian myth in his book *East and West* in the following terms:

> The case put for the invented concept of Asian values is so intellectually shallow. . . . The Asian-values proponents believe that . . . Asians benefit from a difficult culture with deep roots in Confucianism. . . . [Yet,] The discovery of Confucius as the reason for Asians' economic success would have puzzled some of his most faithful followers as well as earlier European philosophers and historians. . . . As Weber argued, it was Confucianism which was responsible for Asia's economic torpor, because it lacked the animating work ethic of Protestantism. (Patten, 1998:149–50; 163–4)

Many managers in the so-called 'Little Dragon/Tiger' economies – Hong Kong, Macau and Taiwan – are becoming closer to their Western counterparts in their managerial practices if not wholly in values. American-inspired management training and socialisation into multinationals' practices have made their mark.

Yet in spite of the controversy over the implications of the Confucian prescriptions for management and business performance (see Hamilton, 2006; Guthrie, 2009), Taiwan, Hong Kong and Macau are probably the custodians of the authentic Chinese traditional values of this heritage – inasmuch as the Mainland is still in the backwash of the discontinuities caused by several decades of the reign of Marxist socialism, which climaxed in the 1960s Cultural Revolution.

Comparing these three societies vis-à-vis each other, Taiwan is perhaps the most Confucian. However, such a legacy is compounded by 'folk religions', like Buddhism and Taoism, as well as the diffusion of Japanese as well as American influences. According to Chow, managerial paternalism was an entrenched practice among enterprises in Taiwan before the 1990s but thereafter there was 'a shift from differential relationship based on paternalistic provisions' to the 'impersonal relationships of the 1990s' (Chow, 2003: 221). This facet is probably explicable by the changing composition of the business elite as members of the second generation of family entrepreneurs are educated abroad, especially in the United States. Like Hong Kong and Macau, Taiwan has adopted American-style management training, with 'business schools' at undergraduate and postgraduate levels (cf., chapter 15). Such schools operate in tandem with extensive in-house training but are mainly confined to the larger firms.

By contrast, Hong Kong has thrived essentially as a refugee society. Its history since its colonisation by Britain in 1842 has been punctuated by episodes of inundations of refugees seeking asylum in the territory (the latest one being the influx of Vietnamese boat-people in the late 1970s and early 1980s). Concomitantly, en masse migration, both into and out of Hong Kong, has added to the fluidity of this society, shaped and reshaped its culture and helped transform management assumptions and strategies. Of particular significance were two 'landmark' movements.

One was the influx of refugees from the Mainland as a sequel to the war of liberation and the changeover of government in 1949. The inflow of capital, technological and managerial know-how and refugee labour enabled Hong Kong to take off in its infancy of industrialisation. The captains of the Shanghai textile-mills transferred their plants to the 'British colony' and inaugurated an entrepreneurial culture which combined Confucian paternalism and Western imported ideas of rationalistic Taylorism (Chen, 2000: 4–6; Wong, 1988). Yet, such an approach of employer benevolence was masked by a pervasive mentality of transient orientation of the working people due to their refugee background. 'Casualisation' was widespread in the labour market, with the proliferation of piecework and daily-rated payment in the firms' hiring practices during the 1950s and through to the 1970s (see chapter 13).

The second demographic movement was the massive exodus of Hong Kong emigrants seeking a 'second passport' or resettling in such 'First-World' countries as Australia, Canada, the United Kingdom and the United States. Stemming essentially from an almost neurotic anxiety about their security and lifestyle after Hong Kong reverted to China, such an 'escape' of its people happened during the 13-year transition period leading up to its reunification with China as a SAR in 1997. The 'brain-drain', inasmuch as these emigrants were preponderantly middle-class professional and managerial personnel and their families, engendered fears about the local managerial competitive advantage. In order to address the manpower gap, many Hong Kong companies, especially the multinationals, began to 'delocalise' and recruit from the international (or, more specifically, the Asian) managerial and professional market. These shifts added to the cosmopolitanism of the city, which was already branded with an element of cultural pluralism by virtue of its British heritage. In short, Hong Kong is now truly a 'melting-pot', where the East and the West meet.

It may be legitimate to postulate that Macau has a somewhat amorphous cultural mix. This place is intrinsically a traditional Chinese community. However, such a native character has been truncated by an array of complex influences. First, the Nationalists and the Communists have each maintained a foothold in this former Portuguese colony. Second, Portugal has left behind a colonial imprint, especially in terms of Catholic ethics and educational missionary work. Third, Macau has always sustained a criminal subculture, inasmuch as secret (*triad*) societies and a 'gangster' community have survived and appear to have maintained covert links with the Mainland and Taiwan. Such elements are associated with, in the fourth place, the 'mainstream' casino industry. Fifth, there is a group of local-borns, and yet of Portuguese descent, labelled as Macanese. They are confronted with a status and 'identity' hiatus. Such ambivalence arises from their desire to secure assimilation with the local Macau Chinese – but they are still greeted by a 'we-they' divide (Hao: 2005; 2011: chapter 4). Sixth, there has always been spill-over from neighbouring Hong Kong, which provides a model for Macau in various domains. A lead example is the almost wholesale transfer of the Hong Kong SAR formula to Macau upon its reversion to China in 1999. Seventh, the arrival of multinational capital, notably that emanating from the United States, to the casino and hospitality industries in the post-handover era has exerted a pivotal impact upon the renewal and innovation of managerial practices in Macau.

The polity and legal system

Ostensibly, politics and the political and legal systems have always played a key role in affecting how business works and the flow of capital and its activities in these three societies. The foremost events in the contemporary political history of Hong Kong and Macau unfolded in the years 1997 and 1999, when both were returned by a colonial administration to China's sovereignty as Special Administrative Regions (SAR). Paradoxically, these processes of 'decolonisation' have stimulated both the economy and business in each place, for two reasons. First, China has been keen to sustain the capitalist system in both places, in order to attest to the viability of its novel 'one-country-two-systems' policy and to enlist these two cities in support of its 'marketisation reforms' (see chapter 5). Second, both territories have attracted more multinational capital with the intention of anchoring upon these two places as a 'springboard' for trading and doing business in the Mainland. Enterprises established by Mainland capital entering Hong Kong are branded as 'red chip' companies, which are managed under a distinctive style reminiscent of PRC multinationals operating abroad.

In Taiwan, the most salient development in its external relations has been the opening of dialogue and economic-cum-cultural mutualities with the Mainland. There has been since the 1990s a mushrooming of Taiwanese businesses trading or investing in industry along the coastal fringe of the Mainland, especially in the south-east provinces of Fujian and Zhejiang. Taiwanese management has been perceived as efficacious in the Mainland context but can be notorious in terms of its propensity for industrial hazards – like fire and workplace accidents.

Another political factor affecting businesses in Taiwan and Hong Kong, and more recently Macau as well, is the democratisation process. In Taiwan, the liberalisation of the government was initiated in 1987 by President Jiang Jing-guo. Politics in Taiwan, as a result, became bipartisan when the monolithic reign of the National Party gave way to an incessant contest between that party and the Democratic Progressive Party. Power was no longer concentrated within a closed oligarchy controlled by a junta of political and military leaders but devolved to a middle-class stratum made up of the business and professional elite and intellectuals. Comprising increasingly the younger generation who are locally born and educated abroad (conspicuously in the United States and Japan), the business elite are enlightened in their managerial ideology and perspective and are also keen to import Western notions and prescriptions of management to reform businesses which are often family estates. Politicisation compounds the practice of management as it becomes attractive for business to seek an alliance with the political elite. Business donations in support of candidates bidding for political offices have become a commonplace, yet this is liable to breed irregular activities such as corruption and bribery. The labour agenda also enters the political arena. Reforms of workplace conditions are widely canvassed by pro-labour politicians, creating an imperative which compels management to make better provision for their employees (cf. chapter 13).

In Hong Kong, the stepped introduction of elected and representative government under the present SAR and the former colonial regimes has transformed the relationship between capital and labour. The shift in power relations is manifested in the domain of the elected Legislative Assembly, as attested by the incessant confrontations and haggling between the two sides in the assembly. A vivid illustration is probably the enactment of the long awaited Minimum Wage Ordinance in 2010, which came into effect the following year. Business has been successful for decades in shelving such a legislative motion on the ground that a lever of this nature would compromise the logic of free enterprise. However, the creeping problem of low wages and the ascending power of organised labour as a stakeholder in elected politics eventually coerced business into making a concession by giving its consent to the establishment of a statutory wage floor.

In Macau, an elected government was also introduced upon the inception of the SAR in 1999. However, political haggling between the various sectarian interests has been less intense than in Hong Kong. Yet the formal system of political governance largely emulates the Hong Kong arrangements. As in the case of Hong Kong, the Macau Basic Law created the office of Chief Executive as the governing head of the SAR and established the law-making Legislative Assembly. Political parties have not yet gestated but instead 'interest groups' representing diverse sectarian divisions secure seats in the Legislative Assembly by direct and indirect election or government appointment. There are three points worth noting in terms of the relationship between the polity and businesses.

The first is the pervasiveness of the theme-gambling-industry, revamped and modernised and transformed into a multinational and pluralistic industry since the reversion of sovereignty. It has become the principal driver of Macau's economic 'take-off' in the first decade of the twenty-first century. The industry also wields formidable political power and influence, being deputised in the Legislative Assembly by the interest group 'Macau Development Alliance' (NUDM) (Lee, 2011: 82).

The second is the secular decline of the traditional associations, including those organising business and labour, notably the Macau Chamber of Commerce and the Macau Federation of Trade Unions. During the Portuguese reign, these bodies acted as the key links and transmission belt between the Portuguese administration, the local Chinese community and the Mainland government (both the central government as well as the provincial government of Guangdong). However, such a role is being increasingly eclipsed and emasculated as a modernised Macau becomes more pluralistic and cosmopolitan and the younger generation emerges as a more inquisitive and articulate population. With an entrenched and growing middle-class, Macau may follow in the footsteps of Hong Kong to evolve into a 'civil society' governed by the 'rule of law'. Such a progression could pose a challenge to the traditional associations which are intrinsically trade and merchant in character. The decline of these associations hence signals that the traditional mode of running and managing business in Macau is withering away and giving way to a more modern and Westernised approach to management.

The third is the rampant volume of corruption which exists in Macau, of which the 'Ao Man Leung' case was symptomatic (Brewer, 2011: 99). To curb this type of duplicity, the SAR government created a high-powered agency, the Commission Against Corruption (CCAC), extensively modelled upon its counterpart in Hong Kong, the Independent Commission Against Corruption (ICAC). If vested with sufficient autonomy and power, the CCAC can exert a powerful impact on reshaping the conduct of businesses and enhancing their quality of governance. Whether Macau will enter a new 'estate of realm' in the eradication of embedded business malpractices chained to corruption will have to await the test of time.

The legal system apparently excels in Hong Kong in providing a hospitable milieu for business. Before 1997, British common law was the cornerstone, which upheld the principle of economic freedom and censured any deeds which would restrain or impede the freedom of trade. Such a legal heritage has been perpetuated beyond 1997, as guaranteed by the 1985 Sino-British treaty or the Basic Law promulgated by China in 1991. In particular, the simple procedures prescribed by the British-inherited Companies Ordinance have been conducive to the formation of companies with limited liabilities and accumulation of capital. The prosperity and expansion of the capital fund market made possible by the above legal permissiveness and a free regime on foreign exchange have encouraged a stampede of local businesses as well as foreign companies into the stock exchange as they aspire for the status and rights of a public company listed for open stock trading and capital formation. Many of these companies are Chinese family businesses, for which corporate governance has always been problematic. Such weaknesses were endemic to the pre-1997 government's regime of moral guidance and non-coercive control. The distress associated with the lack of adequate regulation was exposed in the 1987 crisis, when the shares exchange market collapsed amidst the euphoria of a trading boom.

The lessons of 1987, in the end, caused the government to develop a more legalistic and punitive approach to its control regime. Concomitantly, the individual companies also began to modernise and benchmark themselves against the practices of governance pursued by their Western counterparts. At the macro level of official supervision and surveillance, the regulatory infrastructure went through an almost entire overhaul. The relatively feeble system of legal norms, which had hitherto relied upon the Companies Ordinance and the 1974 Securities Ordinance for exercising a voluntaristic type of gentlemanly control, was visibly strengthened, albeit in a gradual reformist fashion. At the core of these legislative initiatives was the enactment of the Securities and Futures Commission Ordinance in 1989, as the enabling law to create a Securities and Futures Commission (SFC).

The Commission has since then assumed the role of a policing agency with a prerogative to investigate and initiate prosecutions against acts of default in this industry. However, some of its sanctioning abilities have remained surface moralistic rather than legalistic. An example has been the non-statutory Code on Take-overs and Mergers and Share Repurchases which it administers. However, legal prescriptions have become increasingly specific and explicit on the appropriate etiquette governing disclosure of information, especially pertaining to the interests of key corporate officials and dominant shareholders in publicly listed companies, as well as censuring 'insider trading'. The ICAC also plays a cardinal role in complementing the work of the SFC and investigating any governance and managerial misdeeds which have a link to corruption or fraudulence.

Discussion

The brunt of the 1997 East Asian financial-cum-currency crisis unmasked the volatile nature of the stock market, especially because of the growing mutuality between shares and futures trading. In the wake of the crisis, the SAR administration ushered in the merging and integration of the stocks and shares and future exchanges, which was achieved in 2000. It also promptly moved to enact a comprehensive repertoire of legislation to regularise and police securities and future activities.

By comparison, the regulation of corporate governance and ethical business and managerial behaviour is quite different in Taiwan or Macau. In Macau, a stock exchange has been conspicuous by its absence. The notion of a company with limited liabilities has been blurred, rather than made explicit, by legislative codification. The mechanism of enactment is dualistic or 'bi-rail' (Yu, 2011: 60). Parallel to the law-making prerogative of the Legislative Assembly, the Portuguese governor, or since 1999 the Chief Executive of the SAR, is able to promulgate decrees (laws) as administrative regulations. Licences are granted in this connection to the casino operators. The following narrative is an exemplary illustration of the myriad laws and legislative intricacy involved in legitimising businesses in the lead gambling industry:

> The legislature passed a gaming law for the regulation of casino operations in 2001, specifying that three gaming concessions would be granted by the government. . . . However, the government then issued administrative regulations that allowed each concessionaire to sub-contract the right to operate casinos to another group (ibid., 61)

In Taiwan, there are no legal institutions governing the formation of limited companies analogous to those in Hong Kong. However, the presence of the 'visible hands' of governmental intervention in the capital market is pronounced. On various occasions, the official administration has applied discretionary levers to help stabilise the stock market and the exchange rate of its currency. In the heritage of the Republic of China which reigned over the Mainland before the 1949 'Liberation', Taiwan adopts essentially the (European) Continental legal tradition instead of British common law as in the case of Hong Kong. Litigation on business deals and disputes in a complex process can be cumbersome. And it is not clear as to whether a company or an incorporated body can be recognised as a legal person in terms of status. The Japanese system of corporate structure and governance exerts an influence upon the formation of capital (see chapter 7). Although supervising boards can be found in some companies, the corporate culture remains conventional and democratic management of the European type is rarely known, as in most of East Asia.

Conclusions

To sum up, Hong Kong, Macau and Taiwan have each seen rapid economic growth as newly industrialised economies (NIEs) of East Asia. Although they have a common Confucian heritage, they are each quite distinctive in their cultural, socio-political, economic and management systems.

They are also multicultural in their different ways. Hong Kong had over a century of British rule; Macau had an even longer, Portuguese, colonial inheritance; and Taiwan had a complex and diverse Japanese imprint. We have attempted to explore these differences in this chapter and make plain their salient points.

Note

1   The ICAC has been standard-bearing in the eradication of corruption which was notorious previously among such key government departments as the police and public works. Besides, this agency has been instrumental in uplifting the standard of business ethics practised among private businesses. These effects will be discussed in an ensuing section.

References

Brewer, B. (2011) 'Civil Service Reform: Building Basic Administrative Capacity' in Lam, N. M. K. and Scott, I. (eds) *Gaming, Governance and Public Policy in Macao*. Hong Kong: Hong Kong University Press, pp. 89–106.

Chen, E. K. Y. (2000) 'The Economic Setting' in Ng, S-H. and Lethbridge, D. G. (eds) *The Business Environment in Hong Kong*. Hong Kong: Oxford University Press, pp. 3–46.

Chow, W-C. G. (2003) 'Culture and Management in Taiwan' in Warner, M. (ed.) *Culture and Management in Asia*. London: Routledge, pp. 210–27.

Guthrie, D. (2009) *Changing Social Institutions' in China and Globalization: The Social, Economic and Political Transformation of Chinese Society*. London, Routledge.

Hamilton, G. (2006) *Commerce and Capitalism in Chinese Societies*. London: Routledge.

Hao, Z-D. (2005) 'Social Problems in Macau', *China Perspectives*, 62.

—— (2011) *Macau: History and Society*. Hong Kong: Hong Kong University Press and Universidade De Macau.

Lee, A. S. P. (2011) 'Challenges and Threats to Traditional Associations' in Lam, N. M. K. and Scott, I. (eds) *Gaming, Governance and Public Policy in Macao*. Hong Kong: Hong Kong University Press, pp. 75–88.

Maeda, M. and Ng, S-H. (1996) 'The Role of the State and Labour's Response to Industrial Development: An Asian "Drama" of the Three New Industrial Economies' in Nish, I., Redding, G. and Ng, S-H. (eds) *Work and Society: Labour and Human Resources in East Asia*. Hong Kong: Hong Kong University Press, pp. 167–97.

Ng, S-H., Stewart, S. and Chan, F-T (1997) *Current Issues of Workplace Relations and Management in Hong Kong*. Hong Kong: Centre of Asian Studies, University of Hong Kong.

Patten, C. (1998) *East and West*. London: Macmillan.

Turner, H. A. *et al.* (1981) *The Last Colony: But Whose?: A Study of the Labour Movement, Labour Market and Labour Relations in Hong Kong*. Cambridge: Cambridge University Press.

Warner, M. (ed.) (2003) *Culture and Management in Asia*. London: Routledge.

Wong, S-L. (1988) *Emigrant Entrepreneurs: Shanghai Industrialists in Hong Kong*. Hong Kong: Oxford University Press.

Yu, E. W.Y. (2011) 'Executive-Legislative Relationships and the Development of Public Policy' in Lam, N. M. K. and Scott, I. (eds) *Gaming, Governance and Public Policy in Macao*. Hong Kong: Hong Kong University Press, pp. 57–74.

7 The changing nature of management and culture in Japan

John Benson and Philippe Debroux

Introduction

In the post-war period, Japanese manufacturing companies significantly increased their share of the global market of automobiles (Womack *et al.*, 1991) as well as achieving more than 50 per cent of the world market in cameras, video-recorders, watches, calculators, microwave ovens, motorcycles and colour televisions (Oliver and Wilkinson, 1992, p. 5). Much of this success was seen as being due to the 'unique' form of management to be found in Japanese companies, although the industrial structure and the commitment of Japanese workers were also seen as important (Abegglen and Stalk, 1987; Clark, 1987; Dore, 1990; Tachibanaki and Noda, 2000).

Management practices such as lifetime employment, seniority promotion, consensual decision-making and continuous on-the-job training were singled out as it was argued that these practices encouraged the incorporation of employees into the enterprise culture which led to strong employee identification with the firm and a high commitment to improved productivity (Moore, 1987).

The value of these management practices came under increasing scrutiny with the collapse of the 'bubble' economy in the late 1980s, the onset of the recession in the early 1990s and the Asian and global financial crises in 1997 and 2008 (see chapter 2). The decline in economic growth, the lack of consumer confidence and the intense competition from China and other developing economies increased pressure on Japanese companies to reconsider and reconfigure their management practices. Only by doing so, Japanese enterprises argued, would their productivity be improved and their competitive advantage be restored. Yet, Japanese management is embedded in the wider business system, institutions and social values (Clegg and Kono, 2002; Whitley, 1992). This contextual dependency has meant that change would be difficult and slow, and would proceed through experimentation rather than radical changes to the management system (Benson and Debroux, 1997; Benson, 1998; Warner, 2011; Special Issue, Japan, 2012).

The prolonged nature of the 2008 global financial crisis, which has continued well into 2011, has increased the possibility of change in Japanese management accelerating.

This démarche raises a number of questions such as what are the key underpinning factors influencing management today, how has management responded to the current challenges presented by the global financial crisis, what are the constraints operating in Japan to systematic change, and what conclusions can we draw in terms of the structure and form of present day Japanese management?

This chapter will address such issues, although it must be stressed that change in the management practices of Japanese companies is not uniform or clearly transparent. The focus of the chapter will be on the management of human resources – as this is where significant change is taking place and where the environmental contexts are dynamic and fluid. It commences with a brief outline of the historical and cultural context of Japan which is then followed by a discussion of the development of Japanese business and management, and recent economic development. This elaboration provides the backdrop for the following section which discusses why change has been necessary and the difficulties of transitioning to a 'new' management system. The slow and varied rate of transition in Japan demonstrates how corporate and societal culture modifies and reinforces managerial values and behaviours. The chapter concludes with a discussion on how far the dysfunctional aspects of the current Japanese management system are rooted in systemic problems.

The historical and cultural context

The entry-point into modernity for Japan was significantly different to that of Europe and the United States, which subsequently led to a different path being taken in its industrial and technological development. In the seventeenth century, Japan attempted to close itself off from the external world, although this did not stop economic and demographic expansion. This Tokugawa period of relative closure to the world was characterised by a growing importance given to business values and economic problems that ran contrary to the regime's ideal of social stability (Carré, 1995). The *samurai* supporting the Tokugawa government were, during this time, facing a declining income as their 'wages' were based on an allocation of rice which was difficult to sell as the market suffered from overproduction.

As a consequence, distinction in rank and conditions, on which samurai power was based, was increasingly threatened by the economic and social situation. During this time, big trading houses developed and established the goal of business profit as an important social value (Norman, 1940).

Despite strong political control, a pragmatic approach stimulated considerable intellectual activities among a number of *samurai* and members of the bourgeoisie eager to assert their roles and values in society. This facet was most notably illustrated in the interest in Western science and techniques, which introduced the Japanese to the best of Western knowledge that existed at this time (Totman, 1993). This gain may partially explain why during the later Meiji period, the

Japanese elites were able to assimilate, over a period of about 30 years, a modern company system that had been developed over several centuries in Western countries. With the commencement of the Meiji Restoration in 1868, the Japanese adopted and adapted Western practices. Although limited organisational resources were a constraint to growth this forced companies to concentrate their resources in simple and functional organisations with strong collaboration between them. Foreign technology transfers also called for rapid organisational learning which turned companies' ability to adapt and cooperate into a competitive advantage (Fruin, 1992).

It is in such a context that Japan developed a number of management practices, not so much rooted in history and culture, but as a relatively modern phenomenon loosely related to the proto-industrial stage of economic development. Skilled labour was scarce, particularly after the Russo-Japanese war of 1904–5, so employers offered long-term employment and wages based on life stages to attract and retain workers. These practices were critical to securing labour during the subsequent development of the heavy industrial sectors (Taira, 1970).

Similarly, the job-rotation system developed as a response to high levels of absenteeism (Koike, 1988). Likewise, to cope with the shortage of qualified labour in the 1920s, employers attempted to control the labour supply by encouraging the creation of company unions. Over time, these unions became the nexus for exchanging information, bargaining on company-specific working conditions and promoting agreements that were favourable to their members as well as the companies themselves. Thus, it was at the start of the twentieth century that the key features of the modern Japanese approach to managing labour emerged (see Benson, 2008, Gordon, 1985, Kawanishi, 1992).

Japanese culture sees the self to be deeply embedded in social relationships (see chapter 3). As such there exists little confidence in the power of the individual to devise, control and execute his or her own destiny, especially if those plans run counter to prevailing external social and structural norms and conditions (Hamaguchi, 1988). Nevertheless, younger Japanese today are increasingly rejecting notions that the fulfilment of security and stability needs can only occur within the traditional bounds of the closed 'community of fate' (Sugimura, 1997). This challenge to the long standing psychological contract between companies, unions and workers is increasing as young people no longer wish to be bound to, and sacrifice their private life to, a single company (Economic Planning Agency, 2000). These attitudes are also increasingly shared by the wider Japanese society. Employees of all ages are expressing a desire to develop closer relations with their family and friends, as well as to pursue leisure or volunteer-type activities outside the boundaries of the organisation (Economic Planning Agency, 1999). Such a societal transformation is not new as was earlier illustrated with economic modernisation which could not have taken hold so comprehensively and so rapidly from the Meiji period onwards without forces for change and modernisation building up within the 'closed' Tokugawa society. Nevertheless, it is also the case that the Meiji elites sought to limit the penetration of Western ideas through the policy of *wakon yosai* (Japanese spirit, Western technology) and, later, with an extreme form of nationalism. So, modernisation was imposed upon the Japanese people from outside and from above, and the process of modernisation began with changes in the external and material worlds, not from within as happened in the West.

The development of Japanese business and management

There have been, and there remain, two alternative paradigms operating in the Japanese management system. These paradigms reflect the balance between the emphasis on social harmony and the company as a family that has been inspired by Confucianism and Shinto Buddhism, and the stress placed on market rationality and the interpretation, in a Japanese context, of the principles of Taylorism and mass production (see chapter 4). At various times companies would claim to uphold paternalistic principles while at other times they expressed allegiance to the principles of market rationality and emphasised the economic rationale of their management systems.

In general, enterprises emphasised the market rationality of management systems. Horizontal coordination between departments was of utmost importance in terms of knowledge management. The rotation of employees between departments gave companies the opportunity to nurture autonomous problem-solving capabilities and to enhance their employees' ability to process and communicate information back to the production system. At the same time, incentives were devised that allowed individual employees to commit themselves to the collective processes without fear of losing compensation. The trade-off of such an approach was clear in the minds of both parties.

Companies needed long-term, committed employees in the post-war years where a shortage of skilled workers existed. Companies therefore managed the careers of their permanent employees, ensuring adequate training based on their specific needs, and paid wages below productivity in early periods of employment whilst raising them above productivity in the second part of a worker's career. In return, workers could only recoup the early losses if they were diligent and avoided being laid off. Under this system workers no longer had an incentive to retire voluntarily, and so the retirement age had to be specified in advance to control labour costs (Lazeur, 1979).

This démarche led to clear, hierarchy-driven career development schemes where promotions were based on the number of years of continuous employment and merit. This merit component was not based on a particular job or output, but broadly defined by problem-solving and communication skills. Frequent appraisals assessed potential ability, based on adaptability to technical changes as well as soft skills such as loyalty and the ability to cooperate well with other workers. The long-term nature of compensation practices was compatible with the dominant long-term investor relationships. Main shareholders did not pursue short-term profit maximisation strategies and stable cross-shareholdings among affiliated companies prevented hostile takeover bids. As such, companies were able to make implicit commitments such as long-term employment promises and seniority-based wages to their employees, in exchange for employees' commitments in terms of long-term loyalty, ethical behaviour and strong work discipline.

The source of sustainability, in particular the efficiency and effectiveness of the business system (for instance the sustained ability to compete on the basis of quality and responsiveness to customers' specialised needs), was also linked to the sociocultural and historical context. The resultant management concepts and practices, the vested interests that were created and the high social expectations they developed in Japanese society have had an impact that is of considerable importance in understanding the current and future processes for reform of the management system, its pace and orientation and the objectives pursued by the key stakeholders.

At the policy-making level, companies were used as a tool to achieve the overarching public goal of rebuilding the country. The immediate post-war economic and political situation also explained why the Japanese business system developed as it did, but it could be argued that while the universalistic welfare-state developed naturally in the European low-context socio-political and business environment, in the high-context, particularistic Japanese environment, where specific group relationships are very tight and exclusive, it was not surprising that economic revival centred on business organisations.

The idea of private companies being considered as not only economic but also social institutions also permeated the US (Berle and Means, 1932; Galbraith, 1956) and the European (Crosland, 2002) discourse on corporate governance and the position of companies in society, before and after the Second World War. A transformational drive of the capitalistic tenets (the supremacy of shareholders' rights) emerged and lasted until the end of the 1970s and the start of the dominance of the neo-liberal paradigm among the American liberals and the European social democrats (Utting and Marques, 2010). Companies were considered as a kind of public good with shareholders being only one of the stakeholders. Such a view did not, however, get to the point of public authorities, management and unions talking about companies being an organic type of 'community of fate' with symbiotic relationships with society, far beyond the purely institutional devices where management and employees pursued their separate interests based on individualistic utilitarian assumptions.

The official discourse in Japan blurred the line between private and public sectors in its attempt to recreate organisations in the form of the nineteenth-century efficient but also socially responsible Omi merchants (Hirschmeier and Yui, 2006). In this case, corporate growth equalled the realisation of social prosperity and wealth. A system developed in which companies and their employees cooperated and worked collectively to achieve greater economic outcomes that were subsequently spread as impartially as possible. Companies were thus expected to display a benevolent responsibility towards those with whom they had direct relations (i.e. employees, subsidiaries, business partners and customers) as well as the wider community, shopkeepers and service providers who survived on the spending of its employees. In the discourse of a leading figure such as Konosuke Matsushita, the founder of Panasonic, the goal of business was to serve citizens, not just to pursue profit (Matsushita, 2011). Businesses were based on relationship-based psychological contracts emphasising mutual loyalty with interests transcending the interests of the organisations.

It is a *paradox* that no transformational drive towards the legal and fiduciary basis of capitalism, as in the US and Europe, emerged in Japan after the Second World War. The symbiotic type of capitalism was taken as guaranteed and enjoyed considerable legitimacy without needing to have a clear legal basis.

Rapid industrialisation and urbanisation dissolved traditional communities and replaced them with company-based communities and communications. Companies thus became the centre of people's social lives. Whilst work plays a major role in shaping identities and the understanding of societies worldwide, studies have shown that this tendency is the strongest in Japan (Sugimoto, 2010). Long-term employment, seniority promotion and low-income differentials ensured the stability of Japanese society and provided normative reference points in terms of past achievements, current position and the future ambitions of workers and their children. Management enjoyed internal legitimacy linked to these socio-cultural factors.

Japan has been described as a so-called high power distance country run according to a concept of hierarchy in which people of all ranks traditionally accepted the legitimacy of their positions in society. But hierarchy has a meritocratic and not an inherited social privilege-basis (Hofstede, 1991). In credential and status-driven Japanese society, with an education system assuring the production and reproduction of elites on meritocratic criteria, employees were looking at their managers as people who had performed (starting from school) better than themselves in a fair and relevant competition in which they were all engaged on equal terms (Sugimoto, 2010). So, employees were strongly driven to act in accordance with their prescribed roles in a cooperative (mutually beneficial) system rather than engaging in a zero sum (or negative sum) struggle to alter the distribution of power and rewards.

This level of cooperation between labour and management to achieve a flexible and efficient high-skill/high-wage production system had little to do with formal institutions and laws imposing binding obligations (see chapter 13). Japanese corporate law pays scant regard to workers and the principle of shareholder primacy is clearly enshrined in the law (Araki, 2005). Lifetime employment was not an explicit contractual promise or fiduciary duty on the part of companies to protect the interests of employees. The agreement between job stability for employees and flexibility for employers was based only on an 'unwritten guarantee' (Dore, 2000), a 'social norm' (Jackson, 2007) or a 'moral imperative' (Ahmadjian and Robinson, 2001) (Wolff, 2010: 81).

Notwithstanding this lack of formal legal protection, employment agreements subsequently became backed by the state through legal doctrine and court precedents. Permanent employees were dependent on their employers and faced incentives to act in accordance with the long-term interests of the company, lest they would lose their status and fall into the category of the unprotected workforce. But Japan had (and has still largely kept) a legal structure in which the doctrine of employment at-will is not recognised. An employment relationship is normally deemed to be continuous and may only be terminated for just cause. The basic legal doctrine and court precedent is that in contested cases an employer will only be found to have just cause for termination if all less drastic alternatives have been ruled out. In Japan, however, employers who wish to discharge employees for whatever reason usually circumvent the law by asking employees to resign. This is, in most cases, effective as in a collective culture employees often do not want to take a lone stance against their employer. There was, and still is, the possibility for permanent employees in large companies to be transferred to a lesser organisation in the case of poor performance and/or disagreement with supervisors and managers. The employer could back up the request with financial inducements or/and by threats, but in any case the employee almost always had to comply. Therefore, management was clearly in command but there was to some extent an effective balance of power with the state's intervention.

Rationality and sustainability also justified the creation of dual labour-markets. While claiming to uphold the paternalistic approach companies could, in different contexts, integrate the principles of market and economic rationality into their management systems by adopting modes of production driven by cost control. Japan is a society that makes a clear distinction in status and treatment based on the *uchi* (inside) and *soto* (outside) concept which differentiates between insiders' and outsiders' membership of a group. Japanese companies do not consider the use of contingent labour, those workers denied access to fringe benefits and generally working for low wages without job guarantees, and the wide wage gap between large and small companies, as incompatible with the cooperative, long-term work arrangements they have developed with their permanent employees.

Recent economic development

Running parallel to the developments identified above have been significant changes in the economic fortunes of Japan. Agriculture has continually declined in its share of employment since the 1950s and most workers are now employed in the services sector. Real GDP growth has slowed considerably since 1991 and has averaged less than 1 per cent per year. This is in contrast to the 10 per cent average growth rates of the 1960s and the nearly 5 per cent average growth rates of the 1970s and 1980s. Industrial production during this time also experienced a similar decline; from a high average growth of 13.3 per cent in the 1960s to the present low of an average fall of one-third of 1 per cent in the first decade of the twenty-first century. As a consequence, unemployment has steadily risen from between 1 to 2 per cent in the 1960s to an annual average of 4.7 per cent in the last decade. These changes are detailed for the period 1960 to 2010 in Table 7.1 below.

Much of the traditional Japanese management model stemmed from the manufacturing sector, particularly the larger companies. The decline in industrial production, as illustrated above, has had a substantial impact on employment in this sector. These declines were caused by poor consumer demand (Yoshikawa, 2002) and the rising competitiveness of a number of developing countries. This

Table 7.1 Average real GDP growth, unemployment rate and industrial output growth, Japan, 1961–2010 (%)

Time Period	Real GDP Growth	Unemployment	Industrial Production Growth*
1961–1970	Approx 9	1–2	13.3
1971–1980	> 5	Approx 2	7.0
1981–1990	4.4	2.5	4.0
1991–2000	0.9	3.3	0.2
2001–2010	0.7	4.7	−0.3

Sources: Benson, 2005; Ito, 1993; JILPT, 2007 and 2010; JPC, 1995; Nakamura, 1981; Odagiri, 1992; Uchino, 1983.

step has led many Japanese manufacturers to relocate parts of their operations overseas, particularly to other Asian countries. This 'hollowing out' of manufacturing led employment in this sector to fall from 15.5 million employees in 1991 to less than 10.2 million in 2009; a fall of 34.5 per cent in the manufacturing workforce (Benson, 2005: 40; JILPT, 2010: 23). While the loss of manufacturing jobs over the past two decades has been substantial these losses were more than compensated for by an increase in employment in the services sector of 38.8 per cent or 9.4 million employees (JILPT, 2007: 23; JILPT, 2010: 23). Many of these new jobs, however, were of a casual or part-time nature. This shift away from full-time work partly accounts for the rapid increase in non-regular employment in Japan, and the lower wages paid to these workers have raised concerns as to 'whether such employment can support career development and family aspirations' (Whittaker, 2004: 30).

These economic difficulties were exacerbated by some externalities, as alluded to in the introduction. The 1997–8 Asian financial crisis, which developed in Thailand as a result of a drastic fall in confidence in the Thai currency, quickly spread to a number of other Asian countries, including key Japanese trading partners such as Indonesia, Korea, Malaysia and Taiwan. Although the Asian crisis had a severe impact on many of the Asian economies at the time, by 2001 most had recovered. This was not the case for Japan where financial scandals in the latter part of the 1990s, an increase in the consumption tax in 1997 which led to a dampening of consumer demand, a decrease in public spending and the use of public money to support the ailing banking system added to the economic difficulties facing the country.

The Japanese economy did begin to improve after 2002 with economic growth and domestic investment increasing (see Special Issue, Japan, 2012). Exports also increased, although domestic consumption remained sluggish. This outcome resulted in improvements to the labour-market, with increased hiring of employees and improved wages. These factors, in turn, contributed to a subsequent increase in private consumption (Tselichtchev and Debroux, 2009: 337). The 2008–9 global financial crisis, which commenced with a restriction in lending brought about by sub-prime lending in the US, saw Japanese consumption fall (although this had commenced around 2006) resulting in a concomitant fall in economic growth and an increase in unemployment. Although by late 2009, Japan appeared to be out of recession, after a year of negative economic growth, the impact of the Tohoku earthquake and tsunami in April of 2011, and the following explosion at the Fukushima nuclear plant has meant that a great deal of uncertainty now exists in Japan.

Accompanying the economic changes over the past two decades have been a number of other developments that will influence the nature of Japanese employment and labour-markets in the future. The labour-market participation rate for males has fallen from 77.2 per cent in 1990 to 72.0 per cent in 2009 (JILPT, 2010: 20). For women, the rate has also fallen, (cf., chapter 9) but by a smaller percentage: from 50.1 per cent in 1990 to 48.5 per cent in 2009 (JILPT, 2010: 21). In addition, the ageing of the population and the decline in the birth rate has meant that the normal working age population has declined in recent years. This trend will probably continue, as the low birth rate means fewer young people are entering the labour-market. It has been exacerbated by the rise in the number of young people not making an immediate transition from school to full-time employment; in 2002, there were 4.2 million young people who had not gone directly from graduation to full-time employment. Of this group, 1.9 million were 'freeters' – young people working in temporary jobs – 1.7 million were young people without work and 0.6 million were young people not in work (JILPT, 2005: 2). These factors have led to an increase in the percentage of workers who are 65 or more years old, up from 12 per cent of the total population in 1990 to 22.6 per cent in 2010 (JILPT 2010: 18).

Management change and transition

The acceleration of the pace and scope of changes in the Japanese business system since the 1980s has occurred in an environment characterised by a significant transformation of the economic, social and cultural environment. There are two dimensions to this change. On the one hand, during the last decade, Japanese companies have steadily lost ground to Chinese, Korean and Taiwanese firms in industries where they were once the dominant players, such as electronics and telecommunication. Moreover, they also lost ground against the best European and US companies in launching new and successful products and services. In short, Japanese companies seem to have lost their innovative poise and are struggling to remain afloat in a globalised world (Lee and Kim, 2011; Special Issue, Japan, 2012).

On the other hand, the shift towards cultural capitalism in a postmodern economy and society is clearly noticeable (Sugimoto, 2010). The 'Cool Japan' drive, symbolised by the flurry of products and services successfully mixing modernity with traditions, shows the depth of innovative traditions in Japan (Sugimoto, 2010). There are a growing number of workers in knowledge industries and the importance of start-up entrepreneurship to enhance innovation is beginning to be recognised (Jackson and Debroux, 2009). These changes are not only driven by established companies but also by newcomers, especially those in the service and manufacturing sectors. Many new (but also old) companies show a highly flexible and cost efficient use of human resources based on innovations in incentive systems and a systematic diversification of employment patterns.

Despite the social legitimacy of the business system, the seniority-based pay and promotion system has been under scrutiny since the early 1950s. However, it was only since the 1980s that its basic tenets gradually began to be seriously challenged. The cost of such a system began to be higher than its merit because of the *ageing* of the population and the slowing of economic growth. In addition, it was increasingly considered ill-suited to sustain the necessary dynamics in a fast changing business environment (Nikkeiren, 1995). Under such conditions the introduction of performance-related pay was an attractive option to lessen cost pressures and to enhance employee motivation. Such a reform became all the more urgent as the government began to pressure companies to fulfil their social responsibilities by keeping redundant workers employed and offering a longer career span to older workers. This policy-shift proved difficult for these workers as they were losing their mandatory retirement options in a period of rapid market and technological changes which rendered many of their skills obsolete and made it difficult for companies to dispatch them to related companies.

But vested interest and high social expectations of continuity of the old practices explain why the employment practices orthodoxy was not something that could easily be changed simply by wage-engineering. Middle-aged workers resented the introduction of performance-related pay as a breach of the psychological contract and insisted on the fulfilment of their implicit contracts of seniority-based reward. The *noryoku shugi* drive in the 1980s did not overturn the rules governing the age versus pay curve, that is the skill-grading classification and the operational rules for promotions. Rather, it has been argued, it created gaps in the average age versus pay curve with those gaps determined by merit (Ishida and Sato, 2011). The artificial creation of managerial positions accelerated because of the ageing of the workforce. Japanese companies thus continued to go against the trend of what the modern business environment required, namely the development of organisational structures with fewer management layers and flatter hierarchies so as to reduce overall personnel expenditure and turn fixed costs into variable costs. It was only in the latter half of the 1990s that a significant number of companies began to experiment with new appraisal, compensation and promotion elements based on individual performance as part of the revamping of their management systems. The term *seikashugi*, roughly translated as 'performance-ism', was coined in that period as a symbol of the strong belief that a close relationship between the market and management philosophy and practices was a 'must' for the long-term competitiveness of Japanese companies.

This external pressure on companies, brought about by social and economic pressures, was the major factor underpinning attempts to institute market-driven HRM systems in place of organisation-driven personnel systems (see chapter 13). It did not mean, however, that Japanese companies were moving closer to adopting employment practices based on the external labour market. The style of organisational governance in Japanese companies is more sensitive to the product and raw materials markets as well as to the capital and financial markets. It does, however, reflect the growing interdependence with the changes in corporate governance. The coalition of shareholders and employees integrated and mediated by management (Aoki, 1988) in what has been termed symbiotic capitalism started to disintegrate 20 years ago. Ownership of large companies is now largely in the hands of shareholders who are more interested in economic and financial rates of return in contrast to the earlier sales and market shares as indicators of performance. As a consequence, more precise methods of managing organisational performance that reflect the market's evaluation of corporate performance are increasingly being adopted.

Japanese management, and particularly HRM systems, are now more heterogeneous than in the past and practices now differ significantly from company to company. The reform process, necessitated by the changing economic and social conditions, triggered an evolution in the criteria for determining the treatment of employees in organisations including those of age, tenure, gender and education. Increasingly, companies are eliminating or significantly reducing the seniority-related element in pay and retirement allowances and replacing this with a component related to competency. At the same time, companies are increasingly discarding the remnants of the welfare corporatist philosophy by removing traditional allowances such as housing, family and transportation. These actions have lead to the abolition of the ability/skill pay for managerial personnel and the adoption of role and performance-related pay as in the US.

As a consequence, a wider dispersion of wages for the most important and influential group of employees in Japanese companies, the university-educated male employees in medium and large companies, has occurred (Rebick, 2005). As has been pointed out by a number of authors (Debroux, 2003; Takahashi, 2004; Meyer-Ohle, 2009) the adoption of performance-related pay schemes has led to a decline in morale. In many cases, this was caused by the splitting of workforces into predetermined performance bands and a decline in productivity due to the setting of contradictory objectives. The focus on the narrow objectives of 'Management by Objectives' schemes that had been introduced in many companies had the effect of neglecting irregular but important or strategic tasks, which led to an increase in unpaid overtime. In most companies, however, these problems were considered transitory.

The reforms outlined above and the declining employee morale reflect the tensions between the old and new ways of doing business, which raises important questions concerning how companies can most effectively utilise an ageing, yet highly educated and skilled, workforce whose costs are making them less competitive on global markets. In part, this tension (notably that among the older workers) has been simmering over a long period as companies gradually changed the seniority-related system that had been in place for many years. Nevertheless, as generations that have worked in an essentially time-related pay and promotion system retire this problem will lessen, although these systems are embedded in company culture, especially for regular, full-time employees. At the present time, however, the important issue facing management is how to maintain a cooperative and collective management system at a time of considerable decentralisation and individualisation, notwithstanding that future generations of managers will have a better understanding of performance management schemes and can be expected to adapt to the new work rules.

The rapid changes in the external environment of Japanese companies have led to important changes in the mode of employment. As in the US and Europe, a *three-tiered* workforce structure has emerged, composed of a shrinking elite of permanent, long-term core workers, a second group of medium-term skilled workers, increasingly cut off from the traditional welfare corporatist system and a growing third group of casual, short-term, semi-skilled routine workers. This model has worked well for Japanese companies who have over the past decade begun to repatriate factories to Japan after four decades of seeking offshore expansion. Production processes that, due to their labour intensiveness, were once most economically performed in low wage countries can now be performed more economically, more quickly and/or more reliably with flexible automated equipment requiring minimal direct labour in integrated facilities in Japan. This shift allows companies to respond quickly to rapidly changing technology and product markets, and to coordinate production with engineering, product design and marketing. Deskilling of the production processes was made possible by subdividing tasks or by introducing special purpose machines that can be operated with less skilled or educated workers who can be employed as contingent workers with lower wages, fewer benefits and less employment security than regular employees. Such a production approach also is suitable for subcontracting certain functions to small firms that pay lower wages or to independent contractors.

Notwithstanding the tensions outlined above, the process of reform is still, although increasingly less so, reflecting a consensual approach. The transformation is underpinned, to a large part, by both deregulatory and re-regulatory measures that allow some balance to be achieved between job security and flexibility. This 'flexicurity', a model that is receiving considerable attention in Europe, suggests that Japan is not converging toward a market-based, dismissal at-will system of labour regulation (cf., chapter 13). The protection of job tenure (albeit for a declining number of people) remains in place and has been bolstered by initiatives to keep pace with evolving social values concerning privacy, gender equity and work/life balance. After 30 years of limited acceptance. the Equal Employment Opportunity Law is now increasingly integrated into the HRM 'family-friendly' policy of leading companies. In order to balance the expenses of the social security system in a fast ageing society the government now encourages employers to ensure stable employment up to the age of 65 years. Nevertheless, since 2004 the mandatory retirement age has been set at 60 years of age and so companies can still limit the range of workers who are eligible to work beyond this age. The realities of a declining labour force coupled with the changing social fabric of Japan, however, means that companies must take steps to enable workers to work beyond this age.

This mounting pressure to allow people to retire later will, however, have a downside as companies will attempt to decrease their labour costs further through the utilisation of casual labour, technology and reduced working conditions. This step can be seen in recent deregulatory moves that are broadening the powers of employers to deal flexibly with working conditions. The legal maximum limit for an employment contract has been increased from one to three years. Casual labour can now be utilised freely in manufacturing. The section in the Worker Dispatching Law that prohibited dispatching workers to production sites was removed in 2004. These changes are all examples of the erosion of the idealised model of Japanese employment, which has real implications for workers and their unions.

A number of leading Japanese companies have succeeded in gathering support from their core shareholders, who accept the basic tenets of the high performance work systems (HPWS). Adoption of HPWS goes with a compensation differential that remains relatively low (around 1:20 between the rank-and-file workers and top managers) and with long-term job guarantees for a (shrinking) pool of permanent workers. Nevertheless, the accumulation of incremental changes over a number of years has reached the point where some institutional innovations are so different to the legitimated rules on which the Japanese model of HRM was based that it has created new patterns of behaviours. This has led to the emergence of a new management system which is underpinned by 'negotiations' between employer and employee. The resultant employer–employee relationship is now open-ended and is continually being redrafted outside of the societal legitimacy that characterised the past. In short, the gains and losses depend on the bargaining power of the parties and are more uncertain.

The relationship between employer and employee is increasingly seen in market-based terms instead of organisational terms and where the age and capability-oriented principles of remuneration and advancement have diminished and been replaced with a result-oriented approach. Casual employment has risen sharply over the past two decades and these employees, along with their permanent counterparts, are expected to improve their productivity. The level of commitment and ability now demanded means that many employees are working above their current ranking level with little chance of promotion, as would have occurred in the past.

Is such an approach sustainable in the long term? Can workers achieve company demands as well as fulfil their own needs and the changing requirements of society in terms of family, work-life balance and gender equality? These are questions that are difficult to answer at the present time. What can be said is that for many workers their overall perception is that they are being asked to work harder and longer than before with more accountability and responsibility but with uncertain career prospects. In such conditions, the traditional acceptance by employees of management legitimacy cannot be assumed. Moreover, the modernity of the HPWS model appeals to the new generations of Asian managers who see this as a way to overcome obsolete social norms, organisational stagnation, complacency towards bad performers and unfairness to the well-performing workers (Debroux, 2010).

One outcome of the ongoing changes to management practices, with the increased emphasis on the management of performance unit by unit, is the possible negative impact on knowledge management. Knowledge management is a vital part of daily processes with new knowledge being created continuously. The traditional Japanese approach to knowledge management was based on the embodied knowledge that every member of the work group possessed (Nonaka and Takeuchi, 1995). Cultural characteristics, like the importance of face-to-face contacts and communication styles, provide the framework for this distinctive style of knowledge management. According to Nonaka and Takeuchi (1995), Japanese companies relied on the experience of workers, and managing knowledge involved all members of the organisation. In this model, the focus lies on how this can be improved to reach as many members of the organisation as possible. In short, the Japanese knowledge-creating company is built upon the high level of the institutionalisation of personal relationships, and the strong high-context character of the Japanese culture. Tacit knowledge is exchanged through joint activities, such as socialising or living in the same environment, rather than through written or verbal instructions. Communication between workers, which happens outside of formal meetings supports the development of shared mental models of ideas and beliefs and encourages dialogue that is crucial for knowledge creation (Nonaka and Takeuchi, 1995).

Social structures and technological developments shape organisational structures which, in turn, impact on the methods and quantity of information exchange within companies. More recent changes to Japanese organisational structures have led to the perception that the informal exchange of information has decreased. This has created a dilemma for the Japanese company. On the one hand, the need for more emphasis on analysis, individual autonomy and explicit knowledge is considered necessary in the modern competitive environment. Yet, as Collinson and Wilson (2006) argued, the self-sustained, self-contained Japanese organisation has become inflexible as its very high level of cultural homogeneity creates difficulties if it wishes to take advantage of prevailing technologies. Technology changes the way people can exchange information with each other. Traditional working modes within Japanese companies and their related partners are built through intensive interaction among organisational members and are expected to result in the output of innovative products and, subsequently, in economic growth. New media technologies enable virtual dialogues, information exchange and explicit knowledge sharing in new ways which favour the integration of knowledge from different outside players. This démarche has led Nonaka and Toyama (2005) to argue that the organisational *ba* (shared context for knowledge creation) has to be extended beyond the present organisation's boundaries. On the other hand, Japanese companies may be right to continue with their integrated production approach with its focus on the long-term, gradual improvements of products (Itami, 2011). If this is so then this requires the continuation of broad, multifunctional expertise, the long-term dedication of stable project teams and long-term relationships with key partners.

The key question for Japanese management is therefore how to make an efficient, but self-contained, system of production and knowledge management an open system inclusive of all human resources while maintaining the core components of what made it efficient and effective. To take advantage of the open technology model requires the mastering of global mechanisms of exchange, sharing and new collaborative relationships. As Luhmann (1995) argued, organisations survive because they open their boundaries and can manage the balance of mutually opening and maintaining the boundaries. Ehnert (2009) introduced Aristotle's idea of a self-sustaining *oikos* (household) for an economic interpretation of sustainability. The *oikos* has to be self-sustaining to a considerable extent, in that it must not only be consumption-oriented, but must also have a strong focus on reproduction. Up to the beginning of the 1990s Japanese society and its companies were arguably the best illustration of that idea.

Japanese management, companies and their networks have not, however, been entirely self-sufficient. At the societal level, attempts were made to achieve some long-term balance between the internal and external environments. As Ehnert (2009: 147) noted, the

> consumption and reproduction of human resources occurred by fostering both the regeneration of human resources and also by investing in the "origin" of human resources, that is by investing in organisational environments where human resources come from such as schools, universities, education systems and families.

As a consequence companies established close relationships with university professors, not so much to collaborate in research (although that has changed considerably over the past decade) but to have access to their best students. Moreover, despite Japanese women being treated as ancillary workers they performed a crucial corporate role through their activities at home (allowing their husbands to work long hours because they would take care of the household alone) and in the education of their children (in making them well-socialised Japanese fit to enter into the corporate society). In this respect their input in maintaining the sustainability of the corporate system was considerable, albeit not necessarily by choice. This gender-role segregation was largely legitimised in society at large as had been the case before the Second World War. Women had been placed at the centre of the polity but without being given the opportunity to pursue a career of their own (cf., chapter 9).

The economic and social changes that have increasingly occurred since the early 1990s, coupled with increased competition from countries such as China and India, have meant that a mature knowledge-based society and economy such as Japan cannot compete on the standardised product markets. To create products with unique features requires the cooperation of both white-collar and blue-collar workers at the point of production, who have broad integrative skills and problem-solving abilities rather than narrow functional specialties (Shibata, 2009). This is the challenge facing Japanese companies and managers. In a world where the only sustainable advantage is based on knowledge, a cooperative and mutually beneficial management system has to remain the cornerstone of the Japanese company's strategy (Itami, 2011). A mix of modularisation, outsourcing of openly available technology and integrated production is necessary. Competitive advantages based on production acumen and incremental innovations must be kept but the capability of making breakthrough innovations and managing intangible assets such as branding and intellectual property rights has to be improved. It requires a shift from the traditional focus on the embodied knowledge of the individual to codified knowledge as in documents or databases. As Ehnert (2009: 162), however, pointed out the difficulty for Japanese companies in the current situation 'is that tension may occur in balancing the human resource efficiently and effectively today and sustaining the HR base for the future'. This is precisely where the Japanese companies have been since the early 1990s.

However, the strength of the organisational *ba* as a support for the knowledge-creating company resulted from the lack of mobility of Japanese workers which served as an incentive to share tacit knowledge. The increase in non-regular workers employed in companies who tend to have lower organisational commitment, coupled with the growing mobility of knowledge workers, challenges the extent of knowledge sharing. Both categories of workers can take their embodied knowledge with them. The two *ba* supporting socialisation (originating *ba*) and externalisation (interacting *ba*) are the spaces that seemingly become less important for these workers and could lead to a potential decline in the knowledge conversion processes. The shared spaces in which these processes can be facilitated (originating and interacting *ba*) become less identifiable in an organisation. In short, less inter-departmental mobility and, subsequently, less personal communication, means less sharing of a common context about an issue when exchanging information.

The Japanese management model kept open the necessary spaces for discussion, communication and exploration about the kinds of knowledge needed within the organisation but also in society at large. Importance was given to the technical dimension of knowledge but also to its social and cultural dimensions which led to the development of multilevel, integrative networks with constant cross-fertilisation of interconnected knowledge. Yet, the increased casualisation and mobility of the workforce means that less emphasis is placed on cooperation and generic skill training, with more focus on specialist training which will threaten these networks and isolate workers. The problem will probably be most acute in the case of engineers (Nakata and Miyazaki, 2011). The emphasis performance-related pay places on goals in which employee performance is evaluated objectively, and in a horizontal manner, cuts across job descriptions. But in R&D results often take many years to emerge and when they do become clear they are often the result of teamwork which makes the objective assessment of each individual's contribution difficult.

One way these problems could be addressed is through externalising the labour market. In general, Japanese companies want to diversify the points of entry into the enterprise: however, an external labour market has been slow to develop (Benson and Debroux, 2003). Management remains mostly composed of insiders who are graduates of a limited number of elite Japanese universities. Companies are beginning to recruit non-Japanese employees into the managerial track at the headquarters but the obstacles to their integration remain severe. This is not surprising as even the most successful companies have generally been unable to optimise the talent of the non-Japanese employees working in their overseas operations. In Japan, companies are recruiting fewer new graduates than they did 15 years ago but the internal labour-market logic remains the cornerstone of the system. Its social legitimacy has been internalised in Japanese society to such an extent that it remains the expectation of parents and students that large companies will continue to recruit new graduates every year and provide long-term job guarantees and career opportunities. Despite the changes in the corporate governance system that encourage shorter-term horizons for companies' strategy this long-term mindset is so pervasive within the educational system that 20 years of reforms have had little noticeable effect. The long-term orientation of the production and reproduction of the elite can be viewed as an asset or a drawback. The current examination-driven education system assures continuity, facilitates training of the new entrants, decreases the costs of monitoring and is in line with the *kaizen* process of incremental progress (see chapter 15). On the other hand, it creates rigidities, encourages group thinking, tends to become too homogeneous over time and leads to a rejection of diversity.

This provides Japanese companies and management with a dilemma in the current globalised, highly competitive market place. In order to become more agile, Japanese companies have flattened structure and hierarchy which has increased efficiency but has led to fewer promotional opportunities being available. Yet, while employees were willing to acquire firm-specific skills that had value, and to work hard to boost productivity, it was in the context of an expanding company in which they had a stake and prospects of advancement. If companies cannot, however, respond and meet such expectations, in the absence of a vibrant, inclusive external labour market, they will end up with dissatisfied employees, lower productivity and ultimately lower returns on capital. This outcome explains the paradoxical result that the level of employee engagement in Japanese companies is strikingly lower than in US companies that offer much less job stability (Sasaki and Norquist, 2005). These 'trapped workers' may not only be more dissatisfied and less productive but they may also impede the recruitment of better employees that could develop a higher level of engagement.

Management today: dysfunctional aspects and systemic problems

Over the past two decades, Japanese companies have faced a difficult economic environment that has led them to implement new governance and management structures which have incorporated social and environmental issues into strategic planning, business decision-making and compliance and risk-assessment functions. These new practices have, however, not been sufficient to prevent scandals from occurring, as they have been constrained by the traditional business practices. The scandals that have occurred in Japan are different from those that have occurred in Western companies as they were not the result of individual issues, for example the greed of top management, but were systemic. In these cases the wrongdoing occurred further down the company hierarchy and involved a large number of people. Top management did not know or did not want to know. This led companies to adopt a fortress mentality of denial of responsibility, requiring the absolute loyalty of all employees and the minimum disclosure of information to the outside. These responses demonstrated the difficulties Japanese companies have with engaging with a number of parties (for example, non-government organisations (NGOs) or non-permanent employees) because they are not considered as bona fide stakeholders. Under the reforms to management, Japanese companies are now asked to engage more dynamically in stakeholder relations, although this will prove difficult, at least in the short-term, due to their self-sustained and self-contained mindset. In contrast, these same companies find it relatively easy to put in place environmental management systems or engage in philanthropic activities because, although they cost money, they do not affect the company's internal dynamics. In short, companies are much less enthusiastic about initiatives that could engineer changes from outside as such changes could be considered a threat to management authority and control.

In the particularistic Japanese society, it is almost impossible to engage on the basis of general and universalistic principles, linked to social, environmental and human rights-related issues, or to debate such issues objectively. Relationships are based on specific mutual interests that exclude groups such as NGOs and non-permanent workers. In this latter case, it is likely that the situation will become worse. Japanese companies always had a number of non-permanent employees with whom long-term relationships were established. This démarche has led to the integration of some of them as members of the group benefiting from monetary and non-monetary advantages bestowed upon permanent employees. It is less the case now with the utilisation of a large number of transient workers with whom relationships are kept to a minimum. Fundamental tensions between regular employees and non-regular employees have increased with the widening disparity between the role-based pay structure for regular employees and the job-description-based wage system for other employees. Very few Japanese companies have adopted organisational principles that would allow them to internalise these employees by establishing role-based classification systems and codification of the routes by which they could become regular employees.

At the same time, Japanese companies have placed more emphasis on philosophy and guiding principles than on formal administrative processes in the development of a corporate culture. Codified mechanisms for getting information to flow up the chain of command operate poorly and do not encourage the passage of objective information. Filters and channels exist but they are strongly dependent on personal relationships. For example, Japanese companies have introduced childcare and family-care programmes, as well as made efforts to reduce overtime, or at least unpaid overtime. But the existence of those programmes does not mean that it is acceptable to utilise them. Few employees, for example, take advantage of family-care leave because they still assume that taking time off signals to their supervisors or managers that they are not entirely loyal to the company. So far, top managers have not in any meaningful way sought to dispel this notion and so a high degree of ambiguity remains.

The dimensions of the HPWS, promoted strongly in countries like the US, are not alien to Japanese companies. Some of these aspects were inspired by Japanese practices and corporate culture. It is, however, difficult for companies in Japan to adopt such systems as Japanese companies are based on different concepts of organisations and value systems. The HPWS expects more from core employees than purely utilitarian calculation and individual benefit. But the objective of Western firms that introduce HPWS is not to reproduce the Japanese 'community of fate'. High commitment and engagement do not exclude mobility and individual development. Indeed a sense of autonomy is expected and HPWS cannot be based on top–down communication. In this context, teamwork dynamics with empowerment in flat hierarchical structures presupposes a proactive management of conflicts and acceptance of diversity.

Employee mobility linked to employability is a crucial element of cross-fertilisation of ideas and methods between workers. Such mobility fits well with the mindset of a low-context culture (Hall, 1977) where public and private concerns are separated and compartmentalised. In contrast, in high-context cultures such as Japan mobility may create mistrust and feelings of betrayal as relationships are expected to extend beyond functional purposes. 'Impatience with rule' (Storey, 1995) and high discretion in work organisation is difficult to introduce into Japanese companies where respect for hierarchy and a mindset of humility and self-restraint are considered virtues. Self-development and autonomy have always been promoted in the Buddhist and Confucian worlds but it is within a well-defined, hierarchically organised framework accompanied by a subtle social control influencing behaviour and attitudes. Accepting diversity remains difficult, especially in the culturally homogeneous companies and organisations found in Japan (cf., chapter 16). It goes to the core of the reflection on the appropriate boundaries of the organisations and challenges the meaning of belonging to a specific group with its connotations of gender, ethnicity, lifestyle and family relationships.

In the US, the success of HPWS reflects a strong belief in the ideals of individualism and the ethics of self-responsibility and individual competitiveness. Except for a small segment of the working population, concepts and practices simultaneously promoting individualism and collectivism are difficult for Japanese to understand as collective values are still at the centre of private and public life in Japan. As a consequence, the introduction of HPWS could cause a range of dysfunctional problems, and possibly rejection, on the part of the employee. As Docherty *et al.* (2002) observed, HPWS can lead to self-exploitation, burnout and mental problems among the highest committed and engaged employees and managers. Although such problems are not limited to Japan, the increase in work-related mental diseases of employees and managers – for instance cases of *karoshi* (death by overwork) and occupational-related suicides (Furuya, 2007), and occupational psychiatric disorders – show the seriousness of the issue. Whilst *karoshi* is a product of the traditional Japanese management system the fact that it does not disappear with the use of HPWS indicates that it is misused in some companies and has not corrected the problems of the past. Indeed, a significantly lower level of employee engagement is observed in Japanese companies compared to their US counterparts (Sasaki and Norquist, 2005). This facet may reflect the specific situation of the Japanese labour-market, or it could also be considered as an indication of the incomplete fit of the HPWS with the Japanese corporate culture.

Conclusion

After four decades of economic expansion in Japan, the last two decades have been characterised by low levels of growth, a decline in manufacturing, increased competition from other Asian economies, a series of financial crises and considerable social and demographic change. These factors have impacted on the structure and form of Japanese management, although the embedded nature of the management system has meant that change has been slow and uneven. Japanese companies have attempted to adopt some Western approaches such as HPWS and reduce their reliance on expensive full-time regular workers. By doing so some companies have improved their position in the wake of the 1997–8 Asian financial crisis and the 2008–11 global financial crisis. However, for most companies the change has been restricted by the formable barriers inherent in the traditional management system. These barriers, as illustrated above, include the limitations of the internal labour-market, a less than conducive enterprise and societal environment, the lack of opportunities for younger workers and resistance to the individualisation of performance management. This state of affairs has placed Japanese management in a state of flux where the clash between the old and new practices is still being played out and a hybrid system is emerging. This new system is inherently unstable and has been further complicated by the reduction of security for all workers, and especially the increasing number of irregular workers. As such, any new management system that relies on employee loyalty and commitment may be difficult to effectively implement.

References

Abegglen, J. and Stalk, G. (1987) *Kaisha: The Japanese Corporation*. Tokyo: Tuttle.

Ahmadjian, C. and Robinson, P. (2001) 'Safety in Numbers: Downsizing and the Deinstitutionalization of Permanent Employment in Japan', *Administrative Science Quarterly*, 46: 622–54.

Aoki, M. (1988) *Information, Incentives, and Bargaining in the Japanese Economy*. New York: Cambridge University Press.

Araki, K. (2005) 'Corporate Governance Reforms, Labour Law Developments, and the Future of Japan's Practice-Dependent Stakeholder Model', *Japan Labour Review*, 2: 26–57.

Benson, J. (1998) 'Labour Management During Recessions: Japanese Manufacturing Enterprises in the 1990s', *Industrial Relations Journal*, 29: 207–21.

— (2005) 'Unemployment in Japan: Globalization, Restructuring and Social Change' in Benson, J. and Zhu, Y. (eds) *Unemployment in Asia*. London: Routledge, pp. 39–57.

— (2008) 'Trade Unions in Japan: Collective Justice or Managerial Compliance' in Benson, J. and Zhu, Y. (eds) *Trade Unions in Asia*. London: Routledge, pp. 24–42.

Benson, J. and Debroux, P. (1997) 'HRM in Japanese Enterprises: Trends and Challenges', *Asia Pacific Business Review*, 3: 62–81.

— (2003) 'Flexible Labour-markets and Individualized Employment: The Beginnings of a New Japanese HRM System', *Asia Pacific Business Review*, 9: 55–75.

Berle, A. and Means, G. (1932) *The Modern Corporation and Private Property*. New York: MacMillan.

Carré, G. (1995) 'Les Révolutions de la Période Prémoderne' in Sabouret, J-F. (ed.) *L'état du Japon*. Paris: La Découverte, pp. 273–89.

Clark, R. (1987) *The Japanese Company*. Tokyo: Tuttle.

Clegg, S. and Kono, T. (2002) 'Trends in Japanese Management: An Overview of Embedded Continuities and Disembedded Discontinuities', *Asia Pacific Journal of Management*, 19: 269–85.

Collinson, S. and Wilson, D. (2006) 'Inertia in Japanese Organizations: Knowledge Management Routines and Failures to Innovate', *Organization Studies*, 27: 1359–87.

Crosland, C. (2002) *The Conservative Enemy*. London: Jonathan Cape.

Debroux, P. (2003) *Human Resource Management in Japan: Changes and Uncertainties*. Aldershot, UK: Ashgate.

— (2010) 'Human Resource Management in Asia', *Soka Keiei Ronshu*, 36 (March): 13–28.

Dore, R. (1990) *British Factory-Japanese Factory*. Berkeley: University of California Press.

— (2000) 'Will Global Capitalism Be Anglo-Saxon Capitalism?', *New Left Review*, 6: 101–19.

Docherty, P., Forslin, J. and Shani, A. (2002) *Creating Sustainable Work Systems: Emerging Perspectives and Practice*. London: Routledge.

Economic Planning Agency (1999) *Economic Survey of Japan*. Tokyo: Economic Planning Agency.

— (2000) *White Book on National Living Mode*. Tokyo: Economic Planning Agency.

Ehnert, I. (2009) *Sustainable Human Resource Management*. Berlin and Heidelberg: Physica-Verlag.

Fruin, W. (1992) *The Japanese Enterprise System*. New York: Clarendon Press.

Furuya, S. (2007) 'Karoshi and Karojisatsu in Japan', *Asia Monitor Resource Centre*. Accessed at http://www.amrc.org.hk/alu_article/multifibre-arrangement/karoshji_and_karoshijisatsu_in_japan, 11 April, 2011.

Galbraith, J. (1956) *American Capitalism*. Oxford: Blackwell.

Gordon, A. (1985) *The Evolution of Labour Relations in Japan*. Cambridge, Mass.: Harvard University Press.

Hall, E. (1977) *Beyond Culture*. New York: DoubleDay.

Hamaguchi, E. (1988) 'Japanese Management as a Civilization', MITI *Journal*, 1: 46–8.

Hirschmeier, J. and Yui, T. (2006) *Development of Japanese Business: 1600–1973*. London: Routledge.

Hofstede, G. (1991) *Culture's Consequences: Software of the Mind*. London: McGraw-Hill.

Ishida, M. and Sato, A. (2011) 'The Evolution of Japan's Human-Resource Management' in Miyoshi, H. and Nakata, Y. (eds) *Have Japanese Firms Changed?* Basingstoke: Palgrave Macmillan, pp. 70–87.

Itami, H. (2011) 'Restoring Japanese-style Management's Rudder', *JapanEchoWeb*, 5: 1–7.

Ito, T. (1993) *The Japanese Economy*. Cambridge, MA: MIT Press.

Jackson, G. (2007) 'The Turnaround of 1997: Changes in Japanese Corporate Law and Governance' in Aoki, M., Jackson, G. and Miyajima, H. (eds) *Corporate Governance in Japan: Institutional Change and Organizational Diversity*. Oxford and New York: Oxford University Press, pp. 310–29.

Jackson, K. and Debroux, P. (2009) *Innovation in Japan: Emerging Patterns, Enduring Myths*. Abingdon: Routledge.

JILPT (2005) *Labour Situation in Japan and Analysis: Detailed Exposition 2005/2006 – Labour Statistics*. Tokyo: Japan Institute for Labour Policy and Training.

— (2007) *Japanese Working Life Profile 2007/2008*. Tokyo: Japan Institute for Labour Policy and Training.

— (2010) *Japanese Working Life Profile 2010/2011*. Tokyo: Japan Institute for Labour Policy and Training.

JPC (1995) *Practical Handbook of Productivity and Labour Statistics*. Tokyo: Japan Productivity Center for Socio-Economic Development, pp. 95–6.

Kawanishi, H. (1992) *Enterprise Unionism in Japan*. London: Kegan Paul.

Koike, K. (1988) *Understanding Industrial Relations in Modern Japan*. London: MacMillan.

Lazeur, E. (1979) 'Why is There a Mandatory Retirement?', *Journal of Political Economy*, 87: 1261–84.

Lee, S. and Kim, J. (2011) 'Intensifying Competition for Technology in North-East Asia', *Samsung Economic Research Institute Quarterly*, 4: 53–63.

Luhmann, N. (1995) *Social Systems*. Stanford: Stanford University Press.

Matsushita, K. (2011) *Panasonic Ideas for Life*. Accessed at http://panasonic.net/ citizenship/basic_policy/founder/index. html, 17 October, 2011.

Meyer-Ohle, H. (2009) *Japanese Workplaces in Transition*. London: Palgrave MacMillan.

Moore, J. (1987) 'Japanese Industrial Relations', *Labour and Industry*, 1: 140–55.

Nakamura, T. (1981) *The Postwar Japanese Economy*. Tokyo: University of Tokyo Press.

Nakata, Y. and Miyazaki, S. (2011) 'Have Japanese Engineers Changed?' in Miyoshi, H. and Nakata, Y. (eds) *Have Japanese Firms Changed?* Basingstoke: Palgrave Macmillan, pp. 88–108.

Nikkeiren (1995) *Shin Jidai no 'Nihonteki Keiei'* (Japanese-style Management for a New Era). Tokyo: Nihon Keieisha Dantai Renmei.

Nonaka, I. and Takeuchi, H. (1995) *The Knowledge Creating Company*. Oxford: Oxford University Press.

Nonaka, I. and Toyama, R. (2005) 'The Theory of the Knowledge-creating Firm: Subjectivity, Objectivity and Synthesis', *Industrial and Corporate Change*, 14: 419–36.

Norman, E. (1940) *Japan's Emergence as a Modern State*. New York: Institute of Pacific Relations.

Odagiri, H. (1992) *Growth Through Competition, Competition Through Growth*. Oxford: Clarendon Press.

Oliver, N. and Wilkinson, B. (1992) *The Japanization of British Industry: New Developments in the 1990s*. Oxford: Blackwell.

Rebick, M. (2005) *The Japanese Employment System: Adapting to a New Economic Environment*. Oxford: Oxford University Press.

Sasaki, J. and Norquist, M. (2005) 'Grim News for Japan's Managers', *GALLUP Management Journal*, July. Accessed at http://gmj.gallup.com/content/17242/Grim-News-Japan-Managers.aspx, accessed 29 October, 2011.

Shibata, H. (2009) 'A Comparison of the Roles and Responsibilities of Manufacturing Engineers in Japan and the United States', *International Journal of Human Resource Management*, 20 (9): 1896–1913.

Special Issue, Japan (2012) 'Special Issue on Japan', *Asia Pacific Business Review*, 18(2), in press.

Storey, J. (1995) 'HRM: Still Marching On, Or Marching Out?' in Storey, J. (ed.) *HRM: A Critical Text*. London: Routledge, pp. 3–32.

Sugimoto, Y. (2010) *An Introduction to Japanese Society*. Cambridge: Cambridge University Press.

Sugimura, Y. (1997) *Yoi Shigoto no Shiso: Atarashii Shigoto no Rinri no Tame ni* (The Philosophy of Good Jobs: for a New Ethic of Work). Tokyo: Chuko Shinsho.

Tachibanaki, T. and Noda, T. (2000) *The Economic Effects of Trade Unions in Japan*. London: MacMillan.

Taira, K. (1970) *Economic Development and the Labour-market in Japan*. New York: Columbia University Press.

Takahashi, N. (2004) *Kyomo Seika Shugi* (Fallacious Performance Principles). Tokyo: Nikkei PBsha.

Totman, C. (1993) *Early Modern Japan*. Berkeley: University of California Press.

Tselichtchev, I. and Debroux, P. (2009) *Asia's Turning Point: An Introduction to Asia's Dynamic Economies at the Dawn of the New Century*. Singapore: Wiley.

Uchino, T. (1983) *Japan's Postwar Economy*. Tokyo: Kodansha.

Utting, P. and Marques, J. (2010) 'Introduction: The Intellectual Crisis of CSR' in Utting, P. and Marques, J. (eds) *Corporate Social Responsibility and Regulatory Governance: Towards Inclusive Development?* Basingstoke: Palgrave Macmillan, pp. 1–25.

Warner, M., (2011) 'Whither Japan? Economy, Management and Society', *Asia Pacific Business Review*, 17:1–5.

Whitley, R. (1992) *Business Systems in East Asia: Firms, Markets and Societies*. London: Sage.

Whittaker, D. (2004) 'Unemployment, Underemployment and Overemployment: Re-establishing Social Sustainability', *Japan Labour Review*, 1: 29–38.

Wolff, L. (2010) 'Lifelong Employment, Labour Law and the Lost Decade: The End of a Job for Life in Japan?' in Haghirian, P. (ed.) *Innovation and Change in Japanese Management*. London: Palgrave MacMillan, pp. 77–99.

Womack, J., Jones, D. and Roos, D. (1991) *The Machine that Changed the World*. New York: Harper Perennial.

Yoshikawa, H. (2002) *Japan's Lost Decade*. Tokyo: The International House of Japan.

8 The changing nature of management and culture in South Korea

Chris Rowley[1]

Introduction

Post-1960s South Korea (hereafter Korea) developed rapidly from a poor agricultural society into a rich, industrialised 'Asian Tiger' economy. Then the 1997 Asian Crisis hit and 'the miracle on the Han River' seemed a 'mirage'. However, performance recovered up to the post-2008 global financial crisis (see chapter 2). Within this roller-coaster ride of development, management and culture changed from being eulogised to being castigated. So, examining the development and influence of management and culture in Korea is important for several reasons.

First, management plays a role in business, economic development and society but does not exist in a vacuum. A significant work which indicates management variations stemming from culture is a seminal book by Hofstede, 2001). Second, even for some non-culturalists, the concept of culture is recognised (see chapter 3). Cultural underpinnings have consequences for institutional environments, which for Whitley (1991) were via the systems of:

- authority relations, importance of personal ties and conception of appropriate behaviour;
- trust, reciprocity, obligation and enterprise loyalty and commitment;
- organisation and practices of political and bureaucratic state elites, policies and finance.

So, institutional perspectives need grounding in cultural contexts. Third, in contrast to the implications of universalism and convergence-type views, culture remains not only important and diverse, but is portrayed as ingrained, deep and slow-moving.

The format of the rest of this chapter is as follows. The crucial historical setting is followed by an overview of the economic background. Culture, societal and corporate, is dealt with in the subsequent two sections, followed by management in terms of values, behaviour and labour conflict resolution. Final sections on the implications for management and conclusions complete the picture.

Historical background

Korea evolved over a long, sometimes tumultuous, history. The 'Three Kingdoms' (39 BC onwards) were united in the Shilla Dynasty (from 668), followed by the Koryo Dynasty (935 to 1392) and then the Yi Dynasty, which was ended by Chosun's annexation by Japan in 1910. While colonised, Koreans were restricted in organisations to lower positions and excluded from managerial roles. Infrastructure developments, industrial policy imitation, application of technology and operation management techniques and Korean émigrés, were other Japanese influences (Morden and Bowles, 1998). The experience of colonisation, along with the forcible introduction of the Japanese language, names and labour inculcated '. . . strong nationalist sentiments which in due course turned out to be a central psychological impetus for the economic miracles . . .' (Kim, 1994: 95).

With Japan's defeat in 1945 came Korea's partition, with US military governance until the South's independent government in 1948. Further widespread devastation followed with the 1950–5 Korean War. A large US military presence remains, with ongoing tensions and flare-ups and confrontations with the North, such as the North's sinking of a warship and an artillery barrage in 2010 (on North Korean economy and management, see Collins *et al.*, 2012)

The American management system was studied, especially as students going overseas most often went to the US. This focus had impacts on managerial outlooks, views, perspectives and comparisons and sources of practices and examples (see chapter 4). Mixing in with this were military influences and authoritarian rule until 1987. Many executives were ex-officers, while male employees served in the military and had regular training, and companies even maintained reserve military training units.

This Northeast Asian country, formerly known as 'The Hermit Kingdom', now occupies almost 100,000 square kilometres of the Southern Korean peninsula (6,000 miles from the UK). Korea's traditionally very homogeneous ethnic population rapidly urbanised and grew. After the Korean War, there was a baby boom with high birth rates. At the same time, modernising the society brought about 'increased food production, improvement of hygiene and sanitation, development of medical knowledge, technology, and widespread use of antibiotics, resulting in a sharp decline in mortality' (Eun, 2008:7). These events caused a dramatic increase in population. However, in the early 1960s Korea implemented the national family planning programme for the use of birth control. Yet, even though fertility levels began to fall, mortality also continued to decrease amid advances in medical services and health care. As a result, the population continued to increase (Table 8.1). However, this situation has now changed, with falling birth rates (1.2 per cent) and population growth (0.23 per cent) and an increasingly older population.

Rapid industrialisation in the 1960s generated jobs in urban areas and prompted people to migrate from rural areas to the cities (Han, 1978). By 1970 43 per cent of the population was living in urban areas, reaching 80 per cent today. Of the nearly 49 million population, nearly 10 million are in the capital city, Seoul (more

Table 8.1 Trends in population and age structure, 1960–2010 (%)

Age	1960	1970	1980	1990	2000	2010
0–14	42.3	42.5	34.0	25.6	21.1	16.2
15–64	54.8	54.4	62.2	69.3	71.7	72.9
65+	2.9	3.1	5.1	7.2	11.0	15.6
Total population (million)	25.0	32.3	38.1	42.9	47.0	48.9

Source: Korea National Statistical office (http://www.kosis.kr/)

than double the 1960s figure), the destination of 40 per cent of intercity migrants and over 50 per cent of migrants from rural areas, with a further 3.5 million in Busan (Pusan), 2.5 million each in Incheon (Inch'on) and Daegu (Taegu) and 1.5 million in Daejon (Taejon). Seoul is the dominant centre for political, social, business and academic interests and is regarded as 'a case of third-world "glocalization", in which modernity interacts with postmodernity, random development with culture conservation and space dissolution with space reconstruction' (Lee, 2004:112). As a result, Seoul has developed with skyscrapers, residential-commercial compounds that have been called 'dream palaces' and large shopping malls.

Economic background

Korea's evocative nickname of 'the country of the morning calm' became increasingly obsolete with the cacophony of continuous construction rapidly transforming a poor, rural backwater with limited natural or energy resources, domestic markets and a legacy of colonial rule and war with dependence on US aid into one of the fastest growing economies in a rapidly expanding region. For example, gross domestic product (GDP) real annual growth rates of 9 per cent from the 1950s to the 1990s (with over 11 per cent in the late 1980s) took GDP from US$1.4 billion (1953) to US$437.4 billion (1994) (Kim, 2000). Per capita GDP grew from US$87 (1962) to US$10,543 (1996) and gross national product (GNP) from US$3 billion (1965) to US$376.9 billion (1994). From the mid-1960s to the late 1990s annual manufacturing output grew at nearly 20 per cent and exports at over 25 per cent, rising from US$320 million (1967) to US$136 billion (1997) (Kim and Rowley, 2001). Korea became a large manufacturer and exporter of 'ships to chips', in both more 'traditional' (steel, cars) and 'newer' (electrical, electronics) sectors and the world's eleventh largest economy, joining the OECD in 1996. Employment grew and unemployment levels declined to just 2 per cent by the mid-1990s.

This developmental, state-sponsored, export-orientated and labour-intensive model of industrialisation was reinforced by exhortations and motivations, often with cultural underpinnings, such as 'national goals'. These included the need to escape poverty, achieve economic superiority over 'the North', compete with Japan, repay debts and elevate the country's image and honour.

The chaebol

Integral to this economic development was a particular business system and form of business organisation, the *chaebol*. These drivers of the economy were family founded and owned and controlled large business groupings with a plethora of diverse subsidiaries, as indicated in their Korean label, 'octopus with many tentacles'. For example, 'Few people know that Samsung makes summery dresses and blouses. Even fewer are likely to remember . . . it rose to prominence in the 1950s as a woollen mill' (Oliver and Song, 2011:22).

Much of the large business sector was part of a *chaebol* network and it exerted widespread influence. Held together by a variety of means, including cross share-holdings, subsidies and loan guarantees in opaque fashion, there was competitive tension, distrust and rivalry between *chaebol*. They were underpinned by a variety of elements and explained by a range of theories. The state–military links and interactions were important, producing politico–economic organisations substituting for trust, efficiency and the market (Oh and Park, 2002). The state both owned banks (with resultant capital guarantees) which promoted *chaebol* as a development strategy and intervened to maintain labour quiescence. Such close connections have been damned as 'crony capitalism' (Rowley *et al.*, 2002).

A few of the more than 60 *chaebol* dominated. At their zenith in the 1990s the top five (Hyundai, Daewoo, Samsung, LG, SK) accounted for almost one-tenth (9 per cent) and the top 30 for almost one-sixth (15 per cent) of GDP, spread across over 800 subsidiaries and affiliates. Some *chaebol* became major international companies in the global economy, engaged in acquisitions and investments overseas, whose destination was dominated by the US and China (Chung *et al.*, 1997).

Post-1997 there were problems and some, such as Daewoo and SsangYong collapsed, but others prospered and grew, such as Samsung, which overtook Hewlett-Packard in 2009 to become the world's biggest technology company by sales, while Hyundai grew from seventh to fifth largest car maker after the crisis (Oliver and Song, 2011). Recent developments, such as recent mergers at Hyundai, undermine the government's '. . . attempts to shift the economy's centre of gravity away from unwieldy conglomerates that have traditionally weakened themselves by over extending into non-core businesses' (Oliver, 2010:23.). We now give illustrative sketches of three important *chaebol*.

Hyundai began in the 1940s as a car repair shop, spreading into construction, cars (building the first in Korea in 1968) and ships. By 1998 its 63 subsidiaries also included heavy industry, machinery, chemicals, electronics, banking, finance and other services. It was so powerful it was dubbed the 'Republic of Hyundai', with 1996 sales of US$92.2 billion, over 200,000 workers and ranked amongst the world's largest construction companies and producers of cars and semiconductors. The 1997 crisis, however, forced Hyundai to invest in other countries to offset the negative effects and maintain profits, but also enabled it to indicate that it was a global player. However, its post-2000 dismantling saw the motor, engineering and construction, semiconductor and heavy industries parts disaffiliated, pushing it out of Korea's top 20 largest groups. According to Hyundai Engineering's vice president, 'The Chung family has withdrawn from the business. We're no longer a family-run company' (Ward, 2002b). Nevertheless, one of the most successful spin-offs, Hyundai Motor, remains part of the Chung dynasty. The family owns a 22 per cent stake, retaining links by '. . . blood' (Ward, 2002b) to the Hyundai Group, still composed of 63 diverse subsidiaries in: Securities and Investment Trusts; Merchant Marine; Elevator; Corporation; Asan; and Logistics. In 2011 Hyundai Motor took a controlling stake in Hyundai Engineering & Construction (E&C) Group to diversify its business portfolio and to make Hyundai E&C a world leading construction company (Hyundai, 2011). This will allow Hyundai E&C to take advantage of Hyundai Motor's global competitiveness and its high credibility in foreign markets. Indeed, it was argued that these changes at '. . . Hyundai illustrate how family loyalties and rivalries still dominate decision-making in South Korea's biggest companies' (Oliver, 2010:23). In short, 'Bringing Hyundai E&C back under family control is a matter of deep pride for the rival wings of the clan' (ibid.). In 2010, Hyundai Motor's net profits soared to Won5,267 billion (US$4.7 billion), with a market value of US$49 billion in 2011 with other parts of the group valued at: US$36 billion (Heavy Industries); US$33 billion (Mobis); US$9 billion (Steel); US$9 billion (E&C) (Oliver and Song, 2011).

Samsung, the oldest *chaebol*, started as a trading company in 1938 and developed from a fruit and sundry goods exporter into flour milling and confectionery. With roots in the Cheil Sugar Manufacturing Company (1953) and Cheil Industries (1954), Chairman Lee Byung-Chull began the manufacturing business after the Korean War. His business expansion provided 'a roadmap of how the Korean economy and its industrial structure developed over time' (Chang, 2010:59). The company diversified into textiles, paper, fertilisers, retailing, life insurance, hotels, construction, shipbuilding, aerospace, bioengineering. In the 1970s, Samsung expanded exports by switching focus from light industry products to electronics and heavy and chemical industrial goods. With rapid economic growth in the 1980s, Chairman Lee started investing in the semiconductor field and Samsung became the first conglomerate in Korea to introduce a full-scale business unit system (Chang, 2010). Its sales of US$3 billion and staff of 45,000 (1980) ballooned to US$96 billion and 267,000 (1998) (Pucik and Lim, 2002). By the late 1990s, Samsung Electronics alone had 21 worldwide production bases, 53 sales operations in 46 countries, sales of US$16.6 billion and was one of the largest semiconductor producers. By 2002 Samsung still claimed global market leadership in 13 product categories, from deep-water drilling ships to microwaves, television tubes and microchips. By 2010 net profit soared to Won16,150 billion (US$15 billion) from Won9,800 billion in 2009 with the market value of Samsung Electronics standing at US$1,221 billion; Life Insurance at US$17 billion; Heavy Industries at US$10 billion; Fire and Marine Insurance at US$9 billion; Engineering at US$9 billion (Oliver and Song, 2011).

Lucky Chemical Company, founded in 1947, manufactured facial creams then toothpaste and soap. As the company expanded its business to the plastics industry in 1952 it contributed to improving the living culture of Korean society. Goldstar was founded in 1958, going on to produce radios, telephones, fans and consumer electronics, refrigerators, televisions (the first built in Korea), computers, semiconductors and microprocessors. From the 1970s, media, advertising, engineering and petrochemicals were added to its portfolio of businesses. In the 1980s, Lucky Corp. further developed its chemical business in the cosmetics industry and Goldstar Corp. intensively invested in the semiconductor business. To become a global company, LG created 'Jeong-Do Management (the way they display their uncompromising integrity in pursuing LG's management principles)' in the 1990s. LG Electronics alone had sales of US$9.3 billion and 22,800 staff in early 2000. Its 59 branches, 18 sales subsidiaries and 31 manufacturing subsidiaries spanned 171 countries, with 26 R&D facilities in Korea (Kim, 2000). LG has focused on four business sectors since the 1990s: Chemicals/Energy, Electronics/ Information/Communications, Financing and Services. In 2003, LG introduced a holding company structure and committed itself to overcoming chronic problems in circulatory investments between subsidiaries.

The 1997 Asian financial crisis

The 1997 Asian financial crisis hit Korea badly. In 1998 came falls in GDP of –5.8 per cent, GNP of two-thirds, currency of 54 per cent against the US Dollar, number of establishments by 14 per cent (68,014), jobs by 1 million, wage rates by –2.5 per cent (nominal) and –9.3 per cent (real) in 1998 and the stock market by 65 per cent (between June 1997 and 1998). Bankruptcies and unemployment soared, almost tripling to 8.6 per cent (two million) by February 1999.

This economic collapse led to much anxiety and incomprehension as to how quickly and totally things had collapsed and why. Management and culture were quickly implicated as having a role in this downfall (Rowley and Bae, 1998a; 1998b; 1998c). The crisis was due to hikes in labour costs and a decline in international competitiveness. Legalisation regarding labour unions aggravated labour–management conflict and strikes were frequent. The strikes and wage increases resulted in a sharp decline in exports, while at the same time, the government decontrolled the increase of international capital inflows (Heo and Roehrig, 2010).

However, the economy rapidly recovered by implementing reform policies to meet the conditions of the IMF bailout programme. The government enhanced economic openness to attract foreign capital/investment and intervened to improve the profitability of some industries by reducing excessive production capacity and enhancing some regulations. Moreover, the *chaebol* attempted to improve their competitiveness and profitability by pursuing joint ventures with multinational corporations (Heo and Roehrig, 2010). Korea's GDP grew by 10.7 per cent in 1999 and by 2000 GDP was US$461.7 billion, per capita GDP US$9,823 and GNP US$459.2 billion. Growth continued in the early 2000s.

The economy continued its impetus through the decade. Yet, this recovery was fragile. Korean companies remain plagued by adverse publicity and opaque operations. High profile examples included Daewoo's huge debts and accounting fraud, Ford's abandonment of its interest in Daewoo Motor (after six months) in 2000 followed by lengthy subsequent negotiations with GM. Others include lengthy talks between Hyundai's securities and AIG (18 months), Seoul Bank and HSBC and Deutsche Bank (three years) and the Hynix and Micron saga. Then there were the charges against the chairmen of Hyundai (2007) for embezzlement and breach of trust and Samsung (2008) for tax evasion and breach of trust. These events, and the need for a Fair Trade Commission and restrictions on investments in affiliates and cross-investments, indicate problems, especially those that may be more deep-seated or hidden.

The post-2008 global financial crisis

The post-2008 global financial crisis impacted on the Korean economy. Due to the high level of dependence on foreign trade and financial integration with other nations, Korean exports and the domestic sector experienced declines in international demand and 2008's fourth quarter annual GDP growth rate fell to −5.1 per cent. The economy deteriorated and the currency depreciated by over 25.4 per cent in US$ terms. The rise in external debt also has been a main cause of the crisis.

More recently, the economy has slowly improved, with steps to prevent a similar crisis in the future by introducing a low-carbon and eco-friendly economy paradigm, reconstruction of organisations, fiscal policy and banking reforms and balancing export and import growth (KDI, 2010). In terms of regional trade, Korea is located in a more central zone than the US and China, in which Korea plays a key role as a broker. Consequently, today the economy is heavily dependent on international trade (nearly 70 per cent of its economy). Post-1997 trends can be seen in Table 8.2.

Labour markets

The post-1997 employment and unemployment trends can be seen in Table 8.3. This shows the recovery in unemployment levels, from the zenith of 7 per cent in 1998 to 3.3 per cent in 2002, slightly rising to 3.7 per cent by 2005 and falling to 3.2 per cent in 2008 before the post-2008 crisis impact and an increase to 3.7 per cent by 2010.

An important impact on the labour market stems from demographics. The post-1960 trends can be seen in Table 8.1. There has been a halving in the percentage of the population aged 14 or younger, from just over two-fifths (42.3 per cent) in 1960 to much less than one-fifth (16.2 per cent) by 2010. At the same time, numbers in the aged 65 or above category have jumped from a minute 2.9 per cent in 1960 to a substantial 15.6 per cent by 2010. The demographic issues of an ageing population and a declining workforce are critical. The role of women workers is problematic (see chapter 9).

An ageing population is bringing difficulties with less opportunity to engage in productive activities because of earlier retirements and limited job offers. Thus, the proportion of working people aged 50–64 has been declining since 1990, even though there was a slight increase in employment between 2000 and 2005 (Eun,

Table 8.2 Trends in GDP post-1997

	Year													
	1997	1998	1999	2000	2001	2002	2003	2004	2005	2006	2007	2008	2009	2010
Nominal GDP (Billion Korean Won)	506,314	501,027	549,005	603,236	651,415	720,539	767,114	826,893	865,241	908,744	975,013	1,026,452	1,065,037	1,172,803
Real GDP Growth rate (%)	5.8	-5.7	10.7	8.8	4	7.2	2.8	4.6	4	5.2	5.1	2.3	0.3	6.2

Source: The Bank of Korea (http://www.bok.or.kr/)

Table 8.3 Trends in labour force, employment and unemployment post-1997

Labour Force ('000s)	Year													
	1997	1998	1999	2000	2001	2002	2003	2004	2005	2006	2007	2008	2009	2010
Economically active	21,782	21,428	21,666	22,134	22,471	22,921	22,957	23,417	23,743	23,978	24,216	24,347	24,394	24,748
Not economically active	13,070	13,919	14,092	14,052	14,108	14,042	14,383	14,300	14,557	14,784	14,954	15,251	15,698	15,841
Participation rate (%)	62.5	60.6	60.6	61.2	61.4	62	61.5	62.1	62	61.9	61.8	61.5	60.8	61
Employed ('000s)	21,214	19,938	20,291	21,156	21,572	22,169	22,139	22,557	22,856	23,151	23,433	23,577	23,506	23,829
Unemployed	568	1,490	1,374	979	899	752	818	860	887	827	783	769	889	920
Employment rate (%)	60.9	56.4	56.7	58.5	59	60	59.3	59.8	59.7	59.7	59.8	59.5	58.6	58.7
Unemployment rate (%)	2.6	7	6.3	4.4	4	3.3	3.6	3.7	3.7	3.5	3.2	3.2	3.6	3.7

Source: Ministry of Employment and Labour (http://www.moel.go.kr); Statistics Korea (http://kostat.go.kr)

2008). Compared with other countries the employment rate of older people tends to be higher. Yet, more than half of older workers are in the agricultural and fishery industries due to a lack of younger labour, although there are also some in manufacturing or manual labour. Continuing to work into old age is due to the need to sustain their livelihood by engaging even in low-paying manual labour because of the lack of public support or other income sources after retirement (ibid.).

The implications for the management of demographic changes are stark. This is exacerbated by possible alternative sources of labour being constrained, given some of the traditional aspects of society, not least its homogeneity and exclusiveness. However, on some dimensions Korean society is now less homogenous. One example is in terms of international marriages, with 35,000 cases in 2004, 11.4 per cent of all marriages, 7.5 times the 1990 level and 2.9 times the 2000 figure (Kim, 2006). The growth rate of international marriages has accelerated, especially since 2000. There has also been a shift within this trend. In the past, a majority of international marriages were between Korean females and foreign males but now it is Korean males and foreign females. Foreign women came from poorer countries to supplement a shortage of brides. International matchmaking programmes were introduced by local governments to help rural men find marriage partners. As a result, the number of foreigners living with Korean spouses amounted to nearly 75,000 in 2003 (Cho, 2005). Among foreign spouses, the majority were from Asian countries, such as China and Vietnam and the proportion of women was more than 90 per cent.

Another dimension of less homogeneity is indicated by the growth of Korean transnational families or multinational households, which after the IMF bailout increased in many regions of the world. Some well-off Korean families had babies in developed countries, mostly the US, to acquire local citizenship and others educate children overseas; so-called '*gireogi*' families (Cho, 2005). These indicate the changing dynamics of Korean families and reflect Korea's position in the global capitalist economy.

An increase in foreign workers in Korea is another dimension of less homogeneity. Due to labour shortages the government adopted an industrial training system for foreign workers in the early 1990s for utilising them as employees. Since then, the number of foreign workers has risen tenfold, going from about 100,000 (including illegal immigrants) to about one million (including about 200,000 illegal immigrants) (Yoo, 2010). The government has also taken steps to attract talented foreign workers, primarily in the new growth sectors by supporting diverse programmes for multicultural families (Lee, 2011). Therefore, a number of companies have increasingly employed foreigners.

Societal culture

There is a dynamic interaction among political, economic, social and cultural factors and '. . . the selective adoption, absorption and assimilation of some foreign elements; and the selective abandonment, modification and utilization of others' (Kim, 1994: 103). This selectivity occurs through culture or political decisions.

Traditional social values have been identified in Korea (Lee, 1997; Kim, 1994; Cho and Yoon, 2002). These include: absolute loyalty of subjects to sovereigns; close relationship between father and son; separate roles for females and males; precedence of older over younger; mutual trust among friends; unequal inheritance in favour of eldest son; ancestor worship and emphasis on family members in a direct line; faith in the transformability and perfectibility of the human condition; importance of self-cultivation; hard work and frugality as social discipline; duty; reciprocity of respect and authority and public accountability; emotional harmony; hierarchy; discrimination against out-groups. Beneath the Korean people's ways of thinking and values lie a mixture of the easy-going and optimistic behaviours of Confucianism on the one hand and hard-working, '*palli-palli*' ('quickly-quickly'), high achievement and goal-oriented perspective, on the other.

Societal culture can be seen as underpinning development. For example, Shin (1991) argues that rapid economic development was mainly due to the 'progressivism' and 'optimism' of the Korean people. Progressivism means people's orientation towards change and innovation against environmental uncertainty. Optimism means people's orientation towards optimistic views and preparation for the future regardless of the current situation. Work using such concepts compared 1995 and 2006 using the four largest *chaebol*: Samsung, LG, SK and Hyundai (Cho *et al.*, 2007). It is argued this indicates a significant change in employee values for Korean companies, especially after the Asian Crisis (see Table 8.4). It is further argued that this change may be interpreted as a change from a relational psychological contract to a transactional psychological contract in Rousseau's (2001) classification.

Where do these values come from? As we have seen, Korean society experienced many influences. Additionally, Korea's religious and philosophical influences include Buddhism (from 372, and especially 935 to 1392) and Confucianism, the state religion for over 500 years up to the early twentieth century. This influence can be seen in Korean society's rigid Confucian code of personal and social behaviour and its feudal system, maintained by a hierarchical, authoritarian structure, rigidly stratified from top to bottom (Kwon and O'Donnell, 2001). Within this there was the *yangban* (the upper class or ruling class), the *jungin* or *seoin* (middle class), the *sangmin* (peasant farmers and craftsmen) and the *cheonmin* (underprivileged class).

Confucianism's influence remains, with values, ways of thinking and modes of conduct revolving around hierarchy, seniority and respect for education. Education was regarded as one of the best and shortest ways for attaining upper social status and the better way for *jasusungga* ('making one's own fortune'), one reason for expenditure on children's education. Parents educate their children in an intense and uncommon way, commonly depicted as 'excessive fever for education' (Lim, 2007). The structure of Korean education stems from high competition in pursuit of the goal of entering the very 'best' universities, dubbed 'entrance exam hell'. To make matters worse, Korean public education is now facing difficulties caused by '. . . the expanded private tutorial market, the degraded authority of teachers, rising levels of school violence arising from students' stress from entrance

Table 8.4 Trends in education participation (%) and expenditure on private education

		Year													
		1997	1998	1999	2000	2001	2002	2003	2004	2005	2006	2007	2008	2009	2010
Educational Population Rate	Below secondary education	38	34	33	32	30	29	27	26	24	23	22	21		
	Higher education	42	44	44	44	45	45	44	44	44	44	43	43		
	Above higher education	20	22	23	24	25	26	29	30	32	33	35	37		
Monthly average of expenditure on education per person (100 million Korean Won) (private education)												200,400	209,095	216,259	208,718

Source: OECD Statistics; KOSIS (www.kosis.kr)

examinations . . .' (Lim, 2007: 83). These occurrences have become serious social matters in Korea.

There was extensive investment in education, for instance, in terms of the share of education expenditure by central government in relation to GDP. Korea spent 3.6 per cent in 1982, falling to 3.2 per cent in 1990 and 2000 but rising again to 4.2 per cent in 2007, although somewhat below the OECD average of 5.0 per cent. However, Korea has the least favourable ratio of teachers to students at primary and secondary level in the OECD (OECD, 2009). Nevertheless, private spending on education is large (see Table 8.5) and one of the highest in the OECD with a high and rising reliance on private tutoring at primary and secondary levels on the basis of fierce competition for prestigious university places. While fewer are leaving school at secondary level (falling from 38 per cent to 21 per cent since 1997), percentages in higher education are static with a small decline (44 per cent to 45 per cent in the early 2000s to 43 per cent by the late 2000s) but with a large growth in above higher education, which nearly doubled, going from one-fifth (20 per cent) to nearly two-fifths (37 per cent) since 1997. Some of these trends can be seen in Table 8.5. Management education and training, along with the expansion of American style business schools, have also greatly expanded (see chapter 15).

Koreans remain intensely proud of their country. Furthermore, Korean society was traditionally very exclusive towards other countries, people and cultures due to several reasons. First, the single ethnic group and traditionally homogeneous population (albeit with some recent changes, as noted earlier) is one reason. Second, the history of an agrarian society, characterised by passive, closed and dependent views is another. Contributing to these was a climate favouring rice cultivation as this was labour and time intensive and spread along rivers and deltas in communities relatively isolated by mountains and distance. This state of affairs

Table 8.5 Changing values 1995–2006

Values	Year		Statistical significance
	1995	*2006*	
Collectivism	3.08	2.87	Yes
Obedience to senior in company is my duty	2.87	2.67	Yes
Company is my second home	3.31	3.00	Yes
I am willing to follow collective opinion of my colleagues	3.17	2.92	Yes
Optimism	3.05	2.72	Yes
I am proud of being Korean	3.21	2.87	Yes
My generation will be happier and wealthier than parent's generation	3.39	2.93	Yes
I am positive that Korea will become a wealthy country soon	2.90	2.71	Yes
Progressivism	3.11	3.01	Yes

Source: Cho *et al*. (2007)

encouraged cooperation and close-knit groups dependent on each other in the community for survival, with collectivism and inter-group responsibilities (see chapter 10). Third, the antagonistic memories and feelings against foreign interventionist powers persist. For some, this 'one-race-one-culture' mentality produced insensitivity.

Cutting against these societal cultural aspects are some developments, such as experience of education or work in the West, business internationalisation, influx of foreign capital, ideas of importing management 'best practice' and opening up to global cultures. Indeed, in the early 1990s the administration explicitly employed a *segyewha* (globalisation) policy facilitating more communications and interactions with foreign countries. Companies adopted similar policies, sending employees to other countries for exposure to foreign cultures.

However, cultures remain robust and slow-moving. Furthermore, there have been some reactions against Western cultures, with the enhanced power of Korean culture, especially within Asia (Ward, 2002a). Paradoxically, it is argued that this resurgence partly '. . . reflects changes in the country's make-up. Society is becoming more modern and less formal . . .' (ibid: 12).

Corporate culture

There is interaction between social values and corporate culture. The impacts of the traditional social values noted earlier on corporate cultural characteristics are seen in Table 8.6.

The corporate culture of Korean companies is differentially viewed as more collectivist by Westerners versus more individualistic by Japanese (Cho and Yoon, 2002). This is explained by the concept of 'Dynamic Collectivism', an elaboration of traditional notions of collectivism which '. . . applies collectivist norms for in-group members and individualistic ones for out-group members' (ibid.: 71). As a consequence, the boundary between in- and out-group members was reinforced

Table 8.6 Impacts of traditional social values on corporate cultural characteristics

Traditional Social Values	Impact	Corporate Culture Characteristics
Loyalty of subjects to sovereigns	→	Owner management's authority, paternalism
Close relationship between father and son	→	*Inhwa*, belongingness, kinship-based relations
Separate roles of women and men	→	Hardworking, devotion to company (especially male workers)
Precedence of elder over younger	→	Hierarchical relationships among staff, seniority-ism
Mutual trust among friends	→	Trustworthy relations among peers, collectivism
Inheritance, ancestor worship, family emphasis	→	Kinship-based ownership/succession; *Yongo*ism (blood, geography, education-based connections)

Source: Adapted from Lee (1997)

and competition intensified. This is built into corporate culture through the interplay between internal mechanisms (learning, selection and attrition) and external forces (the environment). These forces were:

- 'Culture Legacy', traditional culture embedded in Confucian values;
- 'Social Climate', socio-political situation created by the state economic development stance;
- 'Corporate Leadership', with paternalism and authoritarianism. Their interaction with internal culture management produced Dynamic Collectivism's triple dimensions: 'In-Group Harmony'; 'Optimistic Progressivism'; 'Hierarchical Principle' (ibid.).

We will return to these later.

To further investigate corporate culture Cameron's (1978) competing values and culture quadrant framework (Quinn, 1988) was used in a survey of 2,000 indigenous, US, Japanese and European companies (Bae and Sa, 2003). Some interesting results emerged (see Table 8.7).

All the value quadrants, except Group Culture, were statistically significant at the conventional level. In the case of Group Culture, all company groups had similar levels of the value regardless of the country of origin. US subsidiaries, compared to Asian, had higher values at both Developmental Culture and Rational Culture. The reverse was true for Hierarchical Culture, where firms from Asian countries, on average, had higher values. European subsidiaries were in the middle and US firms the lowest. Asian firms had higher values at Group values and Hierarchical values vis-à-vis Developmental values and Rational values, while the reverse was true in US firms.

Despite an increasing diversity of business ownership in Korea, corporate culture in the *chaebol* remains important and powerful. It retains its high profile, influential and normative nature, with roots in the family. The founders' beliefs permeate organisations, replicated and reinforced by scions of families. Practices

Table 8.7 Culture types and characteristics

Culture Type	Characteristics			
	Place	*Head of Unit*	*Glue*	*Emphasis*
Group	Personal	Mentor/Sage	Loyalty/ Tradition	Human Resources
Developmental	Dynamic/ Entrepreneurial	Innovator/Risk Taker	Innovation/ Development	Growth/Acquiring New Resources
Rational	Production Orientation	Producer/ Technician	Task/Goal Achievement	Competitive Actions/ Achievement
Hierarchical	Formalised/ Structured	Coordinator/ Organiser	Formal Rules/ Policies	Permanence/ Stability

Source: Developed from Cameron (1978); Quinn (1988).

such as long in-house induction with employees staying at training centres, where they are inculcated with company history, events, visions and songs, are important (Kim and Briscoe, 1997). Some *chaebol* dominate localities, even leading to 'company towns', such as Woolsan (Hyundai) and Pohang (POSCO), housing and servicing large numbers of employees.

Examples of corporate culture change

Given the above analysis, how do corporate cultures change? An overview of corporate culture change campaigns in Korea and the reasons for problems and effectiveness notes the need to secure qualified campaign managers and consistency with overall organisational strategy (Park, 2002). For further detail we use examples of corporate culture change in two leading *chaebol*. First, Samsung, which had two distinguishable stages in its establishment. The founder, Lee Byung-Chull, remained its 'leader' until the mid-1980s, with 1983–92 a transition period for the changeover to his son, Lee Kun-Hee. A rational and bureaucratic internal process was emphasised. High rationality and low risk taking were important values, with rules and regulations, thorough analysis and evaluation and hardworking and well-planned processes. These were necessary and sufficient during the high growth stage in a low uncertainty environment. In that period, even though Samsung was the leading company in Korea in most of its markets, its overseas position was relatively low and unstable due to competition from Japanese companies. To surpass its rivals and become a 'super first class' business, Lee Kun-Hee's Frankfurt Declaration (1993) launched the 'New Quality Management' movement in 1993, promoting restructuring and radical organisational, including cultural, change. He made his top managers aware of how poorly Samsung products were positioned in the global market and proclaimed 'quality-first management' at the expense of product quantity. The firm redefined its core business areas by merging or consolidating ten companies and removing or separating 16 companies out of the Group (Chung *et al.*, 1997). Through this process Samsung's direction shifted from 'domestic-centered, rationality' towards 'global player, risk taking' values. Top management were encouraged to take risks, with autonomy and diversity promoted. Samsung's style has moved from utmost caution to riskier approaches and a focus on core businesses and decentralised management. In this way, Samsung developed its hybrid management system from Japanese and Western business practices.

A second example is LG, where *inhwa* (harmony) and solidity were core values, such as 'respect' among members, 'tolerance and trust' and a 'sense of unity and cooperation' stressed. These values had enhanced loyalty and devotion and were key to growth (see chapter 13). However, over time these values made LG more conservative, with passive, easy-going attitudes and behaviours. For example, *inhwa* sometimes meant more lenient evaluations and overlooking of faults. In the late 1980s, an LG survey showed that about 60 per cent recognised LG as a humane and conservative organisation but less than 2 per cent perceived LG as having a high progressive spirit (Lee, 1997). So, a 'Vision Team' to change LG's core values was launched. In 1990, LG's chairman, Koo Cha-Kyung, declared new core values: 'creating value for customers', 'management based on esteem for human dignity' and 'empowerment', by changing its organisational structure and management practices. Simultaneously, LG emphasised autonomy to quickly respond to uncertain environments. By doing so, LG restructured its business based on common product lines or technologies, which enabled it to streamline complex product lines and eliminate duplications of products and labour (Chung *et al.*, 1997). The Group moved towards a better understanding of individual ability, promoting creativity and personal development.

Managerial behaviour

Managerial behaviour stems from a variety of influences. The influence of hierarchical traditional family systems impacts on management behaviour. This includes decision-making, business strategies, organisational structures and HRM (Cho and Yoon, 2002). Companies were centralised and hierarchical with formal structures and vertical organisational principles and family-style relationships. The hierarchical principle made for more predictable behaviour; obligations and indebtedness, contributing to vague roles between personal and public relationships (Cho and Yoon, 2002). Founders organised and managed on the basis of principles governing family life. There was both authoritarianism and paternalism, with companies as 'parents' and employees as 'family'; often they actually were, of course. There was kinship-based recruiting from extended clans (*chiban*) or regions, which dominated positions of power, with kinship-based relationships with owners (*hyulyon*). Ideas of harmony, *inhwa* and family-orientated HRM had seniority as the primary factor, with special allowances for family matters, from marriage and parents' sixtieth birthdays to funerals (Cho and Yoon, 2002). There are impacts on HRM practices, such as appraisals and evaluations, teams, empowerment, and so on.

A group-orientated approach is also often noted. However, practices, endorsed by Confucianism, made in-group members mutually interdependent and emphasised *inhwa*, making the out-group boundary more salient and contributing to strong competition with other groups. This helps explain why '. . . delegation of authority, often espoused formally, is ineffective and why bottom-up and lateral communications are consistently promoted only to fail' (Cho and Yoon, 2002:79).

Managerial behaviours also reflected the high regard for education and supporting a skilled workforce with heavy investment in human resource development. The *chaebol* put strong emphasis on this, with large, well-resourced and supported training centres. These provided induction and ongoing training and a variety of programmes. For example, in 1995 Samsung spent US$260 million on training, Hyundai US$195 million, Daewoo and LG US$130 million each (Chung et al, 1997). In 2010 Samsung educated and trained each employee for 87 hours on average and spent nearly US$10,000 per person for the purpose of training and education (Samsung, 2010). LG has operated 'the LG Training Academy' in the US since 2008 to train engineers, contractors and technicians (LG, 2008).

Furthermore, as education is regarded as the most important criterion of success and social status in Korea, most firms still tend to hire and promote employees according to educational background and achievement (see chapter 15).

Another form of management behaviour relates to mergers and acquisitions. The protracted negotiations with Western companies post-1997 we noted earlier display this. While there are historical, technical, structural and transparency reasons, culture also has a role. This is in terms of the process itself, with concepts such as 'face' and 'shame', along with xenophobia. For example, Koreans rarely see negotiations as 'win-win' propositions, but 'zero-sum' games, implying 'Any agreement means they have conceded too much' (*Economist*, 2002:61). Along with negotiators being criticised in the press for being 'easy' on foreigners, this produces '. . . paranoia and posturing by Korean negotiators' (ibid.:62), who to prove toughness frequently storm out of meetings. Due to corporate culture, such as hierarchical and top–down management, Koreans still seem to be reluctant to work directly with foreigners and find it hard to embrace different cultures and races, despite the fact that more companies need multicultural and cosmopolitan workforces.

The common concepts, meanings and resultant managerial behaviours and managerial characteristics, are outlined in Table 8.8.

Managerial values

Managerial behaviour is influenced by managerial values. Where do these values come from? As we have seen, these include history (i.e. Japan's role), the military and Confucianism. Thus, Korean organisations '. . . are like families as well as armies' (Cho and Yoon, 2002: 79). In particular, Confucianism's influence on values '. . . spilled over to the fundamental underpinnings of the Korean management system and human relationships within Korean companies' (Song, 1997:192).

A late 1980s survey of Korean large companies showed various common core values in their vision statements (Lee, 1997). These included, for nearly one-half, *inhwa*, solidarity, and cooperation (46.4 per cent); and devotion and hard work (44.2 per cent) – and, for just over two-fifths, creativity and development (41.2 per cent). Other common values were: honesty and credibility (28.8 per cent); quality, technology and productivity (16.9 per cent); responsibility (16.9 per cent); progressiveness or enterprising spirit (14.3 per cent); national wealth through business (14.3 per cent); rational and scientific approach (10.4 per cent); and sacrifice and service, etc. (6.9 per cent). However, since then companies have begun to further emphasise the issues of creativity, competitiveness, diversity, customer satisfaction, value-creation, and so on.

In-group harmony is one of the most important managerial values (Chung and Lee, 1989). Korean employees, therefore, tend to respect group opinion and sometimes are even willing to keep silent about their own opinions for group harmony. For the sake of this people sacrifice their own goals for collective ones. In return, companies take care of employees and management helps subordinates

Table 8.8 Cultural influences and paradoxes in Korea

Cultural Influences	Concepts	Meanings	Management Behaviours and Characteristics	Paradoxes
Confucianism	*Inhwa*	Harmony, solidarity	Company as family-type community	Owner-manager-worker distinctions
	Yongo	Connections: *Hyulyon*: by blood *Jiyon*: by geography *Hakyon*: by education	Recruitment via common ties, inner circle solidarity, kinship-based relations with owners	Bounded collectivism and exclusivism
	Chung	Loyalty, subordinate to superior	Paternalistic approach, taking care of employees/families	Hierarchical ranks, authoritarianism in leadership
Japan	*Un*	Indebtedness to organisation/members	Respect, tolerance, patience adhered to	Loyalty to individual not organisation
	Uiri	Integrity to others in everyday life	Long-term relationships	Personal entertainment, gift giving, transaction opaqueness
	Gocham	Senior in service, an 'old-timer'	Seniority-based rewards and promotions	Tension between seniority and ability
	Kibun	Good mood, satisfactory state of affairs	Maintain harmony, not hurting someone's *kibun*	Performance management tensions
Military	*Sinparam*	Exulted spirits	Management and making effort by sentiment-based motivation not rationality	Low commitment without *sinparam*
	Han	Resentment over inequitable treatment	Confrontational and militant labour relations	Passiveness, negativism and suppression
	Chujin	Propulsion, drive, get through	Can-do spirit, driving force, rapid goal accomplishment	Lack rational evaluations and omitting due processes
	Palli palli	Quickly, quickly	Speed of action	Quality, reflection
	Sajeonhyupui	Informal consensus formation prior to final decisions	Collaboration and participation of stakeholders in decision making	Team ethos impacts, slow decisions, impediment to empowerment

Source: Adapted from Song (1997); Morden and Bowles (1998); Rowley (2001).

save 'face' (Cho and Yoon, 2002). Another value is the hierarchical principle, which reinforces particularistic relationships among members (ibid.).

Contrasting company examples of management behaviour and values

Samsung and Hyundai contrast in management behaviour and values. This includes styles, decision-making processes, risk propensity and HRM. Traditionally, Samsung tried to minimise strategic risks, using well-established decision-making systems through utilising professional staff and pursuing standardisation and formalisation, emphasising rationality, analysis and cause-effect relationships. By contrast, Hyundai displayed high-risk propensity and emphasised intuition, totality and contexts and a lower utilisation level of professional staff in decision-making and less standardisation and formalisation. As a result, Hyundai was more tolerant towards cause-effect ambiguity and non-specificity of goals and minimised their efforts for the acquisition and analysis of information.

These behavioural differences can be related to their founders (Lee, 2002). Lee Byung-Chull of Samsung prioritised the pursuit of rationality, arguing that they should emphasise scientific judgements and logical reasoning. Lee was very analytical and cause-effect oriented, stressing philosophy and principles, prior research, thorough planning and well-established systems based on core ideologies. He was a 'risk averter', as mentioned, with a highly cautious approach.

Chung Ju Yung of Hyundai was very different in values and behaviours. Chung disliked sticking to theories, rationality, common sense, fixed stereotyped ideas and logical thinking and discouraged people from clinging to textbook approaches or theories taught in schools. He was a 'crisis generator', believing this helped learning and building up organisational capabilities (Kim, 1998). Chung was intuitive (Lee, 2002) and a 'risk taker' as 'adventures' would inject fresh vigour to inertial organisations.

Why do such firms differ? Carroll (1993) used several perspectives: individual (dispositional and situational), organisational (spin-offs and internal change) and environmental sources and organisational blueprints. Our example is related to individual sources. The founders' values and styles affected organisational characteristics by influencing organisational strategic choice (Hambrick and Mason, 1984) and structure (Miller and Dröge, 1986) and by mediating contextual variables to organisational behaviour (Child, 1972). Thus, founders' values and behaviours were embodied in organisational structure, culture, decision-making processes and systems. However, this organisational architecture is double-edged: well-aligned architecture is a source of competitive advantage; but it can slowly become organisational inertia which can hinder further development and growth.

Example of management behaviour change

Changes in management are contrasted in Table 8.9. A key area concerns employment, much propounded in the literature, regarding ending lifetime employment and seniority-based reward systems (Rowley and Bae, 2002). These are seen

Table 8.9 Key characteristics of traditional and newer management in Korea

Area	Traditional Characteristics	Newer Characteristics
Core Ideology	• Organisation first • Collective equality • Community oriented	• Individual respected • Individual equity • Market principle adopted
Human Resource Flow	• Mass recruitment • Job security (lifetime job) • Generalist oriented	• Recruitment on demand • Job mobility (lifetime career) • Development of professional
Work System	• Tall structure • Line and staff; function-based • Position-based	• Flat structure • Team systems • Qualification-based
Evaluation and Reward System	• Seniority (age and tenure) • Pay equality • For advancement in job grade/job • No feedback • Single-rater appraisal	• Ability, performance (annual) • Merit pay • For pay increases • Appraisal feedback • 360° appraisal
Employee Influence	• Less involvement • Less information sharing	• Involvement of workers • Information sharing

Source: Adapted from Bae and Rowley (2001).

as costly, 'inflexible', unfair and a drag on motivation and development (see chapter 13). There are concerns that junior, younger workers are paid lower and senior, older workers higher, than their 'real' contributions. These characteristics are seen to stifle recognition and reward of performance. By contrast, a flexible labour market model would generate employment and reward performance. Therefore, the frequently argued trajectory is towards greater flexibility and performance in labour markets and remuneration.

A range of anecdotal, quantitative and qualitative evidence indicates management changes here. First, Korean management is moving towards Western management in which personal relationships have less bearing on business operation. In terms of organisational structure and management, it changed from 'efficiency valued' to 'effectiveness valued' seeking horizontal network organisation (Park *et al.*, 2001).

That management behaviour changes were attempted and practised could give strong signals that others might follow this route. However, there were also counter examples of management behaviour continuity. As well as exact coverage in terms of breadth (between and within companies), we can also question the depth and acceptance of changes. The rhetoric may well be different from reality. Institutional theory (Meyer and Rowan, 1977) and isomorphism (DiMaggio and Powell, 1983) play a role (see Bae and Rowley, 2001). Then there are also particular cultural (obligations, loss of face) and institutional (unions, limited unemployment support) constraints (Rowley and Benson, 2002; Bae *et al.*, 2011).

Today, Korean employees have coexisting values from both Confucian and Western cultures (cf., chapter 16). For example, although many Korean workers still perceive a company as a 'second home', they can be unwilling to show strong loyalty or commitment to a company while attitudes and behaviour to improve an individual's value have increased (Park, 2001). Korean employees are not only content to comply with group opinion, but they also want to utter their own ideas more (Chung *et al.*, 1997). However, a recent study showed that Korean workers still have a highly collaborative team spirit (Kwon, 2006).

Labour-management/conflict resolution

Labour-management has occurred in a variety of macro contexts, from authoritarian and military governments to corporatism. Also, labour has played roles at critical points in history, struggling against occupation and for democratisation. In terms of one dimension of conflict, official labour disputes, the frequency has varied, from just 4 in 1970 to 322 in 1990, with peaks of 3,749 in 1987 and 1,873 in 1988. Most of the strikes were fought over wage demands and the freedom to establish the union of a worker's choice. Partly in response to the Asian Crisis, strikes increased by 65 per cent, from 78 (44,000 workers) to 129 (146,000 workers) between 1997 and 1998. Since then, labour disputes increased to 322 by 2002 (Park, 2007). Further figures are given in Table 8.10.

Trade union developments

From the early twentieth century, poor wages and conditions and anti-Japanese sentiments contributed to union formation (Kwon and O'Donnell, 2001). From the 1920s unions grew, reaching 488 and 67,220 members in 1928. Decline as a result of repression for Japanese war production and internal splits followed. Union numbers fell to 207 and 28,211 members by 1935 (ibid.).

The post-war radical union movement, the Chun Pyung, was declared illegal by the US military government, which restricted activities to encourage 'business unions'. The subsequent strikes and the General Strike resulted in 25 deaths, 11,000 imprisonments and 25,000 dismissals. A more conservative, government-sponsored industry-based movement was decreed, signalling labour's incorporation by the state, conflict repression and an '. . . authoritarian corporatist approach . . .' (ibid.:29). Thus, the government officially recognised the Federation of Korean Trade Unions and became increasingly interventionist, enacting a plethora of laws regulating hours, holidays, pay, union forms, the Labour Management Council (LMC) system, more 'cooperative' forms of trade unionism, even prohibiting conflicts in foreign businesses (ibid.).

The diversity of labour-management approaches was partly influenced by *chaebol* growth strategies (Kwon and O'Donnell, 2001). For instance, growth and focus on minimising labour costs resulted in the expansion and concentration of workforces in large scale industrial estates with authoritarian and militaristic controls. Labour resistance was generated, the catalyst for conflict and the re-emergence of independent unions from the 1970s. Employers responded by disrupting union activities, sponsoring company unions and replacing labour-intensive processes by automating, subcontracting or transplanting overseas (see chapter 15). From the late 1980s, companies also softened strict supervision and work intensification by widening access to paternalistic labour-management practices and welfare schemes, subsidised school fees and housing benefits (ibid.). The government declared that labour conflicts should be resolved by employers and employees themselves. Trade union density grew from 12.6 per cent in 1970, peaking at 18.6 per cent in 1989 with nearly 2 million members (Park, 2001).

One study showed that non-unionised firms with fewer labour disputes were more likely to adopt labour-management approaches involving higher wages, better working conditions and other personnel management practices, whereas unionised companies with repeated labour disputes lacked these (Chung and Lie, 1989). Samsung was famous for its 'no union at any cost' policy and adopted specific labour-management programmes, such as a rigorous selection process, employee training and development and so on (Chung *et al.*, 1997). However, there is a causality question here, i.e. is it a threat of unionisation that encourages firms to act that way?

During the 1990s, independent trade unions established their own national organisation, with federations of *chaebol*-based and regional associations. In 1995, an alternative national federation, the Korean Confederation of Trade Unions (*minjunochong*), emerged. It organised the 1996 General Strike (Bae *et al.*, 1997), enhancing its legitimacy. However, the economic whirlwind of the Asian Crisis then hit. Trade union density fell back to 11.5 per cent by 1998 and union membership decreased to 1.6 million by 1996 (Park *et al.*, 2001).

After the Asian Crisis, the government strove to resolve labour problems caused by economic restructuring with a more passive policy-making approach. However, as irregular employment and income instability increased considerably, the labour market faced the most serious problems, which resulted in strike activities at the Korea Minting and Security Printing Corporation, Daewoo and the Artificial Textile Industry (Choi, 2002), amongst others in 1999. Labour-management does not seem to have changed substantially, despite restructuring. Post-1997 trade union membership and density are given in Table 8.10.

Obviously, labour strength and influence also depends on context, such as the locations, legal constraints and opportunities operating and the nature and character of the disputes themselves. In Korea, unions are strategically well located in ship and automobile manufacture as well as power, transportation and telecommunications. As we have seen above, conflicts can be high profile, large scale and confrontational. This characteristic has remained.

This current position is the context for ideas of increased employee involvement, participation and partnership, which have emerged at dual levels. Examples at the macro level include the neo-corporatist type Presidential Commission on Industrial Relations Reform (1996) and the tripartite Labour-Management-Government Committees (*nosajung wiwonhoe*) on Industrial Relations (1998) (Yang and Lim, 2000). At the micro level is the example of LG which looked at practices in plants in the US (Saturn, Motorola) and Japan.

To improve labour-management, trade unions now play two roles: as a management partner and as a negotiator for distribution by moving towards an

Table 8.10 Trends in trade union density (%), membership ('000s) and disputes post-1997

	Year													
	1997	1998	1999	2000	2001	2002	2003	2004	2005	2006	2007	2008	2009	2010
Trade union density	12.2	12.6	11.9	12	12	11.6	11	10.6	10.3	10.3	10.8	10.5	10.1	9.8
Trade union membership	5,733	5,560	5,637	5,698	6,150	6,506	6,257	6,017	5,971	5,889	5,099	4,886	4,689	4,420
Number of members	1,484	1,402	1,481	1,527	1,569	1,606	1,550	1,537	1,506	1,559	1,688	1,666	1,640	1,643
Labour dispute/strike	78	129	198	250	235	322	320	462	287	138	115	108	121	86
Working days lost	445	1,452	1,366	1,894	1,083	1,580	1,299	1,199	848	1,201	536	809	627	511

Source: Ministry of Employment and Labour (http://www.moel.go.kr).

industry-based system (Choi, 2002). The LMCs are becoming more systemised in order to share information about industry trends, helping to support a variety of job stability and training programmes with the public and private sectors. Over time the demand for more public feedback and social consensus has steadily increased.

In sum, the institutions, framework and policies of labour-management all shifted under pressures from political liberalisation and civilian government, ILO (1991) and OECD (1996) membership, trade union pressure and the 1997 Asian and post-2008 global financial crisis. Nevertheless, the frames of reference and perspectives for management remain strongly unitary. By contrast, this is less so for labour, with stronger pluralist, and even radical, perspectives evident. This dichotomy continues (see chapter 13).

Implications for managers

The implications for managers from culture can be seen in terms of not just indigenous, but also other Asian and Western, managers. First, there is the need to recognise paradoxes between concepts and management behaviour and managerial characteristics, noted earlier.

Second, there are variegated implications dependent on management level. Ghoshal and Bartlett (1997) suggested variations in changing management roles and tasks, as follows:

1   Operating level managers from 'Operational Implementers' to 'Aggressive Entrepreneurs'.
2   Senior level managers from 'Administrative Controllers' to 'Supportive Coaches'.
3   Top level managers from 'Resource Allocators' to 'Institutional Leaders'. These models can be applied to some Korean corporations. One issue is that traditional culture facilitated top-down, paternalistic and authoritarian styles of leadership. Yet, given uncertain global environments and more knowledge-based companies, some transition is necessary. This cultural conflict is another task to be resolved.

Third, the influence of the internationalisation of Korean companies and the influx of foreign capital produces tension between managers, in particular those with experience of the West. For example, there may be increased expectations and requirements in corporate governance (such as for transparency) and HRM (such as more rigorous and open recruitment and selection). Also, in terms of the lengthy, strained negotiations with Western companies, management on both sides need to recognise the reasons, which are not just process- or tactical-based, but have cultural dimensions.

Fourth, there is a need for greater understanding of any applicability of Western management concepts. Shifts from more traditional organisational systems, with strong internal labour markets, towards external labour markets, are not 'cost free'. There is the problem of trying to maintain commitment, loyalty and team work with easier dismissals and a focus on individual, sometimes short-term, performance. This issue may partly be due to the traditional dominance of the US in business and educational spheres (and a lack of questioning of Western views). For instance, perceived 'inflexibilities', such as seniority and long-term employment, can generate benefits (even flexibilities) such as willingness to change and stimulation of innovation and long-term development. In contrast, some 'flexibilities' produce problems (even inflexibilities), as when companies look to address problems in a short-term fashion by cutting labour and training at the cost of alternatives and long-term and dynamic growth. If options to follow this latter route are more narrowed, management would be encouraged to consider alternative avenues to pursue. There is also a practical implication in terms of 'first movers' and a critical mass. Who will be first to try such numerically flexible external labour markets and forgo the security and certainties of the internal labour market? What happens if this does not suit or the company fails? There is no going back for employees as previous recruitment was based on limited points of entry and careers and pay on seniority. They must seek more of the same insecure employment.

There are also many problems in 'measuring' performance. These concern performance appraisals in general, when linked to rewards and in Asian contexts. For instance, well known human traits lead towards subjectivity in appraisals. Furthermore, it is common to recommend that appraisals should not be linked with remuneration. Finally, there are cultural biases. For example, *inhwa* and requirements to 'care' for subordinates, encourages tolerance and appreciation of efforts and not being excessively harsh in assessing sincere efforts (Chen, 2000).

Fifth, there is the problem of demographics with an ageing population and declining indigenous workforce. Yet, the traditionally homogeneous and inclusive society makes changes and responses in terms of a multicultural workforce somewhat problematic. The areas of managing diversity (Wei and Rowley, 2011) and the requisite training for it have key roles in this.

Sixth, there is an implication for management in terms of a greater need to recognise varied management perspectives. There are not only unitary perspectives and approaches, but also pluralist ones. In such approaches disagreements and conflicts are not seen as aberrations, but normal, and even useful. Alternative mechanisms for dealing with labour-management can then be explored. There would then be less highly confrontational and entrenched approaches, with greater use of processes such as collective bargaining, negotiation and even conciliation, mediation and arbitration (Rowley, 2011), despite the cultural problems mentioned above.

Conclusion

This overview of the key broad dimensions and developments of management and culture in Korea shows that context is important, despite the rhetoric of 'globalisation' (cf. chapter 16). While institutional perspectives remain important, culture also retains its salience for management and for understanding its behaviour and practices.

The roller-coaster of Korea's development indicates the need for the careful analysis of the roles of management and culture, as they have been both canonised and then vilified. Both of these labels may be too deterministic, stark and naïve. However, what usefully emerges from this is a greater balance as to the roles of management and culture in economies, which ultimately rest on an amalgam of foundations. Also, there may be less hagiography of management and the naïve search for some magic 'one best way' elixir to manage, which, as we should not forget, remains complex and often specific as the power of particular management and culture is pertinent and persists.

Note

1   Acknowledgement: thanks to Hyun Young Jo for kindly checking and updating parts of this and also the tables.

References

Bae, J. and Rowley, C. (2001) 'The Impact of Globalization on HRM: The Case of South Korea', *Journal of World Business*, 36: 402–28.

Bae, J. and Sa, J. (2003) 'The Effects of Human Resource Management Systems on Organisational Performance', *Korean Journal of Management*, 11: 133–69.

Bae, J., Chen, S. J. and Rowley, C. (2011) 'From a Paternalistic Model towards What? HRM Trends in Korean and Taiwan', *Personnel Review*, 40: 700–23.

Bae, J., Rowley, C., Kim, D. H. and Lawler, J. (1997) 'Korean Industrial Relations at the Crossroads: The Recent Labour Troubles', *Asia Pacific Business Review*, 3: 148–60.

Cameron, K. S. (1978) 'Measuring Organizational Effectiveness in Institutions of Higher Education', *Administrative Science Quarterly*, 23: 604–32.

Carroll, H. L (1993) 'A Sociological View on Why Firms Differ', *Strategic Management Journal*, 14: 237–49.

Chang, J. H. (2010) 'Samsung Founding Chairman Lee Byung-Chull's place in Korean Business Management', *SERI Quarterly*, 3: 58–69.

Chen, M. (2000) 'Management in South Korea' in Warner, M. (ed.) *Management in Asia Pacific*. London: Thomson, pp. 300–11.

Child, J. (1972) 'Organizational Structure, Environment and Performance: The Role of Strategic Choice', *Sociology*, 6: 1–22.

Cho, U. (2005) 'The Encroachment of Globalization into Intimate Life: The Flexible Korean Family in "Economic Crisis" ', *Korea Journal*, 45: 8–35.

Cho, Y. H. and Yoon, J. (2002) 'The Origin and Function of Dynamic Collectivism: An Analysis of Korean Corporate Culture' in Rowley, C., Sohn, T. W. and Bae, J. (eds) *Managing Korean Businesses: Organization, Culture, Human Resources and Change*. London: Cass, pp. 70–88.

Cho, Y-H., Kim, K-Y. and Kim, T-J. (2007) 'Ten Years' Cultural Change of Korean Conglomerates: Social Change Effect and Cultural Stability', Proceedings of Ninth Academic Conference of Korean Management Related Society.

Choi, Y. K. (2002) 'Labor Reforms during Restructuring', *Korea Journal*, 42: 100–28.

Chung, K. H. and Lee, H. C. (1989) 'National Differences in Managerial Practices' in Chung, K. H. and Lee, H. C. (eds) *Korean Managerial Dynamics*. New York: Praeger, pp. 163–88.

Chung, K. H. and Lie, H. K. (1989) 'Labor Management Relations in Korea' in Chung, K. H. and Lee, H. C. (eds), *Korean Managerial Dynamics*. Praeger: New York, pp. 217–31.

Chung, Kae H., Lee, Hak Chong and Jung, Ku Hyun (1997) *Korean Management: Global Strategy and Cultural Transformation*. Berlin: Walter de Gruyter.

Collins, N., Zhu, Y. and Warner, M. (2012) 'HRM and Asian socialist economies in transition: China, Vietnam and North Korea' in Brewster, C. J. and Mayrhofer, W. (eds) *Handbook of Research on Comparative Human Resource Management*. Oxford: Edward Elgar.

DiMaggio, P. and Powell, W. (1983) 'The Iron Cage Revisited: Institutional Isomorphism and Collective Rationality in the Organizational Field', *American Sociological Review*, 4: 147–60.

Economist, The (2002) 'Dead Deals Walking', 9 February, pp. 61–2.

Eun, K. S. (2008) 'Population Aging and Social Strategies for Aging Problems in Korea', *Korea Journal*, 49 (3) Autumn: 73–92.

Ghoshal, S. and Bartlett, C. A. (1997) *The Individualized Corporation: A Fundamentally New Approach to Management*. NY: HarperCollins.

Hambrick, D. C. and Mason, P. A. (1984) 'Upper Echelons: The Organization as a Reflection of Its Top Managers', *Academy of Management Review*, 9: 193–206.

Han, W. S. (1978) 'Korean Society: population and development', *Korea Journal*, 18: 22–9.

Heo, Uk and Roehrig, Terence (2010) *South Korea since 1980*. Cambridge: Cambridge University Press, 2010.

Hofstede, G. (2001) *Culture's Consequences: Comparing Values, Behaviours, Institutions and Organizations Across Nations*. Thousand Oaks, CA: Sage (first published, 1980).

Hyundai (2011) 'Hyundai Motor Group completes acquisition of Hyundai E&C', company overview. Available at http://worldwide.hyundai.com/ (accessed 6 Nov 2011).

KDI (2010) *Direction for Development of Korea Economy: Strengthening Security of Economy System*. 1st ed. Korea Development Institute: Seoul.

Kim, D-S. (2006) 'A Conceptual Scheme of International Marriage of Koreans and Analyses of the Marriage and Divorce Registration Data', *Korean Demography*, 29: 25–56.

Kim, J. and Rowley, C. (2001) 'Managerial Problems in Korea: Evidence from the Nationalized Industries', *International Journal of Public Sector Management*, 14: 129–48.

Kim, K. D. (1994) 'Confucianism and Capitalist Development in East Asia' in Sklair, L. (ed.) *Capitalism and Development*. London: Routledge, pp. 87–106.

Kim, L. (1998) 'Crisis Construction and Organizational Learning: Capability Building in Catching-up at Hyundai Motor', *Organization Science*, 9: 506–21.

Kim, S. and Briscoe, D. (1997) 'Globalization and a New Human Resource Policy in Korea: Transformation to a Performance-Based HRM', *Employee Relations*, 19: 298–308.

Kim, Y. (2000) 'Employment Relations at a Large South Korean Firm: The LG Group' in Bamber, G., Park, F., Lee, C., Ross, P. and Broadbent, K. (eds) *Employment Relations in the Asia-Pacific*. London: Thomson, pp. 175–93.

Kwon, O. Y. (2006) 'Recent Changes in Korea's Business Environment: Views of Foreign Business People in Korea', *Asia Pacific Business Review*, 12: 77–94.

Kwon, Seung-Ho and O'Donnell, M. (2001) *The Chaebol and Labour in Korea: The Development of Management Strategy in Hyundai*. London: Routledge.

Lee, D. Y. (2004) 'Consuming Spaces in the Global Era: Distinctions between consumer spaces in Seoul', *Korea Journal*, 44: 108–37.

Lee, Hak Chong (1997) *Cultural Characteristics of Korean Firms and New Culture Development*. Seoul: Bakyungsa (in Korean).

Lee, Hong (2002) 'The Relationship between Features of Business Groups and Founders' Characteristics: Evidence from the Comparison of Samsung and Hyundai Group', *Korean Journal of Management*, 10: 55–94 (in Korean).

Lee, J. Y. (2011) 'Korea considers new immigration office', *The Korea Herald*, 10 July.

LG (2008) 'LG Electronics USA opens training academy in Georgia'. Available at http://www.lg.com (accessed 15 Nov 2011).

Lim, H. S. (2007) 'A Religious Analysis of Education Fever in Modern Korea', *Korea Journal*, 42: 71–98.

Meyer, J. and Rowan, B. (1977) 'Institutionalized Organizations: Formal Structure as Myth and Ceremony', *American Journal of Sociology*, 83: 340–63.

Miller, D. and Dröge, C. (1986) 'Psychological and Traditional Determinants of Structure', *Administrative Science Quarterly*, 31: 539–60.

Morden, T. and Bowles, D. (1998) 'Management in South Korea: A Review', *Management Decision*, 36: 316–330.

OECD (2009) 'OECD Reviews of Innovation Policy: Korea'. Paris: OECD. Available at: http://www.oecd-library.org (accessed 15 Nov 2011).

Oh, I. and Park, H. J. (2002) 'Shooting at a Moving Target: Four Theoretical Problems in Exploring the Dynamics of the *Chaebol*' in Rowley, C., Sohn, T. W. and Bae, J. (eds) *Managing Korean Businesses: Organization, Culture, Human Resources and Change*. London: Cass, pp. 44–69.

Oliver, C. (2010) 'Creditors to Sell $2.6bn Stake in Hyundai E&C', *Financial Times*, 24 September, p. 23.

Oliver, C. and Song, J. A. (2011) 'Evolution is Crucial to Chaebol Survival', *Financial Times*, 3 June, p. 22.

Park, K. S. (2007) 'Industrial relations and economic growth in Korea', *Pacific Economic Review*, 12: 711–23.

Park, W. W. (2001) 'The Corporate Culture Change Campaigns in Korea: Lessons from their failures', *Asia Pacific Business Review*, 7: 89–110.

— (2002) 'Corporate Culture Change Campaigns in Korea: Lessons from their Failure' in Rowley, C., Sohn, T. W. and Bae, J. (eds) *Managing Korean Businesses: Organization, Culture, Human Resources and Change*. London: Cass, pp. 89–110.

Park, W. W., Budhwar, P. S. and Debrah, Y. A. (2001) 'Human Resource Management in South Korea', in Budhwar, P. S. and Debrah, Y. A. (eds) *Human Resource Management in Developing Countries*. London and New York: Routledge, pp. 34–55.

Pucik, V. and Lim, J. C. (2002) 'Transforming HRM in a Korean *Chaebol*: A Case Study of Samsung', in Rowley, C., Sohn, T. W. and Bae, J. (eds) *Managing Korean Businesses: Organization, Culture, Human Resources and Change*. London: Cass, pp. 137–60.

Quinn, R. E. (1988) *Beyond Rational Management*. San Francisco, CA: Jossey-Bass.

Rousseau, D. M. (2001) 'Schema, Promise and Mutuality: The Building Blocks of the Psychological Contract', *Journal of Occupational and Organizational Psychology*, 74: 511–41.

Rowley, C. (2011) 'Dispute Settlement' in Rowley, C. and Jackson, K. (eds) *HRM: The Key Concepts*. Routledge, pp. 55–9.

Rowley, C. and Bae, J. (1998a) 'The Icarus Paradox in Korean Business and Management', *Asia Pacific Business Review*, 4: 1–17.

— (1998b) 'Korean Business and Management: The End Of The Model', *Asia Pacific Business Review*, 4: 130–9.

— (eds) (1998c) *Korean Businesses: Internal and External Industrialization*. London: Cass.

— (2002) 'Globalization and Transformation of HRM in South Korea', *International Journal of Human Resource Management*, 13: 522–49.

Rowley, C. and Benson, J. (2002) 'Convergence and Divergence in Asian HRM', *California Management Review*, 44: 90–109.

Rowley, C., Sohn, T. W. and Bae, J. (eds) (2002) *Managing Korean Businesses: Organization, Culture, Human Resources and Change*. London: Cass.

Samsung (2010) 'Sustainability Performance & Plan'. US: Samsung. Available at http://www.samsung.com (accessed 15 Nov 2011).

Shin, Y. G. (1991) *Mind Setting of Employees in Korean Companies*. Korean Chamber of Commerce: Seoul.

Song, Byung-Nak (1997) *The Rise of the Korea Economy*. Oxford: Oxford University Press.

Ward, A. (2002a) 'Seoul Music Strives for a Global Audience', *Financial Times*, 8 February, p. 12.

— (2002b) 'The Glory Days of Hyundai Sit Firmly in the Past', *Financial Times*, 29 February, p. 26.

Wei, Q. and Rowley, C. (2011) 'Diversity Management' in Rowley, C. and Jackson, K. (eds) *HRM: The Key Concepts*. Abingdon: Routledge, pp. 59–64.

Whitley, R. (1991) 'The Social Construction of Business Systems in East Asia', *Organization Studies*, 12: 1–28.

Yang, S. and Lim, S. (2000) 'The Role of Government in Industrial Relations in South Korea: The Case of the Tripartite (Labour-Management-Government) Committee' in Wilkinson, R., Maltby, J. and Lee, J. (eds) *Responding to Change: Some Key Lessons for the Future of Korea*. Sheffield: University of Sheffield Management School, pp. 113–23.

Yoo, S-G. (2010) 'The Actual Condition Analysis on the Determining Factors of Foreign Workers' Employment in Korean Companies', *International Commerce and Information Review*, 12: 213–34.

Part IV
Issues and challenges in East Asian management

Riches and honours are what [people] desire. If [they] cannot be obtained in a proper way, they should not be held.

(Confucius: Analects, IV, v.)

9 Gender and management in East Asia[1]

Fang Lee Cooke

Introduction

The advancement of women in leadership positions in politics and corporations is essential to achieve gender equality (Schein, 2007). However, according to Schein (2007), 30 years after her revelation of the 'think manager – think male' attitude in the United States, gender stereotypes in management roles continue to exist worldwide, despite some progress. This chapter examines opportunities and obstacles faced by women in three major East Asian countries – the People's Republic of China (hereafter China), Japan and the Republic of Korea (hereafter Korea) – in developing their managerial careers. These three countries were chosen in part because of their geographical and cultural proximities, their relatively similar economic growth stages and the profound historical influence they have exerted on each other in spite of significant differences in their contemporary political systems.

Japan and Korea are developed countries whereas China is an emerging economy with rising economic power globally. Japan and Korea are small countries in terms of geographical and population size and have different industrial structures compared with China. China (see chapter 5) is a socialist country that has been under the control of the Communist Party since 1949. It began its economic transformation in the late 1970s. Japan (see chapter 7) is a modernising imperial country with Western influences, whereas the modern Republic of Korea, established in 1948 (see chapter 8) has been under the control of authoritarian governments with emerging democracy since the 1980s, largely as a result of mass public demonstrations. Japan and Korea were two major driving forces of the Asian economy in the 1970s and 1980s, but were both heavily hit by the Asia financial crisis in 1997 and the global financial crisis in 2008 (e.g. Lee and Lee, 2003; Magoshi and Chang, 2009). Meanwhile, China has emerged as a major power house in the development of the Asian economy since the 1990s (Khanna, 2007). The governments of China, Japan and Korea have all pursued export-oriented economic growth (see chapters 5, 7 and 8). These developments have been accompanied by a substantial fertility decline since the 1980s in all three countries. While the low birth rate in China is a result of the government's 'one child' policy enacted in the 1980s, the low birth rate in

Japan and Korea is largely an outcome of women's choice (the Korean government is providing incentives to encourage women to have more children). Declining fertility is affecting the labour market structure and women's role in it, particularly in Japan and Korea, and the globalising economy of the three countries adds further dynamics to women's choices and constraints on their career and family domains.

Women's education profile and impact on employment

According to the human capital theory (e.g. Becker, 1964), education level is an important determinant of a person's employability and earning power. Lower educational attainment has often been cited as one of the reasons for women's disadvantage in the labour market. In all three countries, women's education levels are relatively high. As we can see in Table 9.1, at the primary and secondary school level females' education level is very close to that of males. At the tertiary level, women's participation levels in Japan and Korea have been high in the last two decades and are getting close to those of men. In China, while a lower proportion of men and women have received tertiary education compared with those in Japan and Korea, the proportion of Chinese women enrolling in tertiary education is now higher than that of their male counterparts.

However, the improved educational attainment of women is not necessarily translated into economic empowerment through their increased participation in the industrial labour force (Brinton *et al.*, 1995; Lantican *et al.*, 1996). This is particularly the case in Japan and Korea. It has been noted that the continuous growth in higher education among women in Japan has not led to 'improvements in women's wages or the greater participation of educated women' (Shimada and Higuchi, 1985: S372; also see Nakata and Takehiro, 2002). This observation reflects to some extent 'the unique features of the Japanese society, such as strong family cohesiveness and integrity, limited promotion opportunities for female workers in employment systems' (Shimada and Higuchi, 1985: S372). In addition, there is a sharp gender divide in the type of higher education pursued by men and women. Men tend to study engineering and science subjects, whereas women tend to diversify into humanities, arts, home economics and social sciences subjects that lead to jobs that are less well-paid (Nakata and Takehiro, 2002). In the next section, we examine women's employment patterns in all three countries in more detail.

Women's employment patterns

China, Japan and Korea have witnessed an increasing or steady proportion of women in employment since the 1980s, with women making up 40–45 per cent of the total workforce (see Table 9.1). Women are also making inroads into public services and management posts and positions in political leadership (see Table 9.1). However, women are still under-represented in managerial and professional positions and are over-represented in firms of certain ownership forms (e.g. the private sector in China) and in irregular employment (Japan and Korea) marked by lower levels of job security and terms and conditions.

China has an above world-average record of women's labour force participation. The vast majority of them are in full-time employment as part-time work is uncommon and those who work part-time often need to do more than one job to make up a living wage (Cooke, 2005). Compared with Japan and Korea, gender segregation is perhaps the least pronounced in China. While women tend to be over-represented in certain industrial sectors such as education, health care and services, they are present in all sectors and occupations in a relatively even pattern (Cooke, 2005). However, Chinese women tend to be under-represented in certain industrial sectors and organisations; for example, mining and construction; due to the physically demanding nature of the jobs, and in government organisations, where power and control continue to be dominated by men (Cooke, 2010). China has a relatively stronger internal labour market than Japan and Korea in that the majority of women have continuous employment with limited career breaks (see chapter 13). In spite of declining job security, those in professional and managerial positions tend to have enhanced job security due to skill shortages in the labour market.

Compared with China, Japan's integration of women into the workforce has been more moderate, although the increasing labour shortage of the country due to declining fertility has provided opportunities for mothers to re-enter the labour market for their 'second career' (Worthley *et al.*, 2009). In general, women's employment in Japan takes an M shape by age and marital status (Houseman and Osawa ,1998; Gelb, 2000). It has a high employment participation rate from young women until they get married and pregnant. Women who have access to family support for child care are more likely to have full-time jobs than those without support. Similarly, those who have elderly care commitment are less likely to work full-time or work at all (Ogawa and Ermisch, 1996). Married women who return to the labour force after an employment break usually find themselves in lower-status positions than they had prior to their break (Steinhoff and Tanaka, 1993). They are generally classified as part-time workers, not because of the slightly reduced number of hours they work compared with full-time workers but because of the absence of job security, career progression opportunities and other benefits that are enjoyed by their full-time counterparts (Steinhoff and Tanaka, 1993; Wakisaka and Bae, 1998). Japanese employers have strong incentives to employ part-time female employees because they 'received only 60 to 70 per cent of a regular female employee's wages, as well as fewer benefits' (Kucera, 1998: 27). The *Nenko* system that rewards employees based on the long service and hard work principle further assumes that this principle only applies to regular male workers but not women even if they are in regular status jobs (Nakata and Takehiro 2002; Yuasa, 2005). Another factor is the weaker bargaining power of women workers in the labour market. In Japan, a widening gender wage gap was observed. A major reason for this is 'the system of seniority-based earnings and promotion, from which part-time, temporary, and non-union employees are typically excluded' (Kucera, 1998: 28).

Table 9.1 A summary of gender profile of China, Japan and Republic of Korea

Items	China				Japan				Republic of Korea			
	1980	1990	2000	2009	1980	1990	2000	2009	1980	1990	2000	2009
GNI per capita (US$)	220	320	930	4260*	10,430	26,960	35,140	42,130	1,810	6,000	9,800	19,890*
Population												
Total (millions)	981.2	1,135.2	1,262.6	1,338.30*	116.8	123.5	126.9	127.45	38.1	42.9	47.0	48.88*
Female (% of total)	48.5	48.4	48.6	48.1*	50.8	50.9	51.1	51.3	49.5	49.7	49.7	50.2*
Participation in education												
Female pupils (% of total)												
Primary	—	—	48	46	—	—	49	49	—	—	47	48
Secondary	—	—	47	48	—	—	49	49	—	—	48	47
Gross enrolment rate in tertiary (% of age group)												
Male	—	4	—	23.8	—	36	51	62	—	51	92	116.9
Female	—	2	—	25.4	—	23	44	55	—	25	53	81.5
Labour force participation												
Total labour force (millions)	503	650	739	786	56	64	68	66	15	19	23	25
Labour force female (% of total labour force)	43	45	45	45	39	41	41	42	37	39	40	42
Unemployment												
Total (% of total labour force)	4.9	2.5	3.1	4.30	2.0	2.1	4.8	5.0	5.2	2.5	4.1	3.6
Female (% of female labour force)	—	—	—	—	2.0	2.2	4.5	4.7	3.5	1.8	3.3	3.0

Employment												
Share of women in total employment		43	44	44	45	41	41	42	37	39	40	42
Share of women in agricultural employment		—	49	—	—	13	9	6	4.2#	39	20	12	7.9*
Share of women in wage employment in the non-agricultural sector		—	38	39	—	—	38	40	41.8#	—	38	40	42.1*
Participation in the labour force (access to economic and productive resources dimension)												
Ratio of female to male labour force participation	81.2	86	84.8	84.5	59.6	64.7	64.5	66.8	57.1	64.2	66.6	69.6
Gender equality in political participation (status and protection under the law dimension)												
% of parliamentary seats occupied by women		—	21	22	21.3*	—	1	5	11.3*	—	2	4	14.7*
% of women in ministerial positions		—	—	—	21	—	—	0	13	—	—	—	6

Sources: Compiled from The World Bank Group (2011); United Nations Development Programme (2011); *figures in 2010; #figures in 2008.

In Korea, women's economic status in the labour market has been significantly improved throughout Korea's economic development process since the early 1960s (Jung and Choi, 2004). Since the 1980s, the Korean tertiary sector has been absorbing large numbers of women workers as the sector expanded significantly (Yoon, 2003). However, like their counterparts in Japan, a large proportion of Korean (married) women have inferior employment status mainly because of their marital status (Kang and Rowley, 2005). Van der Meulen Rodgers' study (1998) revealed that despite rapid economic growth, Korea's gender pay gaps for all education groups had actually widened during the 1970s and early 1980s. This fact indicates that gender discrimination might have increased in Korea. In fact, Jung and Choi's (2004: 577) analysis of the 1997 and 2001 earnings data for full-time, year-round workers employed in manufacturing and service industries in Korea 'confirms the existence of substantial gender wage discrimination, especially in non-knowledge-intensive industries and occupations'. It was not until the late 1980s that the Korean government issued regulations that were aimed to eliminate gender discrimination in employment, although the effectiveness of these regulations remains questionable (Monk-Turner and Turner, 2001).

In addition to societal cultural norms and ineffective legislative intervention (see discussion in the next section), a major reason for the gender inequality displayed in the labour market across all three countries has been the ineffectiveness of the trade unions in representing women workers (e.g. Broadbent, 2008; Cooke, 2008; Hill, 2008; Moon and Broadbent, 2008). In China, trade unions play a largely welfare role with limited capacity and capability in defending workers' rights, in spite of their statutory role to do so. In Japan and Korea, trade unions tend to be more interested in representing male workers (and those) in mainstream employment. In Japan, 'it was mostly married women who drove women's progress in the workplace' during the 1960s and 1970s (Nakata and Takehiro, 2002: 521). In Korea, female factory workers have been 'at the forefront of industrial labour activism', particularly from the mid-1970s to mid-1980s, 'against exploitative working conditions' (Yoon, 2003: 123). However, these achievements have not automatically led to their enhanced political position.

Women in management and entrepreneurship: progress and barriers

Opportunities for and barriers to women's career advancement in China, Japan and Korea are shaped by a broad range of societal, political and organisational factors, and their personal choices reflect these options and constraints. In this section, we examine what progress has been made and what barriers remain in women's managerial career advancement in these three countries.

Women's share in leadership, managerial and entrepreneurship positions

In spite of the relatively large share of women in employment, women in management positions in China, Japan and Korea remain a minority, as is the case in most countries in the world. As indicated in Table 9.1, women make up a very small proportion of those in political leadership positions and progress appears to be negligible. According to the International Labour Organization (ILO) (2003), women's share as administrative and managerial workers in Japan was only 8.9 per cent in the period 2000–2002. This was marginally higher than that in Pakistan (8.7 per cent) and Bangladesh (8.5 per cent), but significantly lower than that in the United States (46 per cent), Thailand (27 per cent) and Malaysia (20 per cent).

In Korea, women's share as legislators, senior officials and managers was about 5 per cent in the period 2000–2002. Korea ranked 48th amongst the Major Group 1 countries, trailing behind Cyprus (16 per cent) and Egypt (11 per cent) (ILO 2003). According to the United Nations Development Programme's Gender Empowerment Measure in 2004, Korea ranked 68th out of the 78 countries categorised (Kim, 2005). The picture in the private sector is even grimmer with few of the top Korean firms having women in their senior executive team (Kim, 2005). As Cho and Kwon (2010) reported, with the exception of the catering and hotel industry, over half of the Korean industries do not have any female managers.

Female entrepreneurship provides an important source, albeit still relatively small in many nations, of economic growth through the generation of employment, business activities and revenue (e.g. Fielden and Davidson, 2005; Lee *et al.*, 2009; Davidson and Burke, 2011). In all three countries, a discernible trend of growth in female entrepreneurship has emerged (e.g. Tan, 2008; Griffy-Brown, 2011; Lee *et al.*, 2011).

In Japan, female entrepreneurship has been growing since the 1990s, aided by government legislative changes in financing businesses (Futagami and Helms, 2009), the women consumers' movement and the digital economy (Griffy-Brown, 2011). It also emerged as a result of the desire of women to combine their motherhood with work and offer other working mothers a better work-life balance (e.g. Leung, 2011). According to Griffy-Brown (2011), normative institutional changes have been taking place in Japan in recent years, including attitudes to women's role in society and attitudes towards marriage, delayed parenthood, non-marital birth and divorce. International education and exposure serves as a further catalyst for women to consider embracing an entrepreneurial career. The emergence of women entrepreneurship is a new addition to the Japanese business landscape that has been dominated by well-established large firms whose high quality, efficiency and innovativeness were the driving force for the country's economic growth (Griffy-Brown, 2011). However, Japanese women entrepreneurs have demonstrated a high level of prudence in the speed and scale in which they wish to grow their firms in order to accommodate their family commitment.

In China, a nationwide survey in 2004 revealed that firms owned by women entrepreneurs are significantly smaller in size, revenue and profit. In addition, Chinese women entrepreneurs tend to have a smaller family size and work longer hours than their male counterparts (Yu 2011). Interestingly, Tan's (2008) study found that women entrepreneurs in the Chinese electronics industry are highly growth-oriented, and they pursue bolder and more risky strategic moves than their male counterparts. In Korea, over a third of enterprise owners are women and the trend is continuing to rise (Lee *et al.*, 2011). However, despite the growing number of women entrepreneurs and increased government support, over 93 per cent of the businesses owned by women entrepreneurs are micro businesses employing fewer than five people. They operate primarily in the service industry and retail trades. In 2004, women entrepreneurs' exports accounted for less than 1 per cent of the total export value of Korea (Lee *et al.*, 2011).

Barriers to career advancement

Despite the considerable progress made in women's managerial careers in all three countries since the 1980s, significant institutional and cultural barriers remain that prevent women from fulfilling their career aspirations and potential, as discussed below.

Labour law and government policy intervention: The elimination of gender inequality necessitates state intervention through legislation and affirmative actions to provide at least the most basic level of protection in principle. For this purpose, the governments of all three countries have introduced gender equality laws and other mechanisms at different stages (e.g. Cooke, 2005; Kang and Rowley, 2005; Yuasa, 2005; Magoshi and Chang, 2009). However, ineffective enforcement of equal opportunity legislation has been a common finding in China, Japan and Korea (e.g. Cooke, 2005; Magoshi and Chang, 2009; Cho and Kwon, 2010).

For example, it was reported that despite the promulgation of the Equal Employment Opportunity Law (EEOL) in 1986, Japan had a much lower proportion of women managers in government organisations than in its corporations in the early 1990s (Steinhoff and Tanaka, 1993). The introduction of EEOL was controversial amongst the legislators, employers and the state at the outset and had 'produced few gains in employment opportunities for women' (Gelb, 2000: 385). There is a widespread consensus amongst scholars in Japan that the government passed the EEOL more as a response to international pressure than as an acknowledgement of the changing social values in Japan (Gelb, 2000). EEOL has been criticised for its 'over-reliance on voluntary compliance' with 'little government enforcement power'. Nevertheless, 'it has led to renewed efforts at litigation, increased consciousness and activism among women, and amendments to the law, passed in 1997' (Gelb, 2000: 385; also see Broadbent, 2008).

For both Japan and Korea, the affirmative action programmes have been adopted only in the 2000s on a voluntary basis with little enforcement power. Private sector employers have the autonomy to decide whether they wish to adopt the programme or not, and evidence suggests that there is little incentive for them to do so. For example, according to Benson *et al.*, (2007), only a small proportion of firms (e.g. just over 20 per cent in 2003) in Japan have adopted an affirmative action programme. Even fewer firms (e.g. less than 9 per cent in 2005) had a training programme specifically tailored for women to develop their leadership skills.

In Korea, the Affirmative Action Programme was first introduced in 2006 'as a major public policy to expand female employment and to rectify gender-discriminatory employment practices' (Cho and Kwon, 2010: 111). Companies with 1,000 or more employees are encouraged to implement the Programme although employers were given a two-year grace period for implementation. However, according to the Korea Ministry of Labour (2007, cited in Cho and Kwon 2010: 122), only 41 per cent of companies took up the initiative in the first year. Lack of vacancies, lack of qualified female applicants and male preference of business partners have been given as the key reasons by employers for not adopting the programme (Cho and Kwon, 2010). This is not only a result of employer discrimination, but also an outcome of the misalignment of education and industrial structure. For example, women tend to choose social sciences and arts subjects for their higher education, while the Korean economy may lean towards industrial sectors such as high-tech manufacturing and the chemical industry (the same is true in Japan). Cho and Kwon's (2010) study further revealed that a high level of distrust of government policies imposed via political processes and the ignorance of the potential benefits of affirmative actions are two other reasons for the Korean employers' apathy towards the programme. Compared with Korea, the Japanese affirmative action policy is even more passive with equally limited effect (e.g. Cho and Kwon, 2010).

Traditional societal value: It has been widely observed that gender stereotyping remains a major barrier to women's progress in management worldwide (e.g. Kanter, 1977; Yukongdi and Benson, 2006; Davidson and Burke, 2011). This problem may be more pronounced in China, Japan and Korea which share a male-dominant Confucian culture (see chapter 3) in which women are subordinate to men socially and economically (e.g. Worthley *et al.*, 2009). Women's primary responsibility is homemaking whereas men are seen as the pillar of the family, socially, financially and spiritually. In all three countries, the home-caring role falls largely upon women, regardless of their employment status (e.g. Cooke, 2005; Kang and Rowley, 2005; Yuasa, 2005). Child care support, from the extended family, state provision or other sources therefore plays an important role in women's access to employment. However, even when women manage to stay in employment, the traditional gender norm presents persistent barriers to their career progression.

As discussed earlier, women and their marital status are crucial sources of discrimination against their employment status and pay in Japan and Korea and to a lesser extent in China. In Japan, the breakdown of the internal labour market, the erosion of the grading system that rewards life-time employment and seniority and the mainstreaming of atypical workers (the majority of whom are women) have not brought sufficient institutional changes for women to break into the managerial rank en masse (Benson *et al.*, 2007). Compared with China, a relatively weaker childcare support system in Japan and Korea adds further constraints to women's labour market participation and career progression.

Employer's perceptions and organisational policy: Employers play an important role in mediating the level of gender inequality. Where firms are facing shortages of labour and talent, they may introduce a proactive human resource policy to attract and retain women workers (see chapter 13). Where the labour market is slack and business competition pressure is heightened, employers often adopt a labour cost reduction strategy to keep operating costs down. And women tend to be more vulnerable than men. For example, in Korea, women are encouraged by companies and union members to resign 'voluntarily' and accept a re-employment contract as an irregular worker with lower pay and less job security when their companies are undergoing downsizing processes (Chun, 2006). In Japan, new opportunities created for women by the equal opportunity law in the late 1980s and early 1990s were then eroded when Japan's economic growth 'bubble' burst after 1992 (Gelb, 2000). It was 'the marginal nature of Japanese women's employment' as a deliberate strategy of the employers that accommodated the core employment system which privileged men during a period of heightened international competition, reduced growth rate, a rapidly ageing workforce and the inflexible hiring and firing system (Kucera, 1998: 28).

Employers in Japan and Korea also exert pressure, albeit now more implicitly following the introduction of equal opportunity laws in the late 1980s, for women to resign when they get married and become pregnant. Age limits are also used to screen out women (Gelb, 2000). Although the 'marriage bar' is far less common in China, employers in private enterprises may impose an (unlawful) age limit on female factory workers. To some extent, if the marriage bar for Japanese and Korean women is aimed primarily at protecting men's jobs and earnings, then age discrimination in China is motivated by increased productivity. In both the private and public sector, women are much less likely than men to be selected for career development (e.g. Lee, 1995; Cooke, 2009).

Research evidence (e.g. Duignan and Iaquinto, 2005; Cho and Kwon, 2010; Xiao and Cooke, 2012) suggests that employers in all three countries appear to share a common (mis-) perception that women employees are less productive or committed to their job/career due to their family commitment. Employers are hence much less willing to invest in the training and development of female employees. A glass ceiling is common to women who aspire to be managers. Even when men and women are allocated to the same (managerial) job category, women are often assigned to positions that make them peripheral to organisational resources and career advancement opportunities (e.g. Kim, 2005; Yuasa, 2005; Cooke, 2009). In public sector organisations in China, women are often promoted to their leadership position for their symbolic value, to fulfil the quotas imposed by the state (Cooke, 2009; Tsang *et al.*, 2011). There is limited organisational support, such as training or mentoring, to enable women to develop their leadership skills. The marginalisation of (married) women in the strong internal labour market in Japan and Korea adds a further structural barrier to women's ability to advance their careers (Benson *et al.*, 2007).

Women role models: Lack of women role models has often been suggested as one of the reasons that account for the shortage of women managers (e.g. Kim, 2005; Yuasa, 2005). However, having female role models may not necessarily help improve the situation, in part due to the distorted image of women managers. Women are generally believed to be less likely than men to possess leadership qualities (e.g. Bowen *et al.*, 2007; Schein, 2007; Cooke, 2005). According to

Javalgi *et al.*'s (2011) comparative study, Chinese men and women displayed the lowest perceptions of women as managers compared to their counterparts in the USA and Chile. Bu and Roy's (2005) study of senior and middle managers in China that compared the composition and social exchange practices of Chinese male and female managers' career success networks (CSNs) found that most of the CSN ties formed by both male and female managers are with men, especially power ties. Bu and Roy's (2008: 1088) study further revealed that whilst Chinese male and female managers generally prefer to form CSN ties with individuals who are older than themselves, 'they are relatively more reluctant to include middle-aged or elder women in their CSN'. In Korea, women managers' mistakes tend to be amplified (Kim, 2005).

Women's career–family choice: Cocooned by institutional, societal, organisational and family constraints, women in China, Japan and Korea face a tough choice between their managerial career and family. Research findings suggest that many women managers ended up in their leadership position 'by accident' instead of through careful planning. They tend to take a passive attitude in their career battles and often adopt a non-confrontational and conciliatory style of leadership in order to gain acceptance (e.g. Cooke, 2009; Tsang *et al.*, 2011). Many of them are struggling to balance their career and family responsibilities, so that when a critical choice needs to be made they will choose their family first and their career second (e.g. Kim, 2005; Yuasa, 2005; Aaltion and Huang, 2007; Tsang *et al.*, 2011). It is therefore important to view women managers' private 'attitude' and 'choice' within the organisation through the mechanisms within which their attitudes and choices are constructed (Yuasa, 2005).

Conclusions

This chapter compared the patterns of women's participation in employment and management in China, Japan and Korea. It examined the political environment and institutional context within which women in these countries have been facilitated or hindered in pursuing their managerial careers. The chapter showed that while considerable progress has been made in the last three decades in women's education, which in some cases has surpassed that of men of the same age groups, this achievement has not been matched by the same level of earnings and organisational/corporate positions. Although affirmative action programmes in various forms have been introduced by the state in each country, which are aimed at enhancing gender equality, the implementation of these policy interventions is hampered by a range of factors, not least by gender-biased work organisation and employment practices.

The comparison revealed a common historical trend of women's disadvantages in employment and in their prospects of a management career, although progress has been made in each country to varying degrees. Institutional structures, persistent patriarchal gender norms and stereotypes and ineffective representation limit women's bargaining power in the labour market (and family) and hold down their financial rewards as well as their career progression. However, the various institutional and cultural factors are not played out to the same strength and each national employment system contains its unique features (see chapter 13). We have tried to highlight the paradox of how strong state intervention is possible and indeed needed to achieve a level of gender equality in patriarchal societies on the one hand, and how the intervening power of the state may be circumvented in East Asian countries where globalisation has had profound impacts on the nation's economy on the other. In the absence of effective law enforcement to enhance gender equality and organisational support to facilitate work-life balance and career development, we cannot be optimistic of the prospects for women in China, Japan and Korea to advance their managerial careers in the near future.

Note

1   Part of this paper draws from Cooke, F. L. (2010) 'Women's participation in employment in Asia: a comparative analysis of China, India, Japan and South Korea', *International Journal of Human Resource Management*, 21, 12: 2249–70, with permission.

References

Aaltion, I. and Huang, J. (2007) 'Women managers' careers in information technology in China: High flyers with emotional costs?', *Journal of Organisational Change Management,* 20: 227–44.

Benson, J. Yuasa, M. and Debroux, P. (2007) 'The prospect for gender diversity in Japanese employment', *International Journal of Human Resource Management*, 18: 890–907.

Becker, G. (1964) *Human Capital: A Theoretical and Empirical Analysis, with Special Reference to Education.* Chicago: University of Chicago Press.

Bowen, C. C., Wu, Y., Hwang, C. E. and Scherer, R. F. (2007) 'Holding up half of the sky? Attitudes toward women as managers in the People's Republic of China', *International Journal of Human Resource Management,* 18: 268–83.

Brinton, M., Lee, Y. and Parish, W. (1995) 'Married women's employment in rapidly industrialising societies: Examples from East Asia', *The American Journal of Sociology*, 100: 1099–1130.

Broadbent, K. (2008) 'Japan: Women workers and autonomous organising' in Broadbent, K. and Ford, M. (eds) *Woman Organising: Women and Union Activism in Asia.* London: Routledge, pp.156–71.

Bu, N. and Roy, J. P. (2005) 'Career success networks in China: Sex differences in network composition and social exchange practices', *Asia Pacific Journal of Management,* 22: 381–403.

— (2008) 'Chinese managers' career success networks: The impact of key tie characteristics on structure and interaction practices', *International Journal of Human Resource Management,* 19: 1088–1107.

Cho, J. and Kwon, T. (2010) 'Affirmative action and corporate compliance in South Korea', *Feminist Economics,* 16: 111–39.

Chun, J. (2006) 'The contested politics of gender and employment: Revitalising the South Korean labour movement', Draft paper for 'Global Working Class Project' in Pillay, Devan, Lindberg, Ingemar and Bieler, Andreas (eds) http://www.nottingham.ac.uk/shared/shared_gwc/documents/South_Korea.pdf, accessed 16 March 2007.

Cooke, F. L. (2005) 'Women's managerial careers in China in a period of reform', *Asia Pacific Business Review,* 11: 149–62.

—— (2008) 'China: Labour organisations representing women' in Broadbent, K. and Ford, M. (eds) *Woman Organising: Women and Union Activism in Asia.* London: Routledge, pp.34–49.

—— (2009) 'The changing face of women managers in China' in Rowley, C. and Yukondi, V. (eds) *The Changing Face of Women Management in Asia.* London: Routledge, pp.19–42.

—— (2010) 'Women's participation in employment in Asia: A comparative analysis of China, India, Japan and South Korea', *International Journal of Human Resource Management,* 21: 2249–70.

Davidson, M. and Burke, R. (2011) *Women in Management Worldwide: Progress and Prospects.* (2nd edn) Oxford: Ashgate Publishing.

Duignan, R. and Iaquinto, A. (2005) 'Female managers in Japan: Early indications of career progression', *Women In Management Review,* 20: 191–207.

Fielden, S. and Davidson, M. (2005) *International Handbook of Women and Small Business Entrepreneurship.* Cheltenham: Edward Elgar.

Futagami, S. and Helms, M. M. (2009) 'Emerging female entrepreneurship in Japan: A case study of digimom workers', *Thunderbird International Business Review,* 51, 1: 71–85.

Gelb, J. (2000) 'The equal employment opportunity law: A decade of change for Japanese women', *Law & Policy,* 22: 365–407.

Griffy-Brown, C. (2011) 'Supporting the emergence of women's entrepreneurship: Regulative, institutional and technological changes in Japan', *International Journal of Gender and Entrepreneurship,* 3: 75–78.

Hill, E. (2008) 'India: The self-employed women's association and autonomous organising' in Broadbent, K. and Ford, M. (eds) *Woman Organising: Women and Union Activism in Asia.* London: Routledge, pp.115–35.

Houseman, S. and Osawa, M. (1998) 'What is the nature of part-time work in the United States?' in O'Reilly, J. and Fagan, C. (eds) *Part-time Prospects: an International Comparison of Part-time Work in Europe, North America and the Pacific Rim.* London: Routledge, pp.232–51.

International Labour Organization (2003) *Yearbook of Labour Statistics.* Available at http://www.ilo.org/public/english/gender.htm, Geneva: International Labour Organisation, accessed 30 November 2011.

Javalgi, R. G., Scherer, R., Sánchez, C., Rojas, L. P., Daza, V. P., Hwang, C. E. and Yan, W. (2011) 'A comparative analysis of the attitudes toward women managers in China, Chile, and the USA', *International Journal of Emerging Markets,* 6: 233–53.

Jung, J. and Choi, K. (2004) 'Gender wage differentials and discrimination in Korea: Comparison by knowledge intensity of industries', *International Economics Journal,* 18: 561–79.

Kang, H. R. and Rowley, C. (2005) 'Women in management in South Korea: Advancement or retrenchment?', *Asia Pacific Business Review,* 11: 213–31.

Kanter, R. M. (1977) *Men and Women of the Corporation.* New York: Basic Books.

Khanna, T. (2007) *Billions of entrepreneurs: How China and India are reshaping their futures and yours.* Boston: Harvard Business School Press.

Kim, Y. (2005) 'Issues and observations: For women leaders in Korea, Gains but miles to go', *Leadership In Action,* 25: 20–2.

Kucera, D. (1998) 'Foreign trade and men and women's employment and earnings in Germany, and Japan'. Available at *Centre for Economic Policy Analysis Working Paper 9,* http://www.newschool.edu/cepa, accessed 16 March 2007.

Lantican, C., Gladwin, C. and Seale, J. (1996) 'Income and gender inequalities in Asia: Testing alternative theories of development', *Economic Development and Cultural Change*, 44: 235–63.

Lee, C. K. (1995) 'Engendering the worlds of labor: Women workers, labor markets, and production politics in the south China economic miracle', *American Sociological Review*, 60: 378–97.

Lee, W. and Lee, B. (2003) 'Korean industrial relations in the era of globalisation', *Journal of Industrial Relations*, 45: 505–20.

Lee, J. H., Sohn, S. Y. and Ju, Y. H. (2011) 'How effective is government support for Korean women entrepreneurs in small and medium enterprises?', *Journal of Small Business Management*, 49: 599–616.

Lee, S. S., Stearns, T. M., Osteryoung, J. S. and Stephenson, H. B. (2009) 'A comparison of the critical success factors in women-owned business between the United States and Korea', *International Entrepreneurship and Management Journal*, 5: 259–70.

Leung, A. (2011) 'Motherhood and entrepreneurship: Gender role identity as a resource', *International Journal of Gender and Entrepreneurship*, 3: 254–64.

Magoshi, E. and Chang, E. (2009) 'Diversity management and the effects on employees' organisational commitment: Evidence from Japan and Korea', *Journal of World Business*, 44: 31–40.

Monk-Turner, E. and Turner, C. (2001) 'Sex differentials in earnings in the South Korean labour market', *Feminist Economics*, 7: 63–78.

Moon, K. and Broadbent, K. (2008) 'Korea: Women, labour activism and autonomous organising' in Broadbent, K. and Ford, M. (eds) *Woman Organising: Women and Union Activism in Asia*, London: Routledge, pp.136–55.

Nakata, Y. and Takehiro, R. (2002) 'Employment and wages of female Japanese workers: past, present, and future', *Industrial Relations*, 41: 521–47.

Ogawa, N. and Ermisch, J. (1996) 'Family structure, home time demands, and the employment patterns of Japanese Married Women', *Journal of Labour Economics*, 14: 677–702.

Schein, V. E. (2007) 'Women in management: Reflections and projections', *Women in Management Review*, 22: 6–18.

Shimada, H. and Higuchi, Y. (1985) 'An analysis of trends in female labour force participation in Japan', *Journal of Labour Economics*, 3: 355–74.

Steinhoff, P. and Tanaka, K. (1993) 'Women managers in Japan', *International Studies of Management and Organisations*, 23: 25–48.

Tan, J. (2008) 'Breaking the "bamboo curtain" and the "glass ceiling": The experience of women entrepreneurs in high-tech industries in an emerging market', *Journal of Business Ethics*, 80: 547–64.

Tsang, A. Y., Chan, P. S. and Zhang, L. (2011) 'Reconciling conflicts: The "accidental" women leaders in contemporary China', *Affilia: Journal of Women and Social Work*, 26: 314–26.

Van der Meulen Rodgers, Y. (1998) 'A reversal of fortune for Korean women: Explaining the 1983 upward turn in relative earnings', *Economic Development and Cultural Change*, 46: 727–48.

Wakisaka, A. and Bae, H. (1998) 'Why is the part-time rate higher in Japan than in south Korea' in O'Reilly, J. and Fagan, C. (eds) *Part-time Prospects: an International Comparison of Part-time Work in Europe, North America and the Pacific Rim*. London: Routledge, pp.252–64.

Worthley, R., MacNab, B., Brislin, R., Ito, K. and Rose, E. L. (2009) 'Workforce motivation in Japan: An examination of gender differences and management perceptions', *International Journal of Human Resource Management,* 20: 1503–20.

Xiao, Y. C. and Cooke, F. L. (2012) 'Work-life balance in China? Social policy, employer strategy and individual coping mechanisms', *Asia-Pacific Journal of Human Resources,* 50: in press.

Yoon, B. (2003) 'Gender politics in Korea: Putting women on the political map', Paper presented at the annual meeting of the American Political Science Association, Philadelphia Marriott Hotel, Philadelphia, PA, Aug 27. Available athttp://www.keia.org/2-Publications/2–4-Adhoc/AdHoc2003/10Yoon.pdf, accessed on 15 March 2007.

Yuasa, M. (2005) 'Japanese women in management: Getting closer to "realities" in Japan', *Asia Pacific Business Review,* 11: 195–212.

Yukongdi, V. and Benson, J. (eds) (2006) *Women in Asian Management.* London: Routledge.

Yu, E. (2011) 'Are women entrepreneurs more likely to share power than men entrepreneurs in decision-making?', *International Journal of Business and Management,* 6: 111–19.

Yuasa, M. (2005) 'Japanese women in management: Getting closer to "realities" in Japan', *Asia Pacific Business Review,* 11: 195–211.

10 Continuity and change in *guanxi* networks in East Asia

Jane Nolan

Introduction

The use of social networks is not unusual in business and is certainly not confined to the East Asian region. There are numerous studies, from all quadrants of the globe, which show that people prefer to do business with those with whom they have existing ties of friendship or kinship (Borgatti and Foster, 2003; Burt, 2000; Uzzi, 1996). Personal connections are universally valuable for gaining access to jobs and enhancing career prospects and for providing organisations with access to a wider range of markets, suppliers and information (Bian and Ang, 1997; Davidsson and Honig, 2005; Granovetter, 1974; Kotabe *et al.*, 2003; Uzzi, 1996). On the downside, if they become too exclusive, networks can stifle innovation as certain core assumptions and work practices become habituated, closing off potentially more productive alternatives. All that said there are those who argue that the form of networking used in China – *guanxi* – is distinctly different from those found in other societies because of its deep cultural roots in the Confucian philosophical tradition (see chapter 3).

Alternatively, there are those who argue that *guanxi* is principally a product of local Chinese institutions which, in turn, are embedded in a society and economy undergoing rapid transformation. Consequently, the 'rules' of *guanxi* are likely to change as those institutions modernise (see chapter 5). If foreign managers develop an *idée fixe* on what constitutes Chinese 'culture' then they run the risk of building networks and making decisions on the basis of outdated stereotypes.

What, then, is really useful to know about social networks in China and in East Asia more generally? Is *guanxi* really immutably fixed in Chinese culture never to be understood or infiltrated by outsiders? And what hazards might guanxi pose to a foreign manager in a rapidly changing global business environment? To answer these questions, this chapter will be divided into three sections. The first will look at the Confucian cultural heritage underlying East Asian business networks generally, including those in China, Japan and South Korea.[1] The second will consider research which focuses on the relationship between *guanxi* and institutional structures. Here we will investigate the question of whether or not the region is experiencing a decline in the importance of *guanxi* networks in light of economic reforms. The third section will offer some evaluation of this debate by arguing that, in global business at least, the continuing need of MNCs to establish links with government officials is a form of *guanxi* networking that needs to be maintained, but that can also prove particularly risky for the foreign manager. Finally, we will evaluate continuity and change in *guanxi* in the post-reform period in China examining both what it is principally used for and who is most likely to still need to use it.

The Confucian tradition and East Asian networks

Over recent decades scholars of East Asian management have repeatedly argued that the economies and businesses of the region need to be understood on their own terms, not simply in terms of their differences to Western models (Hamilton, 2006; Redding, 1990; Tung and Worm, 2001; Warner, 2010). More specifically, most researchers emphasise the need to focus on the continuity of 'civilisational norms' in the region and, particularly, on the enduring influence of the Confucian world view. Briefly, Confucianism is characterised as a philosophical approach which is largely free of the rigid rules and laws which define the monotheistic beliefs which underpin the Abrahamic religions dominant in the West. Instead, Confucianism is based on a set of principles which prioritise 'natural' harmonies and hierarchies in relationships. Five relationships, the *'wu-lun'*, are seen as especially important: the ruler over the subject, the father over the son, the older brother and the younger brother, the husband and the wife and the friend and the friend. If these relationships are pursued with loyalty and benevolence, by all the parties involved, then a harmonious society is believed to be the inevitable outcome (Hwang and Staley, 2005).

In broad terms, many observers of management in East Asia argue, therefore, that organisations in the region are fundamentally ordered around relationships, whereas those in the West are largely controlled by abstract laws. If Western capitalist economies are firm-based, Asian capitalist economies are network-based. Moreover, East Asian organisations are generally seen to place particular importance on respect for age-based seniority in business relationships and on a paternalistic organisational form (Boisot and Child, 1996; Tung and Worm, 2001; Warner, 2010).

All that said, however, there are clearly differences between the nations within the region and, while 'maintaining harmonious relations' is a key uniting theme, there are varying degrees of emphasis which can guide social networking behaviour in different ways in different countries (Alston, 1989). For example, guanxi in Chinese communities emphasises the development of long-term personal relationships based on kinship and regional connections. The Japanese, on the other hand, foreground the importance of group harmonies and social relations and place more emphasis on corporate connections than those based on strictly kinship relations. In Korea, the emphasis on maintaining harmony, or *inhwa,* frequently occurs through kin-based hierarchies and authority relationships, a pattern which is reflected in the 'clan-like' nature of the nation's largest organisations. Each approach will be briefly discussed below.

Guanxi *in China*

In a very general sense the term *guanxi* is often used to indicate the existence of some sort of personal relationship such as a friendship, classmate or kin connection (Guthrie, 2009). However, apart from *guanxi* itself, there also exists a separate phenomenon, *guanxi xue* (or *guanxi* practice), which is used to refer to the material aspect of relationship building or the 'manufacturing of obligation and indebtedness' which can be achieved through gift and favour exchange (Yang, 1994). The codes of practice underlying this element of *guanxi xue* are sometimes argued to have derived from the Confucian desire for respect and harmony, where reciprocity becomes a moral duty and the gift, in this context, becomes an object that materially acknowledges the existence of a ritualised relationship between two people (Ledeneva, 2008). It is, however, always assumed that the nature of the relationship goals (mutual obligation and indebtedness) are to be kept implicit and, furthermore, that there is no real time limit on the 'repayment' of the debt created by the gift. Second, the importance of affect or sentiment (*ganqing*) in *guanxi* is also heavily emphasised.

Those who prioritise the role of culture in understanding *guanxi* take as a foundational assumption that China is a particularistic and collectivist society (Hofstede, 2001; Hofstede *et al.*, 2010; Inglehart and Welzel, 2005) and subsequently seek to describe *guanxi* and *guanxi* practice in relation to other aspects of social life in China, such as human feelings (*renqing*), face (*mianzi*) and reciprocity (*bao*) (Chen and Chen, 2004; Yan, 1996; Yang, 1994). Whilst outside commentators (business people particularly) may emphasise the instrumental nature of *guanxi* practice, Chinese usually emphasise that 'real' *guanxi* must contain an affective element (Gold *et al.*, 2002).

Interestingly, some scholars in this tradition tend to favour the view that the significance of *guanxi* practice in business has increased significantly since the post-1978 reforms (cf., chapter 5). The stresses and strains of the transition to a market economy meant that people needed to utilise informal networks, such as *guanxi*, in order to ensure their economic survival and prosperity. Mayfair Yang (1994) has described the way that *guanxi* practice is used as a way of circumventing newly-established formal rules and regulations. Others have emphasised the intrinsic value of *guanxi* for maintaining and building trusting relationships within an organisation. For example, Wong *et al.*'s (2010) study of employees in joint ventures in southern China shows that a work culture based on traditional *guanxi* influences the nature of Chinese employees' trust in both their supervisor and their organisation. They argue that good subordinate-supervisor *guanxi* is a core HRM concept in China because it influences employees' perceptions of procedural justice and job security and, consequently, their turnover intentions.

Indeed, recent debates have argued for international recognition that HRM practices in China now constitute what can be defined as 'Confucian HRM'. As Warner (2010) notes, although Western-based industrial relations and HRM concepts and practices have been widely taught through management programmes in Chinese universities and business schools, such institutions are also now developing HRM principles based on clearly identifiable 'national guises and incarnations' (Warner, 2003; Zhu *et al.*, 2007). From the phasing out of the 'iron rice bowl' (*tie fan wan*) in the 1980s through to the development of contemporary HRM practices used in large 'learning' organisations in the 2000s, Warner (2010) identifies the emergence of Confucian HRM which takes 'harmony' as the template for interpersonal relationships. In the case of *guanxi*, he argues, HRM correlates lead to both positive and negative outcomes. On the one hand *guanxi* may lead to 'benign horizontal communication or on the other, a less benign form of corruption', a theme we shall develop later in this chapter. Warner (2010) also notes, however, that the identification of Confucian principles in HRM practices in China cannot be explained simply through the 'cultural differences' argument. The term must also be contextualised against the backdrop of the current popular discourse on Confucianism in China which coexists with Sino-Marxism and the CCP's adoption of the concept of the 'harmonious society' to legitimate its current political agenda. Thus, Warner also foregrounds the importance of institutional influences in adapting seemingly stable 'traditional' elements of Chinese philosophy to modern HRM practices.

Wa *and* amakudari *in Japan*

Much of what has been written about business networking in Japan is firmly rooted in the *Nihonjinron* (theories of 'Japaneseness') paradigm which is based on the following assumptions: first, the Japanese, psychologically speaking, are particularly dependent on their superiors' approval for gaining emotional satisfaction; second, maintenance of harmony within the group is essential and extensive effort is placed on sustaining relationships; third, there is a tendency to imply that all Japanese share the attribute under examination to an equal degree regardless of gender, age, education or position in the labour market; fourth, that the attribute is uniquely Japanese in form and has existed in Japanese society for an indefinite period of time (Sugimoto, 2010). Indeed, these assumptions can also be found in much of the East Asian business literature which takes 'culture' as its core explanatory variable (Hofstede, 2001; McSweeney, 2002). It is important, therefore, that the reader retains a critical distance when engaging with studies in this paradigm, despite its intuitive appeal to practitioners and theorists alike.

Nevertheless, with these caveats in mind, there are still some interesting business networking patterns which are worthy of further study. It has been suggested that maintaining *Wa,* or harmony, in Japan tends to occur through group activities in organisations rather than through the dyadic relationships based on family and region ties that are more common in China (Alston, 1989). From a business perspective, one important aspect of this relationship form is that, once accepted into an organisational group, members are considered to be under its permanent protection. This is reflected in the labour market ideal of lifetime protection in an organisation in return for loyalty and high levels of work commitment (Abegglen, 2006; Alston, 1989). Of course, while job security may have been an identifiable characteristic of the Japanese labour market in the past, one in three employees are now in non-regular 'precarious' employment (Sugimoto, 2010). Moreover, in 2006, nine out of ten employees were working in SMEs where the lifetime employment system simply does not operate. Indeed, demographically, the average 'Japanese' is a 'female, non-unionised non-permanent employee in a small business without a university education' (Sugimoto, 2010, p.1). Yet the majority of studies of business networks are based on samples which are largely male, highly-educated permanent employees working in large organisations or of powerful bureaucrats and state officials involved in lucrative business deals (see chapters 7 and 9).

Nevertheless, even among this elite group, some interesting networking patterns can be observed, particularly for those employed in, or associated with, the *Keiretsu* (sets of companies and banks with interlocking relationships and shareholdings). One example is the extensive 'old boy' network of government officials who, post-retirement, 'descend from heaven' (*amakudari*) into the management of private (or quasi private) businesses and public sector organisations (Schaede, 1995). *Amakudari* became particularly prominent in Japanese business when nationalised industries were privatised and bureaucrats retired relatively early (between 50 and 60 years of age). Because traditional Confucian values of hierarchy and respect for authority mitigated against placing senior officials seeking a 'second life' following retirement as the subordinate of more junior staff, such individuals often found themselves placed in positions of disproportionate power and influence (Colignon and Usui, 2003; Schaede, 1995). Unsurprisingly, perhaps, the practice was vulnerable to abuse and led to the development of corrupt practices in that former officials tended to join organisations linked to their former ministry and to collude in helping their new company secure government contracts (Schaede, 1995). Although attempts have been made to curb the influence of *amakudari* and new laws have been passed to limit the appointments of retiring officials, the practice remains widespread (*Japan Times*, 4 May 2011). We will not delve into the historical and institutional structures which may magnify and sustain the problem; suffice to say that the role of Confucian values in relation to hierarchical relationships and respect for authority are important explanatory elements for understanding at least the genesis of this form of networking.

Intra-industry networks, which circle around the membership of professional associations, are another important networking pattern (Witt, 2006). Interestingly, membership of these professional associations is defined principally by the firms themselves, rather than by the individuals who represent those firms. Witt (2006) outlines how organisations appoint specific managers, *madoguchi* (windows), to the role of association networking who, as well as being tasked with establishing connections during the formal meetings of the association, are expected to engage in informal, after-work socialising, or 'bar hopping' (*nijikai*) to gain valuable information. According to Witt (2006) the term 'nomination', a combination of the Japanese '*nomu*' – to drink – and the English word 'communication', highlights the importance of alcohol in these exchanges, confirming the Japanese norm that 'what is said under the influence of alcohol cannot be held against the individual' (p. 99). Interestingly, however, the connections which *madoguchi* develop remain the connections of the firm, rather than of the individual, who will 'pass on' his network to his successor when he leaves the *madoguchi* role. This is an important difference with *guanxi* in China where the network remains the 'property' of the individual, rather than of the firm.

Inhwa *and* yon-go *in Korea*

Much has been written about the distinctive pattern of 'clan management' in Korean corporations (see chapter 8). Known as *Chaebol*, these family-owned organisations are dominated by powerful founding chairmen and run on authoritarian and paternalistic lines (Rowley and Warner, 2005). Companies are frequently viewed metaphorically as 'parents' and employees as 'family', which, in fact, is often a reasonably accurate description of the structure of the organisation (Rowley and Warner, 2005). For example, in the 1980s, one third of executives in the largest business groups in Korea were family members of fellow employees or employers (Alston, 1989). And drawing on one of the most quotable Korean corporate examples, the heirs of Chung Ju-yung, founder of the Hyundai group in 1947, still run all of the named companies in the group.

The influence of Confucianism on Korean corporate life may be most clearly observed through organisational structures, which are based on the establishment and maintenance of harmonious relationships between those of unequal status (Alston, 1989). One of the key business advantages of this practice has been to promote 'in-group' harmony or *inhwa* in the organisational network, leading employees to prioritise collective, corporate goals over individual personal ambition and to make group members mutually interdependent. Consequently, from a business perspective, *inhwa* is seen to reinforce in-group identity and to contribute to the desire to compete with clearly defined 'out-groups' (Cho and Yoon, 2001). In terms of networking behaviour, *yon-go* relations have also been of particular importance for recruitment purposes. *Yon-go* connections are those based on clan, blood, geography or education (Chung *et al.*, 1997) and business owners would traditionally recruit employees from their hometown, school or university in the same way that they would bring their relatives into the organisation. Chung and Jin (2011) note that, historically speaking at least, school and university related connections have been particularly important. These relations are often based on hierarchical seniority which is defined by year of graduation.

There is, however, increasing evidence that, as in Japan, the 'traditional' model of lifetime employment, seniority and recruitment through connections is undergoing significant change (Bae *et al.*, 2011). Due to increasingly difficult economic conditions, numerical and financial flexibility is becoming more common than 'clan' loyalty and age-related promotion (Bae *et al.*, 2011). Moreover, the *yon-go* system has come to be seen as too closely associated with nepotism and favouritism and there is a growing social unease with its use. This issue has seen a shift towards recruitment practices which are now based on more meritocratic systems of assessment and open competition. All that said, there remains an 'enduring preference' for in-group relations (of which *yon-go* is one kind) in business-to-business relationships, such as firm- and supplier-chains, where pre-existing relationships have been shown to increase trust between buyer and supplier and reduce opportunistic behaviour in suppliers (Chung and Jin, 2011). Furthermore, given the intense competition among large companies to recruit top graduates, the *yon-go* system of recruitment from elite universities is still in evidence in the *Chaebol* (Chung and Jin, 2011)

In all of the national case studies cited above, the interaction between Confucian cultural values and political and institutional systems has been hinted at but not drawn out explicitly. We now therefore need to examine this specific issue in more detail if we are to even begin to understand the influence of networking on business outcomes in East Asia. In order to do this, the rest of this chapter will focus on the Chinese example of *guanxi*. First, we will examine the use of *guanxi* in Chinese communities outside of the PRC, and second we will consider whether or not the economic reforms on the mainland have led to an increase or decrease in its importance.

Guanxi *and Chinese communities in East Asia*

Research on the social networks of Chinese communities outside of the PRC, in areas where rational–legal systems are already well established, provides a useful framework for examining the extent to which *guanxi* is a fixed and immutable feature of Chinese culture, or whether it is a malleable system which adapts to shifting local economic and legal conditions. For example, Lin and Ho's (2010) comparison of the use of *guanxi* in Taiwan and mainland China showed that in Taiwan, although *guanxi* remains an important element of business development, managers are less driven to maintain *guanxi* relationships over the long term, adopting a more 'business is business' approach to networking (cf. chapter 6). Lin and Ho (2010) attribute this finding to the more firmly established historical links with Western companies by businesses in Taiwan.

Similarly, Tong and Yong's (1998) study of Chinese business networks in Singapore shows that a 'desire to gain legitimacy in the eyes of international companies, [and] greater systems of trust and acceptance of legal–rationalistic procedures, have effected changes in business principles' (p. 95). In their study, Chinese business people working in Singapore felt that impersonal 'professionalism', rather than the personalism associated with *guanxi*, was the most credible and effective way of doing business. However, they also noted that there was an enduring sense of insecurity and vulnerability amongst some of their participants which led them to continue to rely heavily on *guanxi*, particularly amongst those who were employed in firms where ownership and control was family-based.

Further evidence of the enduring legacy of an insecure past on current networking practices comes from a fascinating empirical study of the 'mindscapes' of Chinese business people in Hong Kong, Taiwan, Singapore and Indonesia carried out by Redding (1990). He showed that, despite their move away from the Chinese mainland, three primary components of Chinese culture and history continued to permeate business practices: paternalism, personalism and insecurity. For Redding, the influence of paternalism was the result of the power of Confucian ideals to encourage rigid vertical order in organisations based on the exchange of obligations. Interestingly, however, he found that trust in business relationships and networks was also, in fact, heavily influenced both by recent personal experiences of insecurity and the perception of enduring widespread insecurity on the Chinese mainland. Particularly, the removal of traditional sources of government support, such as the financial and material stability previously provided by the *danwei* (state owned enterprises) permeated his participants' sense of vulnerability. While Redding is sensitive to the power of Confucian heritage in guiding the preference for personalism underlying the *guanxi* networking practices of his participants, he does not place all of the explanatory weight on culture, arguing for a need to unravel the influence of personal and institutional histories for a fuller understanding. We shall explore this theme further in the following section where we will consider the evidence for change in the importance of *guanxi* in the light of economic reforms in the PRC.

The influence of institutional forces on *guanxi* practices

In the last 30 years, thousands of laws, regulations and resolutions aimed at rationalising business practices and increasing transparency and efficiency in mainland China have been passed by the National People's Congress (China's 'Parliament') (Guthrie, 2002; Nolan, 2010; Wang, 2007). Some argue that this transformation has fundamentally changed the attitude of Chinese managers towards *guanxi*, to the extent that it is now broadly the same as what, in the West, would be called 'social capital' (Gold *et al.*, 2002). A key example of this approach is the work of Doug Guthrie (1998; 2002; 2009) who argues that a conscious attempt on the part of the Chinese government to rationalise business practices, coupled with increasing efforts to reduce the influence of informal networks in public life, means that *guanxi* practice is in decline as China develops a rational-legal system based on formal laws and procedures. Guthrie claims that his data (collected in the mid 1990s) shows that the use of *guanxi* practice in China's urban economy is increasingly 'unnecessary and dangerous', particularly amongst firms which are higher up the state administrative hierarchy. Huang (2008) has also shown that while *guanxi* networks are still important for gaining desirable jobs in the state sector, large non-state sector corporations now rely on a more standardised and transparent recruitment process that can accurately identify the most well-qualified candidates in a meritocratic fashion, regardless of their connections.

It is central to the arguments of these scholars that rationalisation processes, competitive pressures and the nascent development of the rule of law means that Chinese firms and their employees are now much less in need of *guanxi* practice to get things done, be that finding reliable suppliers, accessing new markets or gaining access to good jobs. Not only does legal and institutional change encourage economic actors to change their behaviour, but competitive processes in a market economy shift the emphasis such that the best services, products, people or projects are now more likely to be selected, regardless of the personal *guanxi* relationships of any of the individuals involved. However, there remain a number of scholars who, although also working broadly within an institutional framework, are somewhat more pessimistic that forces of rationalisation and market forces will reduce the influence of *guanxi* practice. Researchers in this camp argue that the continuing impartiality of law enforcement in China means that the economic system is still heavily reliant on 'back-door practices' (*houmen*) and bribery to a degree which remains distinct from what is usually found in Western market economies.

Li (2011), for example, argues that some Chinese managers now use *guanxi* 'discourse' as an informal institutional mechanism to facilitate the contracting process in corrupt exchanges. In other words, those who are being bribed can overcome any sense of moral wrongdoing by redefining their situation as merely part of a 'traditional' cultural heritage. Thus, the term *guanxi* is used as a cultural shield which enables corruption to appear in a morally neutral way to those involved. Similarly, Wank's (2002) research in Xiamen, based on data collected in the mid 1980s and the mid 1990s, uncovered the existence of what he labelled 'symbiotic clientelism' between private businessmen and officials. In his study he shows how the perception that the rule of law remains weak encouraged local entrepreneurs to continue to seek to influence officials through the use of *guanxi* practice. He argues that the more market-orientated regions of China have not seen the elimination of *guanxi* practice, but, rather, a transformation in the scope of its influence. Yang (2002) supports this argument suggesting that the principal decline in *guanxi* practice has been in the need to use such networks to acquire ordinary consumer goods and daily essentials. Such items, for the majority of the population, are indeed now readily available through the normal distribution mechanism of the market economy. For Yang (2002) where *guanxi* continues to thrive, however, is in the relationships between entrepreneurs, managers and state officials. The implications of this pattern for foreign managers in MNCs based in mainland China are discussed below.

Guanxi *networks amongst foreign and Chinese managers*

As well as studies which investigate the use of *guanxi* between Chinese managers and officials, there is also a large literature examining the use of *guanxi* in an international business context. Many of these studies underscore the difficulties involved in running an MNC in a region where access to informal but influential networks remains a necessity (Luo, 2000). For example, Wang's (2000) study of the role of transnational *guanxi* networks in facilitating FDI development in China showed that, for foreigners, *guanxi* are often difficult to sustain and costly to build and, crucially, may depend too heavily on a key individual who may lose their power very rapidly. Moreover, the lack of transparency in *guanxi* networks means that foreigners are particularly vulnerable to the influence of 'phony players' who are not as influential as they claim to be, leading the MNC to significant losses in time and money and to extensive reputation damage.

Furthermore, Langenberg's (2007) work discusses the problem of 'ethical relativism' for non-Chinese MNCs attempting to develop their businesses through the use of *guanxi*. He draws attention to the difficulties involved in trying to reconcile international codes of conduct, which are based on the assumption that there exist universal ethical values, with the multiple local 'exceptions' that managers inevitably encounter in their day-to-day experiences. Langenberg argues that foreigners need to exercise great care when engaging in *guanxi* practices because it is simply not in the interests of the organisation to become involved in activities which may in the long term become harmful to the company as a legal entity. Moreover, he suggests that the importance of developing a good corporate social responsibility profile is becoming increasingly important for MNCs in China and that, in a similar vein to Guthrie, the significance of *guanxi* is very likely to decline both as formal laws become more strictly enforced and Chinese managers with international MBAs seek to run their organisations according to international business norms.

All that said, however, there are numerous examples reported in the financial press of foreign business executives being drawn into seemingly *guanxi*-type relationships with local Chinese officials which have, ultimately, led to their prosecution for fraud and the payment of bribes. One of the most recent examples in the financial sector is the case of Garth Peterson, an American vice-president at Morgan Stanley's property investment office in Shanghai, who was fired in December 2009 on the suspicion that he had violated the US Foreign Corrupt Practices Act (FCPA), a law which aims to eliminate the practice of paying bribes to overseas public officials. In addition, a study by Deloitte in May 2009 reported that nine in ten US businesses were concerned about the possibility of FCPA violations while doing business in China, and an October 2009 report by the law firm Shearman & Sterling showed that at least 24 US companies have had recent FCPA issues involving China (Reuters, 10 November 2010). While such cases may well prove insignificant in the development of rational-legal systems in China over the long term, it is important to note that it is *not* inevitable that China's incorporation into the international economy will lead to the displacement of such practices, not least because of the processes of adaptation which some international managers themselves experience as they adjust their strategies to conform to what they believe to be acceptable and legitimate 'cultural practices' in the local context.

For example, Nolan's (2011) study of Western bankers in China showed that while the network practices of many Western managers may contribute to the adoption of international business norms in China, there is another group of managers who make significant adjustments to local conditions and engage in strategies which actually reinforce some of the existing evasive practices sometimes associated with *guanxi*. Some foreign managers creatively reinterpret the norms of the local context to justify their actions, engaging in 'back-door practices' such as the provision of preferential loans and bribes to certain officials under the assumption that this is what is necessary to advance their business agenda. Moreover, rather than acknowledge the implications of their own actions, some managers transferred responsibility for their behaviour on to domestic actors, arguing that such action was necessary in order to comply with 'cultural norms'. Some managers were, in effect, contributing to the maintenance of informal circumventory practices and were certainly not encouraging convergence towards international norms, a common justification for allowing them access to Chinese markets in the first place (Wang, 2007).

Tung and Worm's (2001) research, which also draws on studies of MNCs that operate in China is, however, more optimistic in tone on the nature and usefulness of transnational *guanxi*. Given that the rule of law is not necessarily enforced impartially in mainland China, they argue that foreign firms are driven by necessity to form relationships with government officials to secure business deals. This fact, in turn, leads to an asymmetry in the balance of power between the two parties which can either favour the government official (who can influence administrative procedures), or the Western company (which possesses the desired expertise and 'know how'). Given the uncertainty of the business environment in mainland China, *guanxi* can increase the efficiency of an MNC because bureaucratic blocks are removed and this, in turn, can create greater stability due to the influx of more reliable flows of information. Moreover, good connections may also increase the legitimacy of the firm, particularly if it is entering a new market.

In short, foreign managers should aim to build personal *guanxi* relationships which meet their organisation's needs for resources, political support and/or legitimacy in a new environment. Other researchers also continue to emphasise the enduring importance of *guanxi* in MNC collaboration, focusing on topics such as its importance for knowledge sharing in R&D collaborations (Hong *et al.*, 2010) and its importance in talent management practices (Hartmann *et al.*, 2010). However, we must conclude by reiterating that foreign managers need to tread carefully in terms of just quite what they are prepared to exchange in order to create the principle of 'mutual indebtedness' commonly associated with *guanxi* practice. In an environment which changes so rapidly they are particularly vulnerable to the downsides of 'bad' *guanxi*; namely corruption, false promises and corporate governance quagmires.

Conclusions

The question of whether or not *guanxi* is changing in form and importance through the course of China's economic reforms is, as we have seen, answered in different ways by researchers who choose to emphasise different aspects of the problem. Some are concerned to track tangible increases and decreases over time, for example through the study of job seekers' experiences or managers' attitudes, while others draw out the subtle ways in which *guanxi* has adapted to changes in the economic system. Authors like Guthrie (2009) argue that, as formal law becomes stronger and the market economy becomes ever more firmly established, the role of *guanxi* practice will diminish in the urban industrial sector. While still acknowledging that *guanxi* is a distinctive cultural practice in China, his overall view is that because *guanxi* is in conflict with rational-legal systems, and is ultimately an impediment to competitive processes, its influence will inevitably decrease over time.

However, there is another position on the role of *guanxi* which argues that what is actually important to understand is what precisely it is used for now and quite who it is used by. As Ledeneva (2008) argues, because of changes in China's state distribution system, 'previously scarce items such as televisions, train tickets, restaurant seats, lean meat, and nursery school space are now easily available through the market, ordinary people [now] have less need to practice *guanxi*' (p.136). However, it is in the sphere of business where both Chinese and foreign managers still often need to engage with figures of political influence (Ledeneva, 2008). As Yang (2002) argues the Chinese state still has strict control 'over state contracts, access to imports, bank loans, favourable tax incentives, access to valuable market information and to influential persons, and exemptions from troublesome laws and regulations. It is here that *guanxi* finds nurture in the new economy' (Yang 2002, 464). While *guanxi* may indeed be of less importance to ordinary Chinese people for the acquisition of essential daily items, it is still a very real 'social fact' for those who are involved in business. It is in the interactions between private entrepreneurs, managers (both Chinese and foreign) and state officials where *guanxi* retains its influence (Nolan, 2011; Yang, 2002).

Social networks are a universal feature of human societies and they play a crucial role in businesses around the world (see chapter 16). *Guanxi* and *guanxi* practice clearly display features that are culture-specific and heavily influenced by the Confucian tradition such as respect for authority, the establishment of long-term relationships, and the formalised exchange of gifts and favours as a means of re-enforcing committed, harmonious associations. In more practical terms, *guanxi* has been used to help people survive in conditions of shortages, to find good jobs, to launch new businesses, to circumvent formal procedure, to negotiate favourable deals, to access and keep clients and suppliers and to contact powerful and influential people. However, there is a fine line between demonstrating sensitivity to cultural norms and developing corrupt and compromised relationships which are cloaked, by both parties, as merely an 'inevitability' of local custom. For the global manager, the benefits of establishing 'good' *guanxi* are significant, but they should also be alert to the dangers of 'bad' *guanxi*; for the time being at least it remains necessary to proceed with caution.

Note

1   Hereafter, Korea.

References

Abegglen, J. (2006) *21st Century Japanese Management*. Chippenham: Palgrave Macmillan.
Alston, J. (1989) '*Wa, guanxi* and *inhwa*: managerial principles in Japan, China, and Korea', *Business Horizons,* March–April: 26–31.
Bae, J., Chen, S-H. and Rowley, C. (2011) 'From a paternalistic model towards what? HRM trends in Korea and Taiwan', *Personnel Review*, 40: 700–22.
Bian, Y. and Ang, S. (1997) '*Guanxi* networks and job mobility in China and Singapore', *Social Forces*, 75: 981–1005.
Boisot, M. and Child, J. (1996) 'From fiefs to clans and network capitalism: explaining China's emerging economic order', *Administrative Science Quarterly*, 41: 600–28.

Borgatti, S. and Foster, P. (2003) 'The network paradigm in organizational research: a review and typology', *Journal of Management*, 29: 991–1013.

Burt, R. (2000) 'The network structure of social capital', *Research in Organizational Behaviour*, 22: 1–28.

Chen, X. and Chen, C. (2004) 'On the intricacies of the Chinese *guanxi*: a process model of *guanxi* development', *Asia Pacific Journal of Management*, 21: 205–324.

Cho, Y. and Yoon, J. (2001) 'The origin and function of dynamic collectivism: an analysis of Korean corporate culture', *Asia Pacific Business Review*, 7: 70–88.

Chung, J. E. and Jin, B. (2011) 'In-group preference as opportunism governance in a collectivist culture: evidence from Korean retail buyer-supplier relationships', *Journal of Business & Industrial Marketing*, 26: 237–49.

Chung, K. H., Lee, H. C. and Jung, K. H. (1997) *Korean Management: Global Strategy and Cultural Transformation.* Berlin: Walter de Gruyter.

Colignon, R. and Usui, C. (2003) *Amakudari: The Hidden Fabric of Japan's Economy.* Ithaca and London: Cornell University Press.

Davidsson, P. and Honig, B. (2005) 'The role of social and human capital among nascent entrepreneurs', *Journal of Business* Venturing, 18: 301–31.

Gold, T., Guthrie, D. and Wank, D. (eds) (2002) *Social Connections in China: Institutions, Culture and the Changing Nature of Guanxi.* Cambridge, Cambridge University Press.

Granovetter, M. (1974) *Getting A Job: A Study of Contacts and Careers.* Chicago: Chicago University Press.

Guthrie, D. (1998) 'The declining significance of *guanxi* in China's economic transition', *The China Quarterly*, 154: 254–82.

— (2002) 'Information assymetries and the problem of perception: the significance of structural position in assessing the importance of *guanxi* in China' in Gold, T., Guthrie, D. and Wank, D. (eds) *Social Connections in China: Institutions, Culture and the Changing Nature of Guanxi.* Cambridge: Cambridge University Press, pp. 37–56.

— (2009) *Changing Social Institutions' in China and Globalization: The Social, Economic and Political Transformation of Chinese Society.* London, Routledge.

Hamilton, G. (2006) *Commerce and capitalism in Chinese Societies.* London: Routledge.

Hartmann, E., Feisel, E. and Schober, H. (2010) 'Talent management of Western MNCs in China: balancing global integration and local responsiveness', *Knowledge and Process Management*, 17: 62–73.

Hofstede, G. (2001) *Culture's Consequences: Comparing Values, Behaviors, Institutions, and Organizations Across* Nations. London: Sage, originally published 1980.

Hofstede, G., Hofstede, G. J. and Minkov, M. (2010) *Cultures and Organizations*: *Software of the Mind.* 3rd edition. New York: McGraw-Hill.

Hong, J., Heikkinen, J. and Blomqvist, K. (2010) 'Culture and knowledge co-creation in R&D collaboration between MNCs and Chinese Universities', *Knowledge and Process Management*, 17: 62–73.

Huang, X. (2008) '*Guanxi* networks and job searches in China's emerging labour market: a qualitative investigation', *Work, Employment and Society,* 22: 467–84.

Hwang, D. and Staley, A. (2005) 'An analysis of recent accounting and auditing failures in the United States on US accounting and auditing in China', *Managerial Auditing Journal*, 20: 227–34.

Inglehart, R. and Welzel, C. (2005) *Modernization, Cultural Change, and Democracy: The Human Development Sequence.* Cambridge: Cambridge University Press.

Japan Times, 4 May (2011) *Utilities got 68 ex-bureaucrats via 'amakudari'.* Available at http://www.japantimes.co.jp/text/nn20110504a1.html (accessed: 1 November 2011).

Kotabe, M., Martin, X. and Domoto, H. (2003) 'Gaining from vertical partnerships', *Strategic Management Journal*, 24: 293–316

Langenberg, E. (2007) *Guanxi and Business Strategy: Theory and Implications for Multinational Companies in China*. New York: Physica-Verlag.

Ledeneva, A. (2008) '*Blat* and *Guanxi*: Informal Practices in Russia and China', *Comparative Studies in Society and History*, 50: 118–44.

Li, L. (2011) 'Performing bribery in China: *guanxi*-practice, corruption with a human face', *Journal of Contemporary China*, 20: 1–20.

Lin, L. and Ho, Y. L. (2010) '*Guanxi* and OCB: the Chinese cases', *Journal of Business Ethics*, 96: 285–98.

Luo, L. (2000) *Guanxi and Business*. London: World Scientific Publishing.

McSweeney, B. (2002) 'Hofstede's model of national cultural differences and their consequences: A triumph of faith – a failure of analysis', *Human Relations*, 55: 89–118.

Nolan, J. (2010) 'The influence of Western banks on corporate governance in China', *Asia Pacific Business Review*, 16: 417–36

— (2011) 'Good guanxi and bad guanxi: Western bankers and the role of network practices in institutional change in China', *International Journal of Human Resource Management*, 22: 3357–72.

Redding, G. (1990) *The Spirit of Chinese Capitalism*. New York: Walter de Gruyter.

Reuters (10 November 2010) *A Morgan Stanley star falls in China*. Available at http://www.reuters.com/article/idUSTRE5A94AY20091110 (accessed: 17 November 2010).

Rowley, C. and Warner, M. (eds) (2005) *Globalization and Competitiveness: Big Business in Asia*. New York: Routledge.

Schaede, U. (1995) 'The "Old Boy" Network and Government-Business Relationships in Japan', *Journal of Japanese Studies*, 21: 293–317.

Sugimoto, Y. (2010) *An Introduction to Japanese Society*. Cambridge: Cambridge University Press.

Tong, C. K. and Yong, P. K. (1998) '*Guanxi* bases, *Xinyong* and Chinese business networks', *British Journal of Sociology*, 49: 75–96.

Tung, R. and Worm, V. (2001) 'Network Capitalism: The Role of Human Resources in Penetrating the China Market', *The International Journal of Human Resource Management*, 12: 517–34.

Uzzi, B. (1996) 'The sources and consequences of embeddedness for the economic performance of organizations: the network effect', *American Sociological Review*, 61: 674–98.

Wang, H. (2007) 'Linking up with the international track: what's in a slogan?' *The China Quarterly*, 189: 1–23.

Wang, W. (2000) 'Informal institutions and foreign investment in China', *Pacific Review*, 13: 525–56.

Wank, D. (2002) 'Business-State clientelism in China: decline or evolution' in Gold, T., Guthrie, D. and Wank, D. (eds) *Social Connections in China: Institutions, Culture and the Changing Nature of Guanxi*. Cambridge: Cambridge University Press, pp. 97–116.

Warner, M. (2003) *Culture and Management in Asia*. London: Routledge.

— (2010) 'In search of Confucian HRM: theory and practice in Greater China and beyond', *The International Journal of Human Resource Management*, 21: 2053–78.

Witt, M. (2006) *Changing Japanese Capitalism: Societal Coordination and Institutional Adjustment*. Cambridge, UK: Cambridge University Press.

Wong, Y. T., Wong, S.H. and Wong, Y. W. (2010) 'A study of subordinate-supervisor *Guanxi* in Chinese joint ventures', *International Journal of Human Resource Management*, 21: 2142–55.

Yan, Y. (1996) 'The culture of *guanxi* in a north China village', *The China Journal*, 35: 1–23.

Yang, M. (1994) *Gifts, Favours and Banquets: The Art of Social Relationships in China.* Ithaca, Cornell University Press.

— (2002) 'The resilience of *Guanxi* and its new deployments: a critique of some new *Guanxi* scholarship', *The China Quarterly*, 170: 459–76.

Zhu, Y., Warner, M. and Rowley, C. (2007) 'Human resource management with "Asian" characteristics: a hybrid people-management system in East Asia', *International Journal of Human Resource Management*, 18: 745–68.

11 East Asian business systems in transition

Michael A. Witt

Introduction

This chapter draws on the analytical framework of business systems analysis (Redding, 2005; Whitley, 1999) to offer a comparative overview of business and its cultural and institutional underpinnings in China, Japan, and South Korea. The overall picture that emerges is one of considerable variety in East Asian economies. China presents itself as a mixed economy that combines several distinct business systems, including a strong private sector and a possibly resurgent State-controlled sector, both operating by different sets of rules. Despite minor institutional changes in recent years, the Japanese business system remains highly coordinated and employee-centric. South Korea retains a business-group-led form of capitalism. Given space constraints, I will be painting with a broad brush and will refer readers looking for more detailed expositions to volumes dedicated to Asian business systems analysis (e.g., Redding and Witt, 2007; Whitley, 1992; Witt and Redding, 2013). This account builds on the topic introduced in chapter 4 and extends its scope by employing, as stated, the "business system analysis" approach.

Business system analysis

A society's way of doing business—its business system—can be understood in the context of three main components: culture, the institutional context of firms, and the rules of coordination inside and among firms (Redding, 2005). Each of these components breaks into three parts.

Culture refers to the social construction of reality (Berger and Luckmann, 1966) in a society; that is, it enables people to make sense of actions and attributes (see chapter 3). Business system analysis explores three aspects of culture: rationale, which expresses the ends and means a society considers acceptable for business; identity, which relates to a sense of belonging and ranges from individualism to collectivism; and authority, which relates to hierarchy in society.

The institutional context of the firm describes the rules governing the ability of actors to draw on three main forms of capital: financial, human, and social. For financial capital, the key questions are where firms obtain their funds and on what conditions. For human capital, the salient points are the availability of skills and the organization of labor. For social capital, the pivotal distinction is between interpersonal trust, which evolves between individuals, usually through positive experiences, and institutionalized trust, which relies on legal systems or generalized social pressure to keep people honest and thus enables strangers to trust one another.

The business system itself consists of three main areas of coordination. The first explores what kind of ownership patterns are present and to what extent owners have control over the management of the firm. The second relates to cooperation across firm boundaries, usually in various forms of alliances and networks. The third considers the internal structure of the firm, and especially the modes of decision-making and promotion.

Interacting with all of this are various actors and influences (cf. Redding, 2005). Prominent among them is the role of the State, which in many societies represents the most important single source of institutions—in the guise of laws and regulations—constituting the overall shape of the business system.

China

China today features several major business systems, differentiated both by ownership of businesses and by region (see chapter 5). The challenge for analysis is to identify sensible broad categories to help interpret the overall picture. In line with much of the literature, we propose that the main business systems in China today are:

The State-owned sector. Once the dominant form of business, its share of economic output has declined to about 30 percent of GDP. Most enterprises in this category are large, capital intensive, and bureaucratic. Many receive special benefits and protection from various levels of government.

The private sector. Private business reemerged rapidly following economic reforms in the late 1970s and now accounts for about two-thirds of GDP. Firms are usually small family businesses.

The local corporates. This category represents a large variety of firms involving elements of both the private and the State-owned sectors, and they may appear in the statistics as belonging to either. Many of them developed from collective enterprises into hybrids blending some aspects of the State-owned sectors with elements of private business. Often, local governments protect and promote these businesses, giving privileged access to financial and fixed capital, labor, and land. Since the characteristics in this group lie in between those of the private and the State-owned sector, I will for the most part bracket it from the discussion below.

These three major forms coexist with a sizable foreign-invested sector. These firms are important contributors to Chinese GDP and are also sources of learning for local firms. They usually represent hybrids between Chinese elements and aspects of the respective home country of the foreign investor. Given our emphasis on Chinese ways of doing business, I will exclude this sector from explicit discussion.

Rationale

There are two main societally accepted reasons for the existence of the firm in China today: generating family wealth, and contributing to Chinese economic development. In the private sector, generating family wealth occupies a central position. This needs to be seen in the context of the need to earn a living, but also of the centuries-old need to use material resources as a buffer against environmental uncertainty. This aspect of Chinese culture was suppressed in Mao's days but re-emerged afterwards and became fully legitimate with Deng Xiaoping's assertion that it was glorious to get rich. Most private entrepreneurs hold that their striving for private wealth also enables them to contribute to Chinese economic development.

In the State-owned sector, the order of priority is reversed. This is particularly salient for the presently 117 so-called core SOEs (or central SOEs) under the control of SASAC (the State-owned Assets Supervision and Administration Commission). These firms cover virtually all industries one might consider strategic or vital. The Chinese State protects and nurtures these firms with the objective of developing leading Chinese firms in these industries, though the State has also pushed them to reform themselves into profitable enterprises.

Identity

Chinese society, like all Asian societies (2010), is collectivist. The key reference group is the family. Concentric circles with a diminishing sense of affiliation follow, extending over the extended family to the clan, friendships of various strengths, and (loosely) people from the same general geographic area. One's company is at best a very weak source of identity for private sector employees, while some sense of belonging may remain in the State sector despite years of market-oriented reforms involving restructurings.

Authority

Chinese society is highly hierarchical, more so than those of Japan and South Korea (Hofstede *et al.* 2010). Authority relations are established on a range of criteria. Some, such as age, education, and sex, have their origins in Confucian ideals of social order. Counter to Confucian ideas that a gentleman would not handle money, wealth has in recent years emerged as a strong status symbol, with respect going to those who make their wealth conspicuous. Communist party membership and office may establish hierarchy, especially in the State-owned sector.

Financial capital

The main orientation of the Chinese financial system is to provide funds to the State-owned sector. State-owned enterprises (SOEs) attract up to 99 percent of commercial bank loans to Chinese firms (Tsai, 2007), and they usually receive funds at low interest rates. SOEs also have preferential access to the stock market.

As a result, the private sector in China finds it difficult to obtain external funding. Most capital seems to stem from savings or informal loans from family and friends. In addition, there is a large shadow banking system providing access to short-term funds, though at high interest rates that in spring 2011 reached 6 to 8 percent per month (*Economist, The*, 2011). One of the major advantages of local corporates is that they usually succeed in circumventing the funding issues of the private sector by maintaining good connections with local government.

Human capital

The overall quality and availability of human capital in the economy has considerable development potential (Sheldon *et al.*, 2011). While the Chinese school system produces locally good outcomes, as demonstrated by the stellar results of the Shanghai region in the 2010 PISA study by the OECD, the average remains weak. Technical skills in particular are in short supply. There is no strong public vocational training system, and on the job training is difficult for firms to sustain because of short-term average employment tenures, especially in the private sector. Unions exist at the company level and are joined together in the All China Federation of Trade Unions (ACFTU). While unions in the West are non-governmental organizations, in China they are a branch of the Communist Party. In labor conflicts, they usually side with the companies.

Social capital

Trust in China is predominantly interpersonal (cf. chapter 10). It follows the same general pattern as identity, with trust being unconditional within the core family and weakening with each concentric circle. People outside the last concentric circle are distrusted and seen as competitors in a zero-sum game. Institutionalized trust in China is for all practical purposes absent. As a result, people do not trust strangers; this acts as a barrier to doing business and to delegating inside companies.

Ownership

Private firms are usually owned and run by private individuals and their families. State-owned firms, by definition, are in the hands of the State. While part of their stock may be listed on the stock exchange and thus be held by domestic and international investors, the State will usually retain operational control and the right to appoint top management. Hybrid firms fall in between, often mixing private and local State ownership and control. Large firms that from the outside look private often have considerable levels of government ownership.

Networks

Despite China's reputation for valuing relationships *(guanxi),* as discussed in chapter 10, non-hierarchical forms of networking among firms are relatively sparse. In the private sector, personal relationships enable so-called production networks in which a number of small firms produce jointly by dividing up the labor among themselves. For simple products such as lighters or toys, this formula can be highly successful (Zeng and Williamson, 2007). Private entrepreneurs may also engage in business associations, which may help them build interpersonal trust. In the State sector, non-hierarchical ties are weak. There are numerous (hierarchical) conglomerates, and the Communist Party nexus permeates the sector.

Management

Major decisions in Chinese firms are usually made at the top of the organization. In private firms, decision-making is in the hands of the owner-manager. In SOEs, ultimate decision power remains in the hands of the State. Delegation in the firm suffers from the absence of institutionalized trust, which implies that strangers are not trusted. Promotion criteria in the private sector include skills and trust. Top positions are usually reserved for family members. In SOEs, seniority continues to matter, and the State appoints top management.

The State

The Chinese State is highly interventionist. At the same time, the central government has far less control over the country than Westerners commonly assume. China features high levels of decentralization of policy-making to local governments, and central government policies and directives have proved hard to enforce. The result is much regional variation in the ways businesses work and the institutions around them evolve. The Chinese State has found these differences useful in that they permit institutional experimentation, which helps evolve information about the feasible direction of central government policy.

Government policy tends to pay relatively little attention to the private sector, though it has in recent years emphasized the need to provide better access to finance. The opposite is true for the State-owned sector. While minor SOEs have been wound up or privatized, the core SOEs already mentioned receive protection and promotion in the context of Japanese-inspired industrial policy measures. In particular, these SOEs have access to ample and cheap finance, are protected from foreign competition, and are encouraged to export or invest abroad (see chapter 12). The ultimate objective for these policies is to create a population of large, competitive, Chinese firms in sectors deemed strategic.

Central government policy for the most part treats local corporates like private firms. Local governments, on the other hand, may provide support and protection similar to those the central government extends to core SOEs.

Japan

Rationale

Japanese firms exist to serve society in general and their employees in particular (see chapter 6). Shareholders have gained acceptance as stakeholders, but few firms would consider them primary. The perceived need to justify business activities to society originates in Confucian values introduced to Japan during the *Tokugawa* era (1603–1868). Trading was seen as a parasitic activity without value added, and merchants were consequently at the bottom of the social order of the time. Their status improved once government needed their funds and business experience to modernize Japan from 1868 onward. After the Second World War, Japanese economic policy refocused on economic growth and spreading economic wealth evenly among the Japanese people. Universal male employment emerged as the Japanese recipe for doing so. In providing for their employees, Japanese firms thus fulfill a societal mandate.

Identity

Like all Asian societies, Japan's is collectivist, as chapter 7 makes clear. The main reference group for Japanese males, and in Japanese economic life more generally, is the company (cf. chapter 9). This is unusual in the Asian context in that this represents an adopted group rather than one the individual is born into. The background of this pattern is that most Japanese men still work for the same company for most of their productive life and tend to spend more time with colleagues than with their family during those years. Family life is mostly in the hands of Japanese women, and accordingly their main reference group tends to be the family. In addition, school ties represent an important source of identity.

Authority

Japanese society is fairly hierarchical, though less so than those of China and South Korea (Hofstede *et al.* 2010). Authority relations continue to be structured according to Confucian principles, which became official government policy during the *Tokugawa* era (1603–1868) in order to help establish and maintain order in society. Determinants of respect are predominantly age, educational attainment, and sex. Of these, age tends to supersede the others; a university graduate behaving inappropriately toward an older person would be considered uneducated, his or her degree notwithstanding.

Financial capital

The main source of financial capital for Japanese firms continues to be banks, meeting around 60 percent of the annual need for new funds. Markets make up for the remainder through stock and bond issues. Allocation decisions involve a combination of market criteria such as credit worthiness, strength of the existing business relationship, and government instructions. The precise mix has changed considerably over time, with the role of government now much diminished and that of market criteria considerably enhanced. Firms usually receive loans for the long term. Unlike Western banks, Japanese banks often do not recall loans from firms in trouble but may offer new loans to help them survive.

Human capital

Skill levels in Japan are generally among the highest in the world. The education system produces high attainment that scores well in international comparisons such as the OECD's PISA tests, though some Asian nations such as South Korea tend to perform even better (cf. chapter 8). Similar to other Asian systems, Japan's has invited criticism for being overly focused on rote rehearsal and test taking rather than on practical application and creative thinking.

Firms usually spend considerable time and resources on training new hires, usually through a rotation system that exposes them to various parts of the company. Firms can afford to do so because employment is long term, which enables firms to reap the benefits of their investments in their staff. Similarly, long-term employment enables employees to develop skills that are valuable to their firms.

Unions are usually company-based. Strikes are rare, and when they occur, they tend to be short and symbolic. Given the rationale underlying the firm, identification with the firm, and participation in decision-making processes, there is generally little reason for employees to strike.

Social capital

Japan features relatively high levels of both interpersonal and institutionalized trust. Personal relationships are important, especially within teams, organizations, and among business partners. Having graduated from the same school, or retired from the same organization, can greatly enhance this form of trust. However, it is relatively less important than in Korea and especially in China.

Japan attains institutionalized trust not through the legal system but through social pressure and collective enforcement. For instance, companies breaching public trust in their products have been driven into bankruptcy by consumer boycotts of their products.

Ownership

Most important Japanese firms are listed corporations. However, about 52 percent of the outstanding stock of the average firm is in the hands of friendly financial institutions and corporations, which tend to hold these shares for the long term. Part of these shares involves cross-shareholdings, that is, companies mutually holding each others' shares. The effect of these patterns is that Japanese firms remain relatively well insulated from pressures from their owners. Other measures blunt shareholder influence even further. For instance, about a quarter of Japanese firms now have poison-pill defenses against hostile takeovers, and many firms hold their annual general meetings concurrently.

Networks

Japanese firms network extensively with one another. There are three main types of Japanese firm networks: first, the business group, also known as horizontal *keiretsu*. These bring together firms from different industries, usually about 30 to 40 of them. Prominent examples have historically included Mitsubishi, Mitsui, and Sumitomo. Recent mergers across group boundaries have blurred the picture and raise the question of whether the groups are reconfiguring or dissolving.

Second, there are supplier networks, also known as vertical *keiretsu*. These tie together firms with their suppliers in long-term sourcing relationships. Third, there are intra-industry loops, in which firms informally exchange information concerning their industries, from market information to technical data. These loops usually develop around industry associations.

Management

Japanese management is unusual in Asia in that non-routine decision-making is consensual and participatory. Major decisions usually involve informal consensus building among the major stakeholders inside the firm before being brought up for a vote at the appropriate forum. Employees are also encouraged to look for possibilities to improve the workings of the company, and systems are put in place to enable employees to feed their proposals into the decision-making process. The drawback of these processes is that decision-making can take a long time. On the other hand, once decisions are reached, implementation is usually quick. Promotion involves a strong element of seniority, which is defined as length of service in the firm. Performance is taken into account through faster performance paths. Less capable employees are sidelined, seconded to subsidiaries, or retired early.

The State

The Japanese State used to be the paradigmatic developmental State. It used to intervene massively in the economy in the context of industrial policy aimed at accelerating the development of the economy. This model had run its course by the 1980s, and the OECD (2011) now rates Japan as a relatively low-interventionist State. However, this probably underestimates the true extent of intervention, as much of it has historically occurred informally (e.g. through "administrative guidance") (Johnson, 1982). The thrust of government policy today is unclear, as political leadership in Japan has been in short supply since the resignation of Prime Minister Koizumi in 2006. The general direction seems to be to move toward a more social welfare-oriented regime, possibly similar to northern European States.

South Korea

Rationale

Korean firms pursue stakeholder value. Key stakeholders are shareholders (especially the so-called "owner families"), employees, and society as a whole (see chapter 7). Underlying this configuration is the need to balance the interests of owners, who want to maximize their returns, against those of the other powerful constituents in Korean business. Employees in Korea are well-organized and proficient at attaining their goals, such as fair wages, through strikes. Society as a whole tends to be suspicious especially of large business in Korea and exerts considerable influence on the State's handling of business through public opinion. As a result, businesses have a strong incentive to try to satisfy all three major stakeholders simultaneously.

A residual and fading element in Korean rationale relates to the development of the nation. While South Korea is now clearly an advanced industrialized country with a per capita GDP that exceeds that of many European nations, Koreans see a continued need for growth and development. Part of the reason for this is that Koreans tend to benchmark their progress against neighboring Japan, which has a relatively high per capita GDP.

Identity

The Korean sense of identity is collectivist, with family as the main reference group, followed by concentric circles of decreasing strength of affiliation along the same general lines as in China (see chapter 8). However, identification with the workplace is in many cases stronger than in China, though it does not reach Japanese levels.

Authority

Korean society is more hierarchical than Japan's but less so than China's. The main variables affecting authority relations are age, education, and sex, which in turn derive from the Confucian value system that constituted the basis of societal order during the Chosun dynasty (1392–1910). In addition, personal wealth has emerged as a status criterion, though the traditional Confucian disdain for wealth has not entirely disappeared from Korean society.

Financial capital

The Korean financial system remains fundamentally bank-based, with on average more than 80 percent of the funding needs of firms being met through direct finance. In fact, despite reforms intended to increase the role of direct finance, the importance of indirect finance has increased since 2000. Even the large conglomerates, the so-called *chaebol*, meet only about 40 percent of their financial needs through direct finance. While they are forbidden to own banks, they usually incorporate a large array of non-bank financial institutions such as insurances and credit card businesses that can be tapped for funds. The overall effect is that large conglomerates have captive, long-term sources of funds while smaller firms are more dependent on meeting creditworthiness criteria to obtain less patient funds.

Human capital

The Korean education system counts among the best performing in the world. In the 2009 OECD PISA tests, Korea ranked on average fourth among more than sixty countries,[1] topped only by Hong Kong, Singapore, and Finland. Tertiary enrollment rates are higher than any country except Cuba. As a result, general skills levels in South Korea are high. On the other hand, technical skills continue to pose a challenge. The vocational training system is weak, and on the job training suffers from the short average employment tenure in most Korean firms. Longer tenures are reported for *chaebol* firms, which in turn should enable higher levels of internal training.

Korea has predominantly company unions, with a unionization rate of about 10 percent. Unlike Japanese unions, Korean unions are notorious for their militancy. Identification with the firm is much weaker than in Japan. In addition, workers usually do not trust managers to treat them fairly, in part because the centralized decision-making structure of Korean firms makes it difficult for workers to verify the claims management makes about the health of the business.

Social capital

Korea has high levels of interpersonal trust centered on the family. Similar to China, this trust weakens as one proceeds through the concentric circles of identity, and there is a tendency toward zero-sum competition among strangers, though it is weaker than in China. Institutionalized trust levels are higher than those in China but lower than in Japan. Social pressure plays a role in enforcement. So do the State and the legal system, though citizens usually do not trust them fully, especially when the interests of major businesses are concerned. For instance, the Korean State has a high propensity to release major business leaders convicted for crimes from prison on grounds of their supposed importance to the Korean economy.

Ownership

Large Korean conglomerates—including Samsung, Hyundai, SK, and LG—usually consist of publicly listed firms. The so-called "owner families" who started these conglomerates usually hold less than 10 percent of the overall outstanding stock in their conglomerates. They remain in control of the entire conglomerate by retaining control of one key enterprise that in turn controls the rest through various mechanisms such as pyramidal or circular shareholdings. As a result, corporate governance is relatively weak when viewed from the perspective of shareholders other than the owner families, and benefits accruing to the owner families are often disproportionate to their shareholdings.

Networks

Korean entrepreneurs tend to build up conglomerates of firms with activities in diverse industries. Though these entities may appear like networks, they remain under the hierarchical control of the owner family and their respective holding company. Other networks across firms tend to be sparse.

Management

Decision-making in Korean companies is top-down and highly hierarchical. Even in large conglomerates, much strategic decision-making happens within the chairman's office. Delegation occurs mostly in the execution of tasks, though some firms such as Samsung and Hyundai appear to have built up professional management cadres. Promotions involve a mix of relationships, seniority, and performance. In general, the top positions in a company are reserved for members of the owner family.

The State

The Korean State used to be a strong developmental State. It followed the example of Japan while arguably streamlining the Japanese model. Businesses were clearly subservient to the State and the policy goal of economic development, as expressed in Samsung's corporate motto (scrapped following the Asian Financial Crisis of 1997/8) that "we do business for the sake of nation building." Firms meeting government export targets—the key metric used to judge performance—would receive support, those falling short would be shut down.

Though State influence has receded, it continues to be a strong, interventionist actor in the Korean economy. Many of its efforts nowadays seem to be focused on taming the enormous economic might of the *chaebol*. Samsung alone, for instance, accounts for about 20 percent of South Korean exports. On the one hand, this suggests a need to break up the conglomerates to reduce the risk associated with any one of them failing. On the other hand, errors in the processes chosen could kill the geese that lay golden eggs for the Korean economy. As a result, State action has at best retarded further economic concentration around the *chaebol* but has failed to stop or reverse it.

Conclusions

Predictions of the future evolution of business systems are always difficult, and seemingly minor events can fundamentally change developments that had previously appeared to be inexorable. With this caveat in mind, I conclude this chapter with some general thoughts about likely developments in the three nations studied in this chapter.

There is a range of uncertainties around the future shape of Chinese business (cf. Redding and Witt, 2011). Of particular interest for the shape of the business system is that after years of letting private business push China forward, the Chinese State now seems to be reasserting a role for State-owned and hybrid businesses. It is possible that policy-makers may have concluded that purely private firms are unlikely to reach the levels of capital and technology intensity necessary to move the Chinese economy further up the value chain. Given the poor historical record of SOEs both in China and elsewhere, the most likely winner of this new development may be the local corporates. Given sufficient State support paired with private leadership, it is possible that in the long run the Chinese business landscape will come to resemble that of South Korea (cf. Redding and Witt, 2009).

The future of the Japanese business system is likely to look very much like its present. While there have been considerable pressures for change, the Japanese business system features such high levels of institutional inertia that large scale change is unlikely (Witt, 2006). The aftermath of the 2011 Tohoku earthquake and resultant tsunami, and especially the nuclear disaster at Fukushima, may yet provide the impetus to overcome the status quo and initiate structural adjustments, including a stronger role for women in business (cf. chapter 9). Failing that, an increasingly assertive China may eventually push Japan into structural reforms.

The main area in need of reform in the Korean business system is, as already mentioned, high levels of industrial concentration. It seems unlikely that government will be able to do much about it, not only for fear of damaging the Korean economy, but also because the *chaebol* owner families will put up strong resistance. In the longer term, however, reform of the *chaebol* will be unavoidable. Family businesses usually do not survive for long unless they succeed in separating ownership from control and turn over the running of the firm to professional managers. Where this does not occur, decline is common, usually around the third generation of owners. The *chaebol* will need to begin tackling this challenge within the next decade. If they succeed, the Korean landscape may begin to resemble that of European business systems, which combine stakeholder value with family owned but professionally run firms.

Note

1   'Country' loosely applied here to include Hong Kong, a Special Administrative Region of the People's Republic of China.

References

Berger, P. L. and Luckmann, T. (1966) *The social construction of reality: A treatise in the sociology of knowledge*. Garden City, NY: Doubleday.
Economist, The (2011) 'The China price', 28 April 2011. Accessed 12 September 2011 http://www.economist.com/node/18620804
Hofstede, G., Hofstede, G. J. and Minkov, M. (2010) *Cultures and organizations: Software for the mind*. New York: McGraw-Hill.
Johnson, C. (1982) *MITI and the Japanese miracle: The growth of industrial policy 1925– 1975*. Stanford, CA: Stanford University Press.
OECD (2011) *Integrated PMR indicator 2008*. Accessed 13 June 2011 http://www.oecd.org/dataoecd/33/12/42136008.xls
Redding, G. (2005) 'The thick description and comparison of societal systems of capitalism', *Journal of International Business Studies*, 36: 123–55.

Redding, G. and Witt, M. A. (2007) *The future of Chinese capitalism: Choices and chances*. Oxford: Oxford University Press.

—(2009) 'China's business system and its future trajectory'. *Asia Pacific Journal of Management*, 26: 381–99.

—(2011) 'Chinese business systems and the challenges of transition' in Sheldon, P., Kim, S., Li, Y. and Warner, M. (eds) *China's changing workplace: Dynamism, diversity and disparity*. London and New York, NY: Routledge.

Sheldon, P., Kim, S., Li, Y. and Warner, M. (eds) (2011) *China's changing workplace: Dynamism, diversity and disparity*. London and New York, NY: Routledge.

Tsai, K. S. (2007) *Capitalism without democracy: The private sector in contemporary China*. Ithaca, NY: Cornell University Press.

Whitley, R. (1992) *Business systems in East Asia: Firms, markets and societies*. London: Sage Publications.

—(1999) *Divergent capitalisms: The social structuring and change of business systems*. Oxford: Oxford University Press.

Witt, M. A. (2006) *Changing Japanese capitalism: Societal coordination and institutional adjustment*. Cambridge: Cambridge University Press.

Witt, M. A. and Redding, G. (eds) (2013) *The Oxford Handbook of Asian Business Systems*. Oxford: Oxford University Press.

Zeng, M. and Williamson, P. J. (2007) *Dragons at your door: How Chinese cost innovation is disrupting global competition*. Boston, MA: Harvard Business School Press.

12 SMEs in selected economies in East Asia

Li Xue Cunningham

Introduction

More than 1.5 billion people, about 38 per cent of the population of Asia or 22 per cent of the world's population, live in geographic East Asia. The region is one of the world's most densely inhabited places, with 133 inhabitants per square km (340 per square mile), being about three times the world average of 45 per square km (120 per square mile). East Asia is the home of the People's Republic of China (hereafter referred to as China), the second largest economy in the world, and three of the four formerly-named 'Little Tigers', namely, Hong Kong SAR, South Korea and Taiwan (see chapter 2). With a sustained high single- to double-digit economic growth and development in recent decades (*CIA World Factbook*, 2010), the region is increasingly playing the role of a global growth-pole and is fast emerging as a manufacturing and information technology hub of the world economy.

One of the key characteristics of the East Asia region is the presence and importance of a large small and medium-sized enterprises (SME) sector which makes up the majority of enterprises in all of the region's economies. Although it is important to recognise that the challenges SMEs face, and the corresponding policies aimed at strengthening their competitive performance, may vary due to a great diversity of economies and development experiences among the countries in the region (Chia *et al.*, 2007), the broad challenges faced by East Asian SMEs are similar. Influences such as globalisation, technological innovation, demographic and social change, the level of technology deployed, innovative ability, financial support and entrepreneurship, can be found in the business environment, impacting as both external and internal factors. Consequently, the way SMEs develop in a changing globalised environment has become a key issue.

This chapter will provide an overview of SMEs in East Asia, by looking at their historical development and examining their current economic situation, with special attention to four main economies in the region: China, Hong Kong, South Korea and Taiwan. The importance of SMEs in their nations' economies is demonstrated. The difficulties, challenges and opportunities for SMEs in the new economic environment after the 2008 global financial crisis are discussed. The chapter shows that institutional support forms a backdrop to the growth in the number of SMEs in East Asia. It also asserts that a strong, dynamic and efficient

SME sector will ensure the nation's sustainable economic development in a changing globalised world.

Definitions

Table 12.1 illustrates that there is no general, legally binding definition for SMEs globally. SMEs have been defined against various criteria, such as different sectors, the number of workers employed, the volume of output or sales, the value of assets employed and the use of energy (*ILO report*, 2003). For example, the OECD (2001) defines establishments with up to 19 employees as 'very small'; with up to 99 as 'small'; from 100 to 499 as 'medium' and with over 500 as 'large'. However, many establishments in some developing countries with 100 to 499 employees, which according to the OECD definition would be considered 'medium', are regarded as relatively large firms (*ILO report*, 2003).

Table 12.1 Some differing definitions of SMEs in most Asian economies

Economy	Category of industry	Criteria/Country's official definition
Hong Kong	Manufacturing	< 100 employees
	Non-manufacturing	< 50 employees
Indonesia	SME	< 100 employees
Japan	Manufacturing, mining and transportation construction industries	< 300 employees or invested capital < £0.42 million
	Wholesale trade	< 100 employees or capitalisation < £0.13 million
	Retail trade and services	< 50 employees or capitalisation < £41,920.843
Korea	Manufacturing	< 300 employees, £10.89 – 43.57 million of capital (assets)
	Mining and transportation	< 300 employees Construction; < 200 employees: Commerce and other service businesses; < 20 employees
Malaysia	Small and medium industries	< = 150 full time workers or with a shareholder fund of < £3.64 million
Philippines	SME	< 200 employees, asset size < £0.63 million
Singapore	Manufacturing	fixed assets < S$ 15 million
	Services	< 200 employees and fix assets < £4.98 million
Taiwan	Manufacturing, mining and construction industries	< £0.93 million and < 200 employees
	Service industries and others	< £1.24 million of sale volume and < 50 employees
Thailand	SME	< = 200 employees or fixed assets < £1.49 million
Vietnam	SME	No fixed definition, generally < 500 employees

Source: Cunningham and Rowley 2008

Table 12.2 National standards on SMEs in China

Sectors	Employee numbers	Annual revenue (RMB million)	Total assets (RMB million)
Industrial	< 300–302,000	> 3,000–030,000	> 4,000–040,000
Construction	< 600–603,000	> 3,000–030,000	> 4,000–040,000
Transport	< 500–503,000	> 3,000–030,000	
Postal service	< 400–401,000		
Wholesale	< 100–200	> 3,000–030,000	
Retails	< 100–500	> 1,000–015,000	
Hotel and restaurant	< 400–800	> 3,000–015,000	

Source: State Economic and Trade Commission, China 2003

Statistics benchmark: The payroll is the year-end employment number; the revenue of industrial enterprises is the annual sales revenue; the revenue of construction enterprises is the year-end completed revenue; the revenue of wholesale and retail enterprises is the annual sales; and the revenue and total assets of enterprises in the transportation and posts sector and hotels and restaurants are operating revenue and combined assets respectively.

In addition, the definitions of an SME differ from one country to another, as they can be based on a nation's economic situation. For example, the European Union defines a SME as having fewer than 500 employees whereas South Korea classifies a SME as having fewer than 1,000 employees. Some countries do not even have fixed definitions of SMEs (for example, Vietnam and the UK) (www.ciionline.org, 2011). Further, within a country or region, definitions of SME are different at different stages of economic development. For example, in China the definitions and criteria of SMEs have been adjusted four times since 1949. On 19 February 2003, a new Small and Medium-Sized Enterprises standards document was published to relevant government agencies with the approval of the State Council in China (see Table 12.2). The standards apply to the government statistics for work and replace the old classification standards, which came into effect in 1988. They also replace the supplementary standards published in 1992.

SMEs in East Asia

Even though the definitions of SMEs are varied, the importance of SMEs in contemporary East Asian economies has been demonstrated. It is evident that East Asian SMEs are the largest source of domestic employment across all economic sectors, in both rural and urban areas (Ganapathi and Joshi, 2008). SMEs are very active in some spheres, engaging in multiple product lines, small-series production and the service industry (Park and Kim, 2011, Hall and Harvie, 2003, Wang and Tsai, 2010). The SME sector is also seen as a major and sustainable generator of employment and income for citizens working outside of the State sector (Cunningham, 2011). SME development holds the added allure of being a key component of wider economic development and poverty alleviation, especially in developing and transitional economies (UNESCAP, 2009). Moreover, a vibrant SME sector helps promote competition and a culture

Table 12.3 The role of SMEs in selected East Asian economies

Economy	Share of total enterprises (%)	Share of employment (%)	Share of exports (%)	Contribution to GDP (%)
1. China	99	40	62.3	60
2. Hong Kong	98	48	94	48
3. Taiwan	98	78.06	17	31
4. S. Korea	99.9	87.5	30.9	49.4

Sources: 1. 2011 figure, http://www.chinadaily.com.cn/, ADB, 2009; 2. 2009 figure, Census and Statistics Department, HK, http://www.censtatd.gov.hk/; 3. 2010 figure, SMEA 2011; 4. 2010 figure, except export 2008, Park and Kim 2011; http://eng.smba.go.kr/

of entrepreneurship, which are both conducive to economic growth (Gries and Naude, 2010).

Table 12.3 describes the share of the number of enterprises, employment, exports and the contribution to gross domestic product (GDP) by SMEs for the four East Asian economies. On one hand, it demonstrates that SMEs have contributed significantly to the overall figure. On average, they represent some 98.7 per cent of all business, provide almost 64 per cent of total employment and contribute over 50 per cent of national exports and 47 per cent of industrial output respectively. On the other hand, statistics also illustrate that SMEs' relative roles and contributions to their national economy differ. For instance, it shows that Taiwanese SMEs are focused more on domestic demand while exporting is still a major business activity of SMEs in other economies. Consequently, the SME sector in Taiwan plays a crucial role as a local job provider and is thus a stabilising force in society rather than a major driver for the nation's export growth. While similarities in economic, historical, institutional and social influences on the development of SMEs are evident in China, Hong Kong, South Korea and Taiwan, underlying conditions and trends are different in each of these four economies (see chapters 5, 6 and 7).

China

China is a communist country which adopted an open door policy in 1979 and has transformed from a planned state to a socialist market economy. Nowadays, China plays a major global role. As the world's second largest economy and the largest exporter, international trade is the largest contributor to the nation's GDP, accounting for 44.2 per cent of the national total in 2009 (SSB, 2010).

The early development of SMEs in China was promoted partly to create employment for recently redundant rural labour and partly to lessen the impact of mass lay-offs from both state-owned enterprises (SOEs) and urban collectively owned enterprises (COEs). Over the last thirty years, the role of SMEs in the Chinese economy has gradually transformed from 'the fringes' to 'a supplement' and then 'an important component' of this market-based socialist economy (Cunningham, 2011). SMEs have become the engines of China's rapid economic growth. Every year they contribute around 59 per cent of GDP, 50 per cent of tax revenue, 68 per cent of foreign trade volume and 75 per cent of urban employment.

They are also responsible for 65 per cent of invention patents and 80 per cent of new products in China. Moreover, Chinese SMEs not only maximise the efficiency of the nation's resource allocation and distribution by mobilising and utilising local human and material resources, but they also stimulate the growth of certain sectors (Cunningham, 2010a). While there is a radical reshaping of the economy in terms of enterprise ownership (see chapter 5), the mindset of the Chinese government is also changing. It has largely de-emphasised ownership and extended support to all sorts of firms, especially SMEs. A 2003 law on SME promotion affirmed SMEs' role in the economy (Xinhua News Agency, 2003). After the global financial crisis in 2008, and in the face of severe survival predicaments, especially the shortage of electricity, labour and capital, the first nation-level special plan for SMEs was issued by the Chinese government on 22 September 2011, so as to build the public service platform network and improve SMEs' capacity (*China Daily*, 2011).

Hong Kong

Hong Kong has been a special administrative region (SAR) of China since 1997. As one of the world's most open trade economies with a very high economic development level, the economy of Hong Kong is made up mostly of SMEs (see chapter 6). At the end of 2009, for example, 98.9 per cent of 12,204 manufacturing business units employed fewer than 100 persons, while 98.3 per cent of the 273,350 service business units were SMEs (employing fewer than 50 persons) (www.gov.hk/en/about/abouthk/Factsheets, 2011).

Due to Hong Kong's geo-strategic position, a channel and an entrepôt for trade in goods and services, Hong Kong's SMEs differ from their East Asian counterparts as they are highly dependent on international trade and finance (Bjerke, 2000). In 2010, the value of the goods and services trade, including the sizeable share of re-exports, was about four times the size of Hong Kong's GDP. Hong Kong's SMEs are also largely involved in the service industry. As the twelfth largest services exporter in the world, Hong Kong's service sector accounted for more than 90 per cent of the territory's GDP and constituted a share of 88 per cent of total employment in 2009 (*CIA World Factbook*, 2010). Furthermore, except in the very broadest sense the Hong Kong government's role is to provide a suitable and stable framework for commerce and industry to function efficiently and effectively with minimum interference (Siu *et al.*, 2006). Economic planning is not practised by the government. Hence, the economic policies of free enterprise and free trade stimulated the huge growth of SMEs, but also exposed them to the global economic slowdown.

Taiwan

Taiwan's SMEs have been recognised as the key driving force of the country's economic development over the past half century (Tai and Huang, 2006). In contrast to China and South Korea, indeed, Taiwan has typically been viewed as a diverse 'small firm' economy (for example, Hamilton, 1996, Bjerke, 2000, Hall and Harvie, 2003, Wang and Tsai, 2010). As family-based or family-like relationships dominate and support social interaction in Taiwan, the majority of Taiwanese SMEs are family businesses (Gabrenya and Hwang, 1996).

The emergence of SMEs in Taiwan is closely associated with domestic conditions, global economic developments and the government's economic, social and educational policies (Siu *et al.*, 2006, Wang, 2007). For instance, the earliest Taiwanese SMEs were encouraged by the Nationalist government as a means to overcome the shortages of food and other essential domestic commodities. The expansion of export-oriented SMEs in labour-intensive industries in the 1950s was the result of an effort by the Taiwanese government to use limited state resources to speed up economic growth (see chapter 6). From the 1970s to the mid-1980s, Taiwan's export promotion policy and its open economy have laid a solid foundation for the further development of Taiwanese SMEs (Ahn 2001). As the government relaxed its grip on the New Taiwan dollar, followed by increasing labour costs and growing environmental awareness, Taiwan SMEs have gone through industrial restructuring and become more service-oriented in the past two to three decades (SMEA, 2011). Some SMEs moved their operations to mainland China and Southeast Asian countries in search of cheaper labour and new business opportunities, while others were forced to become more innovative, upgrade their operations and partner with companies from developed economies to cope with the increasingly adverse conditions. With continued government support, most economists believe that SMEs will maintain their position as the mainstay of Taiwan's economy for years to come (Wang and Tsai, 2010).

South Korea

South Korea presents another variation in comparison with the other three economies. A dual structure, which combines a small number of successful large enterprise groups with the marginalisation of a large number of SMEs, forms the country's industrial development (Hall and Harvie, 2003, Park and Kim, 2011). It was not until the late 1990s that positive measures were implemented to encourage SME promotion in South Korea (Gregory *et al.*, 2002). The increasing focus on the promotion of SMEs has been encouraged on the basis that they offer greater economic benefits than large firms. In 2010, for example, the total amount of production and added value in Korean SMEs accounted for 46.4 per cent and 49.2 per cent of the national total output respectively (SMBA, 2010). Therefore, South Korean SMEs are not only a major player with regard to the total number of companies and overall employment (see chapter 8), but they also play a core part in production and bring added value that contributes to the economic growth (Yang, 2009).

Although the government development strategy has been changed from a '*Chaebol*-led economy' to one that promotes the joint development of SMEs, following the 1997 Asian financial crisis and the 2008 global financial crisis, the political battleground centres on the fact that largely domestic SMEs are still far weaker (*The Financial Times*, 2010). A lack of competitiveness of Korean SMEs was criticised by economists as a key factor behind high youth unemployment and the shrinking services sector (Wang and Tsai, 2010). Moreover, a centre-periphery relationship has gradually formed between Korean SMEs and big business in the long-term export-based industrialisation strategy (*Financial News*, 2011). As vertically integrated organisations, many Korean SMEs have become subcontracting companies for the large conglomerates (Kong, 2000). With vertical rather than horizontal relationships between the conglomerates and the SMEs, it is argued that a contract-based unilateral relationship restrains the expansion of SMEs' business activities and results in a high dependency of SMEs on the conglomerates (Park and Kim, 2011).

Table 12.4 summarises the similarities and differences among the selected East Asian economies, in relation to the SME sector in particular. While most East Asian economies are export-oriented, the SME sector, which fulfils an important economic role in virtually all economies, has been the most vital contributor in the exporting business. In the case of Taiwan and Korean SMEs, even though they do not export, their products feed into the production of goods that are exported. It is estimated that, for instance, SMEs' export contribution ratio in South Korea increases up to 71.5 per cent, if parts and components supplied for the exports of large sized firms are added (Park and Kim, 2011). Moreover, it is clear that SMEs in East Asia are at different stages of evolution in their respective economies. As a result, the variations in the degree of the state's intervention in the economy, the support provided by the external business environment and the social roots of business organisation determine different paths and strategies in SME development across the economies in the region.

Table 12.4 Comparisons among selected economies, East Asia

Economy	Economy character	Development strategy	Export-focused (% of GDP)	SME majority	Gov. support on SMEs
China	Socialist-market economy	A mix of SOEs and PEs	Yes (44.2%)	Privately-owned	Substantial intervention
Hong Kong	Free economy	SME-dominated	Yes (400%)	Service-oriented	Limited support
Taiwan	Capitalist economy	SME-networked	Yes (130%)	Family business	Selective intervention
South Korea	Highly-industrialised economy	Joint-development between big businesses and SMEs	Yes (43%)	Innovation-oriented	Actively involved

SMEs in a changing globalised world

Although constraints and policies vary with each economy, there are similarities in the challenges faced by SMEs across the East Asian countries. Among them all, structural changes due to both internal and external pressures present the most serious challenge to SMEs in the region.

Dramatic decline in market demand

It is argued that, on average, SMEs are more oriented towards the domestic market and therefore are less likely to be the worst-hit by the global economic slowdown in comparison to large firms in the region (ADB, 2009). However, while a strong incorporation into international trade and finance has been the most important contributor in East Asian countries' GDP growth, SMEs account for most businesses in the region (see Table 12.2). Statistics also demonstrate that SMEs, especially those towards the medium-sized end of the scale, play an important role in the process of each nation's economic development in East Asia, especially for the exporting business (see Table 12.3). Further, a number of studies confirm that SMEs are highly sensitive to changing tendencies and environments (for example, Gray and Mabey, 2005, Siu *et al.*, 2006, Cunningham, 2010b). Therefore, the great dependency on exports in most East Asian economies intensifies a high degree of vulnerability of SMEs to the downturn of the world economy.

While it is well documented that SMEs face problems such as difficult access to credit and poor technological and managerial capabilities, the 2008 global financial crisis has indeed exacerbated these problems. Unlike large firms, export-oriented SMEs have little flexibility to cope with plummeting demand, cancelled orders, scarce financing and delayed payments (Economist Intelligence Unit, 2010). Data from the National Development and Reform Commission (NDRC) showed that in the first half of 2008 67,000 Chinese SMEs collapsed, each with sales income exceeding 5 million Yuan, laying-off more than 20 million employees (APEC, 2009). Industry officials attributed Chinese SME difficulties mainly to the growing costs of production (materials and labour), the declining needs of overseas markets and the fast appreciation of the RMB (Renminbi) (Xinhua News Agency, 31 July 2011). While HSBC's survey results reflect Korean SMEs' pessimistic view of the nation's future economy (SMEWORLD, 2008), the study conducted by the Ministry of Economic Affairs in Taiwan found that approximately 55 per cent of their SME respondents were greatly affected by the crisis (Chung, 2010). Business in Hong Kong, mostly SMEs, had also begun shrinking and the profit margin had narrowed in many sectors since 2008. The Federation of Hong Kong Industries (2009) reported that in 2009 nearly 90 per cent of manufacturers had less orders than before, with an average reduction of 36 per cent in order volume and 30 per cent in profit compared with the previous year. A steep fall in GDP growth among the economies in the region, due to the contraction in international trade in the 2008 global financial crisis (Figure 12.1), means that SMEs in East Asia have been severely affected by the downturn in the international economy (see chapter 2).

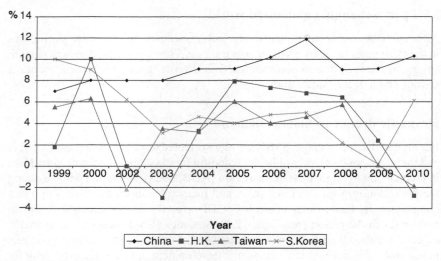

Figure 12.1 GDP growth (1999–2010)

Source: *CIA World Factbook* 2010 (CIA, 2010)

Various approaches and policies have been actively taken by governments to rectify and foster SMEs in the region (Economist Intelligence Unit, 2010). In order to overcome the over-dependency on exports, for instance, Chinese SMEs have started to make a strategic shift to focus on the domestic market rather than Western consumers (Economist Intelligence Unit 2010). SMEs in more advanced economies, such as Taiwan and South Korea, have been upgrading themselves into high-value-added enterprises to achieve high growth (Park and Kim, 2011, Tai and Huang, 2006, Wang and Tsai, 2010). Further, intra-regional trade among East Asian economies has risen considerably in recent years, noted by the Asian Development Bank (ADB, 2009).

While SMEs continue to demonstrate more flexibility than large firms in terms of market entry and exit (SMEA, 2011), however, some scholars have pointed out that the fierce competition in the Chinese domestic market and a fragmented internal market with huge regional differences in consumer tastes and distribution channels have created greater barriers for SMEs to overcome. In addition, other economists argue that the current long supply chain across national borders via intra-regional trade does not insulate East Asian economies from the demand cycle outside the region (Economist Intelligence Unit, 2010). Although the gradual upturn in the economy began in the second half of 2009 (Figure 12.1), with the continued danger of an asset bubble forming and a renewed economic downturn, due to the debt crisis in several consumer nations, uncertainties will remain amid increasingly complicated domestic and overseas conditions. While restructuring industrial competitiveness by shifting the driver of the recovery from an export engine towards more regional- and domestic-focused market demands, SMEs, the major force of all economies in East Asia, are challenged by the rapid pace of change in the global business environment.

More intense competition for human talent

While a number of studies have addressed the significance of a well-motivated, highly skilled workforce as being a key to the success of smaller firms (for example, Storey, 2004, Kotey and Slade, 2005, Sels *et al.*, 2006), finding and retaining skilled staff has been a major and growing problem for SMEs across the world (for example, Hornsby and Kuratko, 2003, Gray and Mabey, 2005, Cunningham, 2010b). In response to the 2008 global crisis, moreover, SMEs in East Asia have been encouraged to transform themselves from labour-intensive manufacturing to innovation-oriented operations (for example, Hall and Harvie, 2003, Park and Kim, 2011, UNESCAP, 2009, Wang, 2007, Wang and Tsai, 2010). As knowledge-based growth depends largely on the quantity and quality of its human resources (SMEA, 2011), human talent has become the main factor affecting SMEs' competitiveness. However, a deteriorating labour market, along with rising unemployment rates and a rapidly ageing population, has intensified the competition for human talent, and the shortages of human talent which have been affecting SMEs have been exacerbated (cf. chapter 13).

Figures 12.2 and 12.3 exemplify the essential social-demographic changes faced by the East Asian economies. It is clear that an increasingly ageing population has become a common phenomenon across all four economies. For instance, the number of people over 65 in Taiwan accounted for 10.9 per cent of the island's total population in 2011, while the population of elderly persons aged above 65 will be 14 per cent of the total population in Hong Kong, as estimated by The Hong Kong Council of Social Service (2011). In the case of China, life expectancy has improved from 48 years in 1960 to 74.51 by 2010 (with women in 2010 having a life expectancy of 76.77 years), while the Under-Five Mortality Rate has

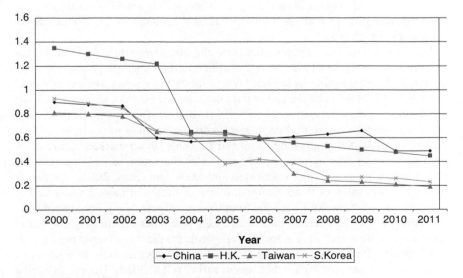

Figure 12.2 Population growth rate (2000–2011)

Source: CIA World Factbook 2011 (CIA, 2011)

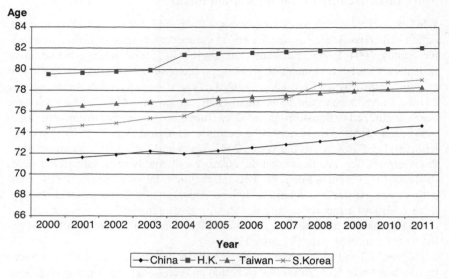

Figure 12.3 Life expectancy at birth (2000–2011)

Source: *CIA World Factbook* 2011 (CIA, 2011)

been reduced from 209 per 1,000 live births in 1960 to 21 by 2008 (SSB, 2010). Whilst population ageing opens up opportunities for economies to invest in human capital formation that may stimulate economic growth and mitigate the possible negative economic effects of an older population, it also results in fiscal problems to the government as well as the potential of a shortage in the labour market (Banister *et al.*, 2010).

In the meantime, the unemployment rate climbed sharply in 2009 in all economies (Figure 12.4). In China, the rise of official urban unemployment to 4.3 per cent in 2009 brought it to its highest level in the last five years. Jobless urbanites jumped to 8.86 million by the end of the fourth quarter of 2008, up more than half a million from the third quarter of 2008 (SSB, 2010). Officially, in the third quarter of 2008 more than 10 million migrant workers lost their jobs, while 670,000 factories closed. Although Hong Kong and Taiwan's labour markets assure inter-sectoral shifts of employment as they are better characterised as integrated and well functioning rather than segmented and inefficient (Ahn, 2001), the rise in unemployment rates in Hong Kong and Taiwan has been more pronounced in comparison to the ones of China and South Korea (Figure 12.4). For instance, the unemployment rate in Taiwan hit a record high of 5.8 per cent in May 2009 after almost a year of consecutive monthly rises, while for the three-month period ending February 2009 Hong Kong registered its unemployment rate as 5 per cent, which was 1.7 per cent higher than a year earlier (CIA, 2010). Hence, an ageing population and high unemployment rates have undermined the labour market.

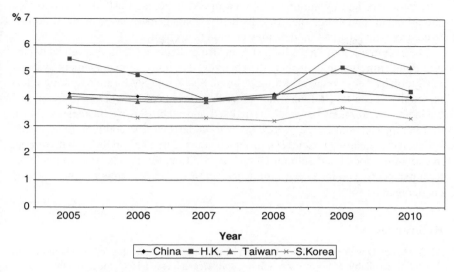

Figure 12.4 Unemployment rates (2005–2010)

Source: *CIA World Factbook* 2011 (CIA, 2011)

Consequently, SMEs are facing more intense competition for human talent while rationalising their operations to enhance the efficiency of resource utilisation and strengthen the overall structure of their business in the coming years.

Overall, the above-mentioned problems are mutually shared and interrelated. They add to the difficulties of and increase the pressure on SMEs. Facing the ever-changing external business environment and a declining internal labour market, how to gain their competitiveness becomes a key challenge faced by not only SMEs themselves but also the economies they operate in.

Conclusions

This chapter examined the issues and challenges to East Asian SMEs in a changing globalised world. Whilst globalisation brings opportunities to SMEs in East Asia in terms of higher efficiency and advanced practices, it poses threats to their development. Yet, the impact of the renewed global business environment did not apply equally to all economies.

In order to enhance SMEs' competitiveness in the subsequent credit crunch and global recession, it is apparent that not only industrial structures but also the labour market and management systems which SMEs operate in need to be reshaped and transformed. Vertical alliances between big businesses and SMEs within and beyond the national border should be promoted so as to ensure a rapid engagement of SMEs in global production and trading. Not only intra-trade but mutual learning from each experience in the region should also be fostered. In so doing, a transitionary and evolutionary change in SMEs across East Asian economies should occur, and simultaneously distinctive management systems, institutional structures, and business models may emerge (see chapter 11).

The examination of SMEs in East Asia also provides a useful theoretical departure point from which to analyse the changing dynamics of management systems in a globalised environment. Although some East Asian SMEs are operating internationally, it can take a long time before the impacts of the change in the global business environment become internalised and stabilised by businesses. Thus, more empirical studies are needed so as to understand the complex relationship between the changing business environment and the impacts on SMEs with respect to economic, social and cultural factors. In addition, future research from a long-term perspective on the changing impacts on SMEs' development in the region is encouraged.

References

ADB (Asian Development Bank) (2009) 'Enterprises in Asia: Fostering Dynamics in SMEs'. Available at http://www.adb.org/statistics (accessed 15 October 2011).

Ahn, C. (2001) 'A search for robust East Asian development models after the financial crisis: mutual learning from East Asian experience', *Journal of Asian Economics*, 12: 419–43.

APEC (2009) 'China gropes for solutions to SME financing difficulties', *Asia-Pacific Economic Cooperation (APEC) e-Commerce Business Alliance*, 30 December 2009. Available at http://www.apec-ecba.org/english/info/Article (accessed 7 November 2011).

Banister, J., Bloom, D. and Rosenberg, L. (2010) 'Population aging and economic growth in China', *Program of Global Demography of Aging*, Working Paper No. 53. Available at http://www.hsph.harvard.edu/pgda/working.htm (accessed 11 November 2011).

Bjerke, B. (2000) 'A typified, culture-based, interpretation of management of SMEs in Southeast Asia', *Asia Pacific Journal of Management*, 17: 103–32.

Chia, H., Fu, P. and Lee, C. (2007) 'Four tigers and the dragon: values, differences, similarities, and consensus', *Asia Pacific Journal of Management*, 24: 305–20.

China Daily (2011) *China issues growth plan for SMEs*. Available at http://www.chinadaily.com.cn/bizchina/2011–09/26/content_13794867.htm (accessed 3 November 2011).

Chung, O. (2010) 'SMEs get equipped', *Taiwan Review*, 7 Jan 2010. Available at http://taiwanreview.nat.gov.tw/ct.asp?xItem=107213&CtNode=1352 (accessed 12 November 2011).

CIA (2010) *World Factbook*. Available at http://www.cia.gov/cia/publications/factbook/index.html (accessed 28 July 2011).

—— (2011) *World Factbook*. Available at http://www.cia.gov/cia/publications/factbook/index.html (accessed 28 July 2011).

Cunningham, Li (2010a) 'Small and Medium Sized Enterprises in China: A literature review, human resource management and suggestions for further research', *Asia Pacific Business Review*, 16: 319–37.

—— (2010b), 'Managing human resources in SMEs in a transition economy: evidence from China', *International Journal of Human Resource Management*, 21: 2120–41.

—— (2011) 'SMEs as motor of growth: A review of China's SMEs development in thirty years (1978–2008)', *Human Systems Management*, 30: 39–54.

Cunningham, Li. and Rowley, C. (2008), 'Human Resource Management in Small and Medium Enterprises in Jiangsu, China' in Barrett, R. and Mayson, S (eds.) *International Handbook of HRM and Entrepreneurship*, Cheltenham: Edward Elgar, 285–301.

Economist Intelligence Unit (2010) 'Towards the recovery: Challenges and opportunities facing Asia's SMEs'. Available at http://www.eiu.com/site_info.asp?info_name = eiu_ fedex_recovery&page = noads&rf = 0 (accessed 15 November 2011).

Financial News (2011) South Korea, 'Han River Miracle' of loss and regeneration, November 10. Available at: http://www.stockmarkettoday.cc/south-korea-han-river-miracle-of-loss-and-regeneration.html (accessed 28 October 2011).

Gabrenya, W. K. and Hwang, K. (1996) 'Chinese social interaction: Harmony and hierarchy on the good earth' in Bond, M. H. (ed.) *The Handbook of Chinese Psychology*. Hong Kong: Oxford University Press, pp. 309–21.

Ganapathi, B. and Joshi, R. (2008) 'Current Status of SMEs and Entrepreneurship Education and Training Intervention in Select South and South-East Asian Countries', *The Icfai Journal of Entrepreneurship Development*, 5: 35–60.

Gray, C. and Mabey, C. (2005) 'Management development: key differences between small and large businesses in Europe', *International Small Business Journal*, 23: 467–85.

Gregory, G., Harvie, C. and Lee, H. (2002) 'Korean SMEs in the 21st century: strategies, constraints and performance in a global economy', *Economic Papers*, 21: 64–79.

Gries, T. and Naude, W. (2010) 'Entrepreneurship and structural economic transformation', *Small Business Economics*, 34: 13–29.

Hall, C. and Harvie, C. (2003) 'A comparison of the performance of SMEs in Korea and Taiwan: policy implication for turbulent times', Conference paper, 16th Annual Conference of Small Enterprise Association of Australia and New Zealand, Ballarat, 28 September–1 October.

Hamilton, G. (1996) 'The theoretical significance of Asian business networks' in Hamilton, G. (ed.) *Asian Business Networks*. New York: Walter de Gruyter.

Hornsby, J. S. and Kuratko, D. F. (2003) 'Human resource management in U.S. small business: a replication and extension', *Journal of Developmental Entrepreneurship*, 8: 73–92.

ILO report (2003) Available at http://www.ilo.org (accessed 6 June 2011).

Kong, T. Y. (2000) *The Politics of Economic Reform in South Korea: A Fragile Miracle*. London: Routledge.

Kotey, B. and Slade, P. (2005) 'Formal human resource management practices in small growing firms', *Journal of Small Business Management*, 43: 16–40.

OECD (2001) 'Definition of SMEs'. Available at http://stats.oecd.org/glossary/detail. asp?ID=3123 (accessed 18 November 2011).

Park, S. and Kim, S. (2011) 'South Korean SME's Entrepreneurship in the Globalizing Economic System focused on Yuyang DNU', 56th annual ICSB world conference, 15–18 June 2011, Sweden. Available at http://www.icsb2011.org/download/18.62efe22 412f41132d41800011448/119.pdf (accessed 26 September 2011).

Sels, L., De Winne, S., Maes, J., Delmotte, J., Faems, D. and Forrier, A. (2006) 'Unravelling the HRM-performance link: value-creating and cost-increasing effects of small business HRM', *Journal of Management Studies*, 43: 2320–80.

Siu, W., Lin, T., Fang, W. and Liu, Z (2006) 'An institutional analysis of the new product development process of small and medium enterprises in China, Hong Kong and Taiwan', *Industrial Marketing Management*, 35: 323–35.

SMBA (Small and Medium Business Administration, South Korea) (2010) *SME Supporting Policy in Korea*. Dejeon: SMBA. Available at http://eng.smba.go.kr/main.jsp (accessed 28 October 2011).

SMEA (Small and Medium Enterprise Administration, Ministry of Economic Affairs, Taiwan) (2011) *White Paper on Small and Medium Enterprises in Taiwan.* Available at http://www.moeasmea.gov.tw/ct.asp?xItem=9699&ctNode=307&mp=2 (accessed 20 November 2011).

SMEWORLD (2008) 'South Korean SMEs to slash capital spending, not workers'. Available at http://www.smeworld.org/story/top-stories/south-korean-smes.php (accessed 15 November 2011).

SSB (State Statistical Bureau, People's Republic of China) (2010) *China Statistical Yearbook.* Beijing: China Statistical Publishing House (2010 and years before).

State Economic and Trade Commission, State Development Planning Commission, Ministry of Finance, and State Statistical Bureau (2003) 'The Small and Medium-Sized Enterprises Promotion Law of the People's Republic of China', 19 February . Available at http://www.stats.gov.cn-18/08/2003 (accessed 28 September 2011).

Storey, D. J. (2004) 'Exploring the link, among small firms, between management training and firm performance: a comparison between the UK and other OECD countries', *International Journal of Human Resource Management,* 15: 112–30.

Tai, D. and Huang, C. (2006) 'A study on relations between industrial transformation and performance of Taiwan's small and medium enterprises', *The Journal of American Academy of Business*, 8: 216–21.

The Federation of Hong Kong Industries (FHKI) (2009) 'Survey on Hong Kong enterprises in PRD'. May. Available at http://www.industryhk.org/english/survey (accessed September 2011).

The Financial Times (2010) 'Seoul tells chaebol sharks to leave small fry', 21 September. Available at http://www.ft.com/cms/s/0/74c19446-c593–11df-ab48–00144feab49a.html#axzz1f5sqYBhC (accessed 2 November 2011).

The Hong Kong Council of Social Service (2011) 'Elderly service in Hong Kong'. Available at http://www.hkcss.org.hk/download/folder/el/el_eng.htm (accessed 15 October 2011).

UNESCAP (United Nations Economic and Social Commission for Asia and the Pacific) (2009) 'SMEs in Asia and the Pacific', United Nations Conference Paper. Available at http://www.unescap.org/tid/publication/tipub2540_chap1.pdf (accessed 7 September 2011).

Wang, J. (2007) 'From technological catch-up to innovation-based economic growth: South Korea and Taiwan compared', *Journal of Development Studies*, 43: 1084–1104.

Wang, J. and Tsai, C. (2010) 'National Model of Technological Catching Up and Innovation: Comparing Patents of Taiwan and South Korea', *Journal of Development Studies*, 46: 1404–23.

www.ciionline.org (2011) accessed 2 October 2011.

www.gov.hk/en/about/abouthk/factsheets/docs/ (2011) Hong Kong: The Facts (accessed 11 November 2011).

Xinhua News Agency (2003) 'Four laws, two judicial interpretations put into force, Xinhua Net', 2 January 2003 (accessed 25 September 2011).

— (2011) 'Survival crisis hits China's small businesses, Xinhua Net', 31 July 2011. Available at: http://news.xinhuanet.com/english2010/indepth/2011–07/31/c_131021370.htm (accessed 9 November 2011).

Yang, J. (2009) 'Small and Medium Enterprises adjustments to information technology in trade facilitation: The South Korean experience'. Available at http://www.unescap.org/tid/artnet/pub/wp6109.pdf (accessed 11 October 2011).

13 HRM strategies, informality and re-regulation in East Asian employment relations

Sarosh Kuruvilla and Sun-wook Chung

Introduction

Although employment relations (defined as labour relations and human resources management (HRM)) institutions and practices generally tend to be stable over long periods of time, that cannot be said to be the case in the three largest economies of East Asia, i.e. China, Japan and South Korea (hereafter Korea), during the last two decades (see chapters 5, 7 and 8). In this contribution, we briefly review the most significant development in East Asian employment relations, i.e. the growth of a variety of non-standard employment arrangements which we subsume under the term 'informality' in all three countries. We see this growth as symptomatic of the 'externalisation' of employment relations beyond the enterprise, a development that imposes major challenges for traditional trade unionism and for employment policy. We argue that the efforts of governments aimed at 're-regulating' employment relations to curb such 'informalisation' are evidence of an emerging 'labour protection logic' in these countries, although we remain sceptical about the effectiveness of attempts at re-regulation.

Our use of the term *informal* is broad and inclusive. We conceive of informal work as work that is not permanent, not always regulated by an employment contract, not always regulated by current law and not always with benefits. Thus, temporary and part-time workers (many of whom receive partial benefits) are included within the scope of our definition. The use of directly engaged contract workers is also covered by our definition. Also included is 'agency work' or 'despatched labour', the *triangular* employment relationship where workers are employed nominally by a labour market intermediary agency, but work at a third location that pays the agency a fee for using the worker. The primary employer in this case remains the agency, but the liability of the employer at the place of work is, in many countries, unclear.

Contextualising non-standard employment in East Asia

The last two decades have witnessed dramatic changes in employment relations systems[1] in all three countries. Perhaps the greatest commonality has been the movement towards a 'logic of competition' (Frenkel and Kuruvilla, 2002) that underlies employment relations, a movement that privileges employers' interests of 'employment flexibility' over worker's interests of employment 'stability'. During the last two decades this movement has been characterised by the adoption of flexibility oriented HRM strategies that have emphasised the use of contingent labour in response to the economic pressures of heightened global competition. The strategies of firms were encouraged and facilitated by institutional changes that permitted the use of such strategies. We focus on the changes in the institutional context in each country below.

In Japan, the economic recession beginning in the early 1990s forced the government to 'deregulate' labour laws in ways that helped firms 'adjust' to declining markets and profits, resulting in challenges to the traditional Japanese employment relations system (see chapter 7). A key deregulation development was the 1999 amendment to the law allowing contracted workers (commonly referred to in the Japanese literature as agency workers or 'despatch workers') to be employed in many industries except five areas (including manufacturing and construction). In 2004, the use of such workers was permitted in manufacturing as well, thereby allowing more manufacturing firms to make use of this flexible work arrangement. In 2007, the law which had only allowed such workers to be employed on temporary one-year contracts in the manufacturing industry was further modified to allow them to be employed on three-year contracts. As was expected, there was a major increase in the use of temporary, casual and agency workers as a result of these changes in Japan as these changes legitimised the movement away from the concept of 'lifetime employment (LTE)' that was a central pillar of Japanese employment relations. Ono (2010) documents the decrease in LTE from a high of over 30 per cent to less than 20 per cent today.

These changes occurred in conjunction with an increase in unemployment, and a continuing decline in 'countervailing protective institutions' such as labour unions and collective bargaining (see Table 13.1). The relative importance of the traditional 'Shunto' (Spring Wage Round) mechanism in national wage bargaining has declined, with the focus of wage bargaining shifting towards the enterprise level (Suzuki, 2010). Increasing differences in the profitability of enterprises, reflecting increased global competition, have been a major driver of this change. The influence of the national union federation RENGO has also declined during the recession, as enterprise unions have been the locus of 'adjustment' bargaining (Yoon, 2009).

The institutional changes in Korea tell a similar story, although the key impetus was the Asian financial crisis of 1997. Although a tripartite commission was formed to deal with the crisis, a key outcome of the tripartite agreement (one of the two union federations did not support this agreement) was the legitimisation of HRM strategies emphasising flexibility (Shin, 2010). As a result, most firms which had maintained Japanese-style long-term employment have abandoned lifelong employment and generous benefits and have increasingly taken on HRM strategies promoting efficiency and flexibility, specifically through the use of temporary and casual workers (Kim and Kim, 2003, Jung and Cheon, 2006). This process was accelerated by legislative changes which justified lay-offs and opened

Table 13.1 Unemployment and union density in Japan

Year	1997	1998	1999	2000	2001	2002	2003	2004	2005	2006	2007	2008	2009	2010
Unemployment (all age groups)	3.4%	4.1	4.7	4.7	5.0	5.4	5.3	4.7	4.4	4.1	3.9	4.0	5.1	5.1
Unemployment (age: 15–24)	6.7%	7.7	9.1	9.1	9.6	9.9	10.1	9.5	8.7	8.0	7.7	7.2	9.1	9.4
Unemployment (age: 25–34)	4.2%	4.9	5.5	5.6	6.0	6.4	6.3	5.7	5.6	5.2	4.9	5.2	6.4	6.2
Union Density	22.6%	22.4	22.2	21.5	20.7	20.2	19.6	19.2	18.7	18.2	18.1	18.1	18.5	18.5

Source: Ministry of Health, Labour and Welfare, Japan Institute for Labour Policy and Training (JILPT).

the way to diverse short-term, indirect employment practices including 'despatch labour' under the Kim (1998–2003) and Roh administrations (2003–8) (Lee 2011). The pro-business administration of the current President Lee (a former CEO of the Hyundai group) makes it clear that its labour agenda is job creation through labour flexibility. As such, a key agenda item in the National Employment Strategy (NES), issued in October 2011, was to expand the occupations and areas in which 'despatch labour' could be used. Furthermore, the Lee administration weakened unionism by enacting long-standing proposals in 2011 to prohibit employers from paying full-time union officials and the introduction of single bargaining agent principles. Finally, the government, public sectors (e.g. schools and post offices) and state-owned enterprises (SOEs) have expanded their use of non-standard work arrangements, as part of their restructuring efforts under the current Lee administration.

In Korea as well (as Table 13.2 indicates), these changes also coincided with an increase in unemployment and a general weakening of trade union power as more Korean firms relocated production to China (see chapter 8). Korean unions did little to organise the largely increasing informal and 'non-standard' workforce, and the decline of large firms significantly affected union density. Importantly, unionism has always been a large firm phenomenon in Korea, although more than 80 per cent of Koreans are employed in small firms with less than 50 employees (unionism in small firms represents only 3.3 per cent of total union membership). In contrast, large firms with over 1,000 employees account for 62.5 per cent of union membership in Korea.

The Tripartite commission, important during the Asian financial crisis, has been gradually declining in importance. The Korean Confederation of Trade Unions (KCTU), the more militant labour federation, was almost never on board with the commission's activities, and gradually the commitment of both employers and the current Lee administration have rendered it toothless. In some industries, enterprise labour unions have now begun to form industry-wide bargaining organisations (Lee, 2011), although here too (with exceptions in the banking and hospital sector), their effectiveness has been limited in view of both employer and government opposition. Thus, institutional developments in Korea have been broadly similar to those in Japan, resulting in creating an environment that has encouraged firms to adopt non-standard arrangements, amidst a decline in countervailing forces such as unions and the tripartite commission.

Unlike Japan and Korea, China has seen a huge expansion in its economy during the last two decades (see chapter 5). In the Chinese case, the institutional transformation has been the break away from the rigid features of the 'iron-rice-bowl' (*tie fan wan*) system. As Kuruvilla *et al.* (2011) suggest,

> in the early stages of reform, the process of "denationalisation", i.e. the withdrawal of the state in the management of state-owned enterprises and the consequent increase in managerial autonomy, the increasing diversity of ownership (the advent of private and foreign ownership), and the numerous joint ventures that are a "recombination of ownership" spawned increasing

Table 13.2 Unemployment and union density in Korea

Year	1997	1998	1999	2000	2001	2002	2003	2004	2005	2006	2007	2008	2009	2010
Unemployment (all age groups)	2.6%	7.0	6.3	4.4	4.0	3.3	3.6	3.7	3.7	3.5	3.2	3.2	3.6	3.7
Unemployment (age15–29)	5.7%	12.2	10.9	8.1	7.9	7.0	8.0	8.3	8.0	7.9	7.2	7.2	8.1	8.0
Union density	12.2%	12.6	11.9	12.0	12.0	11.6	11.0	10.6	10.3	10.3	10.8	10.5	10.1	9.8

Source: Ministry of Employment and Labour.

variation in employment practices, and increasing insecurity of employment, particularly as state enterprises sought HRM strategies that increased labour flexibility to be more competitive.

(Gallagher 2004: 20)

Regional and local government responses to the numerical flexibility strategies pursued by employers were quite varied. Some local governments, to attract foreign investment, emphasised firm autonomy and labour flexibility at the expense of workers' rights, while others, facing political and social pressures, attempted to protect employment by preventing SOE firms from laying off workers. Thus, the initial movement towards informalisation was relatively uneven. As many have suggested, many foreign invested enterprises, whose competitive advantage stemmed from low costs and labour-intensive production, made use of the growing pool of migrant labour willing to work without formal contracts, while SOEs to varying degrees began to lay off workers as part of their restructuring efforts. SOE lay-offs and increased employment insecurity for SOE workers began in earnest in 1997. By the end of the re-structuring period, over 30 million SOE workers had lost their jobs (Kuruvilla *et al.*, 2011).

The second phase commenced with the 1995 Labour Law, seen by many as a decisive step by the Chinese state to 'smash the iron rice bowl' in order to accelerate the restructuring process. This reform, which permitted short-term contracts, was seen as a solution to two different problems. On the one hand, formal labour-contracts would improve the efficiency of state firms by ending the practice of lifetime employment. Second, the legalisation of labour relations through a written employment contract would reduce the potential for labour exploitation, particularly in the non-state sectors by enshrining 'certain rights and responsibilities'. As many have noted, the formalisation of the labour-contract system helped facilitate and legitimise the massive lay-offs that began in the SOE sector in 1997 (Gallagher, 2004), since termination at the end of the contract was done using the language of the law.

The transition to more informal work has 'intensified the process of "commodification and casualization of labour" (Friedman and Lee, 2010), where HRM strategies emphasising flexibility interact with the lack of effective regulation, resulted in plummeting labour standards'. There has been a remarkable growth in the violation of labour standards and in a decline in working conditions including long hours, low pay, lack of social insurance, wage arrears, poor safety and health, illegal firings and so forth during the 1995–2007 period (Lee, 2007). And there is rising dissatisfaction, expressed in a multi-fold increase in labour disputes since 1994 (Hurst, 2009). Thus, although China was growing rapidly, and did not evidence the rise in unemployment that we have seen in Korea and Japan, its countervailing institutions such as trade unions (despite their growth) did not have the power or independence to halt the decline in labour standards. Table 13.3 below shows the dramatic increase in labour disputes during the last decade or so.

Thus, in all three countries the economic pressures of a more competitive environment, combined with legislative changes, opened the door for a general decline

Table 13.3 Unemployment, labour unions and labour disputes in China

Year	1997	1998	1999	2000	2001	2002	2003	2004	2005	2006	2007	2008	2009
Unemployment rate*	3.1%	3.1	3.1	3.1	3.6	4.0	4.3	4.2	4.2	4.1	4.0	4.2	4.3
Number of labour unions (10,000 units)	51.0	50.4	50.9	85.9	153.8	171.3	90.6	102.0	117.4	132.4	150.8	172.5	184.5
Number of labour disputes (10,000 units)	7.2	9.4	12.0	13.5	15.5	18.4	22.6	26.0	31.4	31.7	35.0	69.3	68.4

Source: China Statistical Yearbook, China Labour Statistical Yearbook.

*Unemployment rate: Urban registered employment rate.

in labour standards and a general growth in the informalisation of employment. The ability of countervailing institutions such as trade unions and opposition political parties to arrest these developments has been limited. Clearly competition and flexibility appear to be the dominant logic underlying the employment system transformation in these three countries during the last two decades. We turn in the next section to the impact of this transformation on non-standard forms of employment.

The extent and nature of informal (non-standard employment) in East Asia

As noted, our definition of 'informalisation' of employment is broad enough to encompass any movement away from permanent and stable employment and includes temporary, casual, agency, part-time and despatch workers. Each of the countries uses different definitions of what is non-standard work, hence, the data are strictly not comparable across countries. Despite these definitional differences, it is important to remember that the commonality is that all these forms represent a movement away from a stable, secure job with good benefits.

In Japan, the proportion of people in non-standard employment has increased from 18.3 per cent to 34.9 per cent of the employed workforce (see Table 13.4). Fully half of the non-standard group comprises part-time workers. Table 13.4 shows a dramatic increase in the number of contract workers, who account now for a third of the non-standard workers. What are called *arbeito* workers, now defined as temporary workers (originally it referred to the part-time work done by university students), are also growing substantially.

In particular, non-standard work has crept in to replace regular employment. Table 13.5 below shows the percentage of non-standard workers across a number of occupations in Japan and as the data suggest, even manufacturing, sales and office jobs, which were traditionally unionised and generally permanent, are now increasingly dominated by non-standard employment. In addition, the number of Freeters (or *furita*), defined as the people between the ages of 15 and 34 who lack full-time employment or are unemployed, dramatically increased from 0.5 million in 1982 to 1.78 million in 2009. The trajectory of these young workers represents deviations from the basic school-to-work transition model in Japan, where students become full-time tenured workers upon graduation, with continuous vocational training provided by the company (Reiko, 2006). Although becoming a Freeter was initially a voluntary choice, it currently represents more of a forced choice for young workers in Japan because a shrinking number of Japanese companies recruit new graduates. Currently, a large proportion of young workers work at low-paying, low-skilled jobs in the service industry. And there is also growth in the 'NEET' proportion of the population (neither in employment, education and training), who work informally. Thus there is a growing pool of informal employment, encompassing casual, temporary, part-time, agency and 'despatched' workers, whose wages and working conditions are considerably below the norm.

Table 13.4 Growth of non-standard workers in Japan (1988–2010)

Year	1988	1990	1992	1994	1996	1998	2000	2002	2004	2006	2008	2010
Regular workers (per cent)	81.7%	79.8	79.4	79.7	78.5	76.4	74.0	70.2	68.5	67.7	65.5	65.1
Non-standard workers (per cent)	18.3%	20.2	20.6	20.3	21.5	23.6	26.0	29.8	31.5	32.3	34.5	34.9
Part-time workers	10.7%	11.6	11.9	11.7	12.3	13.2	14.7	14.8	15.5	15.5	16.0	17.1
Arbeito (temporary) workers	3.8%	4.7	4.9	5.0	5.7	6.6	7.3	6.8	6.5	6.3	6.4	6.9
Despatched/contracted workers	3.8%	3.9	3.8	3.6	3.6	3.8	4.0	8.1	9.5	10.5	12.0	10.9

Source: The Statistics Bureau of the Ministry of Internal Affairs and Communications.

Table 13.5 Ratio of regular workers and non-standard workers across jobs (2007)

Job	Regular workers	Non-standard workers	Total
Specialised/ technical work	75.6 %	24.4 %	100 %
Managerial work	92.1 %	7.9 %	100 %
Clerical work	69.1 %	30.9 %	100 %
Sales work	51.6 %	48.4 %	100 %
Service work	29.2 %	70.8 %	100 %
Security work	0.9 %	99.1 %	100 %
Transportation/ communication work	60.3 %	39.7 %	100 %
Production process labour	47.2 %	52.8 %	100 %
Others	9.6 %	90.4 %	100 %

Source: General Survey on Diversified Types of Employment (2007) and Futagami (2010).

Further, 'non-standard' and 'gender' are highly correlated. Women make up 89.7 per cent of all part-time jobs and 62.1 per cent of all 'despatch' jobs in Japan (2007) as Table 13.6 suggests. Women dominate in part-time and non-standard employment (cf. chapter 9), both as a result of a paternalistic employment system and of a paternalistic tax system (Abe, 2008).[2] In addition, there are at least one million foreign workers in Japan, working in a wide range of jobs, and many of them, especially Chinese workers, work informally.

Houseman and Osawa (2003) find that temporary jobs are less likely to be stepping stones to future regular jobs in Japan. Not surprisingly, many temporary agency workers say they would rather be regular, permanent workers. According to Ministry of Health, Labour and Welfare's Survey of the Diversification of Employment Status (2003), while many non-regular workers choose to be so because they are willing to trade compensation and job security for better work schedules, 21.6 per cent of part-time workers and 40 per cent of agency workers worked in non-regular jobs because they could not find a permanent position.

Being in non-standard employment has its disadvantages. A number of Japanese surveys on the working conditions of non-standard workers show that, while they often perform jobs similar to those of regular workers, the wage differentials are widening (JILPT 2008, 2009, 2011).

Table 13.6 Percentage of female workers by employment arrangements in Japan (2007)

	Regular work	Part-time work	Temporary work	Despatched work	Contract work	Entrusted work	Others
Female	30.7 %	89.7 %	49.5 %	62.1 %	48.4 %	37.8 %	51.4 %
Male	69.3 %	10.3 %	50.5 %	37.9 %	51.6 %	62.2 %	48.6 %
Total	100 %	100 %	100 %	100 %	100 %	100 %	100 %

Source: Employment Status Survey (Ministry of Internal Affairs and Communications), Asao (2010).

Table 13.7 Non-standard employment in Korea (2002–2010)

Year	National Statistics Office		Korean Contingent Workers' Centre	
	Number (Unit: 1,000)	*Percentage*	*Number (Unit: 1,000)*	*Percentage*
2002	3,839	27.4 %	7,708	56.6 %
2003	4,606	32.6 %	7,834	55.4 %
2004	5,394	37.0 %	8,130	55.7 %
2005	5,482	36.6 %	8,394	56.1 %
2006	5,457	35.6 %	8,414	54.8 %
2007	5,703	35.9 %	8,576	54.0 %
2008	5,445	33.8 %	8,374	52.0 %
2009	5,754	34.9 %	8,535	51.8 %
2010	5,685	33.4 %	8,550	50.2 %

Source: Non-standard Work Statistics of Korea Labour Institute (KLI), Korea Contingent Workers' Centre (KCWC).

If the level of non-standard employment in Japan is sizeable, the rate of growth of non-standard employment in Korea has been much faster, has happened over a shorter period and the levels of non-standard employment are even higher. Between 1997 (the onset of the Asian Financial Crisis) and 2010, the percentage of employees in various types of non-standard work increased so dramatically that according to some estimates (see Table 13.7) they constitute the largest segment of the workforce.

The differences in wages and benefits between regular workers and non-standard workers are as large as the differences we have seen in Japan. The employment tenure gap is widening as well, from 69.8 months (regular workers) and 24.1 months (non-standard workers) in 2002 to 77.3 months (regular workers) and 23.6 months (non-standard workers) in 2010. Second, and in contrast to Japan where a significant portion of non-standard work is a result of voluntary choices by women and Freeters, a large proportion of non-standard employment in Korea is involuntary. Surveys indicate that many non-regular workers would like standard jobs, but employers are increasingly avoiding regular employment. The percentage of workers who are forced to work in non-standard jobs increased from 48.5 per cent in 2006 to 55 per cent in 2010. It is also notable that most non-standard employment is considered as quasi-permanent, in that most non-standard workers are trapped in their current categories rather than being able to step into regular jobs (Nam and Kim, 2000). Table 13.8 provides some data on the differences between regular and non-standard workers in terms of wages, tenure and benefits.

The growth in the non-standard workforce is mirrored by the growth in the subcontracting of work in the Korean manufacturing industry. Currently 326,000 workers work under subcontracting conditions in numerous industries, including the shipbuilding, electronics, auto, chemical manufacturing and service industries (Kim, 2011). It is noteworthy that both private companies (e.g. Hyundai, LG and

Table 13.8 Wages, tenure, benefits differences between regular and non-standard workers in Korea (2002–2010)

Year		2002	2003	2004	2005	2006	2007	2008	2009	2010
Wage	Regular worker	100	100	100	100	100	100	100	100	100
	Non-standard worker*	67.1%	61.3%	65.0%	62.7%	62.8%	63.5%	60.9%	54.6%	54.8%
Tenure (month)	Regular worker	—	—	69.8	71.8	70.1	71.3	73.9	78.6	77.3
	Non-standard worker	—	—	24.1	23.9	25.1	26.3	24.2	21.2	23.6
Pension	Regular worker	62.9%	70.8%	72.5%	75.7%	76.1%	76.3%	77.3%	78.9%	78.4%
	Non-standard worker	25.7%	30.5%	37.5%	36.6%	38.2%	40.0%	39.0%	38.2%	38.1%

Source: KLI's Non-standard Work Statistics (2010)

* Percentage of wage of regular worker.

Samsung) and state-owned enterprises (e.g. Incheon International Airport Corporation) use subcontracted workers. In the shipbuilding and steel industries, the ratio of subcontracted workers vis-à-vis regular workers is, respectively, 61 per cent and 43 per cent (Kim, 2011).

Further, apart from increased subcontracting and the moving of work to lower cost locations in China, there is a significant increase in the number of foreign migrant workers in Korea. The number of foreign workers doubled between 2002 and 2007. Most foreign workers are unskilled workers employed in the labour-intensive sectors, such as construction, service and manufacturing, and they are doing the low-paid, dangerous, dirty and difficult jobs in South Korea. It is estimated that foreign workers account for more than 5 per cent of the total employees. Although they receive legal protection based on Korea's Labour Standard Act, Minimum Wage Law, and the recently enacted Act on Employment of Foreign Workers in 2010, they are still considered to be the most vulnerable, marginalised group in Korea, as these laws are not well enforced. It is this variation in the different types of non-standard workers that accounts for the different estimates of the number of non-standard workers in Korea. Irrespective of the variation however, it is clear that non-standard work has become the 'new normal' in Korea.

Estimating the quantity of informal work in China is also problematic given that the statistics collected by the government are not very reliable. We know the key source of the growth in informal employment comes from Chinese migrant workers, who work and live in places far away from their home provinces where their *hukou* (household registration) is located. According to the 2010 census, the size of this 'floating population' was 230 million. Most of these migrant workers rely on hometown networks, labour-contracting companies or other labour 'despatch' agencies when searching for jobs in urban areas. Mostly, they end up working in non-standard employment arrangements, such as temporary work, part-time domestic work, 'despatched' work and subcontracted work. A second key source of temporary labour is student interns. Local governments have expanded vocational schools in anticipation of a future need for skilled workers, and the number of interns has increased from approximately 12.5 million in 2003 to 22 million in 2009 (Liang, 2011). Although student interns are supposed to work under the partial supervision of their vocational high schools, they are increasingly seen as a source of cheap labour by employers. These student workers are usually not covered by written labour-contracts and social insurance benefits because they are 'students', not 'workers'. For example, if work injuries occur, they are not entitled to the government's work injury insurance because they are not workers. Until recently, China has not had laws on legal protection for informal and subcontracted work, and even though a new law was introduced in 2008 (discussed later in this chapter), the implementation of labour laws in China varies dramatically across provinces (Kuruvilla *et al.*, 2011).

As noted, formal estimates of informal work in China are difficult to obtain. The best available estimates are from Park and Cai (2011). They analyse a variety of government data bases and conclude that the number of non-standard workers comprises about 40 per cent of the Chinese workforce, as indicated below.

Table 13.9 Urban employment by employer type in China

Year	State-owned	Collective	Co-operative, joint, limited liability, shareholding corporations	Private and self-employed	Foreign and joint venture	Others
1990	61%	21%	1%	4%	–	14%
1991	61	21	–	4	1	13
1992	61	20	–	5	1	13
1993	60	19	1	6	2	13
1994	60	18	2	9	2	10
1995	59	17	2	11	3	9
1996	56	15	2	12	3	12
1997	53	14	2	13	3	15
1998	42	9	5	15	3	26
1999	38	8	6	16	3	31
2000	35	6	6	14	3	35
2001	32	5	7	15	3	38
2002	29	5	7	17	3	39
2003	27	4	8	19	3	39
2004	25	3	8	21	4	38
2005	24	3	10	23	5	36

Source: Park and Cai (2011).

As Table 13.9 notes, the category of 'other' workers or undocumented workers is a residual after counting the number of workers in formal employment.

It is obvious that the wages, benefits and job security of the informal workforce in China will be substantially below that of permanent workers, although unlike in Japan and Korea there are no statistics to indicate the extent of those differences. The abuses that these workers suffer (e.g. such as unpaid or underpaid wages, no work injury compensation and forced, unpaid overtime work) have been well documented (Lee, 2007). Recent empirical studies indicate that these migrant non-standard workers receive one-half to two-thirds the wages of regular workers and make up one-third to one-half of the factory workforce in the auto industry (Zhang, 2010). Although by law the ratio of student interns cannot exceed one-third of the workforce in factories, it was reported that 70 per cent of the workers at a Honda factory in Foshan, where a lengthy strike occurred in 2010, were student interns (Liang, 2011). Thus, migrant workers and student interns are emerging as a cheap, convenient source of labour supply in contemporary China.

In summary, the growth of non-standard work (or informal work as we term it in this paper) has increased substantially in the three largest East Asian economies. The growth in the number of such workers has been clear and measured in Japan, with many workers making voluntary choices to work in non-standard employment. In Korea, the growth has been sudden and dramatic and largely involuntary. In China, the growth of informal employment has seen a major spurt since the 1994 Labour Law changes, and has been driven largely by the rise in its 'floating' population. In all three countries, the definitions of such work differ, making comparisons difficult, but it is clear, particularly in Korea and China, that these departures from regular stable employment now encompass the largest proportion of the workforce. Since these temporary, casual, informal, agency and 'despatched' workers are not in regular employment, their employment relations are largely 'external' to the firm. This externalisation of employment relations poses significant challenges to both traditional unionism, which has not evolved adequate responses to this phenomenon, and government policy, which is only now evolving to take into account these developments. We turn to these issues in the next section.

Responses: apathy, resistance and re-regulation

The growth in non-standard work exacerbates existing divisions within the working class. Trade unions have been historical protectors of workers, and have in most countries attempted to impose standardisation on wages and benefits. However, in both Japan and Korea (see chapters 7 and 8) the dominance of the enterprise union structure has prevented unions from focusing on these 'externalised' employees. Thus, when HRM strategies in enterprises add temporary, or subcontracted or 'despatched' workers, they are not represented by traditional enterprise unions who focus on their core membership, the permanent workers. Thus, by and large, trade unions in Korea and Japan have been either passive or ineffective in protecting the interests of broadly defined informal workers, with some exceptions. In Japan, RENGO included improvements in the working conditions of non-standard workers in its spring wage offensive in 2006 for the first time, despite the long-term growth in temporary and casual workers. It also has made various attempts to recruit and protect non-standard workers, for instance, by the creation of a Contingent Worker Centre in 2007, thereby contributing to increasing the unionisation rate of part-time workers from 3 per cent in 2003 to 5 per cent in 2009.

Although some industrial unions in Korea have had some success in improving the conditions of non-standard workers in banking, janitorial services and sales, Korean enterprise unions have also focused largely on their permanent workers. As can be seen in Table 13.10 below, even though Korean unions have gradually

Table 13.10 Union centralisation and unionisation rate for non-standard workers in Korea (2003–2009)

Year	2003	2004	2005	2006	2007	2008	2009	2010
Percentage of industrial/ regional union members	31.3%	39.4%	40.1%	39.7%	51.3%	52.9%	52.9%	54.1%
Union density of non-standard workers	2.4%	3.1%	3.2%	2.8%	3.3%	3.0%	2.0%	1.9%*

Source: Ministry of Employment and Labour, Korea Contingent Workers' Centre.

* March 2010.

moved into industry-wide bargaining, they have not substantially increased the organisation of non-standard workers.

In China, official trade unionism has an ambiguous role vis-à-vis protecting the regular workforce (for exceptions, see Liu, 2010), let alone temporary workers. Largely ignored by the trade unions, the non-standard workforce in all three countries have had to take matters into their own hands. In Korea, non-standard workers went on strike at Ki-Ryung Electronics in 2005, E-Land in 2007 and Dong-Hee Auto in 2008. These three strikes began spontaneously, without union support, but with help from social justice and civil society groups (e.g. the Contingent Workers' Centre in Korea). Similarly, wildcat strikes and spontaneous protests are increasing in China (see Zhu *et al.*, 2011). These include not only strikes in foreign-owned factories,[3] but also strikes in domestic and state-owned facilities.[4] In addition, Zhang (2010) documents substantial resistance by temporary and informal workers in the auto industry. In China as well, informal workers use the help of labour-friendly NGOs to help them in resolving their issues and grievances (e.g., SACOM and Little Bird). In other situations, they have taken more drastic steps, such as the suicides in Korea Express in 2009 and China's Foxconn in 2010, to draw the attention of the public to their plight (Shin, 2010, Friedman and Lee, 2010).

The most significant response in these countries has come from the government, in response to the growing and increasingly expressed dissatisfaction of a non-standard workforce that constitutes a sizeable proportion of the workforce in all three countries. In Japan, an example is the Revised Part-Time Work Act, which was implemented in April 2008. The major provisions include

- written documentation of employment and working conditions;
- no discrimination regarding equal employment conditions vis-à-vis regular workers;
- encouragement of employer efforts to move part-time jobs towards regular jobs;
- the government's active engagement in part-time workers' grievance procedures through government agencies (Morozumi, 2009).

Since the new ruling party (Democratic Party of Japan) took power in August 2009 after campaigning with a strong emphasis on employment issues, they have introduced a new law concerning 'despatch labour' which is under review in the Diet. The overall focus of the law is to limit the use of such labour. Accordingly, the draft law seeks to

- prohibit its registration except in 26 special areas;
- prohibit it in the manufacturing industry;
- prohibit contracts of less than two months when using contingent work.

In addition, the new draft also seeks to render equal treatment to workers doing the same job (whether they are regular or not) and forces staffing agencies who are the primary employers of 'despatched labour' to notify their employees about their rights and working conditions. Thus, the response of the Japanese government has been to 're-regulate'; i.e. produce new regulations to solve problems created by old legislation.

In Korea, after five years of debate among business, labour and the state, the Protection Law on Contingent and Despatch Labour was implemented in 2007. This law, which focuses on the rights and working conditions of 'contingent' and 'despatched' workers, includes two major provisions: it prohibits employers from using the same worker in temporary jobs for more than two years (i.e. the workers must be made permanent thereafter if the job still exists) and also prohibits discrimination. Not only are these provisions contentious, but they have resulted in unintended consequences, as employers have found ways to engage more indirect labour through direct subcontracting. Given that 'despatched' workers are protected by this law, while subcontracted workers have no regulations to protect themselves with, the employer response was to start using diverse in-house subcontracting, with a nominal subcontractor in the records. With the sudden jump in the use of far-externalised employment practices, and the ensuing protests amongst temporary workers and their civil society supporters, the government has tried to respond with both non-mandatory guidelines and stricter regulations. The guidelines, issued in July 2011, suggest that the principal company

- should give subcontractors a month's warning before the job is ended;
- should improve the working conditions of subcontracted workers;
- should share a greater amount of profits with the subcontracting agency;
- should recognise subcontracted workers' rights to unionise;
- should extend welfare benefits to subcontracted workers.

The normative 'soft law' version of the government's response was strengthened with a new draft 'hard law' effort. This re-regulation initiative, issued in August 2011, proposes to

- prohibit subcontracting in the core work of companies;
- limit the number of subcontracted workers to a proportion of the principal contractor's employee numbers;
- provide them with priority in permanent hiring.

In a similar vein, the Supreme Court's ruling against Hyundai Motor's subcontracting employment in July 2010 has been followed by a series of court rulings at various levels (specifically, about Hyundai Asan in 2010, Korea GM in 2010 and Kumho in 2011). The court ruled in these cases that the companies were using 'disguised subcontracting' (i.e. the illegal use of despatch labour) and forced the companies to transfer the subcontracted worker into regular worker status after two years.

It is in China that we have seen the greatest legislative efforts to control the growing informality of work (Kuruvilla *et al.*, 2011). Under the rubric of a 'harmonious society' (see Warner, 2011) the government implemented a series of labour laws in January 2008 (namely, the Labour-Contract Law, the Arbitration and Mediation Law and the Employment Promotion Law) reinforcing previously nominal IR institutions (e.g. trade unions (the All-China Federation of Trade Unions, ACFTU), collective agreements, wage negotiations and the tripartite system) (see chapter 5). These new laws not only provide a modicum of employment security for workers (through a variety of provisions with regard to employment contracts), but they also expand the rights of workers to file claims for arbitration or litigate them and provide unions with legal encouragement to engage in unionisation and collective bargaining. For example, Articles 10 and 82 of the Labour-Contract Law require that the employer must enter into a written labour-contract with a worker within 30 days of employment. Failure to do so leads to the penalty of paying the worker double wages for any time served without a written contract. If employees work for 12 months without a contract, they must be provided with an indefinite term contract (i.e. made permanent). The changes in the Arbitration and Mediation Law are intended to not only speed up the process of dispute resolution but also to extend the time limit during which the aggrieved worker can file for arbitration (from 60 days to one year), and completely eliminate the arbitration fee, while shifting the burden of proof on to the employer.

Even more far-reaching (relative to efforts in Korea and Japan) are the special provisions in the Labour-Contract Law which try to regulate labour staffing agencies or 'despatch agencies' as well as 'despatched labour'. First, the law requires minimum capital requirements for registration as a staffing agency (0.5 million RMB). Second, it specifies that the 'despatch labour' should only be used for temporary, auxiliary or substitute jobs and that the workers are to be remunerated according to the principle of 'equal pay for equal work'. Several articles focus on the division of responsibility between the 'despatching agency' and the employer, specifying that both share responsibilities for some aspects such as dismissal and workplace injuries. The Law also regulates the conditions of part-time workers, noting that part-time work is specified to be less than 4 hours per day and 24 hours per week (Article 68).

China's legislative efforts have been far more comprehensive than those of Japan and Korea, and in the Korean case the legislative effort is still contested. On the other hand, the implementation of the law in China is uneven. The goals of the central state in controlling the growth of informal work have been undermined by the inability or unwillingness of local governments to enforce the law for a variety of reasons, notably the need to attract foreign investment (Kuruvilla *et al.*, 2011). This problem of the enforcement of the law raises the possibility that the Labour-contract Law may have the unintended consequence of driving even more employment underground into the informal sector (Kuruvilla *et al.*, 2011). On the other hand, there is an increased effort in some parts of China to better enforcement, through the efforts of workers, labour-friendly NGOs and local labour bureaux (Cooney, 2011, Kuruvilla *et al.*, 2011).

In summary, in all three countries it is the governments, rather than the trade unions, that have been the prime movers in developing policy to contain the growth of informal work, and to bolster the rights of informal workers. This legislative effort of the governments is suggestive, in our view, of an emerging and competing 'logic of labour protection' (Frenkel and Kuruvilla, 2002).

Conclusions

What we have identified in this chapter is a clear and significant movement in employment relations and HRM strategies away from stable regular employment to a variety of contingent arrangements in all three countries. These contingent arrangements externalise employment relations at the firm level, creating a new segmentation in enterprise workforces. As such, these new forms of workers do not often come under the purview of bilateral labour relations, as enterprise unions represent only those permanent workers directly hired by the employer. In all three countries, these contingent arrangements account for a significant proportion (if not the major proportion) of the workforce. Their growth represents a challenge not only to traditional industrial relations actors, but also for industrial relations scholarship, apart from government policy.

Given the inability of bilateral employment relations to address these issues (either through labour union action or high road HRM strategies), governments, responding to growing social pressure from these workers, have begun to intervene. In all three countries, the growth in the number of informal workers was the result of government policy and regulations aimed at increasing flexibility. The current efforts represent a significant effort at 're-regulation', i.e. to control the growth of contingent employment unleashed by their prior regulations. It is still too early to estimate the impact of such re-regulation, given that it is quite recent, and also given some evidence that these protective laws are having unintended consequences. However, it is evident that there is a clear 'labour protection' logic underlying these efforts. The challenge for workers and trade unions in these countries is how to capitalise on that 'emerging logic'.

Notes

1   Note that our use of the term 'employment relations systems' includes the variety of labour relations and human resource institutions, policies and practices.
2   If a married woman works part-time and earns less than 1.03 million yen annually, her husband is eligible to receive several types of benefits. These include 1) her social security and health care benefits under her husband's coverage, 2) her exemption for income tax, and 3) an allowance for a low-income spouse from his employer (Abe, 2008).
3   Examples include strikes in Japanese Honda Auto (2010), Taiwanese Wintek (2010), Korean Sungwoo (2010) and American Pepsico Bottling (2011).
4   Examples include a strike in Tonggang Steel (2010), a railway worker strike in Changsha (2011) and a hospital custodian strike in Shanghai (2011).

References

Abe, Y. (2008) 'The Effects of the 1.03 million yen Ceiling in a Dynamic Labour Supply Model', *Contemporary Economic Policy*, 27: 147–63.

Cooney, S. (2011) *Dynamism and Stasis: Regulating Working Conditions in China*. Presented in the Conference 'Regulating for Decent Work', University of Melbourne, 6 July 2011.

Frenkel, S. and Kuruvilla, S. (2002) 'Logics of Action, Globalization, and Employment Relations Change in China, India, Malaysia, and the Philippines', *Industrial and Labour Relations Review*, 55: 387–412.

Friedman, E. and Lee, C. K. (2010) 'Remaking the World of Chinese Labour', *British Journal of Industrial Relations*, 48: 507–33.

Gallagher, M. (2004) 'Time is Money, Efficiency is Life: The Transformation of Labour Relations in China', *Studies of Comparative International Development*, 39: 11–44.

Houseman, S. and Osawa, M. (2003) 'The Growth of Nonstandard Employment in Japan and the United States: A Comparison of Causes and Consequences' in Houseman, Susan and Osawa, Machiko (eds) *Nonstandard Work in Developed Economies: Causes and Consequences*. Kalamazoo, Michigan: W. E. Upjohn Institute, pp. 175–214.

Hurst, W. (2009) *The Chinese Worker After Socialism*. Cambridge: Cambridge University Press.

JILPT (Japan Institute for Labour Policy and Training) (2008) *Labour Situation in Japan and Analysis*. Tokyo: JILPT.

— (2009) *Labour Situation in Japan and Analysis*. Tokyo: JILPT.

— (2011) *Labour Situation in Japan and Analysis*. Tokyo: JILPT.

Jung, E. and Cheon, B-Y. (2006) 'Economic Crisis and Changes in Employment Relations in Japan and Korea', *Asian Survey*, 46: 457–76.

Kim, D-O. and Kim, S. (2003) 'Globalization, Financial Crisis, and Industrial Relations: The Case of Korea', *Industrial Relations*, 42: 341–67.

Kim, I. (2011) *An Investigation Report on Subcontracting Practices in Korea*, Hankyoreh Shinmun (newspaper), 10 October, p. 1

Kuruvilla, S., Lee, C-K. and Gallagher, M. (2011) *From Iron Rice Bowl to Informalization: Markets, Workers, and the State in a Changing China*. Ithaca NY and London: ILR Press.

Lee, J. (2011) 'Between Fragmentation and Centralization: South Korean Industrial Relations in Transition', *British Journal of Industrial Relations*, 42: 1–25.

Lee, C-K. (2007) *Against the Law: Labour Protests in China's Rustbelt and Sunbelt*. Berkeley CA: University of California Press.

Liang, S. (2011) *Cheap Labour in Essence, Students in Name: Vocational School Interns in China*. Hong Kong: Asia Monitor Resource Centre, September 2011.

Liu, M-W. (2010) 'Organizing in China: Still a Monolithic Labour Movement?', *Industrial and Labour Relations Review*, 64: 30–52.

Morozumi, M. (2009) 'Balanced Treatment and Bans on Discrimination: Significance and Issues of the Revised Part-Time Work Act', *Japanese Labour Review*, 6: 39–55.

Nam, J. and Kim, Tae-Ki. (2000) 'Non-regular Labour, Bridge or Trap?', *Korean Journal of Labour Economics*, 23: 85–105.

Ono, H. (2010) 'Lifetime Employment in Japan: Concepts and Measurements', *Journal of the Japanese and International Economies*, 24: 1–27.

Park, A. and Cai, F. (2011) 'The Informalization of the Chinese Labour Market' in Kuruvilla, S., Lee, C. K. and Gallagher, M. (eds) *From Iron Rice Bowl to Informalization: Markets, Workers, and the State In a Changing China*. Ithaca, NY and London: Cornell University Press.

Reiko, K. (2006) 'Youth Employment in Japan's Economic Recovery: "Freeters" and "NEETs" ', *Japan Focus*, May.

Shin, K-W. (2010) 'Globalization and the Working Class in South Korea: Contestation, Fragmentation and Renewal', *Journal of Contemporary Asia*, 40: 211–29.

Suzuki, H. (2010) 'Employment Relations in Japan: Recent Changes under Global Competition and Recession', *Journal of Industrial Relations*, 52: 387–401.

Warner, M. (ed.) (2011) '*Confucianism HRM in Greater China; Theory and Practice*'. London and New York, NY: Routledge.

Yoon, Y. (2009) *A Comparative Study on Industrial Relations and Collective Bargaining in East Asian Countries.* Working Paper no. 8. Geneva: ILO.

Zhang, L. (2010) Dissertation thesis. *From Detroit to Shanghai? Globalization, Market Reform, and Dynamics of Labour Unrest in the Chinese Automobile Industry, 1980 to the Present*. Baltimore PA: Johns Hopkins University.

Zhu, Y., Warner, M. and Feng, T., (2011) 'Employment Relations with "Chinese characteristics": The Role of Trade Unions in China', *International Labour Journal*, 150: 139–58.

14 Management and culture in East, Southeast and South Asia

Comparisons and contrasts

Shaista E. Khilji

South Asia, which we will compare with East Asia (and Southeast Asia in passing) in this chapter in terms of its management and culture, is the southern region of the Asian continent, which comprises an emerging economic giant, India, Maldives with the highest GDP per capita in the region and a number of pre-emerging economies including Afghanistan, Bangladesh, Bhutan, Nepal, Pakistan and Sri Lanka (The World Bank, 2011). With a population exceeding 1.6 billion, South Asia is home to approximately one fourth of the world's population, making it one of the most densely populated regions in the world (The World Bank, 2011). It is also one of the most diverse regions in terms of the multiplicity of its languages and its rich culture (Ahmed *et al.*, 2010). Collectively, the South Asian region has a growth rate of 8.9 per cent, thereby it is also considered to be one of the fastest growing regions in the world. Unfortunately, it is also home to 50 per cent of the world's poorest (The World Bank, 2011). Economic development in the region remains sporadic and uneven, and overall human development is a low national priority (Ghani, 2011). Hence, South Asian countries display stark contrasts; dark slums in the shadows of palatial buildings, highly qualified talent with illiterates and jobless and world-class nimble organisations with an inefficient, bureaucratic public sector. By comparison, East Asia has witnessed systemic economic growth, which is attributed to consistent investment in human development (Tilak, 2002). East Asian growth has fascinated many in the West (Dunning, 1993; Hill, 2007; Singh, 1998) and has been used to draw lessons for leadership, strategy and organisations for many businesses in the West (Chen and Miller, 2011).

Unlike East Asia, the South Asian region has been slow to progress and is faced with several socio-economic challenges in terms of population growth, poor infrastructure, terrorism, corruption and elitism (Khatri *et al.*, 2011). However, East Asia (because of its geographic proximity) and some countries in Southeast Asia (including Malaysia and Singapore) have served as a shining example to many struggling South Asian countries, which look up to the economic development in Taiwan, China, Japan, Hong Kong, Malaysia and Singapore, and often debate if they should emulate a Western or an East Asian Model (Ghani and Ahmed, 2009). Nevertheless, the East Asian countries themselves are in a state of flux, following a period of Asian crisis and the recent global economic downturn. Studies have shown that management is being reformed in East Asia (Zhu *et al.*, 2007; Nowland,

2008). For example, the rise of China is influencing corporate Japan, which seems to be in relative decay along with South Korea and Taiwan.

Although East Asian philosophy may be powerful, a growing number of companies there are pursuing an amalgam of East–West management practices (Chen and Miller, 2011; Hill, 2007; Lin and Hou, 2010). Companies in rapidly growing India have also caught the attention of management scholars in recent years, who have attributed their success to the India Way, a unique management philosophy that places a strong emphasis on investment in human capital (Cappelli *et al.*, 2010). Given these developments in the continent, it is important to evaluate what represents a contemporary Asian model, and how it can contribute to the development of management thought and practice globally.

In this chapter, we first present South Asia as a region that is similar to East Asia in some respects, but is also different in others. We identify contemporary management behaviour, business ethics issues and management practices in order to evaluate the impact of globalisation in South Asia. The challenges and strengths of South Asian organisations are captured. Based upon a discussion of Indian and Chinese approaches, we argue that successful global management behaviour is ambicultural, which exhibits the hybridisation of values – taking the positive from indigenous local culture and the West. We conclude with a note to enhance learning between East and South Asia and across East/South Asia and the West in order to develop approaches that are appropriate for a complex global environment.

Socio-economic and cultural environment in South Asia

As many Western (including the USA, the UK, Germany and France) and East Asian countries (including South Korea, Japan and Taiwan) grappled with the recent global crisis, the South Asian region witnessed a robust economic rebound (see chapter 2 in this volume). It grew between 7 per cent and 9 per cent in 2010 and 2011, exceeding other regions around the world and even surpassing the high growth rates (6.5 per cent annually) experienced between 2000 and 2007 (The World Bank, 2011). Many economists have rebutted the argument that South Asia is relatively less integrated with the outside world, and that has helped protect it from the global recession. Instead, they have attributed South Asian economic growth to India's unprecedented growth and various governments' efforts at making their respective economies more open (Dorji *et al.*, 2007; The World Bank, 2011).

Such an impressive performance, when several other more developed countries around the world (including Greece, Italy, South Korea, Taiwan and Japan) show signs of decline and stagnation, offers optimism to businesses within South Asia. According to a World Bank Report on *Doing Business in South Asia* (2007), which compared business regulations in the region with 175 economies around the world, governments in South Asia have taken consistent steps to improve the investment environment and introduce wide-ranging reforms; from land registration in Bangladesh to reducing the time, cost and hassle for businesses to comply with legal and administrative requirements in India (The World Bank, 2007). The most transformative change actually took place in Pakistan. Modelled on Malaysia, South Korea and Singapore, the Higher Education Reforms were initiated in 2002. These changes focused upon improving the research and education infrastructure in Pakistan; and led to upgrading research labs, strengthening research support, providing lucrative salaries and scholarships for academics, initiating global faculty exchanges, establishing quality assurance and accreditation processes and developing the best digital library in the region. The progress placed Pakistan's higher education programme as 'the best practice example for developing countries' (Michael Rode, UNESCO Chairman quoted in Hayward, 2009). Science Watch (2009) also ranked Pakistan as a rising star in five disciplines, more than any other country in the world. As a result of some of the aforementioned steps, four South Asian countries have been included in the Global Competitiveness Index (GCI) since 2002, including India, Sri Lanka, Bangladesh and Pakistan (Hallward-Driemeier, 2007). Most recently these countries are ranked 56, 52, 108 and 118 respectively. Nepal was ranked 130 in the GCI 2010–11 report (World Economic Forum, 2011).

Despite its impressive growth, many weaknesses persist within South Asia. Most notable among these are weak institutions, underdeveloped infrastructure and a feeble knowledge economy (World Economic Forum, 2011). A rigid labour market with high redundancy costs is also an area of major concern. Although India has branded itself as the provider of services in information technology, it lags on most indicators of knowledge economy, in particular education (Ahmed and Ghani, 2006). For example, in 2004 gross enrolment rates for secondary education were 49 per cent for South Asia compared to 69 per cent in East Asia (Ahmed and Ghani, 2007). In a recent survey of global companies, CEOs said that their fourth biggest concern was the shortage of high-skilled workers in India (*The Economist*, 2007).

In contrast, East Asian economies fare much better on the GCI, highlighting better-developed infrastructure and more sophisticated institutions. For example, Japan is positioned at number 9, Hong Kong at 11, Taiwan at 13, South Korea at 24 and China at 26. Japan has a major competitive edge in business sophistication and innovation. Hong Kong has consistently maintained its leadership in financial market development because its economy has proven resilient post the recent global crisis, and offers one of the world's most friendly business environments. China continues to show its strength in its large and growing market size, macroeconomic stability and steadily improving businesses (see chapter 5). On the other hand, much like South Asia, a majority of East Asian countries present rigid labour markets. For example, business leaders in South Korea face extreme difficulty in hiring and firing employees. The World Bank (2011) estimates that the average severance pay for dismissing an employee is now equivalent to 91 weeks of salary. This fact leads companies to resort to temporary employment, thus creating precarious working conditions (see chapter 13).

History and culture

Throughout South Asia's history and primarily because of its strategic location (in between Central Asia and the Middle East and providing a passageway to East

Asia), several countries in South Asia (including Pakistan, India, Afghanistan and Bangladesh) have served as major cultural and trade hubs. Consequently, the region has been invaded, occupied and settled by many different peoples, including the Aryans, Greeks, Arabs, Turks, Mongols and the British, who colonised the entire United India, until the Indian subcontinent (Bangladesh, India and Pakistan) gained independence in 1947. Therefore, its people have been exposed to many different cultures and influences. The region historically shared a common Vedic culture, and later absorbed Islamic, Buddhist, British and American influences (Khilji, 2002).

Levi-Strauss (1951) argued that the peaceful and interactive coexistence of diversity was a distinct cultural feature of the region. However recent history proves otherwise. For example, the 1947 partition of the Indian subcontinent into Muslim majority Pakistan and Hindu majority India led to extreme religious violence, killing over half a million people on both sides (Butalia, 2000). Since then Pakistan and India have fought three full-fledged wars, and Hindu Muslim riots remain common occurrences in several Indian states. In recent years, the USSR invasion of Afghanistan and a growing partnership with Saudi Arabia where a more orthodox form of Islam is practised, also led to a gradual radicalisation of some Islamic societies, such as Pakistan, Bangladesh and Afghanistan (Wong *et al.*, forthcoming). Here tensions in balancing the many influences have become apparent, as these countries are struggling to achieve harmony between liberal (Sufi-influenced) and orthodox forms of Islam. It has often resulted in violence, creating unrest (and fear) amongst the general public and hurting their socio-economic development.

In contrast, East Asia has been influenced by Buddhist, Confucian and Taoist principles (Hill, 2007), although it is often described in terms of a strong Confucian ideology with an emphasis on maintaining harmony and balance within all relationships (Chen and Miller, 2011). Confucianism teaches *Zhong he*, or 'balanced harmony' for obtaining prosperity. In the Book of Means, Confucius writes, 'If balance and harmony are reached, heaven and earth will be in place, and all things will grow' (Chen, 2001, p. 88). Many scholars have attributed the economic prosperity of East Asian cultures (including Japan which shares a close affinity with the Chinese culture – House *et al.*, 2004) to Confucianism. It has been argued that family ties, combined with a high regard for intellectuals have been the primary driving force behind East Asian commitment to education and learning (Khilji *et al.*, 2011). Chen and Miller (2011) explain that for the Chinese opposites does not exist in the 'either/or' form known to many of us. Rather opposites are inseparable where they interdependently unite in a 'both/and' framework to create a new possibility (see chapter 16). This feature is the key to holism practised by Chinese cultures, but it appears to be lacking in South Asia as discussed previously (see chapter 3). On the other hand, much like East Asia, the social set-up in South Asia is family-centred. The head of the family is often a male member.

Traditionally, the role of a woman is to perform household chores and to bear children; however, this practice has been changing in urban areas as female enrolment in colleges/universities is rising (see chapter 9). Family-like ties are also created with persons who are not biological relatives but who are socially integrated into their groups. Family/social allegiance is abiding and generally takes precedence over rules. Conformity to a group is an extremely important value (Lyon, 1993).

Traditionally, South Asian culture has been characterised as collectivist (with an in-group orientation), hierarchical with a high power distance, masculine, ascription-oriented and with a high uncertainty avoidance and a low context (Hofstede, 1980; Khilji, 2002). A review of Trompenaars' (1993) work indicates that South Asians and East Asians are both outer-directed, and ascription-oriented; however, Indians, Nepalese and Pakistanis prefer less of an organisation as a system than a social system, compared to Chinese from the Mainland and Hong Kong. The GLOBE (2004) study found India to be lower on performance orientation, higher on power distance and more humane oriented than other East Asian economies, including Japan, Taiwan, South Korea, China and Hong Kong. India was also less future-oriented than Japan, but more than China, Hong Kong, Taiwan and South Korea, more male dominated than all East Asian countries (except South Korea), less assertive than South Korea and Hong Kong but more than Japan, China and Taiwan, and less collectivist than all East Asian countries (except Hong Kong).

Recent studies however indicate that individual values are in transition, and find evidence of converging values especially among the young adults in Asia. For example, Khilji's (2004) and Davis *et al.*'s studies of Pakistanis and Indians (2006) show that younger individuals are more open to change and more achievement-oriented (Lyons *et al.*, 2005) than their older counterparts. Kwong (1994) also noted that individualism had been growing among the younger groups of Chinese, which is in sharp contrast to older Chinese who grew up in 'seclusion' under socialist regimes. Egri and Ralston's (2004) study supports these arguments and shows that American and Chinese youth have more similar values orientations than do Chinese youth and Chinese older workers.

Globalisation and change: contemporary management behaviour, business ethics and management practices

Since the South Asian economies deregulated and opened up for foreign direct investment (FDI) in 1992, the region has witnessed a substantial increase in multinational activity. Exposure to the global marketplace brought about a re-conceptualisation of work values, organisational processes and approaches. This step gradually led to changes in management behaviour, and business ethics, as multinationals transferred their policies and practices to local companies that emulated and learnt from the global companies (Khilji, 2004; Chatterjee and Pearson, 2000). Below, we discuss contemporary management behaviour and business ethics.

Management behaviour and practices

In 2000, Chatterjee and Pearson's study of Indian managers indicated that a cadre of senior managers was more influenced by the market culture and economic reforms, and less bound to tradition. They concluded that Indian organisations were at the crossroads, and needed to balance tradition and market-oriented culture in order to become competitive. A decade later, some South Asian companies (including Biocon, Infosys, Reliance and Tata from India and TRG from Pakistan), have become strong global competitors. In particular Indian companies are not only attracting FDI or innovating, but they are also acquiring other global companies. Cappelli *et al.* (2010) argue that many Indian companies have blazed their own path. Their two-year study of the 100 largest companies in India proposes a new framework for managing in India, which they refer to as 'the India Way'. It includes a focus upon social mission (versus shareholder value), investment in human capital, adaptability, a unique approach to problem solving (referred to as '*juggad*') and pursuing a strategy from within for building internal capabilities first and foremost. Cappelli et. al. (2010) suggest that the source of the distinctiveness of the India Way rests heavily upon the careful and long-term development of people, their empowerment and motivation to work hard at solving problems bit by bit until they break through. It is clear that Indian companies and their management have gained confidence in their own ability. They have also learnt from the West and East Asian companies (such as Samsung, Sony, ACER, Toyota, etc.), which they looked up to in their initial years of growth.

The concept of frugal innovation (also referred to as reverse innovation), popularised by *The Economist* (2010), is an illustrative example of management excellence in South Asia (in particular India) where companies are reconfiguring and re-bundling products and processes (Henderson and Clark, 1990). They are also leading the redesigning of products and processes to cut unnecessary costs and make them available to poorer populations who, otherwise, may not have access to these products. Nanocar by Tata, a hand-held electrocardiogram by GE in Bangalore, GasFans (to overcome electricity shortages in Pakistan) and Telenor Pakistan's Easypaisa to carry out financial transactions via mobile devices are some of the examples of product trends emanating from South Asia. The recent Global Innovation Efficiency Index by INSEAD has placed Pakistan at number four, India at nine and Bangladesh at ten in terms of their innovation efficiency (Innovation Excellence, 2011; INSEAD, 2011). China has occupied the third place on this index, and also offers many examples of frugal innovation, including BYD with its low cost lithium ion batteries and electric cars, which has been supported by the most respected American investor, Warren Buffet.

In contemporary management literature, Indian companies are being labelled as a 'compelling example of a model that succeeds financially while succeeding socially' (Cappelli *et al.*, 2010, p. 22), 'worthy of emulation', a 'change agent' (Kristie, 2010: 29) and offered as an alternative to the Western management models. It is a tall order even within India where for every exemplary organisation there are hundreds of private and public sector organisations that are caught in a cultural paradox – either maintain a traditional mindset or adopt a global economic order in order to achieve international standards of performance, professionalism and quality. Sinha *et al.* (2002) argue that this situation has created a dissonance among Indian managers. It has also been witnessed in other South Asian countries, where many managers are trying to balance tradition with global demands (Khilji, 2004). It is particularly apparent in the bureaucratic public sector, which still suffers from poor managerial efficiency. For example, studies have reported a lack of managerial autonomy (Batra, 1997) and difficulties in regulatory compliance, human resource management and IT management. Public sector reforms in Pakistan, although focused on public participatory orientation in policy development, strategic planning and awareness of public needs, have not led to satisfactory results as training practices there still remain ineffective (Rehman *et al.*, 2011). Similarly, a study of the public sector reported low efforts at employee retention and lack of transformational leadership in Sri Lankan public sector organisations (Gill *et al.*, 2011).

Business ethics

Corruption is widespread in South Asia, and remains a huge challenge despite much economic development. It is often argued that corruption has severely undermined the economic growth, political structures and general well-being of South Asians (Khatri *et al.*, 2011). Nepotism, bribery and administrative corruption are most commonly practised within these societies (Thakur, 2000). The hierarchical structure of organisations often inhibits transparency and traditional management practices promote favouritism in the workplace (cf. chapter 10). In addition, the collectivist culture (with an in-group orientation) can legitimise patterns of behaviour, in that it makes it difficult to detect bribery or nepotism because the entire group might approve of these practices due to pluralistic ignorance and overall group conformity (Mujtaba, 2011). These practices have resulted in inefficiencies, delays and distrust among people. Administrative corruption, driven by complex rules and procedures, is particularly detrimental to doing business in these countries. Clearly, corruption and cronyism weaken the fragile institutions, which need to be strengthened in order to support a competitive global economy. The Transparency International Corruption Perception Index (2010) placed all South Asian countries in the red zone (for example, India is ranked 87, Sri Lanka 91 and Pakistan 143 among 178 countries) indicating high levels of corruption and lack of transparency in doing business.

Some regulatory developments have taken place within Sri Lanka, which were aimed at improving the level of corporate governance. However, it is still the case that multinational companies are more aware of ethical concerns than local companies (Batten *et al.*, 2007). A study of corporate social responsibility reporting from Bangladesh also indicates that although there are pressures from the international market, companies have only produced cosmetic responses (Belal and Roberts, 2010). More robust codes of ethics, the effective use of monitoring systems and the consistent enforcement of high ethics with social support within South Asian organisations may improve ethical behaviour and encourage the focus on the right things to be done by employees. A study of business ethics in Pakistani public and private sector organisations showed that employers are aware of the negative consequences of unethical behaviours on stakeholders, and emphasised the need for ethics education within organisations (Mujtaba, 2011).

Challenges faced by South Asian organisations

Despite the impressive growth of the South Asian region (mainly driven by India) and a recent fascination with the India Way in the West, there are many challenges that South Asian organisations are faced with. First, operating in a fast changing environment has necessitated a fundamental transformation in their orientation to focus more upon quality, professionalism, customer satisfaction, performance and employee well-being. Managers are being pressured (by the younger generations, and the success of some companies) to reconcile a traditional cultural mindset (hierarchical, in-group oriented and reactive to change) with the growing demands to become global. These diverging characteristics are generally seen as incompatible, and have resulted in a cultural paradox for these organisations. Organisations that have learnt the need to balance global integration with local adaptation have blazed the trail by exhibiting a creative new management philosophy (or the India Way). Second, despite very large populations, organisations in South Asia are being stretched to recruit qualified professionals. Even within India with its large population in the region, *The Economist* (2007) has estimated that there will be a shortage of half a million IT professionals by 2012. This shortage is partly due to the impressive growth of the IT sector, and also due to a smaller percentage of highly skilled local workers who have the relevant expertise in managing global transactions. At the same time, a competitive higher demand for the same kind of skills has created an employee labour market for top talent resulting in high labour mobility. Consequently, organisations are experiencing difficulties in retaining employees who have been trained and exposed to leading complex projects. Third, managers in local indigenous organisations are constrained in the actual implementation of effective management practices, because of widespread resistance, poor organisational design and lack of visionary leadership (Balasooriya *et al.*, 2010; Khilji and Wang, 2006; Subedi, 2006),

At a macro-level, a bureaucratic government structure, cumbersome trade tariffs and rigid business/labour policies generally hinder the growth of smaller entrepreneurial firms (see chapter 12), resulting in frustration among managers. Perceptions of poor business ethics and continuing business scandals also damage business potential in the region. The global community (and the regional) is pressuring organisations to reform its management systems to become more transparent in order to gain investor, employee and customer confidence. Terrorism and internal conflicts in some countries (in particular Afghanistan, Pakistan and Sri Lanka) have posed a distinct challenge to foreign investment and economic development. In addition, terrorism has altered the business environment by consuming organisational and managerial resources to prevent and guard against possible violent attacks. Finally, South Asia is one of the least integrated regions in the world, because of a long standing rivalry between India and Pakistan. These traits are systemic, rooted in uneven socio-economic development. Unfortunately, they are also reflective of local governments' inability to prevent an ascent of extremism in society and fully engage in a deliberate development agenda through macroeconomic reforms, efficient governance and restructuring measures.

A comparison with Southeast Asia

It was mentioned previously that the countries of Southeast Asia, in particular Singapore and Malaysia, have served as models of human and economic development to countries in South Asia. We have also shown that Higher Education Reforms in Pakistan, considered exemplary in the modern era, were modelled after Singapore and Malaysia. Hence it is important that in order to develop a complete discussion of South Asia, we also need to draw up a comparison with Southeast Asia.

Southeast Asia is composed of 11 countries, including Brunei, Burma, Cambodia, East Timor, Indonesia, Laos, Malaysia, the Philippines, Singapore, Thailand and Vietnam. It has a total population of 593 million people. Indonesia has the largest population, followed by the Philippines and Vietnam. Much like South Asia, Southeast Asia has also served as a major cultural and trade hub for centuries. Consequently, it has been invaded, occupied and settled by many different peoples, including Indians, Chinese, Arabs, Japanese, Dutch, French, Portuguese and Spanish. The dominant religions in Southeast Asia include Hinduism, Buddhism, Christianity and Islam. Over the past two decades, many Southeast Asian countries have gradually upgraded their economies and export structures from being commodity-based to becoming more related to high-technology (Ahlstrom *et al.*, 2010). Furthermore, Singapore and Malaysia have a rapidly growing service sector (Economic Surveys Series, 2011; Economy Watch, 2010). Newly industrialised countries include Malaysia, Thailand and the Philippines; Indonesia is the largest regional economy and is a member of the G-20. Singapore has become one of the wealthiest economies in the world (Ahlstrom *et al.*, 2010). The rest of Southeast Asia is heavily dependent on agriculture; however, Vietnam is notably making steady progress in developing its industrial sectors. ASEAN provides an effective framework for the integration of commerce, unlike the South Asian Free Trade Association (SAFTA) within South Asia, which suffers from barriers against the flow of goods to and from several countries in South Asia (Asian Development Bank, 2009).

There are some distinctive features of Southeast Asian businesses, including high levels of state direction, low levels of state capacity, the presence of large conglomerates and the dominance of a Chinese minority (Tipton, 2009). Typically, large business groups dominate the Southeast market and are controlled by families, with both shareholders and stakeholders excluded from influence. With the exception of Singapore, this has generally prevented established institutions from being reshaped according to changing global needs. However, in recent years, following the 1997 financial crisis, governments have launched reforms to improve the overall efficiency, responsiveness and dynamism of their economies. Although a majority of Southeastern countries have a relatively lower state capacity, the reform agenda in the direction of export-oriented industrialisation (EOI) has strengthened their economies, in particular within Malaysia, Indonesia, Thailand and Vietnam. The only exception is Singapore, where state capacity and direction are both high enough to develop a distinct model of coordinated 'liberal market economy' that is both entrepreneurial and dynamic in nature. Finally, the ethnic Chinese minority plays a disproportionately dominant role in Southeast Asian economies. For example, in Malaysia they hold 61 per cent of the listed share capital and constitute 60 per cent of private sector managers; and in Singapore and Thailand they own 81 per cent of the listed capital (Tipton, 2009). Some scholars have argued that it is not possible to understand the Asian miracle without understanding the Chinese minority. Drucker and Nakauchi (1997) have also argued that the growth and economic power of the overseas Chinese has no precedent in history. They are scattered all over Southeast Asia and are concentrated in family businesses kept together by strong collectivist ties, hence the Chinese value system (Confucianism and Taoist principles of harmony, loyalty, thrift, self-sacrifice, respect for elders and the primacy of relationships) serves as a major influence on Southeast Asian culture and management practices.

Significant growth within Singapore, Malaysia, Indonesia and Thailand has been spurred by ethnic Chinese firms (Haley *et al.*, 2009), which are often characterised by simple and flat structures, focus on high volumes–low margin business and frugal family leaders. However, there is also evidence to suggest that companies in the region have moved away from a traditional relation-based model to a market-based model in order to overcome the vulnerability that was exposed during the Asian financial crisis. Hence, much like South Asia, management and culture in the Southeast is being constantly shaped by globalisation in terms of attitudes, symbols, rituals and behaviour (Fang, 2010).

Conclusions

Management in East Asian companies, such as ACER, is based upon the principle of shared value, or 'creating value which benefits others' (Lin and Hou, 2010, p. 7). Chen and Miller (2010) show that managers in East Asia embrace the best of both worlds, that is, taking the best from Chinese and Western philosophies and businesses, while deliberately avoiding the negatives. A look at Stan Shih's management style at ACER indicates that he has taken a holistic and community driven orientation from the Chinese culture and fused it with decentralisation and empowerment from the West to successfully lead the second largest computer company in the world. It is an integrative approach, which in international management has been observed for many years in different parts of the world, and referred to as the crossvergence of values (Ralston, 2008). Khilji's (2002) study of multinational companies in Pakistan also showed that changes in management culture are complex and are facilitated by both global convergent influences and cultural divergent factors. Organisations that succeed in a global environment develop integrative approaches to managing change.

The success of the Indian IT industry is attributed to the deregulation of the Indian economy, its dynamic, mobile and well-educated workforce, the entrepreneurial spirit and innovation of the employee-base and a transformational leadership. It has boosted the confidence of investors globally and trickled down to many other industries in India, including steel, automobiles, the financial sector, telecommunications and biotech. The Indian approach to management (among the top 100 companies) has been found to be distinct from the Western business model and deeply rooted in a culture of scarcity, shared values, employee engagement and investment in people (Cappelli *et al.*, 2010). Managers in these organisations have avoided the negative aspects of in-group orientation, such as ascription and lack of trust, hierarchical decision-making and top-bottom approaches to managing. They are aware of the environment within which they operate and have adopted some Western management practices. In fact, they have used their unique constrained environment to develop new products and services. They have also avoided some local cultural practices while maintaining a strong collectivist orientation, much like successful dragon multinationals from East and Southeast Asia.

In essence, a successful Asian management model reflects a high awareness of its local culture and the global environment (see Nankervis *et al.*, 2013). It exhibits a blend of East and West philosophies to accentuate the positives of both while avoiding the negatives of both. It has 'learnt from, absorbed the richness and enthusiastically embraced the best models of governance, leadership, and administration from both East and West' (Chen and Miller, 2010, pp. 21–2), and adopted an ambicultural approach to managing. As Western companies struggle with the recent economic crisis, an ambicultural Asian model could offer new ideas for management (cf., chapter 16). Global managers need to open their minds and engage in deliberate learning between East, Southeast and South Asia and across East/South Asia and the West. In addition, as Fang (2010) has argued, 'Asian philosophies and changing institutional and cultural contexts can serve as an important source of inspiration for cross cultural theory building' (p. 159).

The success of many Indian companies offers hope to managers and organisations throughout South Asia, which like India, operate in a constrained environment with limited government support. An ambicultural Asian model could serve as a good framework for all struggling South Asian organisations and likely position them as role models for future generations of global managers. It also presents them with the possibility of contributing where local governments have failed, i.e. addressing the inconsistencies and disparate social development found in South Asia.

References

Ahlstrom, D., Chen, S-J. and Yeh, K. (2010) 'Managing in ethnic Chinese communities: Culture, institutions and contexts', *Asia Pacific Management Journal*, 27: 341–54.

Ahmed, S. and Ghani, E. (2006) *South Asia: Growth and regional integration*. Washington, DC: The World Bank.

— (2007) *South Asia: Growth and regional integration*. Delhi: Macmillan.

Ahmed, S., Kelegama, S. and Ghani, E. (eds) (2010) *Promoting economic cooperation in South Asia: Beyond SAFTA*. Thousand Oaks, CA: Sage.

Asian Development Bank (2009) *Study on intraregional trade and investment in South Asia*. Available at http://beta.adb.org/publications/study-intraregional-trade-and-investment-south-asia (accessed 27 September 2011).

Balasooriya, A., Alam, Q. and Coghill, K. (2010) 'State vs. market in search of good governance: The case of Sri Lanka telecommunications industry reforms', *Thunderbird International Business Review*, 52: 369–89.

Batra, G. S. (1997) 'Management audit as a service to public enterprise management: A study of management audit and the memorandum of understanding (MOU) system in India', *Managerial Auditing Journal*, 12: 148–55.

Batten, J. A., George, R. J. and Hettihewa, S. (2007) 'Is corporate ethical practice changing?', Evidence from Sri-Lanka, *Asia Pacific Business Review*, 13: 59–78.

Belal, A. and Roberts, R. (2010) 'Stakeholders' perceptions of corporate social reporting in Bangladesh', *Journal of Business Ethics*, 97: 311–24.

Butalia, U. (2000) *The other side of silence: Voices from the partition of India.* Durham, NC: Duke University Press.

Cappelli, P., Singh, H., Singh, J. V. and Useem, M. (2010) *The India way: How India's top business leaders are revolutionizing management.* Boston, MA: Harvard Business Press.

Chatterjee, S. and Pearson, C. (2000) 'Indian managers in transition: Orientations, work goals, values and ethics', *Management International Review*, 40: 81–95.

Chen, M-J. (2001) *Inside Chinese business: A guide for managers worldwide.* Boston, MA: Harvard Business Press.

Chen, M-J. and Miller, D. (2010) 'West meets East: Toward an ambicultural approach to management', *Academy of Management Perspectives*, 24: 17–24.

— (2011) 'The relational perspective as a business mindset: Managerial implications for East and West', *Academy of Management Perspectives*, 25: 6–18.

Davis, H. J., Chatterjee, S. R. and Heuer, M. (eds) (2006) *Management in India: Trends and transition.* New Delhi: Response Books.

Dorji, D., Mitra, A. and Patel, P. (2007) Foreword in Ahmed, S. and Ghani, E. (eds) *South Asia: Growth and regional integration.* Delhi: Macmillan Publishing.

Drucker, P. F. and Nakauchi, I. (1997) *Drucker on Asia: A dialogue between Peter Drucker and Isao Nakauchi.* Newton, MA: Butterworth-Heinemann

Dunning, J. (1993) *The Globalization of Business.* London: Routledge.

Economic Surveys Series (2011) *The Service Sector.* Available at http://www.singstatgov. sg/stats/themes/economy/biz/services.pdf (accessed 18 November 2011).

Economy Watch (2010) *Malaysia GDP.* Available at http://www.economywatch.com/gdp/ world-gdp/malaysia.html (accessed 18 November 2011).

Egri, C. P. and Ralston, D. A. (2004) 'Generation cohorts and personal values: A comparison of China and U.S', *Organization Science*, 15: 210–20.

Fang, T. (2010) 'Asian management research needs more self-confidence: Reflections on Hofstede (2007) and beyond', *Asia Pacific Management Journal*, 27: 155–70.

Ghani, E. (2011) 'The South Asian development paradox: Can social outcomes keep pace with growth?', *Economic Premise*, 53: 1–6.

Ghani, E. and Ahmed, S. (eds) (2009) *Accelerating growth and job creation in South Asia.* New York: Oxford University Press.

Gill, A., Mathur, N., Sharma, S. P. and Bhutani, S. (2011) 'The effects of empowerment and transformational leadership on employee intentions to quit: A study of restaurant workers in India', *International Journal of Management*, 28: 217–29.

Haley, G. T., Haley, U. V. and Tan, C. T. (2009) *New Asian emperors: The business strategies of the overseas Chinese.* Singapore: John Wiley & Sons (Asia).

Hallward-Driemeier, M. C. (2007) 'Improving the climate for investment and business in South Asia' in Ahmed, S. and Ghnai, E. (eds) *South Asia: growth and regional integration.* Delhi: Macmillan. Available at http://www.ucm.es/info/eid/cursodcd/IMG/ pdf_SouthAsiaGrowthandRegionalIntegration.pdf (accessed 27 September 2011).

Hayward, F. M. (2009) 'Higher Education Transformation in Pakistan: Political & Economic Instability', *International Higher Education Quarterly*, 54: 1–12.

Henderson, R. B. and Clark, K. B. (1990) 'Architectural innovation: The reconfiguration of existing product technologies and the failure of established firms', *Administrative Science Quarterly*, 35: 9–30.

Hill, H. (2007) 'Regional development: Analytical and policy issues' in Balisacan, Arsenio M. and Hill, Hal (eds) *The Dynamics of Regional Development: The Philippines in East Asia*. Northampton: Edward Elgar, pp. 68–92.

Hofstede, G., (1980) *Culture's Consequences: comparing values, behaviors, institutions, and organizations across nations*. Thousand Oaks, CA: Sage.

House, R. J., Hanges, P. J., Javidan, M., Dorfman, P. W. and Gupta, V. (2004) *Culture, leadership, and organizations: The GLOBE study of 62 societies. Journal of Cross-Cultural Psychology*, 36 (5): 628–30.

Innovation Excellence (2011) *Global innovation index 2011 – Country rankings*. Available at http://www.innovationexcellence.com/blog/2011/07/10/global-innovation-index-2011-country-rankings (accessed 27 September 2011).

INSEAD (2011) *Global innovation index 2011*. INSEAD Issues. Available at http://knowledge.insead.edu/contents/documents/GII2011_30June.pdf (accessed 27 September 2011).

Khatri, N., Syed, J. and Khilji, S. E. (2011) 'Cronyism and corruption: Evidence from South Asia', *Academy of Management,* San Antonio, TX, August 2011.

Khilji, S. E. (2002) 'Modes of convergence and divergence: An integrative view of multinational practices in Pakistan', *International Journal of Human Resource Management*, 13: 232–53

— (2004) 'Whither tradition: An evidence of generational differences in human resource satisfaction from Pakistan', *International Journal of Cross Cultural Management*, 4: 141–56.

Khilji, S. E. and Wang, X. (2006) 'Intended and implemented HRM: The missing linchpin in strategic international human resource management research', *International Journal of Human Resource Management*, 17: 1171–89.

Khilji, S. E., Oh, C.H. and Manikoth, N. (2011) *People lead to stronger performance: The secret to Samsung' success*. Ivey Business Case, Ivey Business Publishing.

Kristie, J. (2010) 'May this "India Way" paper be a change agent', *The Academy of Management Perspectives*, 24: 28–30.

Kwong, J. (1994) 'Ideological crisis among China's youths: Values and official ideology', *British Journal of Sociology*, 45: 247–64.

Levi-Strauss (1951) 'Foreword to documents on South Asia', *International Social Science Bulletin*, 3: 1–10.

Lin, H-C. and Hou, S-T. (2010) 'Managerial lessons from the east: An interview with Acer's Stan Shih', *The Academy of Management Perspectives*, 24 :6 –16.

Lyon, P. (1993) 'Epilogue' in James, P. (ed.) *Pakistan Chronicle*. London: Hurst, pp. 211–22.

Lyons, S., Duxbury, L. and Higgins, C. (2005) 'Are gender differences in basic human values a generational phenomenon?', *Sex Roles*, 53: 763–78.

Mujtaba, B. (2011) 'West and east's ethics comparison: America's business ethics influence in Afghanistan, Pakistan and Iran', *International Leadership Journal*, 4: 16–27.

Nankervis, A. R., Cooke, F. L. C., Chatterjee, S. R. and Warner, M. (2013) *New models of HRM in China and India*. London: Routledge (in press).

Nowland, J. (2008) 'Are East Asian companies benefitting from Western board practices?', *Journal of Business Ethics*, 79: 133–50.

Ralston, D. A. (2008) 'The crossvergence perspective: Reflections and projections', *Journal of International Business Studies*, 39: 27–40.

Rehman, A. U., Mansur, A. and Khan, R. A. (2011) 'Measuring training effectiveness: A case study of public sector management in Pakistan', *Journal of Diversity Management*, 6: 39–48.

Science Watch (2009) *Rising Stars*. Available at http://sciencewatch.com/dr/rs/09may-rs (accessed 27 September 2011).

Singh, J. (1998) 'Growth: Its Sources and consequences' in Thompson, G. (ed.) *Economic Dynamism in the Asia-Pacific*. London: Routledge.

Sinha, J. B., Vohra, N., Singhal, R. B. and Ushashree, S. (2002) 'Normative predictions of collectivist-individualist intentions and behaviours of Indians', *International Journal of Psychology*, 37: 309–19.

Subedi, B. (2006) 'Cultural factors and beliefs in influencing transfer of training', *International Journal of Training and Development*, 10: 88–97.

Thakur, R. (2000) 'Corruption undermines India', *Japan Times*, Tokyo. Available at http://search.japantimes.co.jp/cgi-bin/eo20000701a1.html (accessed 27 September 2011).

The Economist (2007) 'Asia's skilled shortage: capturing talent', *The Economist*, 16 Aug 2007: 22.

— (2010) 'First break all the rules: The charms of frugal innovation', 15 April 2010. Available at http://www.economist.com/node/15879359 (accessed 27 September 2011).

The World Bank (2007) *Doing business in South Asia 2007: Overview*. Available at http://siteresources.worldbank.org/SOUTHASIAEXT/Resources/Publications/448813–1171300070514/overview.pdf (accessed 27 Sept 2011).

— (2011) 'Moving up, looking east', *World Bank South Asia Update. Advance Edition*. Available at http://siteresources.worldbank.org/SOUTHASIAEXT/Resources/223546–1269620455636/6907265–1275784425763/SAREconomicUpdate7June2010.pdf (accessed 9 September 2011).

Tilak, J. B. G. (2002) *Building human capital in East Asia: What others can learn*. Available at http://siteresources.worldbank.org/WBI/Resources/wbi37166.pdf (accessed 27 September 2011).

Tipton, F. B. (2009) 'Southeast Asian capitalism: History, institutions, states and firms', *Asian Pacific Journal of Management*, 26: 401–34.

Transparency International Corruption Perception Index (2010) *Corruption Perceptions Index 2010 Results*. Available at http://www.transparency.org/policy_research/surveys_indices/cpi/2010/results (accessed 27 September 2011).

Trompenaars, F. (1993) *Riding the waves of culture: Understanding cultural diversity in business*. London: FT Books.

Wong, D., Kessler, E., Khilji, S. and Gopalakrishna, S. (forthcoming) 'Cultural mythologies and global leadership: Evidence from India, Indonesia, Pakistan and USA'. *South Asian Journal of Global Business Research*.

World Economic Forum (2011) *The global competitiveness report 2010–2011*. Available at http://www3.weforum.org/docs/WEF_GlobalCompetitivenessReport_2010–11.pdf (accessed 27 September 2011).

Zhu, Y., Warner, M. and Rowley, C. (2007) 'Human Resource Management with Asian characteristics: A hybrid people management system in East Asia', *International Journal of Human Resource Management*, 18: 44–67.

15 Management education and training in East Asia

China, Japan and South Korea

Malcolm Warner

Introduction

In this chapter, we look at management education and training in Asia, focusing in particular on three countries, namely the People's Republic of China, Japan and South Korea. All are core economies in East Asia and are major players in the expanding trade and growing well-being of that part of the world. We will also refer to a number of Overseas Chinese domains in the region, such as Hong Kong, Macau and Taiwan, if only in passing (see chapters 5, 6, 7 and 8).

East Asia has seen unprecedented rates of economic growth over recent decades, with China leading the pack, although many of the other regional players are now advancing, but less rapidly relative to their giant neighbour. Extensive economic, industrial and structural reforms have taken place, nonetheless. Such changes have led to quite different educational and training requirements from those in place in earlier years.

As one Special Report put it:

> China could overtake America in the next decade. Its economy has grown by an average of more than 10% a year over the past ten years. As the country gets richer and its working-age population starts to shrink, that growth rate is likely to tail off to perhaps 8% soon. For the American economy the calculation assumed an average annual growth rate of 2.5%. (*Economist, The*, 2011a).

The countries all differ in terms of their economics, demography and politics. Of the three countries, Japan is currently the richest with a GDP per capita of US$34,780 in purchasing power parity (ppp) terms, South Korea comes next at US$29,010 and China at US$7,570; in terms of income inequality, paradoxically, China has the highest Gini-coefficient, in rounded figures, at 0.47, with Japan at 0.37 and South Korea at 0.31 (World Bank, 2011).

In demographic terms, China now has 1.3 billion people, Japan 127.5 million and South Korea 48.7 million. Of these, China has 25 per cent of its secondary-educated cohort in tertiary education, Japan has 59 per cent and South Korea has 100 per cent. Tertiary education, 'whether or not to an advanced research qualification normally requires, as a minimum condition of admission, the successful completion of education at the secondary level' (World Bank, 2011).

In terms of politics, China has long been led by a top-down Marxist–Leninist Chinese Communist Party (CCP), Japan is a liberal democracy but for a long time was dominated by only one, business-friendly, political party, the Liberal Democratic Party (LDP) and is now dominated by the breakaway Democratic Party of Japan (DPJ) and South Korea, which was for many years a military dictatorship, is now governed by the Grand National Party (GNP) which has a parliamentary majority.

In the respective countries, better trained managers have increasingly become de rigueur, to cope with the fast globalising world, as firms seek to keep up with their rivals and enhance competitive advantage. A new breed of international managers is needed, able to manage both at home and abroad, equipped with foreign languages and a knowledge of foreign markets and workforces. Since investment in management education and training is only one variable in boosting both micro- and macroeconomic performance, however, it is very difficult to evaluate its specific contribution. The number of trained managers, especially top ones, is small vis-à-vis the aggregate size of the labour-force. Identifying significant statistical relationships is thus a major challenge. Even so, the contribution of education and training should not be underestimated.

Management education and training: background

Business schools and similar institutions in Asia are now to be found almost everywhere. The fastest expansion of management education and training in the world is now to be found in that region (see Warner and Goodall, 2009). In accredited Asia Pacific business schools, there has been a 14.6 per cent increase in such enrolment from 2008–9 to 2010–11.

The AACSB International – The Association to Advance Collegiate Schools of Business – was set up to accredit management education establishments. Only 5 per cent of schools worldwide earn its approval, namely 1,182, in all. Out of its recent listings (AACSB, 2011), the US has 651 member-institutions, China has 26, Japan has 6 and South Korea has 22 (of Overseas Chinese ones, Hong Kong has 7, Macau has 1, Taiwan has 27).

In any model of management education and training at the macro-level, the initial drivers are likely to be the modernisation process, economic growth and the need for trained managerial personnel. However, such a model has to be seen in the context of its historical, cultural and institutional experience.

A number of major determinants, such as lateness of entry, nature and pace of industrialisation, pre-industrial social and cultural norms, socio-political system, social class, as well as social geographical mobility, amongst others, may help influence the configuration of management education models that take root in a specific cultural and societal context (see Warner, 1992: 104).

An initial hypothesis might be to predict 'convergence', for if given industrial societies are becoming more alike, they might choose a common institutional and organisational solution as to how best train their managers. Is this likely to be the case, as the convergence–divergence debate might surmise? Will it be true of

Asian economies which appear to have experienced modernisation and industrialisation, albeit over different timescales? Will their 'solutions' be, plus or minus, comparable? Or will there be only 'soft' convergence as institutional and organisational transfer only occurs within cultural parameters?

On the face of it, the three Asian economies presented here have much in common. They are all successful players in the respective East Asian markets, they have all had impressive economic growth-paths and they all seek highly educated workforces. They also share, in part, a Confucian and a Neo-Confucian cultural inheritance and its consequences for the development of education and governmental systems (Bol, 2008). The legacy has been a focus on an interdependent collectivistic social behaviour code in the East rather than an independent individualistic mode as in the West (see Luo, 2000).

The Chinese Imperial examination system has long had an extensive influence throughout East Asia over the centuries (Elman, 2000). The meritocratic Chinese Imperial examination system in addition had important influences outside Asia; for instance, it was admired by the eighteenth-century Enlightenment *philosophes* in Europe and later most significantly shaped the Northcote-Trevelyan Report (1857) in the UK on the reform of the Civil Service in British India and later in the United Kingdom. The Chinese may indeed be said to have invented bureaucracy.

It was used as a model by both the Goryeo and Joseon dynasties in Korea, too, until the country's annexation by Japan. Japan also used the Chinese Imperial examination system as a template in the Heian period but the influence involved only the minor nobility and was subsequently replaced by the hereditary system during the Samurai era. Its contemporary bureaucracy has its roots in these origins.

There are thus precedents for contemporary developments in management education and training, in terms of the notion of highly selective elite schools but with varying degrees of continuity linking past and present. There may of course be 'family resemblances' from one country to another but they may not be exactly alike.

Where the three countries differ is that Japan modernised earlier than the other two after 1868 with the Meiji Restoration. In their respective ways, China and South Korea might be described as 'late developers' experiencing their significant industrialisation in the 1950s. Although China has left its mark on much of East Asia over the many centuries, in recent years the waves of Japanese imperialism led to the export of its institutions to Manchuria in 1905, as well as to Korea after 1910. Even today, there is an organisational legacy in both places. In the north of China, in the Manchurian case, the Japanese enterprise model, which took the form of the lifetime employment 'golden rice-bowl' (*jin fan wan*) system morphed into the later Chinese 'iron' (*tie fan wan*) variant; similarly, in South Korea, the (*chaebol*) corporations resemble their Japanese counterparts in many ways.

Thus, we find many overlapping influences in trying to make sense of contemporary developments in management education in East Asia. There are, in effect, three overlapping influences, namely traditional Chinese, later Japanese and even later Western ones (see Figure 15.1). Amongst these Chinese influences, Confucianism has of course been central (see chapter 3).

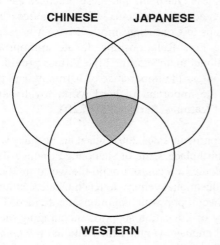

Figure 15.1 Influences on management education and training in East Asia.

Standing back, it is possible to model the respective influences *grosso modo*. We can hypothesise that the more recent Western influences will now have a greater impact on training than the past Asian ones exercise, on the overlap at the centre of the diagram. We can see from the Venn diagram above, how these overlaps are configured.

China

The People's Republic of China is the first case we examine here in detail (see also chapter 5). Traditional belief-systems, such as Confucianism, have had a continuing influence in the 'Middle Kingdom' for well over a millennium, as we have previously noted, in promoting the study of bureaucracy and organisation (see Child and Warner, 2003). The philosopher, Confucius, 551–479 BC (Kong Fuzi) may well be regarded as 'the uncrowned emperor' of China (Ronan, 1978:79). His influence has been pervasive, if at many times diffuse, over the *longue durée* (see Warner, 2011). Once thought demoded, as reflected in the 1912 'New Culture Movement', Confucianism has now sprung back into prominence. Although there are other major streams of thought in Chinese thinking, such as the Legalists and the Daoists, the Confucians still retain their niche, even in the 'harmonious society' of today's China (Bell, 2008).The Master also casts a shadow on contemporary Chinese management theory and practice:

> When one describes the managerial approach of the Chinese, some of the more commonly mentioned characteristics include collectivism and harmony, centralised control, authoritarian and paternalistic leadership, family-staffed businesses, expectation of hardworking employees, and strong organizational networks and business connections. These characteristics are practiced both

in China and overseas by the Chinese Diaspora, and these practices can be traced to the value system dictated by Confucius. These practices are influenced by the Five Relationships of Confucianism, the Five Virtues, and the Confucian Work Ethic. The Five Relationships dictate appropriate behaviour and roles for organizational members; the Five Virtues provide a moral framework for society and stress the importance of harmony; and the Confucian Work Ethic stresses the important of hard work, loyalty and dedication, frugality, and a love of learning (Rarick, 2007:22ff).

The Party has now in effect co-opted Confucius since 2001, when his birthday was officially once again celebrated in his birthplace, Qufu in Shandung Province. The Chinese set up Confucius Institutes *(kongzi xueyuan)* around the world in 2004, particularly in universities and other educational venues, to teach Chinese culture and language, as a vehicle for 'soft power' upon which opinions are divided. The non-profit making body, with Ministry of Education support, encouraging these developments, the Office of Chinese Language Council International (*Hanban*), aspires to have 1,000 of them by 2020.

The Imperial Civil Service examination was first set up in the sixth century AD, inspired by Confucian thought and practice. The elite Hanlin Academy, was established in Beijing in the eighth century AD and produced its last graduates in 1911. This body trained scholars and administrators for over 1,300 years (see Warner and Goodall, 2009:15).

The curriculum covered the 'Five Classics' (*Wujing*), as well as agriculture, civil law, geography, military strategy and taxation, amongst others. The term *jing* was used to refer to the interweaving of the vertical and horizontal threads of a loom, analogous to what ties a community together. The choice of this descriptor suggests that the Classics were considered the key unifying underpinning factor in Chinese society. In this format, the examinations were institutionalised to last for many centuries. They are regarded by most historians as the first standardised tests in recorded history which were solely based on merit. They built up a critical mass of qualified individuals with knowledge and skills able to run the high offices of the nation. The examination system attempted to select men on the basis of merit rather than of their family or their political connection. The notion of a state ruled by men of ability and virtue was thus a likely direct spin-off of Confucian philosophy.

After the 1911 Nationalist Revolution, the leadership under Sun Yat-sen established a new selection system for the reformed bureaucracy called the Examination Yuan, which had continuities with the older traditional one. It was suspended in the Civil War and Second World War but was revived in 1947 until the communist takeover in 1949 and is still extant in Taiwan.

The growth of management education and training in modern China has been remarkable since Deng Xiaoping introduced his economic reforms in 1978 (see Goodall *et al.*, 2004; Warner and Goodall, 2009) not long after Mao Zedong died in 1976. The new leader launched the 'Four Modernisations' *(sige xiandaihua)* and 'Open Door' (*kaifang*) policies which were designed to shake up the old command economy system (Child, 1994). The reformers wanted to reinvigorate the system with incremental, market-led policies. Deng famously argued that it does not matter what colour the cat, as long as it catches mice, in proposing his pragmatic reform programme (Vogel, 2011).

He was to achieve this goal with great success over the 1980s. This démarche also had consequences for management education (see Warner, 1986; 1992). Previously, management cadres (*ganbu*) as they were known were trained on Soviet lines, appropriate to the state-owned enterprise (SOE) model in part taken from the USSR (see Kaple, 1994). China had adopted the 'command economy' model but with modifications from the Soviet template.

Such industrial firms epitomised the 'iron rice bowl' (*tie fan wan*) model, which more or less institutionalised lifetime employment and a mini-welfare state within the enterprise (Ding *et al.*, 2000). It was a model which dominated Chinese industry from the early 1950s onwards. Although the Sino–Soviet split in 1960 put an end to such close collaboration, the SOE model took a long time to wind-down and its accompanying training system limped on until the late 1980s. It took two forms: one, a network of regional training centres for senior cadres; two, a wide range of in-house management training courses. It was not until the 1990s that major changes were introduced (See Warner, 1995).

Eventually, education and training in the People's Republic was reformed root and branch and was slowly replaced by a more market-oriented initiative. Delegations had sent to the US, Western Europe and Japan in the early 1980s to see what might replace it. But the Chinese were reluctant to adopt one single foreign model and wanted to avoid being too dependent on the Americans, so they diversified their mentors. Help was sought from both Western and Eastern countries, although in the end the US business school model prevailed, as adapted 'with Chinese characteristics'.

A major field of innovation was centred on the development of MBA courses in China. The US Government helped to set up an MBA education centre at Dalian, in 1984, in the North-East of China, in collaboration with the State University of New York (SUNY) at Buffalo. This step constituted a very useful 'learning experience' for the Chinese side. It was to signal the confirmation that the MBA could be taught in the Chinese context and that relevant materials could be developed which would be meaningful for Chinese managers.

China also looked to Western Europe for assistance. A European Union (EU) initiative, developed through the European Foundation for Management Education and Development (EFMD), resulted in the setting-up of the China EU Management Institute (CEMI) in Beijing in 1984. Its philosophy was one of 'action learning', a mixture of theory and practice promoted by its early Directors, namely Professors Max Boisot and John Child, both teachers of management from the United Kingdom, mixing theory with practice. It went on to become the China Europe International Business School (CEIBS) eventually to be moved to a different location in Shanghai, in 1994.

This change in strategy resulted from a mission that the present writer undertook with Professor Edouard Vermeer of Leiden University, on behalf of the EFMD, to seek out a university campus home for CEMI, as it was originally located in a State management education centre in the capital. Six noteworthy Chinese universities were visited and their suitability for hosting the European venture was evaluated. The final recommendation was made by the Vermeer–Warner team. It involved a relocation of facilities from Beijing to Shanghai so as to improve access to multinational corporations, many more of which were to be found in the latter than the former city. In the end, Shanghai's Xiaotong University was selected.

The Vermeer–Warner report recommended that the Beijing-based CEMI be transplanted to a university environment, with a new partner in Shanghai. The role of the municipal government there was very encouraging and its support with matching funds clinched the deal. The new institution, CEIBS, opened its doors there in 1994, has moved house several times in the city since and has ended up in a 'state of the art' campus designed by the famous Chinese-American architect I.M. Pei, in the district of Pudong. It is now recognised as the 'number one' in all of Asia, although it only deals with postgraduate management courses. Its mission statement runs as follows: 'To prepare highly competent, internationally oriented managers who are capable of working within the Chinese economic environment while adapting to the forces of business globalisation, international competition and international cooperation'.

By 2000, 62 universities in China offered MBA courses, such as Beijing (*Beida*) and Tsinghua in the capital, as well as others such as Nanjing and so on. By 2004, nearly 90 institutes and schools were offering MBA degrees. By 2011, over 35,000 were registered for MBA courses at 236 universities (*China Daily*, 4 November, 2011: 24). McKinsey estimates a need for 75,000 Chinese top managers with global experience in the near future; the country has perhaps a tenth at present. The Chinese government has also set a goal of 1.4 million MBAs to fill the talent-gap, an ambitious task to achieve.

As a recent account noted:

> The programs are set up to offer professional and practical training for experienced managers. Some experts say China's programs need to reduce their focus on theory and improve their practical training. And some students find the expansion of business contacts they make is at least as valuable as their lessons. Whatever the shortcomings, Chinese enterprises have come to value MBAs as they hire management personnel (*China Daily,* op. cit.).

Nearby, in the same district, is the China Pudong Cadre Academy, opened in 2005 by President Hu Jintao, which is run by the Party for top officials and which also offers an MBA. The Central Party School in Beijing also offers management courses.

As of 2009, one school, namely CEIBS, alone had graduated over 8,000 MBA and EMBA graduates and completed management training for over 80,000 executives. Additionally, a wide range of undergraduate and business and management courses is now offered in Chinese universities, both famous as well as less well known. The top universities mentioned above set standards for the others.

The upshot of all this is that China has now trained an impressive core of professional managers, although there is still a shortfall not only of senior executives but even those further down the line. It is evident that their very rapid rate of economic growth has created a demand for highly trained personnel across all fields and at all levels and that the system of training has not quite managed to keep up. The supply side efficiency is now particularly acute in respect of skilled workers, as well (see Warner 2009, 2011).

China's universities are now coming up in the world rankings but only slowly. Peking University is now rated at 49th and Tsinghua at 71st in the *Times Higher* top 100 list of 2011; in the *FT* rankings, CEIBS was the only one for Mainland China listed in the Top 100 Global MBA category, at 17th (with HKUIST at 6th and Macau not at all); it scored 11th in the FT Global EMBA list; in the Eduniversal list, CEIBS, Fudan, Tsinghua, Peking and Shanghai Jiaotong were entered in the top classification for China; in the *Asiaweek* one, only CEIBS was rated in the top 20 for Asia; and it was the only mainland Chinese one, rated 91st, in *The Economist*'s '100 Top MBAs' list, with the University of Hong Kong at 36th, HKUIST at 62nd, and the Chinese University of Hong Kong at 88th and no Macau mention (see *Times Higher* 2011, *FT*, 2011, *Eduniversal*, 2011, *Asiaweek*, 2011, *Economist, The*, 2011b).

To sum up, as Chen and Yang (2010) put it:

> It was found that successful practices such as the National MBA Education Supervisory Committee, the top-down approach by the government, the emphasis on international collaborations and faculty development, national MBA entrance examinations, and other related measures have maintained the MBA education system on its current development course, while challenges from the ever-changing context, the balance between internationalization and localization, curriculum design with the Chinese characteristics will continue to shape the future of MBA education in China (Chen and Yang, 2010:128).

Japan

Japan is the second case we examine here (see chapter 7). At first, Japan shared the experience of Imperial China in setting-up a Confucian model of education and training and we find here similar precedents for contemporary practices. The classical autocratic state required an educated bureaucracy. During the Taika Reforms (645 AD), Chinese political systems (from the Sui (581–618) and Tang (618–907) dynasties) were imported to establish a legal–political system called the *ritsuryo* system that would last some five centuries and set the scene. The *ritsuryo* government established what they called the *daigakuryo,* a school that trained administrative bureaucrats in the capital. It also established schools in the outlying regions.

Later, both Buddhist, Confucian and Shinto influences coexisted. These precepts centred upon the ruler–subject relationship, key to Confucianism, the importance of piety from Buddhism, the disciplines of everyday living and the importance of education. After the *Meiji* Restoration in 1868, Japan moved towards modernising not only its education system but also its government administration. Although British and American liberal ideas circulated, French and German statist notions found greater favour in Imperial circles (*Education in Japan*, 2011).

The evolution of modern management education in Japan has been rather different from that of the Chinese model. It was very slow to adopt the North American business school model. Instead, it proceeded on something similar to German experience, with vocational technical education and engineering degrees as the main influence. After the Second World War, the big business conglomerate groupings (*keiretsu*) were largely uninterested in establishing business schools and the Japanese system remained resilient to the North American model in spite of the US Occupation regime. There was the widely held view that American methods did not suffice and Japan must develop its model based on an emphasis on technical competence, as in the German case. Over 40 per cent of school leavers went to university or college and they were expected to have a higher standard of general education with a strong emphasis on mathematics and science.

Students who wanted to get on studied economics or commerce, not management. Those in the elite who went to top universities like Tokyo pursued studies in law or engineering. University was seen as providing a rounded education and later on company-specific skills could be taught in-house. As Locke and Spender (2011:45) put it; 'Companies spend much time and money on in-house training, job rotation and multiskilling that impart tacit and explicit learning tailored to the firm's environment'. Training programmes in-house fell into four categories: programmed training, cafeteria-type training, a combination of the above and cafeteria-type training with supervisors' advice.

A major body providing a certification was the Japanese Management Association (JMA), the oldest such entity in Japan: during the war the Nippon Industrial Management Association and the Nippon Scientific Management Association had merged in 1942. Its activities include open programmes, in-house training, distance learning, and publications.

The absence of North America-style business schools in Japanese universities is remarkable; there are only a few comparable to the US model, such Keio University's. Although there have been some shifts in recent years, there is still a great deal to do vis-à-vis internationalisation.

Compared with other Asian countries (including China), Japan produces only a limited number of home-grown MBAs (see Warner and Goodall, 2009:4). The QS Global Top Business Schools 2009 listing featured only three Japanese schools amongst the 200 schools that constitute the MBA elite in Asia: Waseda Business School (WBS), International University of Japan (IUJ) and Ritsumeikan Asia-Pacific University (APU) although 78 institutions teach management studies at graduate level. More and more of these teach the course entirely in English. But it is clear that there is a dearth of Japanese MBA candidates or practising managers attending Western business schools, whether in Cambridge, England or Cambridge, Massachusetts.

On the other hand, the Harvard Business School Japan Research Center (JRC) was established in Tokyo almost a decade ago, in January 2002. Its primary aim is to support HBS faculty research and case-writing activities in that country:

> Through its activities in Japan, HBS strives to deepen faculty's understanding of and exposure to Japanese management issues, trends, and practices, as well as developing locally relevant case-studies and course materials for use in MBA and Executive Education programs around the world (HBS, 2010).

Japan's universities do not fare that well in international rankings, such as the *Times Higher* top 100 list, but Tokyo University achieved a reasonable status at 30th place and Kyoto at 52nd; no Japanese business school featured in the '100 Top Global MBA' or EMBA category in the *Financial Times* (*FT*) current management education institution ranking in 2011, or at Masters level (or others) globally, or even for Asia; *Eduniversal* recently mentioned three business schools in their top ranking for Japan, namely those of the University of Tokyo, Keio and Waseda; and in the *Asiaweek* list, there are two listed for Japan in their top list: International University of Japan and Waseda are featured as 13th and 16th; no business school from Japan was to make the top 100 in *The Economist*'s 100 Top MBAs (see *Times Higher*, 2011, *FT*, 2011, *Eduniversal*, 2011, *Asiaweek*, 2011, *Economist, The*, 2011b).

Accreditation agencies have problems in Asia with the Japanese educational bureaucracy, as the Ministry responsible appears to be reluctant to deal with them.

South Korea

South Korea is the third case we examine here (see chapter 8). As in its Chinese neighbour, there was a long tradition of Confucian education which passed on the scholarship, as well as the theory and practice, of bureaucracy in the Korean dynasties. This not only influenced the governance of the country but also passed on a legacy of organisational hierarchy to be incorporated in business administration, past and present.

South Korean business is dominated by big formally structured business groups known as the *chaebols*. The word itself means 'business family' or 'monopoly' in the Korean language. Its structure can cover a single large company or several. Each is controlled, managed and/or owned by the family dynasty, generally that of the group's founder. We find giant indigenous MNCs such as Hyundai, LG Group and Samsung are among the biggest and most noteworthy.

After the Japanese occupation ended in 1945, Korea ended up divided into the north (the Democratic People's Republic of Korea (DPRK)) and the south (the Republic of Korea (ROK)), with the former under Russian hegemony and with the latter under American military government. A destructive localised war in 1950 ensued, with disastrous consequences. The north consolidated its Soviet-style economic system, with Russian and Chinese backing, with its own kind of development of management education and training for its cadres (see Collins *et al.*, 2012) in the Central School for High Ranking Cadres (see Kim, 2006:167) and upgrading of institutions is being considered with UN advice (see DPU, 2009). An American-led recovery plan was launched to rebuild the south in 1953, which laid great emphasis on training needs in the widest context and has borne substantial returns as will be seen below.

Many South Koreans went to study in the US, and therefore Western management practices were adopted there (see Rowley *et al.*, 2005), as adapted to the local cultural environment. Although Westerners perceive corporate culture in Korea as typically Asian and highly collectivistic, the Japanese however see it more as being individualistic, as they do vis-à-vis the Chinese equivalent. Some commentators see this as 'Dynamic Collectivism' (see Rowley and Bae, 2003:193–4).

Management education and training in South Korea has largely been based on US lines for some decades now. In recent years, its business schools have tried to gain wider recognition in the Asian market. The best known business schools are at public institutions such as the Seoul National University (SNU) and KAIST Business School at Korea Advanced Institute of Science and Technology, as well as seven private schools: Yonsei School of Business (YSB) at Yonsei University; Korea University; Sejong University; Sogang University; SungKyunKwan University; Hanyang University; and Ewha Woman's University. Yonsei has been teaching management since 1915. Its Global MBA Program was inaugurated in 1998 as the first English-only-speaking one in the country.

A recent commentator argued that:

> South Korea's Yonsei University, which touts its expertise in *chaebol,* or the management of family-run enterprises, has offered its services globally. The *chaebol* curriculum reflects the work of well-known American researchers, but the program works only where it reflects indigenous value systems (Lovett, 2010: 1).

International rankings of South Korean universities remain very low as they have very few international faculty-members and students and little internationally published research. Pohang Institute of Science and Technology achieved 53rd position in the *Times Higher* 100 list, with KAIST at 94th; only one Korean business school featured in the top 100 of the Global MBA *FT* listings in 2011, however, namely KAIST as 99th; in the *FT* Global EMBA listing, Korea University was placed at 23rd, Yonsei scored 57th; in the recent *Eduniversal* list, Seoul, Korea, KAIST and Yonsei are rated as top Korean schools; in *Asiaweek*, Seoul was listed but was low down in Asia rankings; and in *The Economist's* Top 100 MBA list, Yonsei was the only one noted, at 76th (see *Times Higher*, 2011, *FT*, 2011, *Eduniversal*, 2011, *Asiaweek*, 2011, *Economist, The*, 2011b).

Salaries have been on the low side for many years, compared with other professions. Recently, there has been a determined effort to improve matters, with an attempt to recruit more foreign faculty-members, especially English-speaking ones. As a response to globalisation, a number of Korean universities and business schools are beginning to teach in English. Yonsei (YSB) has now embarked on this course of action as noted above, as well as a number of others, such as the SolBridge Business School outside the capital, in Woosong.

Conclusions

It would be unwise to generalise too sweepingly about the links between past and present. Indeed, a degree of caution is needed when considering the origins of business schools in general and in Asia in particular. However, we will now present some broad conclusions.

Taking their evolution in sequence, we find that the newer participants in the modernisation process we have looked at seem to have a greater attraction to the North American business school model, namely China and South Korea, compared with Japan (see Jenster, 2009). Given that the Japanese started earlier in their modernisation process in the late nineteenth century, it is understandable that they might not have adopted a particular mode of education and training which was only just emerging in the US around the turn of the last century, bearing in mind that the HBS only came into being in 1908. The later development of both South Korea and China perhaps made them more open to what were, by then, well-established Western management education and training modes, namely full-blown business schools.

Even so, teaching in such training institutions in the three Asian countries remains largely glocal rather than global and is often in the indigenous language, with only distinct exceptions. Most business schools in East Asia teach their main courses in their own tongues; Chinese, Japanese or South Korean. A good part of the instructional materials are filtered by the local culture, are in its language and any case-studies written are mainly locally focused ones. This emphasis is even more marked in such schools in provincial locations, where the bulk of management teaching takes place and where the majority of management graduates have jobs in nearby enterprises, usually not MNCs. Cases are Western-based only where appropriate, such as in 'International Business' courses. Textbooks are also often ones published by indigenous authors in the local language, with a minority of Western texts used in translation or in English, although more so the latter case at the higher-status schools.

We may therefore conclude that the 'convergence' theory does not fully resolve the issue in this context. Modernisation and industrialisation do not have the same impact on these countries' systems of management education and training. Neither does the cultural and historical legacy of Confucianism point to overly common outcomes. The cultural resilience of the Japanese system seems to protect it more from exogenous influences compared with the Chinese or South Korean. One irony is that American-style business schools have diffused more widely in communist China than in anti-communist Japan. If 'soft' convergence does occur, it might be likely to do so within cultural parameters but possibly in unanticipated ways.

References

AACSB (2011) *The Association to Advance Collegiate Schools of Business, Data Trends.* Available at http://www.aacsb.edu/publications/businesseducation/2011-data-trends.pdf (accessed 11.11.11).

Asiaweek (2011) *World MBA Ranking.* Available at http://worldranking.blogspot.com/2008/09/top-asia-mba-schools-by-asiaweek.html (accessed 11.11.11).

Bell, D. (2008) *China's New Confucianism: Politics and Everyday Life in a Changing Society.* Princeton, NJ: Princeton University Press.

Bol, P. K. (2008) *Neo-Confucianism in History.* Cambridge, MA: Harvard University Asia Center.

Chen, X. and Yang, B. (2010) 'Copying from others or developing locally?: Successes and challenges of MBA education in China (1990–2010)', *Journal of Chinese Human Resource Management,* 1: 128 –45.

Child, J. (1994) *Management in China During the Era of Reform.* Cambridge: Cambridge University Press.

Child, J. and Warner, M. (2003) 'Culture and management in China', in Warner, M. (ed.) *Culture and Management in Asia.* London and New York, NY: Routledge, pp. 24–47.

China Daily (2011) 'Masters of business take on the world', *China Daily,* 4 November, 2011: 24.

Collins, N., Zhu, Y. and Warner, M. (2012) 'HRM and Asian socialist economics in transition: China, Vietnam and North Korea,' in Brewster, C. J. and Mayrhofer, W. (eds) *Handbook of Research on Comparative Human Resource Management,* Cheltenham: Edward Elgar (in press).

Ding, D., Goodall, K. and Warner, M. (2000) 'End of the "iron rice-bowl": whither Chinese human resource management?', *International Journal of Human Resource Management,* 11: 217–36.

DPU (2009) *Economic Management Training for North Korea* (Keith Sargent), DPU Associates. Available at http://www.dpu-associates.net/node/121 (accessed 19.11.11).

Economist, The (2011a) 'Special Report: Becoming number one. China's economy could overtake America's within a decade', *The Economist,* 24 September, p. 6.

— (2011b) 2010 Full Time MBA Ranking. Available at http://www.economist.com/whichmba/2010/free-ranking-tool (accessed 11.11.11.).

Education in Japan (2011) Education in Japan – Bibliography. Available at http://science.jrank.org/pages/7648/Education-in-Japan.html> (accessed 11.11.11).

Eduniversal (2011) *Business School Rankings.* Available at http://www.eduniversal-ranking.com/business-school-university-ranking-5palms.html (accessed 11.11.11).

Elman, B. A. (2000) *A Cultural History of Civil Examinations in Late Imperial China.* Berkeley: University of California Press.

FT (2011) *Financial Times Global MBA Rankings.* Available at http://rankings.ft.com/businessschoolrankings/global-mba-rankings-2011 (accessed 11.11.11).

Goodall, K., Warner, M. and Lang, V. (2004) 'HRD in the People's Republic: the MBA "with Chinese characteristics?"', *Journal of World Business,* 39: 311–23.

HBS (2010) *Harvard Business School.* Available at http://www.hbs.edu/global/research/asia/center/japan/ (accessed 11.11.11).

Jenster, P. V. (2009) 'The Future of Management Education and Business Schools in China', in Warner, M. and Goodall, K. (eds) 2009 *Management Training and Development in China: Educating Managers in a Globalized Economy.* London and New York, NY: Routledge, pp. 175–97.

Kaple, D. (1994) *Dreams of A Red Factory*. Oxford and New York: Oxford University Press.

Kim, S. G. (2006) *North Korea under Kim Jong Il: From Consolidation to Systemic Dissonance*. Albany, NY: SUNY Press.

Locke, R. R. and Spender, J. C. (2011) *Confronting Managerialism: How the Business Elite and their Schools Threw Our Lives Out Of Balance*. London: Zed Books.

Lovett, C. M. (2010) 'American Business Schools in the Post-American World', *Chronicle of Higher Education*. Available at http://chronicle.com/article/American-Business-Schools-in/124256/ (accessed 11.11.11).

Luo, Y. (2000) *Guanxi and Business*. Singapore: World Scientific.

Rarick, C.A. (2007 'Confucius on Management: Understanding Chinese Cultural Values and Managerial Practices', *Journal of International Management Studies*, 2: 22–8.

Ronan, C. (1978) *The Shorter Science and Civilization in China (with J. Needham)*. Vol. 1. Cambridge: Cambridge University Press.

Rowley, C. and Bae, J. S. (2003) 'Culture and Management in South Korea', in Warner, M. (ed.) *Culture and management in Asia*. London and New York, NY: Routledge, pp. 187–210.

Rowley, C., Benson, J. and Warner, M. (2005) 'Towards an Asian model of human resource management? A comparative analysis of China, Japan and South Korea', in Warner, M. (ed.) *Human Resource Management in China Revisited*. London and New York, NY: Routledge, pp. 301–18

Times Higher (2011) *World University Rankings*. Available at http://www.timeshigher education.co.uk/world-university-rankings/ (accessed 11.11.11.).

Vogel, E. F. (2011) *Deng Xiaoping and the Transformation of China*. Cambridge, MA: Harvard University Press.

Warner, M. (1986) 'The "long march" of Chinese management education, 1979–84', *China Quarterly*, 106: 326–42.

— (1992) *How Chinese Managers Learn*. London and New York, NY: Macmillan.

— (1995) *The Management of Human Resources in Chinese Industry*. London and New York, NY: Macmillan.

— (ed.) (2009) *Human Resource Management 'with Chinese Characteristics'*. London and New York, NY: Routledge.

— (ed.) (2011) *'Confucianism HRM in Greater China; Theory and Practice'*. London and New York, NY: Routledge.

Warner, M. and Goodall, K. (eds) (2009) *Management Training and Development in China: Educating Managers in a Globalized Economy*. London and New York, NY: Routledge.

World Bank 2011 *Miscellaneous*. Available at http://web.worldbank.org/WBSITE/ EXTERNAL/EXTABOUTUS/0,pagePK:50004410~piPK:36602~theSitePK:29708,00. html (accessed 11.11.11).

Part V
The future and conclusions

When rulers love to observe the rules of propriety, the people respond readily to the calls on them for service.

(Confucius: Analects, XIV, xlv)

16 The future of East Asian management

Rosalie L. Tung

Introduction

It is both exciting and intimidating to speculate on the future of East Asian management. It is 'exciting' because it presents a wonderful opportunity for me, as one of the first Western management scholars of Chinese descent to undertake systematic research on China and Japan, to set forth my perspectives on the way that things might be in the future. It is also 'intimidating' – since forecasting is always daunting particularly in times of very rapid and dramatic changes. Perhaps the best example of a seismic change that has occurred in the last quarter of the twentieth century is the meteoric rise of China, the world's most populated nation. In the late 1970s, China was one of the poorest countries on earth; yet within the course of three short decades, it has become the most 'cash-rich' nation and has assumed the status of the world's banker. The fact that European leaders turned to China for assistance in solving the EU sovereign debt crisis is a clear sign that that country has already become 'a dominant global power' whose scope and magnitude of influence is 'far greater . . . than anyone imagines' (Alderman and Barboza, 2011).

This chapter will first briefly identify some of the forces that have contributed to the transition from 'West leads East' to 'West meets East' (Chen and Miller, 2010: 17) before speculating on the future of East Asian management.

From 'West leads East' to 'West meets East'

Beginning with the Industrial Revolution that began in the second half of the eighteenth century, the West (first, the UK, then followed by much of the rest of Europe and subsequently the US) has been upheld as the model of economic development around the world. China and India, two countries once known for their economic and military prowess in the centuries preceding the Industrial Revolution, were reduced to a semi-colonial or colonial status, respectively. From then onwards, industrial/business practices in the West (particularly those in the US) became synonymous with efficiency resulting in superior performance and were hence emulated worldwide.

This status quo was maintained for almost two centuries until the end of the Second World War when the rapid ascendancy of the Japanese economy in the world attracted widespread attention – researchers and practitioners alike were keen to unravel the factors that have contributed to the economic miracle that has transformed Japan from the ruins of the Second World War to its emergence as the second largest economy in the world in a few short decades. These factors included Japanese institutions, such as the Ministry of International Trade and Industry (MITI), that transformed Japan into an efficient export machine that generated huge trade surpluses for that country (Johnson, 1982). Others asserted that the secret of the Japanese economic miracle lay in its superior management practices and leadership styles as epitomised by the publication of *Theory Z* by William Ouchi (1981). Concepts such as quality control circles (QCC), just-in-time (JIT) inventory systems and zero-defects (ZD) movements – typically associated with Japanese management practices although they may not necessarily have originated in Japan – received worldwide attention (see chapter 7). Yet others have argued that the formula for success could be found in Japan's ability to harness and leverage its human capital to compensate for that country's lack of natural resources (Tung, 1984).

Japan's ascendancy was rapidly followed by the emergence of the 'Asian Tigers' consisting of Hong Kong, Singapore, South Korea (ROK or Korea, in short) and Taiwan (see chapters 6 and 8). While significant differences abound among these countries, they do share certain common cultural characteristics. In their correlational analysis of cultural dimensions and rates of economic growth worldwide for the 1965–85 time-period, Hofstede and Bond (1988) found that the cultural dimension that has the most significant explanatory power for variations in economic growth rates around the world is Confucian Dynamism (CD). CD was subsequently relabelled as Hofstede's fifth cultural dimension, long- versus short-term orientation. The characteristics associated with CD included persistence, thrift, the ordering of relationships in society and a sense of shame (Hofstede and Bond, 1988:17).

Just as the Japanese economy began to lose its momentum and direction, commonly referred to as the 'lost decade(s)', two other East Asian countries quickly took Japan's place. First, there was Korea and then the People's Republic of China (PRC or China, in short). Despite the yet unsettled political situation on the Korean peninsula, South Korea has produced several *chaebols*, such as Samsung, Hyundai and LG, which have become major manufacturers or leaders in semiconductors, electronics, automobiles and construction on a worldwide basis. The per capita GDP in Korea expanded from $87 at the end of the Korean War (1950–3) to its current rank as the fifteenth largest economy in the world (2009 World Bank data). The Asian financial crisis that erupted in that region in 1997 marked the entrance of China as a formidable force that has to be contended with in the world economic arena (see chapters 2 and 5). Within the course of three short decades, China was transformed from a backward country that was brought to the brink of economic bankruptcy at the end of the Cultural Revolution (1966–76) to become the second largest economy in the world in 2010 and the holder of the largest foreign reserves in the world. China is projected to overtake the US by 2030 or perhaps before then (*The World in 2050*, 2011; Ferguson, 2011).

The 2008–9 global financial crisis (GFC), with its epicentre in the US, followed by the sovereign debt crisis that continues to plague countries in the European Union, has exacerbated the gap in economic growth rates between the industrialised countries, on the one hand, and the emerging markets, particularly those of China and India, on the other. Even though the US

- continues to dominate the ranks of *Fortune*'s Global 500 companies
- still leads the world in terms of publication in scientific journals
- is home to some of the most innovative and admired companies in the world (such as Apple, Google and Microsoft) and
- remains as the most attractive destination for pursuing studies in science, technology and business administration, the winds of change are gathering force that challenge the West to make way for or, at the very least share the world stage with, Asia[1].

These forces of change include, but are not limited to

- the widening disparity in rates of economic growth between the industrialised vis-à-vis the emerging markets;
- the rising competitiveness of non-Western multinationals;
- the increasing awareness in Western countries of the need to understand and perhaps learn from their Asian counterparts;
- the surge in scientific knowledge generation in the emerging markets, as evidenced by the growing share of publications in science and scholarly journals by researchers from China.

Each of these factors is briefly discussed below.

Widening disparity in economic growth rates

As noted earlier, the epicentres for the 2008–9 GFC and the sovereign debt crisis are the US and Europe, respectively. These crises have crippled the economies in these two regions and have resulted in negative or very low rates of growth in each of the past four years. In stark contrast, China and India have continued to experience high rates of growth. In fact, since 2003–4, the rates of economic growth in the emerging markets have surpassed those of the industrialised countries, (TD Economics, 2009) and this gap is expected to widen further in the years ahead (Bremmer and Shalett, 2011). To reflect this new world economic order, the industrialised West has finally realised the futility of attempting to chart the course of world economic development among the G-7 member countries alone (US, Germany, UK, France, Japan, Italy and Canada), particularly when some of them are the source of the current financial woes. The substitution of the G-7 by the G-20 countries (the G-7 plus the BRICS countries and other emerging markets) means that the emerging markets, particularly those countries with hefty foreign reserves and strong economic growth, will have a broader say in world economic affairs. In short, the formation of the G-20 represents a crisis of confidence in the developed West's ability to lead the world. As Ferguson (2011:5) has aptly described it: '. . . the West has suffered a financial crisis that has damaged not only the wealth of the Western world, but perhaps more importantly the legitimacy, the credibility, even the self-esteem of the West'.

In fact, because of the persistent problems in the US and EU economies, there has been growing talk of the need to decouple the Asian economy from those of the US and Europe so that the growth in the former group of countries will not be hampered by the lingering economic woes in the latter regions of the world.

Rising competitiveness of non-Western multinationals

Earlier on, reference was made to the emergence of Japanese and Korean multi-nationals after the 1950s. Products by Toyota, Nissan, Sony, Samsung, Hyundai and LG have become internationally recognised brands that challenge and, in some cases, surpass those that emanate from the West. In the more recent past, multinationals from other emerging markets have also made substantial inroads into the international marketplace. Table 16.1 presents the growing representation of Global 500 companies in *Fortune's* 2011 list that emanate from the emerging markets (*Fortune*, 2011). For comparison purposes, those from the G-7 countries will also be included in this table.

Some of the emerging market multinationals (EMMs) have become active players in the mergers and acquisition (M&A) arena including the acquisition of some leading international brands. Examples include Lenovo's purchase of IBM's PC, Tata's acquisition of Jaguar and Tetley Tea, and Zhejiang Geely Holding

Table 16.1 2011 Fortune's Global 500 companies from BRICS, Asian Tigers and G-7

Country/Economy	# of Global 500 Companies
BRICS:	
Brazil	7
Russia	7
India	8
China*	61
South Africa	0
ASIAN TIGERS:	
South Korea	14
Singapore	2
Taiwan	8
G-7:	
US	133
UK	30
Germany	34
France	35
Japan	68
Canada	11
Italy	10

Source: *Fortune*, 25 July, 2011.

* This includes four firms located in Hong Kong, SAR.

Group's purchase of Volvo. M&A aside, some of the home-grown firms in the emerging markets have very sizeable market valuations. Examples include China-based Alibaba, one of the largest B2B e-commerce companies in the world; Baidu (market valuation of US$37.3 billion), the biggest internet search engine in China; and Huawei which is poised to overtake Ericsson as the largest network equipment maker in the world ('Huawei near to overtaking Ericsson, sees consumer devices' (*Economic Times*, 2011). Given the rapid rise and expansion of indigenous emerging market companies, three of the largest markets for initial public offerings in 2010 were Hong Kong, Shanghai and Shenzhen (Sorkin, 2011).

Awareness of the need to understand and perhaps learn from Asia

Just as the motto for China after its humiliating defeat by Western powers in the mid-nineteenth century was 'to learn from the West to defeat the West', in light of the rise of Asia and the emerging markets it appears that the West has finally awakened to the need to understand and perhaps learn from Asia. As Hexter and Woetzel have observed (2007: 7): 'As China emerges into the world economy, best practices there will become best practices globally. More products developed in China will become global products; more industrial processes developed in China will become global processes'.

This crude awakening first surfaced in the 1980s in the form of the desire to unravel the secrets of the Japanese economic miracle alluded to earlier in the chapter. In the more recent past, in light of the phenomenal growth of the Chinese economy – economic growth rates of at least 9 per cent for three continuous decades – the West, including the US, has finally awakened to the need to understand China. Some indications of this growing awareness include the following. One, in his 2009 visit to China, US President Obama unveiled his '100,000 initiative', the objective of which is to send 100,000 American students to study in China in the next 4 years ('Obama pledges to send 100,000 students to China in the next 4 years', *Chronicle of Higher Education, The*, 2009).

Two, the growing enrolment of international students in Asian universities is now of key importance. While Asian students are still very much attracted to North American universities, in the recent past a growing number of non-Asian students have been lured to Asian universities for two primary reasons: the economic ascendancy of Asia and the rapid rise in the rankings of Asian universities ('Asian Universities Become Draw for Foreign Students', *Chosun Ilbo, The*, 2010) (see chapter 15). For example, the number of international students in China doubled from 110,844 to 223,500 between 2004 and 2008. At the National University of Singapore, an estimated 20 per cent and 60 per cent of its undergraduate and graduate students, respectively, are foreigners. At the University of Hong Kong, a high percentage of its students are from overseas; it plays host to around 5,300 mainland Chinese and international students, out of just 22,000 students in total.

Three, there is a growing forum for research on Chinese and/or Asian management; for example, the mission of the *Asia Pacific Journal of Management* (*APJM*) is to publish 'original manuscripts on management and organisational research in the Asia Pacific region, encompassing Pacific Rim countries and mainland Asia'. *APJM* had attained an impressive 3.36 impact factor in 2010 (*Asia Pacific Journal of Management*, 2011). Other examples include the establishment of the International Association for Chinese Management Research (IACMR) and that association's journal, *Management Organization Research (MOR)*, as well as the *Asia Pacific Business Review (APBR)*. Even the top-ranked management journal, the *Academy of Management Journal (AMJ)*, will devote a special issue around the theme of 'West meets East: New Concepts and Theories' (based on Ming-Jer Chen's theme for the 2010 AOM annual meetings). The objective of that special issue is to move beyond the North American-centric research paradigms and concepts to 'tap into the empirical phenomena of the East and its cultural, philosophical and broader intellectual tradition to create a richer, more robust and "powerful" field of Management, in terms of understanding and managing organisations and behavior globally' (Barkema *et al.*, 2011). This growing attention to Chinese and/or Asian management practices by Western or Western-trained scholars will undoubtedly translate into greater knowledge and awareness and, most probably, have an influence on management literature in general.

Growing share of publication by Chinese scholars

The 2011 British Royal Society report entitled *Networks and Nations: Global scientific collaboration in the 21st century*, confirmed the emergence of China as a scientific power that rivals, and in some cases surpasses, the traditional 'scientific superpowers' of the US, Western Europe and Japan (British Royal Society, 2011a). Table 16.2 presents the comparative proportion of global publication authorship by select country for the top ten countries in two time periods, 1999–2003 and 2004–8.

It is important to note that the aforementioned statistics may mask higher numbers for China since a country's publication record is determined by the country of affiliation of the authors as opposed to citizenship and/or ethnic background. A cursory review of management journals' publication attests to the exponential growth in ethnic Chinese authors among our ranks. Brazil and India

Table 16.2 Comparative proportion of global publication authorship by country

1999–2003	2004–8
US: 26.4%	US: 21.2%
Japan: 7.8%	China: 10.2%
UK: 7.1%	UK: 6.5%
Germany: 7.0%	Japan: 6.1%
France: 5.0%	Germany: 6.0%
China: 4.4%	France: 4.4%
Italy: 3.5%	Canada: 3.6%
Canada: 3.4%	Italy: 3.5%
Russia: 2.6%	Spain: 2.7%
Spain: 2.5%	India: 2.5%

Source: Royal Society's Knowledge, Networks and Nations report, 'Would Einstein get funded today?' (2011).

are also catching up and São Paulo is now ranked among the world's top 20 cities for research output ('Royal Society's Knowledge, Networks and Nations report: Would Einstein get funded today?', British Royal Society, 2011b). While quantity is not necessarily synonymous with quality, the sheer increase in the volume of publication in refereed scientific journals by scholars from emerging markets does attest to the rising competitiveness of emerging markets in research.

The same British Royal Society report also projected that China may likely overtake the US as the global leader in scientific output by 2013. Since 1999, China has increased its investment in R&D by 20 per cent per year to reach over US$100 billion in 2007 (or 1.44 per cent of that country's GDP). China's R&D budget in 2020 is projected to reach 2.5 per cent of its GDP. In 2010, China embarked on the National Medium- and Long-term Talent Development Plan (2010–20) that established a blueprint for creating a highly skilled national work-force over the next decade (Wang, 2010). Foreign-educated Chinese talent is an obvious target. The growth in the emerging markets has meant that immigrants and their offspring may be returning to their countries of origin in pursuit of career opportunities. In fact, because of the continued weakness in the US economy contrasted with the growing strength of the emerging markets, this reverse migra-tion has already begun. Setting aside reverse migration, to capitalise on the growth opportunities in the emerging markets, there is a growing trend among high-tech immigrants to establish dual beachheads of businesses in the US or Canada, i.e., their adoptive country of residence and their country of origin. Saxenian, author of *The New Argonauts: Regional Advantage in a Global Economy* (Saxenian, 2006), noted that by the end of the 1990s, Chinese and Indian immigrants accounted for 29 per cent of all IT start-up companies in Silicon Valley. Another study in 2005 by Duke University and released in 2007 has indicated that the percentage of immigrant start-ups in Silicon Valley has risen to 52 per cent (Labriet-Gross, 2007). The migration of human talent to the emerging markets is not confined to immigrants and their children. In fact, Beijing and Shanghai have become attractive destinations for a growing number of American graduates in search of jobs and/or career development opportunities (Seligson, 2009).

The future of East Asian management

In light of the rise of Asia and the growing role that it currently plays in the world economic arena, there is much speculation as to what the future will hold in terms of management styles and practices in East Asia and how these developments can, in turn, affect the rest of the world (see chapters 4 and 11). To put it differently, with the transition from 'West leads East' to 'West meets East', does it mean that Western management theories and practices will be eclipsed and replaced by East Asian management paradigms and styles? Some have raised the spectre that Western dominance may be over – see, for example, Paul Kennedy's *The Rise and Fall of the Great Powers* (Kennedy, 1987) and the six-part television series hosted by historian Niall Ferguson entitled, *Is the West History?* which examine these issues, albeit on a grander scale that encompasses political, economic and socio-cultural dimensions. Others, however, have pointed to the continued ingenuity of the West, particularly the US (see Gupta and Wang, 2011, for example) and have suggested that the current economic woes confronting the West are merely temporary hiccups that will be resolved in time.

It is not the intention here to debate whether the East will eclipse the West or vice-versa; rather, the focus here is on what will East Asian management practices look like? In my view, East Asian countries, China in particular, will not be so foolish as to discard completely what Western management styles and practices have to offer; at the same time, however, given China's rich cultural heritage combined with its new-found success and confidence, it will continue to espouse East Asian fundamentals and principles including elements of the so-called CD cultural dimension that have served the countries in this region well in the past. In other words, on the surface, Chinese management practices will appear to resemble those of the West but with Chinese characteristics, thus giving rise to a diversity of styles characterised by eclecticism, perhaps with more women managers (see chapter 9).

In making this assertion, I am reminded of Takeo Fujisawa's response to the question as to how Japanese management practices are different from those of the West: 'Japanese and American management is 95 per cent the same and differs in all important respects' (Pascale and Athos, 1981, p. 85). Takeo Fujisawa is the co-founder of Honda Motor Company. His answer while short is a very profound one indeed because it captures the essence that while East Asians, in general, are 'savvy' enough to absorb the best from the West and the rest of the world, they are at the same time fully aware of the futility of the wholesale appropriation of foreign techniques and principles as the context/environment differs significantly from country to country. Furthermore, it is foolish to abandon principles and values that have served them well in the past. For example, many East Asians, including those who have emigrated to foreign lands, continue to cherish many of the attributes associated with the Confucian Dynamism dimension (Hofstede and Bond, 1988), such as persistence, emphasis on education, hard work and savings (see chapters 3 and 11).

In a comparative analysis of savings rates and attitudes towards money of Chinese in China, Canada and Australia, and Caucasians in Canada and Australia, Tung and Baumann (2009) observed that the savings rate and attitude towards money of overseas Chinese resembled that of their counterparts in China as opposed to that of the Caucasians in their current country of residency.

As such, the future of East Asian management, particularly Chinese management, would most likely exhibit the following characteristics or traits:

1   A more intense scrutiny of Western management practices, particularly their pitfalls, and as they apply to the context of the institutional environment specific to a given country.
2   A more bidirectional flow of knowledge from East to West and vice-versa as distinguished from the more unilateral flow from West to East prevalent in the past.
3   A diversity of styles and practices characterised by eclecticism.

Each of these traits is briefly discussed below.

More intense scrutiny of Western management practices and principles

As noted earlier, the GFC and sovereign debt crisis have negatively affected the 'wealth', 'credibility', 'legitimacy' and 'self-esteem' of the West (Ferguson, 2011:5). As such, East Asian nations that are bent on the path of economic development are intent on avoiding the same mistakes that have contributed to the financial woes that currently plague the West. In the near future, at the very least, East Asians will continue to study in the West, particularly the US which continues to be the breeding ground for some of the most innovative and creative companies around the world and whose business schools are still in the forefront of knowledge generation as far as management strategies and practices are concerned.

However, East Asians will henceforth be more discerning and carefully scrutinise what works and what does not, particularly in the context of the peculiar institutional environment that each of these countries is confronted with. In fact, this approach resembles a 'latecomer effect' whereby the more recent adopters of the latest technologies and techniques, in this case East Asia, have the advantage of observing decades of development and experimentation in the West during which process the flaws and limitations associated with such systems have been exposed. In other words, East Asian societies have the advantage of distilling decades of trial-and-error in the West, observing what works and what does not and thus leapfrogging decades of progress/development to selectively implement what should be preserved and discard those elements that do not fit their own country, as in management education and training (see chapter 15).

In terms of selective learning from the West to suit the local situation, even before the outbreak of the current financial woes, the Chinese have always insisted on adapting foreign concepts and principles to fit their country's conditions (see chapter 5). For example, Mao Zedong, the founder of the People's Republic of China, asserted that the brand of socialism to be implemented in China would take on 'Chinese characteristics' (Schram, 1963).

More bidirectional flow of knowledge

Until the recent past, the flow of management knowledge has been primarily unidirectional, namely from West to East. At least two eminent scholars have lamented this sad state of affairs. James March (2005:7), for example, has called for the fostering of a 'multidisciplinary, multinational, multilingual community' to better prepare us for a 'future world of scholarship less dominated by North American research'. Similarly, Bruce Kogut has exhorted the US 'to re-import ideas at the same level as we export ideas' (Kogut, 2005).

The current economic turndown has become a clarion call to many in the West that this complacency on its part may no longer be tenable in the long run. This crude awakening has become a catalyst for change and has contributed to the recent surge in interest to garner insights from some predominantly East Asian phenomena that may be better able to capture the realities of the new economic order. Take, for example, the 'either-or' mindset that is dominant in the West. Because Western thinking and the Western civilisation have been largely influenced by Greek Aristotelian logic that favours linear thought, such as induction and deduction, matters are typically viewed as possessing *either* one set of attributes *or* another but not both. These include concepts such as 'competition' versus 'cooperation', 'good' versus 'evil', and so on. By contrast, Eastern thought, as represented by Taoism, a major philosophical tradition that originated in China, is based on the complementarity of opposites. In *yin-yang* philosophy, for example, 'darkness' and 'light' are complementary; the 'male' should be complemented by the 'female'; similarly, good coexists alongside evil, and so on. With the changed calculus in global competition where firms have to concurrently 'think global and act local' and where companies in strategic partnerships with other external entities (whether domestic or international) have to simultaneously cooperate and compete in order to succeed, Western management is thought to have become more receptive to paradoxical thinking (Smith and Lewis, 2011). Paradoxical thinking allows for the unity of opposites and can accommodate such dualistic and contradictory constructs such as 'glocalization' and 'coopetition' (Chen, 2008) to capture the realities of the new economic reality. In other words, East Asian philosophical traditions can be a 'potential fount of managerial wisdom that can help the renewal of Western economies' (Chen and Miller, 2010:217).

Another example of the influence of East Asian thought pertains to the current interest in studying networks and social capital in the management literature. While these two constructs are neither inherently nor uniquely East Asian constructs, the important role that networks and social capital, such as *guanxi* in Chinese, *kwankye* in Korean and *kankai* in Japanese (see Paik and Tung, 1999) have played in bringing out such remarkable economic transformations in China, Japan and Korea within a relatively short period of time has translated into a more intense desire to understand the comparative dynamics and processes associated with these two phenomena across societies (see chapter 10).

Stan Shih, a native of Taiwan and founder of the multi-billion dollar electronic empire known as Acer, embraces the best practices associated with Chinese and Western management practices and epitomises the 'ambicultural approach to management' advocated by Chen and Miller (2010). Shih retained Chinese values such as long-term orientation, harmony and collectivism while discarding other Chinese attributes that are not conducive to successful performance in the global context. These dysfunctional aspects include mistrust, secrecy, centralised authoritarianism and ethnocentrism (Lin and Hou, 2010).

Diversity of styles characterised by eclecticism

Despite similarities, salient differences and diversity exist across the East Asian countries of China, Japan and Korea. Even within China, given the geographic spread, strong regional differences exist (Tung *et al.*, 2008). Furthermore, in light of different types of ownerships (state versus private ownership), it is naïve to assume that there will be one style of management that fits all situations.

Throughout history, the Chinese have been eclectic in their approach to religion and philosophical traditions. During the *Tang* dynasty (618–907 AD), for example, Buddhism was introduced from India to China and Buddhism has continued to remain an important religious influence in many aspects of Chinese society. Even today, many Chinese do not see any contradiction in venerating their ancestors (often erroneously translated as 'ancestral worship') and conversion to Christianity.

In a similar vein, many Chinese subscribe concurrently to the principles of Confucianism and Taoism, two major philosophical traditions that appear to be diametrically opposed to each other. The former prescribes a moral code of conduct or ethical behaviour to be observed in a civil society whereas the latter focuses on the pragmatics and realities of life and living. In my 1994 article entitled, 'Strategic management thought in East Asia' (Tung, 1994), I outlined the twelve principles that have served as a handbook or 'bible' for many business practitioners in China, Korea and Japan. From the Western perspective, many of these principles appear to resemble the cunning and wiles that are characteristics of the preaching of Machiavelli in *The Prince* and hence are diametrically opposed to the teachings of Confucius that emphasise ethical behaviour and conduct. This Western perspective stems from the 'either-or' thinking described earlier whereas the Chinese perspective is one of dialectic harmonisation that suggests that in the presence of contradictions we should 'project ourselves into a situation where conflict and antagonism will disappear through an overall process of adjustment of ourselves to the world' (Cheng, 1991:195).

As noted above, a major tenet of Taoism is the *yin-yang* philosophy that accepts inherent contradictions in all things and matters. This philosophical tradition has enabled the Chinese to embrace Hegelian dialectics, as adapted by Karl Marx, and explains the coexistence of socialism and market capitalist principles in today's Chinese economy (Lin, 2011; Warner 2011).

Conclusions

The foregoing discourse suggests that the East Asian countries, China in particular, in their attempt to maintain their economic development will most likely not completely abandon the wisdom from the West in favour of a home-grown tradition, at least not in the foreseeable future (see Warner, 2011). In fact, the title of Ferguson's six-part television series *Is the West History?* is a very Western concept based on the 'either-or' mentality associated with Greek Aristotelian logic. Rather, the most likely scenario is one where East Asian management concepts and practices exist on a more equal footing with those from the West to result in a more truly bidirectional flow of knowledge from 'West leads East' to 'West meets East'.

This optimism stems from the fact that, in general, most Chinese are very introspective. As Ferguson (2011:15) noted, the Chinese leaders are keen students of history – 'more historically minded than Western leaders. They're more historically educated'. As such, they are eager to learn from, and hence avoid, sins of commission and/or omission by their ancestors as well as mistakes made in other countries. As Charles Zhang, founder of Sohu.com (a leading internet portal in China) observed, after China's humiliating defeat in the First Opium War (1840–2), that country has been engaged in 150 years of soul-searching of what went wrong and in the process it 'has been the best student because it has continuously sought to understand what went wrong and learn how to correct the situation' (Zhang, 2004:148). This situation will most likely hold as long as the Chinese do not lapse into the 'hubris born of success' trap that they fell victim to several centuries ago. As the popular saying goes, 'Pride goes before a fall', a phenomenon that Collins has documented in his book, *How the Mighty Fall: And Why Some Companies Never Give In* (Collins, 2009), which identifies the deadly sins associated with the collapse of large corporations.

In the final analysis, perhaps no organisational entity or nation can progress in a straight line. As Ferguson (2011:19) has astutely observed: 'the process of historical change is non-linear and it is characterised by a really high level of unpredictability. It's not a question of smooth trend lines that you can project forward to 2050'. After all, a fundamental tenet of East Asian wisdom, the *yin-yang* principle, supports the duality of all matters and so can accommodate the coexistence of diametrically opposed management thoughts and trends.

Note

1   Besides China and other East Asian countries, other emerging markets such as India and Brazil have attained rapid economic growth. Given the emphasis of this book and chapter, the focus here is on East Asia, particularly China.

References

Alderman, L. and Barboza, D. (2011) 'Europe Tries to Lure Chinese Cash to Back Rescue of Euro'. *New York Times*, October 28. Available at http://www.nytimes.com/2011/10/29/world/asia/europe-seeks-chinese-investment-in-euro-rescue.html?nl=todaysheadlines&emc=globasasa2 (accessed 8 November 2011).

Asia Pacific Journal of Management. (2011) Available at http://www.springer.com/business+%26+management/business+for+professionals/journal/10490 (accessed 8 November).

Barkema, H., Chen, X.P., George, G., Luo, Y. and Tsui, A. (2011) 'West meets East: New Concepts and Theories', *Academy of Management Journal*. Available at http://journals.aomonline.org/amj/research-forums

Bremmer, I. and Shalett, L. (2011) *The Great Global Shift: New World, New Rules*. New York: Merrill Lynch Wealth Management.

British Royal Society (2011a) 'Networks and Nations: Global scientific collaboration in the 21st century'. Available at http://royalsociety.org/uploadedfiles/royal_society_content/influencing_policy/reports/2011-03-28-knowledge-networks-nations.pdf (accessed 1 April 2011).

— (2011b) 'Royal Society's Knowledge, Networks and Nations report: Would Einstein get funded today?' 29 March. Available at http://www.telegraph.co.uk/science/science-news/8412074/Royal-Societys-Knowledge-Networks-and-Nations-report-would-Einstein-get-funded-today.html (accessed 30 March 2011).

Chen, M-J. (2008) 'Reconceptualizing the Competition-Cooperation Relationship: A Transparadox Perspective', *Journal of Management Inquiry*, 17: 276–81.

Chen, M-J. and Miller, D. (2010) 'West meets East: Toward an Ambicultural Approach to Management', *Academy of Management Perspectives*, 24: 17–24.

Cheng, C. Y. (1991) *New Dimensions of Confucian and Neo-Confucian Philosophy*. Albany, NY: SUNY Press.

Chosun Ilbo, The (2010) Asian Universities Become Draw for Foreign Students. Available at http://english.chosun.com/site/data/html_dir/2010/01/13/2010011300261.html (accessed 13 January).

Chronicle of Higher Education,The (2009) 'Obama pledges to send 100,000 students to China in the next 4 years', 18 November. Available at http://chronicle.com/blogs/ticker/obama-pledges-to-send-100000-students-to-china-in-the-next-4-years/8903 (accessed 8 November 2011).

Collins, J. (2009) *How the Mighty Fall: And Why Some Companies Never Give In*. New York: HarperCollins.

Economic Times (2011) 'Huawei near to overtaking Ericsson, sees consumer devices', August 15. Available at http://economictimes.indiatimes.com/tech/hardware/huawei-near-to-overtaking-ericsson-sees-consumer-devices/articleshow/9612032.cms (accessed 8 November 2011).

Ferguson, N. (2011) *The West and the Rest: The Changing Global Balance of Power in Historical Perspective*. London: Chatham House.

Fortune (2011) Global 500, July 25. Also available at http://money.cnn.com/magazines/fortune/global500/2011/countries/Australia.html (accessed 23 September 2011).

Gupta, A. and Wang, H. (2011) 'China as an Innovation Center? Not so Fast', *Wall Street Journal,* 28 July, p. 16.

Hexter, J. and Woetzel, J. (2007) *Operation China: From Strategy to Operations*. Boston, MA: Harvard Business School Press.

Hofstede, G. and Bond, M. H. (1988) 'The Confucius Connection: From Cultural Roots to Economic Growth', *Organizational Dynamics,* 16: 5–21.

Johnson, C. A. (1982) *MITI and the Japanese Economic Miracle*. Stanford, Ca: Stanford University Press.

Kennedy, P. (1987) *The Rise and Fall of the Great Powers*. New York: Vintage.

Kogut, B. (2005) 'Acceptance speech as Eminent Scholar in the International Management Division', *Annual meeting of the Academy of Management*, Honolulu, August 5–10.

Labriet-Gross, H. (2007) 'Study finds foreigners ahead in the Valley', *The Standard*, February 8. Available at http://www.thestandard.com.hk/news_detail.asp?we_cat = 9&art_id = 37823 &sid = 12112655&con_type = 1&d_str = 20070208&fc = 8 (accessed 9 February 2007).

Lin, H. C. and Hou, S. T. (2010) 'Managerial lessons from the East: An interview with Acer's Stan Shih', *Academy of Management Perspectives*, 24: 6–16.

Lin, N. (2011) 'Capitalism in China: A Centrally Managed Capitalism (CMC) and its Future', *Management and Organization Review*, 7: 63–96.

March, J. G. (2005) 'Parochialism in the Evolution of a Research Community: The Case of Organization Studies', *Management and Organization Review*, 1: 5–22.

Ouchi, W. G. (1981) *Theory Z: How American Business Can Meet the Japanese Challenge*. New York: Avon Books.

Paik, Y. S. and Tung, R. L. (1999) 'Negotiating with East Asians: How to Attain "Win-Win" Outcomes', *Management International Review,* 39: 103–22.

Pascale, R. T. and Athos, A. G. (1981) *The Art of Japanese Management*. New York: Simon & Schuster.

Saxenian, A. (2006) *The New Argonauts: Regional Advantage in a Global Economy.* Cambridge, MA: Harvard University Press.

Schram, S. R. (1963) *The Political Thought of Mao Tse-tung.* New York: Praeger.

Seligson, H. (2009) 'American Graduates Finding Jobs in China', *New York Times*, 11 August. Available at http://www.nytimes.com/2009/08/11/business/economy/11expats. html (accessed 12 August 2009).

Smith, W. K. and Lewis, M. W. (2011) 'Toward a Theory of Paradox: A Dynamic Equilibrium Model of Organizing', *Academy of Management Review,* 36: 381–403.

Sorkin, A. R. (2011) 'For deals, Wall Street goes East'. Available at http://dealbook.nytimes. com/2011/09/28/for-deals-wall-street-goes-east/ (accessed 28 September 2011).

TD Economics (2009) 'The global economy of tomorrow: Better, stronger, faster', 2 December. Available at http://www.td.com/document/PDF/economics/special/ td-economics-special-rk1209-global.pdf (accessed 25 September 2011).

The World in 2050 (2011) *The accelerating shift of global economic power: challenges and opportunities.* London: Pricewaterhouse Coopers. Available at http://www.pwc.com/ en_GX/gx/world-2050/pdf/world-in-2050-jan-2011.pdf (accessed 1 February 2011).

Tung, R. L. (1984) *Key to Japan's Economic Strength: Human Power.* Lexington, Mass.: Lexington Books, D. C. Heath.

— (1994) 'Strategic Management Thought in East Asia', *Organizational Dynamics,* 22: 55–65.

Tung, R. L. and Baumann, C. (2009) 'Comparing the Attitudes toward Money, Material Possessions and Savings of Overseas Chinese vis-à-vis Chinese in China: Convergence, Divergence or Cross-vergence, vis-à-vis "One Size Fits All" Human Resource Management Policies and Practices', *International Journal of Human Resource Management,* 20: 2382–2401.

Tung, R. L., Worm, V. and Fang, T. (2008) 'Sino-Western Business Negotiations Revisited – 30 Years after China's Open Door Policy', *Organizational Dynamics,* 37: 60–74.

Wang, H. (2010) 'Attracting Talent Globally for the Future', *China Daily*, 15 September. Available at http://www.chinadaily.com.cn/opinion/2010–09/14/content_11297892.htm (accessed 15 September 2010).

Warner, M. (ed.) (2011) *'Confucian HRM in Greater China; Theory and Practice'.* London and New York, NY: Routledge.

Zhang, C. (2004) 'China's leading Internet guru Charles Zhang, chairman of SOHU.com Inc., on how the Internet has changed the world's most populous nation', *Academy of Management Executive*, 18: 143–50.

17 Managing across diverse cultures in East Asia

Conclusions

Malcolm Warner

Introduction

In this edited volume, we have set out to examine the problem of managing across diverse cultures in East Asia. We looked at the underpinning influences at the macro-(economy) level, as well as at the micro-(firm) level, which were related to the economy, culture and management in these countries and how far each societal case provides a unique story within the parameters of diversity. We also tried to link dysfunctions in these societies to changing values and analyse the positive and negative characteristics of these. Rather than deal with the region in its entirety, we concentrated on the major players, such as China, Japan and South Korea, as well as in passing the Overseas Chinese (*Nanyang*) enclaves of Hong Kong SAR, Macau and Taiwan. The rationale for this choice has been spelled out in chapter 1.

In the region as a whole, we have dealt with a number of major dimensions, such as the cultural, economic and political ones which we would argue are the key shapers of management in its various guises found there. We will now take each in turn to sum up their broad-brush characteristics and try to relate them to their specific management implications.

Cultural

Many scholars have suggested that there is a common traditional cultural influence in most of East Asia (see for example, Holcombe, 2011). The phenomenon dates back many centuries as China advanced and retreated across the region (see Maddison, 2007; Moore and Lewis, 2009). We have noted here that the most significant belief-system shaping values in East Asia has arguably been Confucianism (see Warner 2011). The degree to which culture, or specifically the thoughts of Confucius (see Kwon, 2008; Lin and Ho, 2009), might be *the* key independent variable determining economic and related behaviour in this society, is, however, moot. Social scientists and others differ in their opinions regarding its importance for contemporary affairs. Even so, we have given a considerable emphasis to it in this volume, with caveats duly noted. Chapter 3, for example, notes how Asian values, such as the emphasis on education, have been crucial for many centuries.

Scholars in the region have reflected on economics and management, either directly and indirectly, since ancient times (see Chen, 1911; Rindova and Starbuck, 1997; Trescott 2007), for example. As Asia has asserted itself in recent times, there has even been a determined attempt to present 'Asian values' as an almost ideological platform, and with an implication of moral superiority. But as Tung (in chapter 16) puts it:

> Rather, the most likely scenario is one where East Asian management concepts and practices exist on a more equal footing with those from the West to result in a more truly bidirectional flow of knowledge from 'West leads East' to 'West meets East'.

The phenomenon of culture has also been a significant key to disentangling the twin threads of *convergence* and *divergence* (see Warner, 2003, 2011). Cultural variation may characterise diversity and give it its flavour. We have made it clear that we do not accept 'convergence thesis' as such, and prefer to speak of 'soft' convergence/divergence. Globalisation finds its roots in many common drivers of change but nonetheless specific Asian societies still retain their distinctive characteristics. The typical Chinese shop-floor sometimes looks like its Japanese or Korean counterpart but what stands out is the 'socio-technical system'. Not only is the language different but there are nuances of culture. Most East Asian management structures are hierarchical but still vary in their specifics.

How culture impacts upon management has been made clear in almost all the chapters in this book. Most experts in the field would not find this surprising given its Asian context, since we are dealing with relationship-based societies. *Guanxi,* for example remains very important in Chinese life (see chapter 5), as does its equivalent in Japanese and Korean society (see chapter 10). Further, a great deal has been written on the subject of culture across the board. The bibliographies of the contributions presented above testify to the amount of academic interest in this field in recent years. It would perhaps be invidious to suggest that culture is a more important variable than others, as it varies from one place to another to another but the ways in which it manifests itself are clearly different here and there. We have seen in the earlier chapters (5, 6, 7 and 8) in the book detailed accounts of how this relates to management in China, Hong Kong, Japan and South Korea for example.

In one sense, it may be said that Asian societies are perhaps blending (see Rowley *et al.*, 2005), in that they may be becoming less collectivistic and more individualistic. This may, however, be debatable as there is mixed evidence regarding intergenerational changes in the values. Few would deny that women's participation in the labour force in Asia is now expanding too, as chapter 9 points out. This trend is increasingly observable within the ranks of management but may vary greatly between societies. Asia is also said to be now building a new 'consumer-driven' society on the back of its formerly production-oriented one. China's managers and workers are now motivated by monetary rewards, as never before. Even so, the legacy of past habits dies hard and Asians still save much more of their incomes than their Western counterparts (see chapter 16) often as much as half again. This habit, it is said, may be due to the lack of a robust welfare state, which is the case across Asian economies, and the need to prepare for the unforeseen.

Notable too has been the rise of an Asian middle class, especially in East Asia. It has been evident in Japan, Hong Kong, South Korea and Taiwan for many years now. But the development of such a class in China has also been growing in recent years. It consists of those who derive their wealth and income from entrepreneurial activity as much as those who benefit from their roles and status as managers and administrators. This new middle class is in many ways a 'meritocracy', in great part deriving its position from education and training. But although China had a traditional elite education system for hundreds of years, it was not until the twentieth century that opportunities opened up for the many. Today, China has expanded its colleges and universities on a massive scale to encourage the development of talent. Indeed, educational investment both at the personal and the national level characterises all East Asian economies. We have seen in chapter 15, for example, how a subset of this has been channelled into management education and training.

Although the numbers of managers are relatively small compared with the huge labour force, they constitute an elite which is growing in importance. Whether or not there has been a 'managerial revolution' is debatable but it is evident that top managers in China now have very high status (see Redding and Witt, 2007). Entrepreneurs and businessmen/women have also come into prominence, which is quite a change from the lowly status they were traditionally accorded.

Social stratification in what were formerly feudal societies has now changed considerably. It has been transformed into one increasingly based on merit and achievement. Managers selected by competitive processes, including formal examinations, are now more and more legitimised, as they are in the West, on the one hand. But this is mitigated by dysfunctional behaviour which seems to be very prevalent in all East Asian societies, relating to corruption and favouritism. It becomes most visible when it makes the headlines involving senior executives at the top corporate level. So, as Nolan suggests earlier in this volume, there is 'good' *guanxi* and 'bad' *guanxi*: 'For the global manager, the benefits of establishing the "good" one are significant, but they should also be alert to the dangers of the "bad"; for the time being at least it remains necessary to proceed with caution' (see chapter 10).

Economic

It is now becoming conventional wisdom that Asia has become the 'powerhouse' of the global economy. In chapter 2, Das notes that: the '[E]mergence of the Asian economy as a dynamic economic growth-pole over the preceding four decades is an event of historic significance'. East Asia in particular contains the new economic superpower, China, which has displaced Japan as number two, at least in terms of aggregate GDP, vis-à-vis the USA. If one had predicted a couple of decades ago that this would have been the case, it would have seemed quite improbable, as it would with India (see Nankervis *et al.*, 2013). Even so, a communist state has outperformed a capitalist nation, albeit one with a statist history. This might have appeared even more improbable given the debris of the Cultural Revolution years. Much of the credit must be laid at the feet of Deng Xiaoping. His bold démarche in initiating the 'Open Door' and 'Four Modernisation' policies in 1978 laid the foundations for the later successes. The next three decades were to see a seemingly unstoppable period of rapid economic growth, sometimes a little uneven but most of the time at full speed. The net result was to increase the standard of living of all classes in the PRC; all are now equal citizens in China's new 'harmonious society' but some are more equal than others. The 'economic rent' the elite claims there, due to the scarcity of resources and talent amongst other considerations, has led to one of the widest degrees of inequality of wealth and income in the Asian societies. The Gini-coefficient is 0.47, meaning that Mao's levelling down to 0.24 is in the dim and distant past, with a steeper 0.53 in Hong Kong. Japan's position is somewhat more egalitarian but it is still 0.37; South Korea comes in at 0.31 (World Bank, 2011).

The economic growth of East Asia has wide implications for its management. In the detail, the picture varies from one country to another. The relentless expansion of the Chinese economy and its sea-change from being a 'command economy' to becoming a 'market' one has had enormous consequences, as we saw in chapter 5. The nature of the enterprises was to change from being under state control to becoming a mixture of public and private in various combinations. China now even has its own MNCs that operate on a global basis. This new *status quo* requires a new breed of managers and a new kind of management education and training (see Warner and Goodall, 2009). Japan had earlier presented a model which many countries East and West looked to (see chapter 7); but this became less convincing when its economy entered its decade of *stasis*. In the case of South Korea, its reputation slid after the Asian Financial crisis, but it has bounced back in recent years, as chapter 8 notes.

Political

China's 'peaceful rise' (or 'development' as they prefer to call it) has now become a familiar phrase in the editorials. The PRC has now become the dominant player in terms of both 'hard' and 'soft' power in the region. Given the history of the twentieth century, it has had an uneasy relationship with its neighbour, Japan, and an equally complex one with the two Koreas, North and South. Today, it is increasingly asserting its hegemony over the region.

Politics, both internal and external, have a wide influence on both micro- and macro-management in the respective economies. In the case of China, there was a deliberate political choice to switch from a 'command' to a 'market' economy (see Lin, 2011). With its idiosyncratic form of Party-led capitalism, strategy still comes from 'on high'. Japan had earlier its own statist form of development (see chapter 7) as did South Korea, (see chapter 8). In both countries, there is also a close nexus between the political and business elites.

At the micro-level, the political balance between the managers and the managed is moderated by workers' representatives in different configurations in the respective East Asian workplaces, as we see in chapter 13. There is only one trade union management in China which is the official one, the ACFTU; the position in Japan is more differentiated, with enterprise based unions; similarly so in South Korea (see chapter 13).

Conclusions

The implications for management of the above cultural diversity are indeed complex, as has been seen in the above three-dimensional analysis. We have attempted to sum up what has been said in the book, why it was important and where it is leading to. *Culture*, it may be argued, still influences the parameters of Asian values within which management functions. *Economics,* especially the quite extraordinary growth in GDP in recent times, has also been a driver of what specific kinds of management have emerged. *Politics*, too, still plays an important role in how the system works, with the State interacting with the market but now perhaps less so. The 'devil' is, however, always 'in the details'.

References

Chen, H. C. (1911) *The Economic Principles of Confucius and his School*. New York: Columbia University Press, 2 vols. Reprinted 2009, New York: General Books.

Holcombe, C. (2011) *A History of East Asia: From the Origins of Civilization to the Twenty-First Century*. Cambridge: Cambridge University Press.

Kwon, K. (2008) 'Economic development in East Asia and a critique of the post-Confucian thesis', *Theory and Society*, 36: 35–83.

Lin, N. (2011) 'Capitalism in China: A centrally managed capitalism (CMC) and its future', *Management and Organization Review*, 7: 63–96.

Lin, L. H. and Ho, Y. L. (2009) 'Confucian dynamism, culture and ethical changes in Chinese societies – a comparative study of China, Taiwan, and Hong Kong', *International Journal of Human Resource Management*, 20: 2402–17.

Maddison, A. (2007) *Chinese Economic Performance in the Long Run, 960–2030 AD*. Development Centre Studies, OECD, Paris.

Moore, K. and Lewis, D. L. (2009) *The Origins of Globalization*. London and New York, NY: Routledge.

Nankervis, A., Cooke, F.L., Chatterjee, S.R. and Warner, M. (2013) *New Human Resource Management Models from China and India*. London: Routledge and New York (in press).

Redding, G. and Witt, M. A. (2007) *The Future of Chinese Capitalism: Choices and Chances*. Oxford: Oxford University Press.

Rindova, V. and Starbuck, W. (1997) 'Ancient Chinese theories of control', *Journal of Management Inquiry*, 6: 144–60.

Rowley, C., Benson, J. and Warner, M. (2005) 'Towards an Asian model of human resource management? A comparative analysis of China, Japan and South Korea' in Warner, M. (ed.) *Human Resource Management in China Revisited*. London: Routledge, pp. 301–18.

Trescott, P. B. (2007) *Jingji Xue: The History of Western Economic Ideas into China, 1850–1950*. Hong Kong SAR: Chinese University Press.

Warner, M. (2003) 'China's HRM revisited: a step-wise path to convergence?', *Asia Pacific Business Review*, 9: 15–31

— (ed.) (2011) *Confucianism HRM in Greater China; Theory and Practice*. London and New York, NY: Routledge.

Warner, M. and Goodall, K. (eds) (2009) *Management Training and Development in China: Educating Managers in a Globalized Economy*. London and New York, NY: Routledge and New York.

World Bank (2011) *Miscellaneous*. Available at http://web.worldbank.org/WBSITE/EXTERNAL/EXTABOUTUS/0,pagePK:50004410~piPK:36602~theSitePK:29708,00.html (accessed 11.11.11).

Glossary

(includes *Chinese, Japanese and Korean terms*).

amakudari, 'descend from heaven'
bao, reciprocity
cai hai, 'taking the plunge' [into business]
chaebol, business family, Korean conglomerate
daigakuryo, bureaucrat's training school
danwei, work-unit
dingti, inherited posts
dongbei, North-East
ghaizi, 'changing the system'
gong-guan, public relations
gonghui, trade union
gongzi biaozhun, wage standards
guanli, management
guanli renyuan, manager
guanxi, connections
guojia zhuren, 'masters of the country'
guoyou qiye, state-owned enterprises
inhwa, kin-based hierarchies
jin fan wan, 'golden rice-bowl'
jingji gaige, economic reforms
jingji guanli, economic management
juyou Zhongguo tese, 'with Chinese characteristics'
kankai, relationships, in Japan
kaifang, Open Door
kaisha, Japanese corporation
keiretsu, Japanese big business grouping
kexue guanli, scientific management
Kongzi xueyuan, Confucius institutes
Kong Fuzi, Confucius
kwankye, relationships, in Korea
laodong, labour

lingdao jieji, 'leading class'
mianzi, face
mingsheng, reputation
munojo jeongchaek, Korean 'no-labour union' policy.
nanyang, Overseas Chinese
Nihonjinron, theories of 'Japaneseness'
nonmingong, peasant workers
palli-palli, 'quickly-quickly'
poka-yoke, mechanism in Japanese lean manufacturing
renli ziyuan guanli, Human Resource Management, (HRM)
renminbi, people's currency
renshi guanli, personnel management
san xiang zhidu gaige, the three-systems reforms
segyewha, Korean globalization policy
shifu, Master
shijie datong, 'viewing the world in a harmonious state'
shiye, unemployment
sige xiandaihua, Four Modernizations
tie fan wan, 'iron rice bowl'
tudi, apprentice
wa, harmony
won, Korean currency
xaihai, 'to jump into the sea'
yen, Japanese currency
yon-go, connections
yuan, Chinese currency
zaibatsu, Japanese big corporations
Zhongghuo, Middle Kingdom
Zhonghua Renmin Gongheguo, People's Republic of China
zhuren, 'masters'
xiagang, worker redundancy

Index